Men and the Water of Life

The salmon on the cover represents the Celtic "Salmon of Knowledge" that gains wisdom while swimming in the sacred pool amid the nine trees of knowledge. According to the myth, when the nuts on the tree are ripe, they turn scarlet. When the fish in the pool are struck by the falling nuts, they absorb the knowledge of the tree.

Whoever could catch a Salmon of Knowledge would be flooded with inspiration by one taste of it. The inspiration would reveal all that had happened in the past, whatever was transpiring in the present, and what was about to happen as well. The salmon was considered the oldest of animals and therefore the oldest ancestor. Within that salmon was the knowledge of how to release the son of the earth, who was trapped among the rocks at the bottom of the water, and the knowledge of how to stop a battle that has already commenced.

Men and the Water of Life

INITIATION AND THE TEMPERING OF MEN

Michael Meade

HarperSanFrancisco
A Division of HarperCollins*Publishers*

HarperSanFrancisco
and the author, in association
with the the Rainforest Action
Network, will facilitate the
planting of two trees for every
one tree used in the
manufacture of this book.

Copyright acknowledgments begin on page 443.

Text design by Margery Cantor

FIRST EDITION

Library of Congress Cataloging-in-Publication Data
Meade, Michael.
    Men and the water of life : initiation and the tempering of men /
Michael Meade.
        p. cm.
    ISBN 0-06-250542-4
    1. Masculinity (Psychology)—Cross-cultural studies.
    2. Initiation rites—Cross-cultural studies.   3. Men—Folklore—
Cross-cultural studies.   I. Title.
HQ1090.M4   1993
305.31—dc20   92-56405
                                                          CIP

93 94 95 96 97 ❖ HAD 10 9 8 7 6 5 4 3 2 1

This edition is printed on acid-free paper that meets the American National Standards
Institute Z39.48 Standard.

*This book is dedicated to my father,
who has gone ahead to the place of ancestors,
and to my mother, who has always insisted
that we came from a land of promise and holy wells.*

Contents

The Forest of Stories

Myth is the foundation of life; it is the timeless pattern, the religious formula to which life shapes itself. . . . Whereas in the life of mankind the mythical represents an early and primitive stage, in the life of an individual it represents a late and mature one.

THOMAS MANN

INTRODUCTION

Just as myths begin with origin stories, I want to begin this book by talking of beginnings—by describing the origins of this book in my own life and in the wider work from which it has grown. For over a decade, I have been working with men in workshops and conferences throughout North America, England, and Ireland. What is now called "men's work" began for me when Robert Bly invited me to teach hand drumming and mythology at a workshop for men at the beginning of 1981. That workshop was one of the first gatherings of its kind, and I didn't know what I was getting into. It was also the first of a long series of collaborations with Robert Bly, James Hillman, Terry Dobson, and many men now associated with this work. At that time, news of such events spread by word of mouth, and no one was sure how to name or describe these retreats. Most of the men attending had little or no experience with drumming, myths and symbols, or initiation and ritual. But that was due to change.

As interest in such events spread steadily, I had the opportunity to work with thousands of men of all ages and experience. At first, the groups consisted primarily of "white" men, although Etheridge Knight frequently visited carrying poems and songs, black roots, scars, and wisdom. Eventually, men of all colors and many cultures were involved. Executives, ex-cons, priests, war veterans, doctors, healers of all kinds, students, craftsmen, professors, and artists of every description have now struggled joyously with drumming patterns, have wandered and labored in the "forest of stories," and have relived life's wounds as if they were all just waiting for the invitation to begin. There was a great surprise in the willingness of men to experiment in the study and practice of myth, music, emotional expression, and ritual forms—all of which I had been studying on my own for twenty years. Through these conferences, I felt as if a territory that had been lost was found again, as if a path had opened up that led from the present to the age-old grounds of the masculine psyche. And the path also led me back to the beginnings of my interest in myths and ritual.

When I was in high school, the divisions between the adult world and the world that my friends and I inhabited, between school and the street corners we claimed as our own, between weekdays and weekends, were sharp, full of oppositions, and unexplained. We were able to move through the daily world governed by teachers and family, but our real lives took place on a different plane, where all feelings and events were intensified. Each week culminated in the rituals of the weekend—our rites of attraction to and fear of gang wars on Friday night, costume-drama romances on Saturday night, and church on Sunday.

During the 1950s in New York City, local neighborhoods were being redefined as "turfs" by the gangs that lived in and roamed through them. This re-visioning and renaming made the streets the territory of youths, to be defended against adults, authorities, and outsiders of all kinds. We were in an unguided experiment that moved in and out of the realm of initiation and myth, although we didn't realize that. The gangs were named after royalty—the Dukes, the Crowns, the Kings, the Knights—or after animal totems—the Blackhawks, Sharks, Cobras. Their names alone separated them from the banality and predictability of daily life. Friday night was the time for "rumbles," for preplanned or impromptu battles with neighboring gangs. Whether or not there was an actual battle, the air was thick with expectation, testosterone, the ring of challenges and boasts, and the rhythms of back slaps, handshakes, and fast feet.

It was a baffling world of light and dark. One moment we were suffused with the warmth of friendship and thankfully contained in a band. Then we were a reckless crew animated by our symbolic name, walking our mythical turf. The next moment that world was torn open by enemies trying to cut into our territory, destroy our bonds, intimidate us, or defame our name. Our bodies and our imaginations leapt at the feelings of belonging to the gang, the more so because it was separate from parents, school, police, children—history itself! We had created a world that existed in the same physical space as the worlds of family and society but was somehow on a different plane. In some respects, this world coincided with the neighborhood, but its boundaries were not simply physical. You could enter it unawares and violate its rules unknowingly. You could threaten it by not recognizing it or by misusing its name. It was mythical and literal, imaginary and concrete at the same time. If those inhabiting this world had listed its characteristics, it would have sounded like something out of *The Odyssey* or *The Iliad*.

On Friday night, the gang would wander like the Fianna, the ancient Irish bands of warriors that guarded borders and broke boundaries. On Saturday, we gathered together to review the night before— what could have happened, what did happen, what would happen the next time. It was also time to get ready for the "heart of Saturday night." There would be a dance, a party, or just hanging out—but somehow there was always music, and if possible in any way, girls, and if lucky, pretty girls, and if this was really "it," sex. But if not actually sex, then talking of it, preparing for it, using the language of it, telling stories of finding it, of getting it, of losing it. And not just sex, but the romance of it, the imagination of it.

Music and dance were doorways to the rituals of desire. Ritual costumes had to be shaped from everyday clothes: unusual shoes, polished to shine the flashing feet; socks to match the shirt, as if to say we were subtle; contrasting pants, to say we were not. Hair was slicked up and back as if to show the speed at which our minds were moving, and shirts were open to the winds of summer or winter, for these were rituals of exposure and display. Wild and tentative dances led us into the mysterious world of girls, where slow songs and melodies softened the edges of the mind. Girls whose shapes had barely been visible hours ago were now voluptuous. Our world was no longer defined by the borders of our turf but by the inches between bodies and the extensions of time and space made through promises of "always," "anywhere," "anytime," and "everything." The separations between boys and girls dissolved, and we entered a temple where a different dance was required. Instead of defending our turf, we now engaged in surprising rituals of self-revelation.

On Sunday, we told stories of what had or hadn't happened, could have happened or should have happened, except that now we were going to church. Sunday was God's day, the end of one week and the beginning of the next. It was the last day of creation. God rested; we paused. Retelling the events of Friday and Saturday was a way to mythologize what had happened. We embellished the facts, enlarging them to mythic proportions, and we got pulled into the mythic aspects of ourselves. Sometimes we hung around outside the church, making our myth as the faithful inside were reviewing theirs.

God was everywhere in his effect on this morning. The newspaper was a great, heavy summary of the creations and destructions of the week; stores were closed in honor or in fear of God. Another world appeared that belonged to a god who accepted silence and money, prayers and songs, excuses and sinners. Despite the dogmas and the preachings, we each met some god on our own, in some secret inner way. While we entered together the ritual of the church, what happened to each of us was uniquely cleansing, uplifting, downcasting, frustrating, damning, or ecstatic.

Into this temple were brought the aggressions of Friday and the delicate dance of Saturday, mixed with the aspirations and melancholies of the rest of the week, all wafting through the air of the church as if inhaled and exhaled on the breath of God. In my church, the father god was distant and hard to see; the young son was held by the mother herself; and all were surrounded by the bloody and pious confusion of saints. Our own confusions, joys, wounds, and losses seemed to be deepened by the steady rhythms and repetitions of the church rituals. The neighborhood and the turf, the gang and the family were all held together inside a world that had power by rite, by art, by movements repeated by ancestors, by secrets confessed, by births blessed, by deaths mourned, and by marriages celebrated. The past, the present, the wounds carried in and out, even the jokes we made about it—all were consecrated, whether or not we believed. Even if we mocked it, we knew that this world was sacred and that here we shared our souls with some god and some goddess.

Then Monday would come, and schoolbooks would rise up like barriers to the mysteries that absorbed us. School itself seemed to deny the outer and inner intensities and violent complexities of the other realms we lived in. Occasionally, something was said or read in class that would cause the room to vibrate for a moment, and the boundary between the world of school and the worlds we mostly inhabited would dissolve. But most of the time, the rhythms, feelings, and purposes of our activities were contrary to those of family, school, and the routines of daily life.

On my own, I poured through books and newspapers looking for hints about these apparently parallel and separate worlds, searching for the links that connected them. I could find none. Apparently, these different and even antagonistic realms were to be experienced like classes in school. You went from literature to science to religion. When the bell rang, you simply switched realms. After school, you went home to family, and from family to gangs, to dances, to church. At church and in school, there were bells to let you know when to switch realms; the others had more subtle signals that had to be studied and learned. But there were no thresholds, no evident connections; one world didn't even recognize the existence of the others.

I found another world on my thirteenth birthday when my aunt gave me a copy of Edith Hamilton's *Mythology,* an anthology of Greek myths and legends. I was stunned by the stories, which I read and reread. The tales of gods, goddesses, and humans caught in extreme and mysterious situations seemed more like life than anything else I had heard or read. The stories seemed to explain what was happening within me as well as in the world around me. But they did not "explain" in the sense of making the events and meanings of my life plain and clear; rather, they mirrored the complications and dramas of the life I was experiencing. That book reshaped my mind. The stories gave a form to my internal life and opened a vast dwelling place within, where the imagination and emotions denied by family, school, and church were accepted. In many ways, I've never stopped reading that book.

Later that year, I was in a movie theater with a few friends. We were trying to be a "crew," a small, local gang. We were cool; we had a street corner where we hung out and some older guys to watch and emulate. One of our rules was that we couldn't pay to get into the movie theater; we had to enter some other way. The management of the theater had set up elaborate defenses to try to keep us out or make us pay. On this particular day, we had walked along the train tracks, climbed a fence, slid down a hill, jumped from the top of a wall to the alley behind the theater, and tapped on the rear fire door until some kid had opened it, and we slipped in.

During the movie, I got up to go to the bathroom and suddenly found myself surrounded by six older guys. They escorted me to the bathroom, which was upstairs behind the projection room. They threw everyone else out and shoved me to the floor by the white urinal.

While one guarded the door, the other five stood over me. The leader held a sharpened monkey wrench in my face; the others held pipes. They were from a nearby neighborhood. I recognized the leader; he had a reputation for having put someone in a hospital and for carrying a homemade zip gun. His hand shook as he angrily accused me and my crew of calling his gang punks. Now he was going to show us what happened to anyone who challenged them. At first I was too startled to understand what he was saying. Then I realized that they had mistaken me for a friend who had recently tangled with them and got away. This was the payback; they were going to mess me up.

As my eyes went back and forth between the sharp, curved edge of the monkey wrench and the mad eyes of the kid holding it, my mouth began to talk on its own. I hurriedly explained that I wasn't the one who had called them names. Why would I be fool enough to challenge them? They were older and armed, I said, and everyone knew they were tough. Our crew was just forming; we wouldn't challenge them. But listen, I went on; I know what happened. My friend was cursing you, looking for a fight. Now, there are things you don't know about him. He's crazy, I said. He does this shit all the time. His older brother beats him, and it makes him crazy. Actually, their father beats both of them, but the older one won't take it anymore, so my friend is getting beat up by his father *and* his brother. So he's crazy, and what he says doesn't make sense. It's like he's just going around yelling. It doesn't mean anything.

I was talking fast, and I could see the leader's eyes waver and the wrench drift a little away from my head. I kept talking. The more I talked, the more they calmed down. They got caught up in the story of this guy's family and forgot about messing me up.

They wound up letting me go. I was to tell my friend to apologize; they would be waiting outside the theater after the show. I walked back to my seat, still in great fear. I told my friends. We crawled on the sticky floor of the theater, pushing everyone's legs out of the way. We got to the side door, burst through it, and tore down the alley. Before the movie was over, we were standing on our corner discussing what had happened, rehashing it, figuring out what to do next.

Someone once asked me how I became a storyteller, and this was the event that suddenly came to my mind. The tool that had been made into a weapon, the mistaken identity, the strange way in which I was as caught up in the story I was telling as my attackers were, and the way the telling of one tragedy had seemed to avert another—all these elements were compelling to me. But to my friends other parts were important: How did they surround you? Were they all in different aisles waiting for you? Would they have taken any one of us? What did the wrench look like? Who else is dangerous in that crew?

My friend was angry because I had talked about him and his family. He felt that this was just going to make his life worse. He wanted to go right back and have it out with them. We pointed out that he would die on the spot and that this would accomplish nothing. What happened next was strange. He went home instead and attacked his older brother, putting the blame back on him. If his brother hadn't beaten him, he said, he wouldn't have cursed that crew. The protective side of the older brother awakened, and he went out, got some of his friends, and they confronted the monkey-wrench gang. Those guys didn't want to mess with the bigger, older guys, so they agreed not to do anything. It was all over. We could even go back to the movie house.

The turns in these events left me a lot to think about. There seemed to be stories within stories, and strands woven together in a way I couldn't quite grasp. Our plan to get in and out of the theater without paying or getting caught by the manager reminded me of the story I'd read in the mythology book about Odysseus escaping the Cyclops by hiding under the sheep. But inside that was the story of my being cornered and threatened with death, and again inside that was the story of my friend and his family. That story wasn't actually the "truth" about why he had challenged the gang. My friend's brother probably hadn't hit him just before the encounter with the crew; he was carrying this rage all the time, most of us were. What I had told was a story of why my friend was so hurt and angry and maybe why they, too, were so touchy and felt they had to be armed. Facts, psychology, and myth were all mixed together, and all unfolding while the movie flickered on the screen. I didn't understand it, but could see that what had happened was more complicated than anything anyone was saying on the screen, on the corner, at home, or at school.

My sense of the complications in the patterns of life was enhanced that same year when I began to ride the subway from my neighborhood in Queens to an all-boys high school in the center of Manhattan. Where I caught the subway, it was an elevated train; then, at a certain station, it plunged from daylight into darkness and entered the underground. This became for me the "underworld," described in the mythology book as a place of descent, inhabited by shadows and accessible only through caverns and deep lakes. Most days I climbed up from it along with the hordes of workers who surfaced at Grand Central Station, then walked to school. But sometimes I would travel on and return to the surface in another part of the city—in another world.

At that time in New York, many of the old ethnic neighborhoods were still intact. I could ascend from the underworld into Little Italy, Germantown, Spanish Harlem, Little Ukraine, Chinatown, and so on. Each area had strange foods whose smells filled the air. The old people talked their native languages and wore clothes that defied modern styles. Snatches of each culture's music could be heard, and traditional costumes hung in store windows. Some newspapers that the inhabitants read were written in scripts that looked simply like designs to me. It was like finding encampments of lost tribes all over the city.

I got after-school delivery jobs and found that within each neighborhood there were layers upon layers, worlds within worlds. Some people were trying to hold onto the patterns of the past; others were reinventing themselves day by day, creating new languages and cultures. In the elevators that creaked up and down the dark shafts of the old buildings in the garment district, for example, the men shepherding racks of bright, newly designed clothes spoke a language unintelligible to the people who bought those clothes in the showrooms and department stores. At first I thought that these black men were another foreign group, since I couldn't understand their rapid, rhythmic speech. It took me weeks to figure out that these men were adding new designs to an existing language as they spoke it. They were mixing words that I knew with phrases from the deep South and lacing all with the language of industrial New York, sped up to allow rapid exchanges as carts and racks were pushed past each other. It took as much attention to learn their language as it did to learn Latin at school. One was a dead language; the other, a "street Latin" that was being born daily.

Glimpsing the multiplicity of old and new cultures striving between subway stops all over New York ended any belief I had in a singular interpretation of life's events. The many layers of cultural heritage and cultural invention that seemed the true commerce of the city matched the many-layered stories of myth. Every group seemed to have rites that wove the members together and bits of myth that were shared. I found that myth was intricately woven into the art, music, and ceremonies of each culture.

For the next twenty years, I studied myth, religion, anthropology, and traditional music. In college, I majored in literature and philosophy, but I studied myth and religious anthropology in my spare time. While fathering four children, marrying twice, and working a wide variety of jobs, my home served as a museum and a stage, where the art on the walls, the displays on the tables, and the music playing changed frequently to match the myths and folktales of whatever culture I was studying at the time. These studies of ritual art and tribal music led to the practice of various forms of traditional drumming, chanting, and storytelling.

Eventually, I was so full of tales from ancient places that the stories had to find a way out into the world again. Attached to the stories in my psyche were explanations of myth and symbols and chunks of anthropology and psychology. I began to perform the stories before audiences while drumming; then I added poems, proverbs, and discussions with the audience on the meaning of the stories. The discussions developed into workshops on myth and symbolic imagining.

From the very beginning, it was clear that most people reacted to the stories as more than just "entertainment." I began to see that people were looking for opportunities both to relive and reexamine personal traumas and to discover meaningful experiences of community.

Unraveling the threads of fairy tales and myths caused people to reveal hidden pieces of their personal stories and experience the emotions of living through them again. I found myself studying developmental and interpersonal psychology in order to understand and assist in the emotional reactions and experiences of participants. I needed, too, to explore my own increasingly strong reactions to myths and to people's personal stories. And I began to dig in the grounds of anthropology as it became clear that what was missing from most people's lives were opportunities to participate in the great symbols of life, to encounter the great passions, and to immerse themselves in meaningful human community.

When I entered the nascent world of workshops for "modern" men, I was heartened to find other men who were starving for the sense of meaning that only comes from grasping the mythological levels of life and from participating in rituals where there is enough safety to explore neglected emotional and spiritual lives. This was the great surprise, that behind the boardroom, the locker room, the waiting room, and the barroom, there was a forest of emotional, imaginal life that modern men were just waiting to enter. As men entered that forest, the armor that choked off their emotional, imaginal, and spiritual lives would crack, loosen, and fall clattering to the ground.

I never expected to find a place in the modern world where the proceedings begin with drumming and singing, the language carries emotions and images, and what can't be said is danced and sung. It was as if a threshold had been located that allowed re-entry to the unfinished initiations of youth and the timeless forest of symbolic adventures.

Albert Camus said, "A man's work is nothing more than to rediscover, through the detours of art, those one or two images in the presence of which his heart first opened." If we open up the word *art* to include myth, emotion, and ritual, then modern men, through "men's work," are trying to rediscover the doorways to their hearts and the territories of the soul. In these gatherings, modern men reconnect to men in tribal cultures throughout time, as they try to locate and return to those moments when the heart was fully open to life. Often men are seeking the rediscovery and deepening of those initiatory events that in fact constitute the source of individuality and genuine spirituality. It was in these experimental gatherings that I began to understand the instincts and expectations that inspired our neighborhood gangs and our earlier experiments with reckless emotions and ritual attitudes. We had been exploring the gaps in the daily world in order to open our hearts and minds. We had been seeking initiatory breaks in order to find out who we were, and sometimes we were willing to face death to learn.

Initiatory events are those that mark a man or a woman's life forever, that pull a person deeper into life than they would normally choose to go. Initiatory events are those that define who a person is, or cause some power to erupt from them, or strip everything from them until all that is left is their essential self. I mean initiatory events in the sense of Van Gennep's "Rites of Passage": There is a departure from daily life, a suffering of ordeals and dramatic episodes, and a return as a marked and different person. Initiation is the dramatic way the psyche shifts the ground and orientation of an individual or group in response to the expected and the unexpected breaks in life.

Within each individual there is an expectation and a desire for self-revelation and periods of change, life living itself out through stages and cycles. Mircea Eliade says, "Initiation is a creative death." So that moving from one stage to another requires a brush with death, a sense that one stage dies and the next grows out of it, leading to greater life. From this point of view life can be seen in classic stages: birth, childhood, youth, maturity, elderhood, death—with initiations occurring between stages.

But, the dynamics of initiatory change can also be provoked by any unexpected, dramatic event: accident, divorce, abortion, the death of a loved one, the loss of a career, an eruption from nature that destroys the shape of a life. All severe separations in life evoke the sense of initiation in the psyche and open a person to psychological and mythical territories of unusual depth. Initiation is the psyche's response to mystery, great difficulties, and opportunities to change. The ground of the psyche shifts and breaks and opens. Past and future frame this opening—the past can be re-viewed and the future can be glimpsed and felt. Once the opening has occurred, the psyche is animated with the expectation that this beginning will be carried through to a new organization of inner and outer life. However, the radical changes that initiation precipitates take a long time to learn and to realize. The "eye of initiation," the way of looking through one's life to see where the initiatory breaks occur, requires reimagining one's own biography. Traumas, shocks, mistakes, and losses that we are encouraged to "put behind us" and "get over" often contain detours that did, and can again, open our hearts and our inner resources for change.

Initiatory experiences carry a person away from what they know and outside the normal rules, beliefs, and boundaries. While in that separated state outside of normalcy, radical change can occur and radical healing is possible. Initiation involves both suffering and healing, makes the "self" a territory of great learning, and connects a person to the essential mysteries of life. Initiation makes a person mysterious.

Tribal initiations include intentional woundings that leave scars which mark the initiate physically and concretely. Often the scars are visible and remind everyone that the marked one has entered a new stage of life, for initiation changes a person's relationship to everyone. Through a mixture of reality and artifice a line is drawn that ends one stage and begins another. From this a new person emerges who is growing further into life and also moving a little closer to their knowledge of death.

Modern initiatory experiences may leave a physical mark, or they may only be located through psychological scars and emotional traumas. In the psychology of initiation, experiences that change a person's life and mark that person as an individual are opened up and re-examined to learn who a person is and who they are trying to become. The wounds work as thresholds between inner and outer realities. Seeing into the wounds and scars reveals that everyone is wounded and teaches one how to see the person coming out of the wound.

Without the reopening and re-visioning of the events that mark a person's soul, life seems chaotic and more disorderly than it actually is. You could say that those feelings of chaos within life are actually calls from areas of unfinished initiation. Initiatory experiences inhabit the same deep psychic ground as birth and death. When the stages of life and the radical occurrences in the life of an individual are not marked, old age becomes confusion and chaos. Dwelling with the little deaths in life changes the size and shape of the big death. Seen through the eye of initiation, death is not the opposite of life, death is the opposite of birth. Both are aspects of life.

The process of initiation also gets activated when there are shocks to a group or culture. Major breaks and changes open a culture to past and future at the same time. At the threshold where one epoch ends and another begins, initiation becomes the dominant style of the psyche. Change can erupt like a river undammed by the shifting of psychic ground.

Seen through the eye of initiation the scars of initial woundedness and of life-changing events turn out to be the openings to imagination and the heartfelt experiences of life. When these experiences are contained in art, in poetry, story, song, and dance, the limits of the individual and of time are shed, and the timeless territory of the heart and the imagination opens.

We enter the territory of the heart by going into our wounds and reliving them. By "wounds," I mean those blows from life that stun and injure one's spirit or lacerate and mark the tissues of the soul. There are three major sources of wounds for men: the hurts suffered in childhood, the blows received in initiatory circumstances, and the losses in life that become the cloth of the cloaks of the elders. The eye of initiation sees darkly and sees in the darkness of suffering the glint of survival and the glimmer of emerging wisdom.

Men's work began with men coming together over their wounds and losses. In these divided times, when we talk of "men's wounds," the questions immediately leap up: What do men, especially white men, have to feel wounded about? Haven't *they* presided over the wounding—of women, children, people of color? Is their gathering together a source of further wounding of others? From the point of view of the psychology of initiation the answer is no, not if the wounds of those gathering are opened and kept present, not if each man's woundedness and beauty are involved. The way to guarantee that someone will continue to wound others is to keep him ignorant of his own wounds. The wounded wounder knows vaguely that there is a wound somewhere, but he can only see it when it appears in someone else. Wounding another makes the wound clear for a moment and seems to move the pain of it from inside the wounder to out in the world. Faced with the monkey wrench, I found a story that moved the focus of all those in that bathroom in the opposite direction—from a passing on of injuries to the examining of wounds. For a moment we all shared a knowledge of our wounds, and hearing about woundedness replaced the need for further wounding. The stories in this book and the stories men rediscover in conferences are narratives of childhood wounds, initiatory blows, and scars of life revisited for their capacity to heal from within and change the course of a life.

It is no accident that the average age at these gatherings is about forty—no accident because the "midlife crisis" represents another period of initiation, when all the smoldering issues of previous life stages as well as those of the present are ignited. The man standing before the door to the second half of his life is visited, often attacked, by the demons of his early adulthood, his youth, and if he allows it, by the specters of childhood and infancy. The wounds of these earlier periods must be reexamined and carried over the threshold. This means that the suffering and losses that come with such life-marking episodes as divorces, career failures, deaths, accidents, lovers long lost, and desires long avoided must be viewed anew. Moreover, those at midlife stand at the middle of their culture as well and face forces that strike them from both directions—they inherit the crises of the elders that preceded them and they are being pushed by the generation that follows.

On the other side of the threshold is the "territory of the elders"— the area where life experience, if held in one's consciousness long enough, turns to wisdom. As a man passes through the elders' gates, his focus shifts from personal striving and status building to attending to the mysteries at the core of the community. In tribal communities, those in their forties become the "practice elders," maintaining the rituals of the community and debating issues that stir or threaten the tribe. Eventually, the "practice elders" are pushed into the positions vacated by elders who die. This push starts from the group of youths just crossing the threshold of initiation. Seen that way the elders are connected to the youth, not simply opposed to them.

Contemporary gatherings of men echo this process, and the acknowledgment of elders at the right time can bring an outpouring of emotions. Tears fall and hands applaud as older men move into positions of respect and take ritual seats from which they can appraise the community. Often these elders are being called to take their places for the first time, and they are surprised by the powerful feelings that the recognition of them evokes. The younger men, too, are surprised by their enthusiasm for having and honoring elders.

Then, if a young man speaks of his fears and struggles in this world, where institutions are decaying and nature itself is threatened, the older men suddenly feel again the pain of youth, standing uncertain and humble before the challenges of life. Meanwhile, the men at midlife are flooded with waves of feeling that wash back through the memories of their own youth and rise toward the respect and honor of an elderhood they secretly aspire to attain.

All of these feelings—of the young, the old, and the middle-aged—flow like a river just below the surface of men's lives. Whenever men find themselves in a situation safe enough to allow these feelings to become conscious, they descend and the waters rise up and flow out to all those present, reconnecting them to each other and to the cyclical stages of life. Through rituals of descent men can find emotional connections among the generations that remind us that besides the fires that can threaten and divide, there is the Water of Life that can flow into and fill the gaps that inevitably occur between generations, genders, races, and cultures.

It is not surprising that a man must first experience this reconnection with other men, that he gathers other men around him in order to re-enter the suffering that he could not bear in his youth, in his bewildered isolations, in his single-minded pushing through life. What is strange and distinct about modern cultures is that the men who gather around these inevitable wounds often don't know each other from earlier stages of their lives. These are impromptu communities of "sudden brothers" trying to piece together emotional histories and open the territories of the heart. Clearly, the need for this work is so elemental, so long overlooked, and so desperate that "strangers" will suddenly thrust themselves into the most vulnerable, delicate, and risky involvements, which ordinarily would only occur among close relatives, lovers, and old friends.

In the retreats, the telling of an ancient tale contains each event. Personal stories and memories are poured into the old tales and contained therein. Eventually, it becomes clear that the men are stepping through the scenes and images in these old stories, through the stories of their personal woundings, and into the timeless forest that is part of our human heritage. The forest is not only the symbolic landscape in which the stories are set but it is also the place where our ancestors lived and where men's retreats have been held for the past ten years. This forest contains both masculine and feminine areas, symbols, and characters. The feminine is encountered, but it is inevitably seen through masculine eyes.

This book is divided into six parts. Each part contains stories that spring from the gound of the psyche and lead into an important territory of masculine imagination and human life. No single interpretation can capture any of the stories. They have lived long lives because they carry mystery and living symbols. These are stories of trouble, of the difficult initiations life requires before revealing glimpses of beauty and meaning. Taken together they represent a narrative track, a pathway, a songline that wanders through the forest of the male psyche.

A chorus of voices enters repeatedly, wandering from story to story, representing the reactions and responses that typically emerge during week-long retreats. No one retreat has provided all these comments, nor are they the exact words of any one man. Instead, they represent the kinds of comments made over and over by hundreds and hundreds of men as they have gathered around the scenes in these stories. Their comments reveal surprising differences between the outer world of facts, opinions, and expectations about men and the inner imaginal and emotional worlds that men also inhabit. The chorus of men announce, argue, and illustrate themes that recur throughout the book: the anguish between fathers and sons; the mysteries and fears of the mother, the feminine, of beauty; the recurring struggle for manhood; the devastation caused by loss of meaning and authenticity in men's lives. Again and again, these themes connect the men's current, personal stories with timeless and symbolic myths. Like a dream, each story elicits a variety of emotions, memories, and interpretations.

Part One and Part Two are excursions "the son of the family" takes into the land of fathers and mothers. In each story he wanders into the mysteries and troubles that must be engaged and survived before getting out of the villages of childhood and onto the roads of life.

The first two stories set off into the territory of fathers and sons and establishes the style of hunting and questioning that are typical in gatherings of men. The next tale follows a boy on a narrative path right into the territory of the Great Mother, the mysterious feminine force behind life and encountered here in the form of a half-giantess. The next tale gathers an entire community around a fire in which the fates of a young man and a young woman are intertwined and in question.

Each story raises basic questions about the relationships between fathers and sons, mothers and sons, and sons and lovers, but these tales don't provide answers or fixed solutions to the questions they raise. The point of these stories is to move us from the strictly biological and historical sense of "father," "mother," and "lover" to the mythical sense and thus to bring us closer to the ancestral symbols of initiation.

All four stories—"The Hunter and His Son," "The Sweetness of Life," "The Boy and the Half-Giantess," and "The Lizard in the Fire"—

are African "dilemma tales." Traditionally, they are told when the community is in trouble. Unlike European fairy tales, these stories don't end with the promise that everyone will live happily ever after. Rather, they end in questions; they pose dilemmas. The purpose of this kind of story is to provoke discussion, to bring underlying conflicts to the surface, to force everyone to take a position, and to remind everyone that mysteries are at the core of life in any community.

At the center of the cultural village a fire burns. It fills the gap between generations and genders. It can raise the heat enough to move life along or it can burn out of control. When one figure in the psychic family moves through the fire, everyone changes position. Each major change requires heating in fire and cooling in water. The rest of the book will follow stories of the heating and cooling of the individual and cultural psyches.

Parts Three, Four, and Five follow various roads through the territories of initiation, often seen as the education of the prince in a man's psyche. There is no single, exemplary initiation story. There is no single initiation that makes a person forever complete. But in the area of men and masculine forces, I believe that initiations by fire and water are essential. A man must be tempered; he must have his temperament made and remade through repeated immersions in fire and water. Too much fire and a man becomes brittle, rigid, given to explosions, liable to crack under pressure, or constantly burning others in order to get rid of some of his heat. Too much water and he never gets to the point, can't end what needs ending, cools out when he needs to heat up, smoothes over what should have a clear edge, or drifts along when certainty is required.

The process of initiation is, to me, the lifetime spent in finding oneself over and over through ritual immersions in the intense fires of desire and the stunning waters of surrender. These two exist as parallel realms, ruled by different rhythms and images. When in the fire, the sense of loss and sorrow that inhabits water is forgotten. When in the water, the drive of purpose and anger disappears like mist. Men can get caught in one realm or the other, or they can get stuck in-between. When a culture forgets that men need to go back and forth, it polarizes into violence on the one hand and passivity on the other.

Part Three introduces initiation more fully by entering the forest of symbols through the story of an exiled prince. Parents and the expectations of the daily world are left far behind as the road descends to the underworld, where fire and water mix with one another, where spells are broken and innocence is traded for a darkened knowledge that restores the soul below and renews the world above.

Part Four erupts in the extreme tests of fire and power that are caused by the flight of the Firebird; they lead to a boiling cauldron that will make a new king or have none at all. Part Five begins the search for the Water of Life that alone can cure a dying father and king and reverse the conditions of the Wasteland. When generativity, creativity, generosity, and the capacity to embrace life dry up, the Water of Life has gone underground. At such times, the earth becomes arid, life becomes devoid of meaning, the ground of culture cracks and splits, and gaps develop among peoples and between people and nature. Only water can bring the pieces back together, awaken seeds hidden in the ground, and enliven the parched Tree of Life.

The story in Part Six follows the road of the strange Companions. This road leads to images found in the depths of the individual psyche and in stories of all cultures that bring men together in a search for beauty and meaning. The appearance of the companions is always strange, but they are in touch with the roots of community. They insist that the incurable conditions of life be accepted and the impossible desires for community be felt. The weird companions are at the root of all male initiation groups, from street gangs to music groups to sacred brotherhoods. They are also the tap roots of courage and compassion that nourish the elders, who alone can remember the essential role of beauty in life. They also carry the message that what will shatter this world more certainly than anything else is the loss of the threads that connect the here and now to the "other world."

Only when these ancestral figures of unity and inclusiveness are found will the Old Queen of the psyche release her daughter to the world. Unless she returns, the Wasteland will spread. Her return depends on ritual accomplishments. The weekend rites of conflict, romance, and worship I experienced as a youth are refound in the depths of the psyche as rituals that carry the fires and water of life. Unless the fires of conflict are ritualized, unless the sorrows of life are allowed to flow into grieving, joy recedes from the world. With the appearance of the companions the rituals that contain and carry anger, grief, and joy return.

The purpose of initiations begins to be visible when the return to community begins. The road of return is as dangerous as any road in the psyche. On this road it's always the last hour when things could be lost. Either the roots of community will be touched again, or all will be for naught.

The most lost and dangerous people in this world are those who are not emotionally bonded to family, community, and humanity as a whole and those who have acquired personal power without being initiated to a sense of the source of that power and the value of individual life. The collapse of traditional cultures, the loss of shared myths and rituals that enfold the individual into the group, and the spread of modern industrial societies are producing generations of unbonded children and adults who are not initiated to the purpose and meaning of their own lives. News reports of murderous child-soldiers, drive-by shootings, increased racism and intolerance, the spread of child abuse, and the steady increase in the rape of women in the very centers of the culture are bulletins from the child-men whose bodies grow apace while their psyches remain outside the touch and blessings of human community.

In many tribal cultures, it was said that if the boys were not initiated into manhood, if they were not shaped by the skills and love of elders, then they would destroy the culture. If the fires that innately burn inside youths are not intentionally and lovingly added to the hearth of community, they will burn down the structures of culture, just to feel the warmth. Each generation is a fire of individual and collective heat that only learns its purpose by burning. No proliferation of laws, no adjustment of the curriculum of early education, no private, hopeful prayer is going to remove the threats that modern society will be destroyed by its own youth. But the most certain signals for lighting the fires of destruction are sent when the old people of a group lose their memories, consume like youths, and neglect the rites of grieving and burial.

The individual life is "made" in those initiatory moments when the individual sees both ways into their own soul. The validity of that vision can only be verified by a return to community. A man cannot look back accurately enough or look forward long enough if he is standing alone and isolated; there is just too much confusion, illusion, and disillusionment to be able to face it alone. Unless enough men can gather together and hold the genuine threads of their lives so that the pattern of community and of elders can be seen, even temporarily, there's no promise of healing waters ahead.

The Road
of the Two Fathers

... two old roads, curving and white.
Down them my heart is walking on foot.

CÉSAR VALLEJO

THE HUNTER AND HIS SON

Pay heed to this tale of the father and son!

A hunter and his son went to the bush one day to pursue their occupation. They hunted all morning and found nothing to sustain them but one small rat. The father gave the rat to the son to carry. It seemed of no consequence to the son, so he threw the rat into the bush. The rest of the day they saw no other game. At dusk the father built a fire and said, "Bring the rat to roast, son; at least we will have something to eat." When he learned that the son had thrown the rat away, he became very angry. In an outburst of rage, he struck the son with his ax and turned away. He returned home, leaving his son lying on the ground.

Late in the evening, the son rose up from the ground and returned to his father's village. He stood at the edge of the village until everyone was asleep. He went to his parents' hut, gathered up his few belongings, and left. He walked into the night, following a long path that led to another village. He arrived at this large village in the dark of the night. Everyone was asleep. He went to the center of the place and came to the chief's hut. The chief was awake. The son of the hunter entered the hut of the chief naked, without trousers.

The chief said, "From where do you come?"

"From that other village," the son told him.

The chief asked, "How goes it with you?"

The son said, "My father and I went into the bush to hunt. We found only one rat. He gave it to me to carry. It was small, and I threw it into the bush. In the evening, we built a fire. He told me to roast the rat. I said that I had thrown it away. He became angry and struck me with his ax. I fell down. In the night, I rose up and came here. That's how it is with me."

The chief said, "Will you keep a secret with me?"

The son said, "What secret?"

The chief said there had been a war and his only son had been captured and killed. He said, "Now I have no son. I wish to say that you are my son who was captured in the war, that you have escaped and returned home. Will you keep that secret?"

The son said, "This will not be difficult."

Then the chief began to play his drum—boom, boom, in the middle of the night. The mother of the house was awakened; she came out and said, "O King Lion, he who causes fear, what is the drum you are playing in the middle of the night?"

The king said, "My son has returned."

Then the mother raised the sound of joy, the whole village was awakened. Everyone was saying, "What has happened at the king's hut that they are playing drums and singing in the middle of the night?" A messenger was sent round, telling everyone that the king's son had come, that he who had been captured in the war had returned. Some of the people were joyful; others doubted it, saying, "Indeed, indeed."

At dawn, the son was bathed, anointed with oil, and dressed in fine new clothes. The chief gave him gifts and brought him before the whole village to be welcomed. Some of the chief's counselors said, "It is not his son." Others said that it was. The doubts of some grew; they said, "Indeed, indeed."

The counselors summoned the sons of the village, dressed them in fine garments, and called for their great war-horses. The counselors said, "Go to the house of the chief. Call the chief's son. Tell him to bring his horse and a sword. Say you are taking the horses for exercise. Ride out to the clearing. Dismount there, and taking your swords, slay your horses. Observe what the son of the chief does, and report to us here." Each counselor gave a sword to his son, and the young men set off for the chief's hut.

Now, there was a talebearer present who heard the counselors' plan and quickly informed the king. The king made preparations, saying, "If the naked man can dance, how much better can the man with a cloak?" He called the son to him and said, "Take this horse and sword. When the sons of the village call for you, go with them. Whatever they do, you do it as well." The sons of the counselors came and called for the king's son. They all set off. They rode to the clearing and dismounted. When the son of the king saw the other sons slay their horses—well, he did it, too.

The sons of the counselors returned to their fathers and reported that the king's son had slain a valuable mount, saying, "Only the son of a king would display such magnificent disregard for property and wealth."

The counselors still had their doubts and said, "Indeed, indeed." They decided on further tests. The next day they gave each of their sons a slave girl. They instructed them to invite the son of the chief to bring his slave girl and go with them to the clearing. Once there, they should slay the slave girls and observe what the son of the chief did. Once again, the talebearer was present. He informed the king, who told the son to take his slave girl when they called for him, and "Whatever you see they have done, you do it as well." In the clearing, the sons of the counselors took their swords, and each slew a slave girl. The son of the king? Well, he did it, too. And the sons returned to the counselors and reported what had happened, saying, "Only the son of a king would act as he has done." This time the counselors were satisfied. They offered no more tests.

Time went on. The son lived with the king. Then, one day the hunter came looking for his son. He questioned people, saying, "Have you seen one who looks like this, who acts like such and such?" The people said, "No, we don't know him, we haven't seen your son. But there is a son in the king's hut who looks like that." He was sent to the hut of the king. He entered and greeted the king, who was seated with the son at his side. The hunter said to his son, "Will you get up and return with me and live as before?" The son remained silent. The king said, "Hunter, if you will keep the secret with me, I will give you whatever gold you wish." The hunter refused. The king offered one hundred times whatever gold the hunter would request. The hunter refused despite all the entreaties of the king. The son? Well, he remained silent.

Then the king called for three horses to be saddled and one sword to be brought. The three of them—the hunter, the king, and the son—then rode off to the clearing. When they reached that place, the king gave the sword to the son. He said, "We are here unarmed, but you hold a sword. There is nothing else left to do. Either you must slay me and take my goods and return with your father to his village and his world, or you must slay your father and return with me and live as we have been in my village."

The son did not know what to do.
If it were you, what would you do?
Kill the father, or kill the king?
What would you do?
Off with the rat's head!!

CHAPTER I

THE HUNTER AND HIS SON

THERE'S A STRANGE relationship between a storyteller and a story. Looking for a story is like hunting. I often set out seeking a story for a certain occasion and wind up being hunted down myself by a different kind of story. I found "The Hunter and His Son" in a paperback collection of African stories hidden in a corner of a used bookstore. The book had been out of print for over twenty years, and its pages were yellow with age. It cost fifty cents. I read all the stories in it and put it away. Eventually, this story began to pop into my mind. I tried to get rid of it, but just as the rat in the story won't stay forgotten, this tale kept coming back to me after I had thrown it down.

When I first stumbled across this collection, I had been looking for tales that could engage an entire class of high school students prone to distractions and interested in anything other than what was being presented to them. The stories needed to be brief and powerful, and I realized that the type of story usually called a "dilemma tale" might have just the right amount of intrigue. I hoped that the students would feel compelled to answer the questions or solve the mysteries that lay in the stories. So I gathered together a pile of dilemma stories and read through them. Two of them kept coming back to me: one told how a young woman was undervalued by her father, her husband, and a would-be lover and the other was this rat's tale. At the school, I told the story of the young woman. The students jumped into a discussion of what it meant to be devalued, not seen for what you are truly worth. Everyone wanted to speak from the position of the woman, and it was fine.

Meanwhile, I couldn't forget the story of the rat. The image of the father and son setting out together struck me and stayed with me. I recognized the universality of the scene. I could see my own father with me following him, and then immediately I could see myself as the father with my children following me. And I could see that what held those images together was the wound. I could see my father's back as he disappeared after dropping me off at the induction center during the Vietnam War. I could feel the uncertainty in my own back as I walked away from my sons after an angry exchange. I could smell and taste the earth, as one does when struck and suddenly knocked to the ground. The story sent me back to football games and fights, where I found myself on the ground with that taste of earth and grass and blood in my mouth and that metallic ringing in the head that accompanies a wound.

So, instead of telling this story to the high school students, I found myself recalling my own confusion and my own sense of feeling abandoned in the world when *I* was a student. I remembered that I had known that I was wounded at the time, and that feeling returned, as well as the feelings of being unable to express what the wound was, how I had received it, and why and how it was to be carried. The more I dwelt with this confusion, the more apparent the wound became. The more I stayed in touch with the wound, the younger I felt. The wound seemed to be pulling me back into earlier and earlier experiences of myself. This story began to stalk my imagination, and I would find it popping up before me as I stood at a street corner, as I got ready to leave the house, or as I thought of one of my children. I decided to tell it at a gathering of adult men to see how they would react to it. I needed to toss the rat to them and learn if they were pulled into the complexities of the wound from the father. I needed to see if they were pulled two ways as I was, back into my own childhood and further into my own experience as father.

When I first told the story, there was an uproar at the end. Everyone had something to say at once. Men wanted to change this, or describe that, answer this, or question that. The room was immediately full of emotion and confusion. It became apparent that the common entry point was the scene where the father delivers a blow to the son. There everyone could find himself semiconscious, unconscious or rising out of the unconscious and lying alone on the ground. We began to work seriously on what is happening in this scene.

Often in telling this story, I'll stop right after the father has struck the son, the son has fallen to the ground unconscious, and the father has turned away and left him there. The idea isn't to discuss victimization or to blame the father for the blow. The point is to stop the story on the ground where the wound has occurred, to stop the story in the place where the father and the son are both joined and separated by this inevitable wound. The point is to gather on the ground of a common wound rather than through heroic effort or shared success. One of the strengths of this story is that the wound appears at the beginning.

When a group of men begins to discuss this scene in the story, they are coming together where a son gains consciousness of himself as one who is wounded. He is not just hurt; he enters his own life through that wound. And all the son's actions—indeed, the whole rest of the story—are driven by the emotions generated by that wound. A genuine community of men forms around shared wounds. When this woundedness is denied men grow further apart.

When I tell this story now, I hear not only the voices of those present but the chorus of men who have spoken their lives into the story before. I usually pose the question, "Where did the father strike the son?," and a man will answer, "Right in the head." "With which part of the ax?" "The blunt end of the ax on the left side of the head." "Is that what everyone saw?" "No!" And then a proliferation of descriptions pours out: right side of head, from behind, top of the head, sharp end of the ax in the heart, in the genitals, flat of the ax in the face, on the right shoulder blade, and so on. Each man will touch the area he mentions in an impulsive gesture that not only explains but also resembles the way someone will describe an injury right after it happens. These gestures are lively, as if the body has something to say and wants to participate in the description.

The second time I told this story and stopped to ask these questions, one man insisted that I had said outright that the ax had hit the boy in the head and knocked him unconscious. I said it was the certainty of his own imagination that filled him. He disagreed. Since the event was being tape-recorded, we played it back. There was no mention of the head at all. But he wasn't the only one surprised by the certainty of his imagination; many other men had heard words that had not actually been said. It's like the scene of an accident or crime, where each observer mixes the outward events with inner images and memories. The rush of emotions stir up inner stories that become intermingled with what was actually seen. In the same way, each listener provides specific details and emotions to match the symbols and events that appear in a story. The scene of the father striking the son will immediately release some memory inside a man of being threatened or struck by his father. Or he will be struck by the image of his father turning away, avoiding, ignoring, abandoning him to some darkness. Often the memory is stored in an area of the body, and the place where it is held is symbolic, for this is not only where the wound is carried but also where a blessing is sought.

Once this type of talk begins, more and more statements about fathers begin to come out, and more and more emotions pour forth. Each man has, stored in his body, memories of dramatic interactions with his father, and as these memories are awakened, a surge of emotion and energy is released. The mention of the wound brings back the wounding, brings the father into the room, brings the son out of the mouth of the man. Suddenly, a composed audience of modern men has erupted into a gesturing, angry, sorrowful, resentful, fearful group. It is as if all present had in fact been hunting with their fathers, and what connected them to their fathers and connects them now to each other is this wound that has been reopened. For even if the wound was an accident, it is an accident that has happened to almost every man.

In such moments, the "normal" distinctions, divisions, hierarchies, and agreements among men disappear. The differences now consist of the different woundings and the different feelings that have emerged from those wounds, but all are the same in having been wounded. Each man feels an increasing pressure to tell out, among strangers, his most painful memories and feelings. Most men can immediately name the age they were when a particular blow was received.

At one end of the spectrum there are stories of the son who is so brutally and repeatedly beaten by the father or by a series of stepfathers that he still feels the presence of the ax all the time. At the other end are the stories of men whose fathers were either physically absent or emotionally distant. These men simply can't form the image of the father striking his son. Often, one of these men will say that he envies the man who can vividly describe the blows delivered by a brutal or raging father. He would prefer the clarity of the physical wound to the invisible blows of omission. At this end of the spectrum, the "blow" consists of the absence of touch, the absence of a passionate mistake. Often as a result of this wound, men feel an indecisive and vague connection to life.

Some men are surprised that the son in the story gets up again. They had felt sure he had received a death blow, so they hadn't heard anything that was said after that point in the story. Something in these men was killed off by their fathers, and the story has caused this experience to be repeated. What the father did so stunned their psyches that returning to that event almost literally knocked them out. They didn't literally die, of course, but a major part of their childhood ended, and when they approach this moment again, they look confused and disoriented, not sure of what is being said around them. The story continues without them, they are being left behind, and they don't know what to do about it.

A man says, "Wait!" He wants to keep the scene right there where the boy is lying on the ground alone. This man was beaten daily by an out-of-control father. He has been running away from that boy and his pain for years. He doesn't want to rush on now, not when there are others willing to talk about that kind of isolation and pain. He stops the scene from moving, puts everyone in touch with the dark earth and with a child isolated in the dark. The rage the story evokes becomes palpable, as if a fire is being made from the pieces of story being brought out by the men.

Indeed, from the beginning of the story, the father and son have been heading toward a fire. Across it they face each other in a moment when the deep, confused emotions between them burst to the surface. The rat and the fire are the father's gifts—food and warmth. But they are never enough for the son's burning desire for life.

In a sense, father and son have been hunting each other. When the story opens, the father has set out to hunt, and the son is coming right behind. The son can glean from his father the skills and techniques of hunting, but whenever a father teaches his son, the experience throws them both into a wild state of anticipation and tension.

In addition to learning a skill, the son gets exposed to the attitudes and emotions of the father. The father's temperament as a teacher and as a hunter is also revealed to the son. Not only does the son follow the father into the world but he is also following the *way* in which the father goes into that world.

This story is very old, and the situation primal. If the hunt is successful, something will die to sustain their lives. Thus, the father's footsteps lead the son into the issues of life and death, or—to put it another way—the imagination of the son hunts for the purpose of his father's life and for the purpose of his own life by stepping into the tracks made by his father. If the father's world is humdrum and predictable, the son will hunt the reason for that predictability and will become keen about anything that disrupts the predictable. If the father is mostly absent, the son will hunt into that emptiness; he will absent himself from many things in order to get to know the space that the father has left empty. If the father erupts and flies off repeatedly, the son will study those eruptions and wait where the comings and goings occur. Somehow the son knows that even before his own birth, he came out of the track that his father was making through life, and he knows that he will one day pick up that track again. All of these elements are what flush the rat out of his hole in the earth.

For the son is after something, and at first he thinks he can find it in his father. The father usually comes to believe this as well—until one day, he hands the son a rat. By the time the son is able to hunt along with his father, his own hunting imagination has already been activated. He already sees beyond the father, though he may not realize it. The father has been to the bush many times. Some days he has returned empty-handed, coming home with only disappointment. The father's expectations have been changed by his exchanges with the bush, by his exchanges with life. The newness of the hunt provokes great expectations in the son, however; the son's hands are full of promise, and there's no room in them for an ordinary bush rat.

To the father, the rat represents survival. Literally, the father counts on this first presentation from the bush as food. He knows from experience that the bush may provide no more for days, and he has learned this through hardship. Throughout his adulthood, the father has been learning the art of survival and how to negotiate with the uncertainties that life presents. The son has received the benefits of the father's efforts without experiencing the father's struggles. The father may be willing to accept the rat, but the son is certain that there's bigger and better game ahead. His eyes are big with the future, with the potentials of his life. The rat seems inconsequential. What is a rat when an elephant or an elegant antelope lies ahead? The whole day is ahead, anything can happen, even at the last minute game may appear. The son is ready for the wonders of life, and the possibilities are increased by his closeness to his father. If they were to do something great, they would share in it together. It would somehow explain their relationship; it would attribute a great meaning to that relationship. Catching something great together would explain many mysteries and enclose them from the uncertainties that surround them. It's easy for the son to throw the rat away; it's even an act of faith in his father and faith in his father's world.

Meantime, the father has been walking in his own tasks, in the knowledge of the limitations of his life. He is reassuring himself that if this is one of those days that brings no good news, at least they have the bush rat. Perhaps the son will learn something of the uncertainty of this life. He will remember the weight of that rat and learn the value of carrying whatever life happens to provide. Maybe he will even see the wisdom of a father who takes what is given. Together they can enjoy the story of a day that has given so little, but one in which they, at least, knew how to hold onto what they got. In the life of a hunter, there isn't an eland behind every bush. Hunting is the art of survival; they will survive this day, too, and survive it better because of the bush rat.

Of course, the father goes all the way through the preparing of the fire and the son waits all the way to the last minute to tell of tossing the rat. The whole scene is lit by the fire of expectation, but the expectations of the father and son are different. When the story comes out, each thinks the other has failed in some way, and each has indeed failed the other's expectations. The son imagined that there would be some great treat for dinner, that his sense of what is possible would be satisfied. The father imagined that there would be some rat to eat and that they would be satisfied in the knowledge that it was better than nothing. Neither one expected that there would be only this fire and an emptiness between them. The father is speechless. There's nothing to say. Maybe it's all been said before. Maybe the father would have been able to face an evening of nothingness alone, but he cannot now, in front of his son. Maybe he had invested more in the rat than he realized. Maybe he had lived with too many empty promises for too long. Somehow, at any rate, this is the last straw. He strikes the son down and walks away.

A story reveals its gifts only to those who enter into it. The stories and the makers of stories have to be approached on their own ground. In its own way, a story reads us as much as we read it. As the old hunters of Australia say, "You can't hunt in the tribal lands until the country knows you!" The key to learning from a story is to find a doorway into its interior.

One of the ways I've learned to do this is to actually lay the scenes out in the room where the story has been told. I set the scenes up as stations along the path of the story, which winds its way through the room. People then go to the scene in the story that speaks to them the most. The story becomes embodied, and the people are inhabiting the story. Then, everyone speaks from the place in which they are standing. The story is told again, but through the voices of the people standing in the story. The audience, the listeners who took the story in, now speak it back, mixing it with their own emotions and memories.

Once, when we had laid out this story of the hunter and his son, there were a hundred men arranged throughout the room according to their chosen detail from the story. Only one man was in the place that represented the road between the village of his parents' hut and the village with the king's hut. For some reason, no one else had taken a place on that road. A large group of men had gathered where the father had given the blow with the ax to the son, and an even larger group had crowded at the scene where the son stood with the sword having to decide whether to use it against his father or against the king. But on the road between the two villages, there was only one man. It was as if the story itself had been made visible. The two large groups stood like villages full of people; the lone figure of the man between them looked out of place, exiled, lost.

This man began to talk about his life, describing how a couple of years before he had separated from his wife and children, how he had begun to live more and more by himself, how he was overcome with shame and couldn't explain even to his children why he had remained away so long. Only now, when he found himself as the solitary man in the long stretch of path in this room full of men, did he realize how isolated and alone he had become. Everyone was drawn to the sadness in his voice.

Another man said that actually he, too, was at that place in the story, but he hadn't known it until he felt the weight of this man's sorrow. This second man had grown up without a father, so he had initially felt that he wasn't even in the story; he was somewhere at the beginning of the story, still looking for the footsteps of his father. But now, hearing the sadness of the other man's voice, he realized that he was on that dark road walking back toward the village where he had grown up. He was trying to find those things that had fathered him and was even now looking for a blow from those things that had fathered him and left him on this dark road.

After these two men had spoken, everyone began to take a turn describing the time that they had spent walking in one direction or the other on that dark road. One man said that he had hit that road running, having to escape conditions that would have destroyed him. He wondered why everyone in the village was able to sleep while his parents raged at him and he wailed in pain. Standing at the edge of the village, he now watched the house of his parents with a mixture of sadness and hate. Then another man began to tell how he had returned to the parents' house over and over, each time picking up some small piece of himself, gathering that which belonged to him and carrying it out to the road.

At first the parents' hut and village are the world of the son. Inevitably, harshly in some cases and mysteriously in others, the father gives a blow to the world of the son. The blow may be literal; it certainly is psychological, and it has mythic dimensions. The son's head is turned from the hut of his father to the greater world outside and to the separate world within himself. The crown that the son sometimes saw on his father's head fell with the swing of the ax. The son steps into the darkness outside his parents' village looking for the crown. Though he feels empty and alone, he walks the same road all other sons have walked. It's a road of few belongings, many shadows, and many missteps.

CHAPTER 2

THE KING'S HUT

WHEN THE SON stands at the edge of the new village, the story is about to change direction. The son left his parents' village when all were asleep. This village is asleep, too. The son goes to the center hut, enters, and—is the chief awake or asleep? Is he a chief or a king? Why is he called chief and then King Lion?

Stories are full of codes and hints that speak directly to the irrational parts of the psyche and announce that the story is changing direction. The second village is deeply different from the first. The son has stepped across some line that changes everything. One meaning of the story at this point is that everyone at both the old and new villages is asleep to what is about to happen between the son and the king. What happens next is between the only two who are awake to the painful issues that the son is carrying. There is something to which both the chief and the son are awake, something that they both seek. If the story is seen to occur within the son's psyche, then all the rest of his psyche is asleep, and these two have encountered each other at the center of the psychic forest. The son has entered a door that opens when all else in him is asleep. It is the opposite of the door of his parents' hut. In this strange hut, the qualities of being alone, unknown, and dispossessed are useful.

In leaving the father, the son has awakened a king, or a king has awakened because the son has left his father. When the father turns away from the son, the son turns toward a king. The separation from his village of origin, from the world of the father and the mother, awakens something in the psyche that is connected to images of royalty. The parents are no longer ruling the psyche. In some stories, royalty is represented by a king; in others, it's a queen or a sultan. It can be a master of wondrous skill or a master thief. Even in stories where the father gives his son away to the master of all thieves, the son still becomes a figure of great accomplishment and wealth, much to the surprise of the father.

The dynamics of this story reflect the instincts in the depths of the human psyche, for somewhere we know that if we accept loss fully, we open up to unknown possibilities both within and without. When the son walks the dark road away from his family, he walks toward that which the family cannot see in him. Somewhere along that dark road, the son gives up some of his expectation of being fully recognized by his parents. In the language of the story, the wound, the separation from his village, and the journey on the dark road have awakened something in the son that resonates with something in this king, who waits awake in the center of his psyche. The son is looking for something that will father what is royal in him. The sleepless king waits for someone who is like the son that he has lost. When they see each other, the questions and tests begin.

The hunter's son has stepped into another world where simple things carry greater weight than usual. In a fairy tale there might be stronger signals that he has crossed the line into the inner, other, underworld. In this folktale the signs of the otherworld are subtle: the story simply says that everyone in the village was asleep, but the king at the center was awake, and that the son entered the chief's hut "naked, without trousers." Soon the chief will be called "King Lion" and no one will question the son's physical resemblance to the missing king's son. In the dark night of the son's soul the story has shifted to the "otherworld," and the three simple questions that the chief asks carry unusual weight. In other stories three similar questions are asked by spirit animals, who will help if the answers are honest and direct. Here they are asked by King Lion.

The first two questions are simple, as simple as the doorway of a hut, but they separate one world from another. "From where do you come? How goes it with you?" The answers to these questions will determine whether or not the third question will be asked. If the son's answers are evasive or superficial, nothing much may happen. If the son has not worked his own story through to the point where he can say, "This is what happened to me," the king may dismiss him. The questions are tests that determine the course of the story.

Huts like this exist in the psychic forest. They appear when genuine change is possible. But they have their rules and dangers. If it is a hut of the Baba Yaga, the Old Hag of the World, the witch who tests the seeker for the suppleness of heart and soul needed to handle the power she guards, the question will pose a dilemma: "Are you running toward something or away from something?" A simple choice of one horn of this dilemma will stick the seeker onto that horn. If the answer is running away, one has to return. If the answer is running toward, one gets a wild goose chase until you are ready to say a third thing that accepts the dilemma.

Like Baba Yaga's hut, the hut of the king is also a place of questions. The king puts questions of past, present, and future to the son: where are you from, how are you now, will you keep a secret from now on? The son understands because he answers the second question by telling the story of the hunt with his father and the blow he received. If he had talked of other aspects of his life, he might have been sent back to those aspects, or the hut might simply have disappeared. For this is a hut of radical change; if the son lies about where he is coming from, he can't go forward. What's going on here is subtle, but if the son denies that he is driven forward by the wound he carries, the chief may not make the offer. The son can only be the son of a king if he knows in what way he is wounded. Ultimately, denying his woundedness will deny him access to the king in himself.

The circumscribed hut where the three questions are asked can also be seen as a "therapy hut." The three questions set up a recapitulation of the son's psychological life: Where has he come from, what has happened that causes trouble, how is he coping with his wounds? Within the contained hut of therapy the questions of origins, woundedness, and inner royalty are raised privately, even secretly.

The chief accepts the self-examination of the son and says, "Will you keep a secret with me?" This question represents a danger because anything that must be secret is dangerous. The son has just revealed how he was wounded by his father, that he has no home and doesn't know where he is going. He is completely exposed to this king. The last son the king had was killed in a war—will keeping the secret lead him to the same fate? As many stories will show, every encounter with a king has intimations of fate and danger mixed with opportunity.

When the son of the hunter agrees, the queen raises the sound of joy, and the entire village joins in the joyous return. Apparently, the queen mother in the psychic village was waiting for a candidate for "royal son" to arrive as well. She makes everyone aware of the "return of the son." There is joy everywhere, except among the counselors, who say "Indeed, indeed."

The story evokes many "indeeds" when a group of men hear it and respond to this exchange in the chief's hut. There is always a lot of shouting. Is this a secret or a lie? Is the chief a legitimate king or a betraying older male misusing his power? If the king's son is dead, why does the king want a pretend son? Is the son entering an abusive situation where the secret is not to reveal the abuse? Why should the son pretend he's better than he is? How can anyone trust a chief who makes secret deals? Why doesn't everyone just tell the truth and get on with their lives? Isn't this just more fatherly falsehood? Isn't the village just another patriarchal set-up secretly intended to harm everyone?

The fact that the son accepts the secret draws forth widely divided opinions from the story's listeners. The chorus stirs into action—the arguments go back and forth as if a meeting of the counselors had begun. It is as if the men, in response to the king's questions, have taken up various positions inside the chief's hut and are observing the exchange between the son and the chief. It becomes clear that most men have attended this type of conversation both inside themselves and in the outside world. The angle from which each man perceives the dialogue between son and king reveals much about where he stands with questions of authority and self-esteem.

If a man has never dealt with the wounding that comes from his own father, he may forget or deny how often he wished he had a different father or was the son of some other man. He may identify with the father and king in the story. But, once a man enters the story through the wound as felt by the son, his attitude to the secret becomes important and revealing. The scene in the hut has psychological and mythic implications. As the men begin to examine and explain their views of the secret, deeper layers of the question appear.

One man says, "It's simply a lie. I'm not the son of a king or a chief, and I never was. I'm simply the son of a rat hunter, and he couldn't even accept me and my mistakes." All of this is true, and there's a factual directness to this man's position. But it is also harshly literal, and the phrase *never was the son of a king* has a sound of despair and longing in it. As this man works the story through his imagination, it becomes clear that his hopes have been crushed. His capacity for trust in himself and in other men ended with some blow from his father. He has been left unconscious of anything in him that may have a touch of royalty. His psyche is still flattened by the blow from the ax. The image of himself as no more than a rat hunter like his father has stopped his life flow. He is carrying so much of his father with him that he is flattened continually. He is depressed, pressed down by the weight of the father's blow; the hopes he had when he threw away the rat were so severely squashed that any offer seems simply false, a lie. Besides, even if there was any truth to his being the son of a king, no one else would believe it, and it would only lead to more troublesome burdens.

From the opposite side of the king's hut, a man says, "Why shouldn't I just take whatever I can? I've been hit so many times from so many directions that I don't know who I am anyway. The whole deal is phony, and all the rules are made by fools to be followed by fools. Truth is in the eye of the beholder. What you grab is what you get. If this fool is willing to make me a prince, I'll take it. Rules are made to be broken. In a world that is so unjust that I don't know where I come from, don't know who my father really was, don't know what he really did for his living, don't know what kept him alive, what's the difference? All deals are crooked; I may as well be the son in this man's crooked system as in any other."

Another, who was seriously beaten or sexually abused by a father or uncle or stepfather, will see the deal as yet another seduction before mistreatment. He will either be compelled to accept it because resisting is even more painful, or he will refuse it completely because there can be no trusting of any man who offers pleasure, wealth, or power.

When the chief says, "Will you keep a secret with me?", one man says yes with no thought of where things may go, and the other says no, certain of where things will go. Both wind up back on the road to the parents' village needing to piece together some personal belongings, needing to wait until the first two questions can be answered more thoroughly. The first job on this Road of the Two Fathers requires putting one's "personal belongings" together, being able to answer the questions: What are your origins, what wounds are you carrying, where are your scars, and to what group of sons do you belong?

Until the son enters the hut of the king, the story could be read as a report of something that actually happened. There's very little of the psychological and nothing of the mythical in the narration. But when the son enters the village and the king's hut, the tone changes. The chief of the sleeping village is "King Lion, he who causes fear." The queen of joyous sound accepts a youth she has never seen before as her own son. Clearly, it is not her "real," biological son who is being announced. There is something going on here that has psychological depth and that moves into mythic territory.

The modern idea is to take the past literally: "It happened, it's over—I'll put all that behind me." But in the psyche, time is an ocean that can wash things that were cast away back on shore. As in many other stories, going forward depends on going back. Turning to the past to look for traumatic events and the causes of present conditions is one of the great movements of the psyche. It is also one of the styles of the psyche to pretend that something in the past has literally caused something in the present. It's as if bottles wash up on the shores of consciousness with little messages curled inside them calling for help. The bottles continually land on the shore. One day we notice one and open the message. One purpose of that message is to bring some deeply meaningful event from the past to a mythic aliveness in the present. At a certain point in the interview in the king's hut, the son, the rat, the wound, the king, and the secret are all present. Past and future are present in a symbolic event that temporarily turns the hunter's son into the son of a king. The change from one to the other requires a review of the past, a suspension of literal-mindedness, and the willingness to imagine a secret self hidden in the heart.

Until a man can talk clearly of the rat that passed between him and his father, potential kings will keep turning out to be wounding fathers. Denying what actually happened between his longings and his father's reactions to him keeps him returning to his father's hut. A man has to get out of his parents' village with his longing intact. Facing the wound from the father makes clear the unfulfilled longing and makes a man's inner life more real. It's as if each man has to talk to an inner king about the longings that became conscious during childhood that his father couldn't or wouldn't bless.

The chorus in the king's hut speaks it over and over: "At one memorable point in my life, the rat was more important to my father than I was. That's how it looked, how it felt, how it still feels when I approach something new and begin to feel enthusiastic." "Just when I was feeling high-spirited, full of imagination, and grand with the potential just ahead of me, my father saw the rat as more important than me." "Any time I felt great my father would cut me down to size." "My father dismissed everything I did with a platitude." "Mine said I'd never amount to anything."

The father can rarely see what is potential and grand in the son. Unless a man can travel the road of his father's mistake, and feel the wounding and the separation again, he can't get back to the core of grandness in his own psyche. The king becomes the second father by accepting the grand imagination that seized the son and caused him to toss away the rat. The sense of self-importance that flooded the son with spirit and feeling is the secret that is shared by the king and the son. And this sense of his own grandness allows the son to step into a symbolic world where he has another father.

The hunter's son answers the king's third question with "What secret?" Every family has skeletons in the closet, hidden deals. If there is a heavy family secret to carry, then lies become necessary in order to keep the secret safe. Carrying shameful family secrets requires a psychic effort that limits growth and blocks the imagination. Underneath the family guilt and shame waits the carefully guarded belief that somewhere in the core of the soul there is a seed of royalty. Around that core the soul grows. Life is a slow revelation, with occasional outbursts, from that core.

In the old Celtic imaginings, a person was born through three forces: the coming together of mother and father, an ancestral spirit's wish to be reborn, and the involvement of a god or goddess. Thus, at some core level everyone feels sovereign, but the need to fit into a family and a village group forces that sense of royalty deep inside. The infant wails and demands like a tyrant and sits beatifically in state like a true sovereign. Then the demands of life and the years of dependency cause that grand self to remain deep inside. There, each person has a royal heritage, an inherent claim to a mythic life. Part of what all humans hold in common is the sense of a royal birth and the subsequent sense that their extraordinary qualities are lost and left behind.

The people who are destined to become royal—the kings, queens, and heroes of stories and cultures—are at first hidden or abandoned.

What is hidden or abandoned must be visited in secret; so everyone maintains a path that leads to this secret sense of self. Moreover, the feeling of abandonment forces a person to be close to the part that is hidden. When all else is gone and there's nothing left to lose, then what is left and what cannot be completely lost or even thrown away is truly one's self. What was abandoned by others remains part of the genuine self and cannot be abandoned by me; rather, it comes out in times of loss. And what stays secret inside everyone is that somewhere he is a king, somehow she is a queen.

The poet William Stafford finds this secret revealed in a corner in the rain:

A STORY THAT COULD BE TRUE

If you were exchanged in the cradle and
your real mother died
without ever telling the story
then no one knows your name,
and somewhere in the world
your father is lost and needs you
but you are far away.

He can never find
how true you are, how ready.
When the great wind comes
and the robberies of the rain
you stand in the corner shivering.
The people who go by—
you wonder at their calm.

They miss the whisper that runs
any day in your mind,
"Who are you really, wanderer?"—
and the answer you have to give
no matter how dark and cold
the world around you is:
"Maybe I'm a king."

Each of us carries inside a "story that could be true," that can get more revealed as one stands in the rain and wind, robbed of one's usual coverings. The hunter's son stands "naked, without trousers," before the chief. The son has been carrying the secret that despite the blows of life and the loneliness of the wanderer's road, or because of them, he is a king's son.

The chief, on the other hand, is awake because of the loss of his son. In many cultures, a king could not continue to rule unless he had a son to inherit the kingdom. A king without offspring was thought to lack in creativity and generativity. A king without a son would not be keeping a careful enough eye on the future of the realm, and a king who was not preparing for the future of the realm would be dangerous to his subjects.

Once the hunter's son has accepted the secret, has accepted that he is the son of a king, or at least has agreed to play at being prince, the queen-mother proclaims him her son. He is washed and anointed, given new clothes, and brought out before all the people. He is also exposed to the critique and testing of the counselors, who have a stake in whether he is royal or not. The whole village gets involved, the whole psyche wakes up.

In the psyche of the listener, the story at this point describes those occasions when we do something or step into something that blesses us, washes clean the wounds and weariness, and anoints the soul afresh. When occasions of renewal occur, part of us exults, and another part brings up doubts and questions. Our inner counselors immediately begin to consider what this renewal means to them and to their positions in the psyche. They are masters at reminding us of what things were like before we put on the new clothes. They are supremely aware of intrigue and are not moved by joy, except to question the genuineness of its source and the shortness of its duration. They are uneasy with change, committed to the status quo, enamored of tests, and distrustful of everything. They question the qualifications of anyone who would assume a station above their own sons—that is, above the image of the self that they have created. In some people, these inner counselors act like a powerful modern bureaucracy that blocks any attempt at change, that grinds any new developments into smaller and smaller questions and concerns, and that slows almost to a standstill the dynamic motion kicked off by the chief's recognition of the son.

The work of these counselors can be seen in the outer, as well as the inner, worlds—in schools, corporations, family businesses, and sports, for example. Political parties and entire nations can become obsessed with the question, Is this the king's son or not? Even in the United States, where there is no monarchy, any new candidate for major office is examined for signs of sovereign qualities and common weaknesses. The media assume both the role of the queen-mother and that of the critical ministers. At the first appearance of a royal son or daughter, they raise the sound of joy; they anoint the new candidate and quickly present him or her everywhere. Then they begin to say, "Indeed, indeed." Perhaps because most people are so distant from their own inner sense of sovereignty, the outer counselors of disbelief are emboldened.

It's extremely common for men who come to conferences to talk about the huge number of inner critics who sit on their shoulders and stifle any attempt to try something new, or to grow, or even to descend into genuine sorrow. Many men despair of ever finding an authentic voice, a genuine sense of purpose in life. The voices of the inner critics tear apart any attempts at authenticity. Many men, entering into the story of the hunter's son, feel that they are driven away from the hut of the king before they even get to the tests. In the same way, the counselors, like our inner critics, become an extension of the blow from the father. They are a reminder of any and all mistakes; they serve as extensions of the wrath of the father. They can keep a man from entering any king's hut. They can drown out the voice trying to speak out the woundedness inside. They can block the route that leads to help, to therapy, to a mentor, and to the importance of an inner life.

Because the hunter's son has accepted the secret that he is also the king's son, the entire psychic village wakes up. Anything that reaches to the core of grandness in a person awakens *all* the villagers in the psyche. The secret is out and people want to celebrate it or criticize it. Messengers spread the news, the horses of the psyche begin to stir. The whole village awakens. The lights are on, the rumor mill begins running, the counselors listen to conspiracy theories, swords are being gathered. It's the opposite of the sleeping village that the son walked away from and the opposite of the quiet when he entered this village. The talebearer goes from one place to another keeping the parts of the village in touch, keeping the doubting critics in the psyche connected to the grand sense of self. The king instructs his new son, "If the naked man can dance, how much better can the man with a cloak?" If a man has a sense of what the tests in life are about, there's the possibility of dancing through some of them, and a weight is lifted from his spirit.

the world? Aren't the ministers, the sons, and the king all guilty of the most outrageous destructive behavior? How can any chief or king allow this cruelty? And who wants to be the inheritor of this aberrant bloody mess?

Often a man will say, "I dropped out of the story at that point. I wouldn't kill a horse or a woman—I'd rather die." An animal rights activist will say, "This is exactly what we're against, exactly the arrogant attitude that endangers species after species. The need to make men superior by the destruction of innocent animals is the problem, not the cure!" Other men will begin to tell stories of their involvement with horses and other animals. Still others will say that this is a typical example of the kind of destructive behavior into which young men feel pressured by their peers; they point out that this is the kind of loss of personal choice that leads to mob behavior. Others will rail against a story that seems to justify male violence against women. A whole contingent of men have said that this handing of swords from fathers and kings to their sons is the cause of all the violence in this world. They refuse to accept the swords as their fathers did. It's time for a new village that has no swords and no violence toward women, children, or animals! Other men will disagree: you've already agreed to do what they do, so you have to do it. How do you know that they won't simply kill you if you don't kill the horses? And besides, if the youth is not the literal son of a king and queen, then the horses and slave girls are not literal either.

The arguments often heat up and become fierce. Someone will say, "Kill the ministers"; another, "Kill their sons," or "Kill the tale-bearer," or even "Kill the storyteller." Strangely, even those who are outraged at the idea of killing the horses are often able to imagine killing the ministers. The feeling that something needs to be slain prevails. As the arguments intensify, more swords come out.

Suddenly everyone listening to the story seems to have entered the clearing outside the village, and all find themselves with sword in hand, facing the question, What does it mean to be the son of a king? People feel tricked and upset to find themselves inside the story, to sense that they are a part of the wanton slaying that is going on. There is a clash of swords as everyone begins to cut away at the literal interpretations of the images of horses and slave girls. The emotions provoked by the story catch everyone in the story; even contrary emotions mark the spot where people fully engage the images. The dilemma story is serving its purpose, catching everyone up and causing them to suffer and discuss the issues plaguing the group. For the images in this story mirror those that appear in newspapers and documentaries, on city streets, and in the farms and fields of the real world. People may have trouble imagining a chief or a king these days, but no one has trouble imagining the massive slaying of animals, the enslaving of women, the constant demeaning of women into girls, and the brutalization of actual girls.

When I first found this story, I was caught up in the wounding of the son and in the dilemma of the son, with sword in hand, faced with the opportunity to slay father or king. I knew I had to tell the story in order to learn more about it. But I felt I couldn't tell about the tests of slaying animals and slaves; they seemed archaic, shameful, and repulsive. Then I realized that these responses were also reasons to tell the story, that the dilemma at the end of the story starts here. At the end of the story the question is, Kill the father or kill the king? If the images are taken as literal "real people," not many would actually choose to kill either and some would have no choice to make. People would say that it's illegal, immoral, even physically impossible because their fathers are already dead and they don't know any kings. For the most part that doesn't happen because the king and the father are seen as images, as symbols that focus the emotions, attitudes, and inner stories of the listener. But there is a strong tendency to literalize the horses and the slave girls, as if the cultural imagination gets stuck.

If only a literal interpretation applies to the scenes in the story, then the wound to the son would be reduced only to cuts and bruises of the body and not relate to conditions of the soul. Tests, questions, and dilemmas abound in this story. They begin with, Am I wounded? As a man, am I wounded in relation to my father and therefore in my sense of the masculine? This question sets us on a road that leads to another question: am I in any way connected to a king? The test that will answer this question takes place on the field of the slayings. And part of the test lies in whether or not I can find the symbolic layer of this story—and, indeed, of my own story.

Because of our ability to amass information and the facts of modern life, people can carry statistics and accounts of human tragedies that stun the imagination. Hard facts and statistics about human suffering are sometimes carried like weights that must get moved before the emotions and imagination can move. Often at conferences we will designate one group as the "Men Who Handle Ugly Facts" or the

"Men Who Don't Deny Ugly Facts"; this group announces the facts that the other men carry. The first thing to be slain in the clearing beyond the village is the idea that the ugly facts of this life can be avoided or ignored. The image of the "great war-horses" produces a litany of violence and destruction. There is no denying the persistence of wars and the increasing slaughter and devastation exacted by the machines of war. There is no denying the spread of warfare into cities that are supposed to be at peace; there is no denying the ravages of racism and colonial dominance or the prevalence of and increase in the abuse of women and children.

Hearing this part of the story, some women have said, "That's right—men start out as boys hurting animals and each other, then move on to women and children." Men of all colors have said that the big wars consist of men of one group killing men of another group while the little, constant wars consist of men of the same group killing each other. Many men carry with them the statistics on how many women are raped each minute, and they know that the rapes are an enslavement of women by fear and a killing of both the body and the feminine spirit.

Whatever causes this flood of violence, it is most often enacted by men. In the United States, violence has reached epic proportions as swords are traded for guns and horses for high-horsepower cars, and the ugly facts include the statistics on how many young men die from gunshot wounds and car crashes. The suburban white youth is more likely to be slain by a car or commit suicide, and the urban black youth is not only much more likely to be slain but also more likely to be slain by a gun. Men are more likely than women to be killed and more likely to kill. Boys are likely to be threatened and beaten at home, at school, and in the streets. And of course, men are likely to wield great violence against women. In the clearing, everyone can make a sword of the ugly facts that cut him or her the most.

The accumulation of tragedies, abuses, and corpses is undeniable and increasingly unavoidable in daily life. But to get the whole story, the hard ground of literal facts must break open. The emotional and imaginal must break through the literal views of this world, or real change can't occur. The aggressions in men must be engaged before, not after, they become violent. The wound with which the story started is one source of the breakthroughs. The wound connects and separates the son and the father, the son and the king, the son and the other sons. The slayings must, finally, be seen through the wound.

If a man doesn't know he is wounded, he can deny the facts forever. One fact about a man who doesn't know he is wounded is that he can't see that others are wounded. More than that, he'll put his wound into others because of his vague sense that there's a wound somewhere. He'll only see it when he puts it into someone else and will feel strangely better when he sees it there. Then he'll lose touch with it and have to stick it on someone again. If the sense of the wound received at the beginning of the story is present vividly enough in the listeners, then they will be able to move beyond the literal meaning of the slayings in the clearing. Stories are full of swords and of heads rolling, for this is how the psyche changes—by being cut off and then growing again. Entering the deeper layers of the psyche means that heads are going to roll and that anger, anguish, and fear will arise. Changing one aspect of the deep psyche changes every relationship in the psyche, masculine and feminine.

Inevitably, someone begins to refer to the horse as a symbol. What does the horse represent for the psyche? Someone says, "Instinct." The slaying of the horse then becomes the slaying of some instinctual human behavior. What behavior? Charging about? Domesticating animal energy and harnessing it for human power? Horses are a continual presence in most men's lives through the horsepowered vehicles they own or desire—the Mavericks, Broncos, and Mustangs. Men are driven to great lengths by their desire for a given model of car, truck, or motorcycle; they judge and are judged by horsepowered vehicles. Thousands gather to watch them race, on the verge of being out of control. Thousands more lose control and crash into one another. Horses are a metaphor for instinctive power, but also for freedom, speed, and dominant masculine force.

The horses in the story are called the "great war-horses." Indeed, the horse changed the nature of warfare, and at one time, whoever achieved the greatest skill with horses was able to rule the widest area. There's a sense in the story, then, that the son of the king must be able to slay certain instinctive drives to power, certain tendencies to charge about, to get on his high horse, to get caught up in the trappings of power. A modern man might need to slay his attachment to his Bronco or his dreams of a Porsche. Another may need to rid himself of his habitual means of escape from relationships, from speed limits, or from facing responsibility or authority. Another might need to slay his obsession with risk before he can access his genuine feelings of being special, lucky, royal. A man may have to cut through the habit of gambling everything on a long shot in order to have a moment in the "winner's circle" and the right to "live like a king."

Another man may need to slay the image of himself as a "work-horse," a draft animal that is always pressed into service. Another may have to stand before the image he carries of himself as only a "horse's ass" or someone who is always "mule-headed" or ornery as a mule. In short, it is whatever horse the man has ridden to the field that will have to be slain—that is, whatever has carried him or even driven him to this point in his life will now prove him to be something other than the son of a king. "Only the son of a king would have such disregard for wealth and power."

In other words, the horse stands for an image the son has had to adopt in order to continue to be the son of his parents. As a psychological move, slaying the horse moves the son away from the village of his parents' opinion of him and toward the king. What is viewed as the epitome of wealth and power in the upperworld can be the opposite in the inner, underworld. Whatever adaptation has carried him this far will now block his connection to the king. If he is to remain close to the center of grandness, generativity, secrecy, and creativity in the village—and in himself—he must slay whatever image he was saddled with as a boy. Slaying the horse is a symbolic ritual that moves him closer to being the son of a king.

After this first test, the sons of the ministers report that the son of the chief has acted in a kingly way. The ministers say, "Indeed." They require a second test, for there remains another symbolic part of the son to be seen. As the men at the conferences begin to work on this part of the story, they find it difficult to talk about female slaves. The anguish that they feel over the cultural treatment of women is revealed, along with an awkward sadness over the lack of language available to describe the distance between modern men and women. At this point, someone usually begins a protest that the story shouldn't be told in this way, that it is demeaning to women, that it raises the specter of colonial slavery, that there are no women present to speak for themselves, that even uttering the phrase *slave girl* does double violence to women.

But, there's also a question:

What's the connection between the slave girl in the story and the profusion of female suffering—the incest, rape, battering, and discrimination in modern cultures? What happens when each man is seen as heading for the clearing with a slave girl? The literal vision is horrifying, yet people line up night after night, year after year, to see slasher movies and horror films where women are reduced to helplessness and then killed. A movie that depicts men enslaving and cannibalizing women wins "best picture" awards and newspapers report actual cases where men keep girls trapped and enslaved in hidden chambers in suburban houses.

It's as if men can carry the sense of undeveloped yet threatening inner "feminine" characteristics as a slave girl. If the inner image is not brought to consciousness, if a man's inner sense of the feminine is not released, it becomes more literal and more dangerous to women. In India, a place where feminine deities are visible and worshipped in public, there are still "dowry slaves." Young women are married into families for social reasons and their dowry is paid over time. If the dowry payments stop the bride is beaten and humiliated. She may even be killed for lack of the dowry. Despite the presence of feminine deities actual women lack protection. The endangered bride also appears in fairy tales of the Bluebeard type, where hidden rooms are filled with the bones of former brides kept under lock and key. Literal, historical, and imaginal figures meet in the image of "slave girl," an inner slave figure that is projected onto the outer world.

When the men working within the story start to approach the slave girl as a symbol connected to themselves, personal images get released. At first, men resist the idea that the slave girl could be within them. It's as if the heroic ego in the psyche must keep defining "girl" as something outside itself yet controllable, as if the ego cannot accept the idea that part of the psyche is treated as a slave girl. But some men argue that the oppression of women is related to the oppression of the feminine inside men. What, then, is enslaved or enslaving in men, and what is the "girl" in the man? Each man reveals something important about himself in his answer to "What is a slave?": property, a servant, a sexual slave, always ready to serve, does whatever I want, does the dirty work, always submits to me, feeds me, takes care of me, works for nothing, and so on. As each man defines his slave, he also indicates what he is a slave to.

If the master-slave relationship lasts long enough, the master eventually is no longer able to do the job expected of the slave. Then both are in chains, and each is dependent on the other. Each son brings to the clearing some aspect of his life where he is at times the master, at times the slave. The man who answers that the slave is a sexual object is enslaved to objectified sex. If he's caught in pornography, he may try to be the master or to feel masterful, but he can only do so if a woman is forced out of all mastery of her body. And the more he engages with the pornographic material, the less he can master his obsession with it; he becomes enslaved or addicted to the material itself.

In the psyche of the individual, the slave represents a habitual way of doing and seeing. In other words, the aspiring son will be kept from the king unless he can cut through some habitual ways of seeing and acting. And the clue to where this slavishness exists lies in his attitude toward "girl," toward his own immature, feminine self. Thus, the story is saying that the hunter's son must cut through two areas in the psyche that he habitually takes for granted: the area of instinct, force, and power and the area of his inner feminine. And the story suggests that there's a logic to the order in which the discriminating sword should be used in the psyche. If the "war-horses" in a man have never been cut down, he'll be unable to cut through his habitual views of the feminine. Paradoxically, if a man has never ridden his own horses, has been kept away from all stallions, or was knocked off before he felt in charge, he will probably carry an exaggerated view of the feminine and of women. In the logic of the story, slaying the horses is necessary to uncover the habit of enslaving the inner feminine of the man. After consciously engaging the inner feminine, a man becomes less likely to demean others and releases himself from a too heroic attitude toward life.

The two slayings in the psyche to which the story points are extremely important. If a man can avoid having his horse cut out from under him, he will be overbearing to everyone, especially women, and people may say that they wish to "cut him down to size." The forty-year-old man who claims never to have had a real failure is still riding the horse of youth. He received a horse from some king, but he denies knowledge of the clearing where the other sons have sacrificed their horsepower. Moreover, a man who denies failure in himself can't abide it in others. It's only as he is walking back from the loss of the charging horse of masculinity that a man begins to see his dependent relations with women and with the feminine within. What needs to be cut through with the two slayings are the literal layers of the masculine and feminine in order to open the full emotional and imaginal life of the man.

The son's internal feminine components connect him to the world and integrate his own basic emotional style with the attitudes of his family toward life and with elements of his fate. If something doesn't cut through to this grand sense of the feminine, the youth will be enslaved to a narrow sense of what it means to be alive. The "slave self" is that sense of oneself that responds predictably even to surprising circumstances. Whether the slave self is always charming and seductive or is haggard and overworked doesn't matter as much as the fact that it is automatic, on call, and dutiful. The slave self can't break the fetters that bind it to its routine chores and that keep it from the freedoms and responsibilities of a larger life. The slave sense of self is the opposite of the sense of grandness in the self. Slaying this slavishness satisfies the village that he can be the son of the king.

The son's relationship to the feminine, symbolized by the slave girl in the story, is a problem that is partially connected to his father. The son acquires his relationship to the feminine partly through his own father's view of his mother, partly through the views of women held by fathers throughout the culture, and partly through the son's own view of the world. In the story, the way he sees the world is being tested. Slaying the slave sense of self completes the tests and precipitates the return of the father into the story. When the son settles into the king's hut, that seems to awaken his father's interest in him. The father's world and the threads of feeling between father and son are affected by the son being recognized by a king and the son moving towards the deeper masculine and feminine images in his soul. By consciously engaging and expanding his attitudes toward power and the feminine, the son's relationships to father and king change. The next test will find him standing between the two of them.

By the time a group of men have argued about and discussed the rituals in the clearing, it's clear that each man has received a complex inheritance from the world of fathers. Each has a wound, a war-horse, a sword, and a slave girl. Each area of inheritance comes with curses and potential blessings. Wishing to be, trying to be, secretly agreeing to be the son of a king forces the troubles in each area of inheritance out into the open and makes changes in the psychic village possible.

The father walks back into the story as if drawn to the fully awake village where the son waits. The road between the village of the father and the one where the son waits remains a dark road. The darkness is made from the wound they share. Many attempts to reach the other's village only go part way, one or the other gets lost in the dark. Each attempt to reach the other awakens the wound and spreads the darkness. The day the father reaches the village of the son a third test begins.

CHAPTER 4

A FONDNESS FOR SWORDS

Aᴛᴛᴇʀ ᴛʜᴇ ᴛᴇsᴛs, the ministers seem satisfied, the psychic village calms down, and the son of the hunter lives with the king. For a time, life goes on and a man may forget he has unfinished issues with his father and that he carries a wound through life. But, the father issues always return. One day the father arrives in the village looking for his son. The villagers say they haven't seen such a son, but they send him to the chief's hut. Everyone in the village seems to recognize this double fatherhood, and that the son remains subject to further testing. The father enters the chief's hut and calls for the son to return with him. It's as if the father cannot see the king, as if the father cannot see the son in relation to the king. The son sits silently between the two fathers. The hunter offers the son life as before. The chief offers the father gold and great wealth to leave the son in the new village. The father continues to call to the son, refusing the wealth of the king and refusing to accept the secret that the king and the son share. The son silently refuses to choose between the two.

In the logic of stories, elements are repeated ritualistically, often three times. The king now calls for a sword and three horses. Twice before the sons of the ministers have called for swords. On the same ground where the horses and the slave girls were slain, the father, the son, and the king face each other over the sword. The king gives the son a sword for the third time. This time the instructions are not to do "whatever they do" but to choose what to do himself. Slay the king, return with the father, and live as before, or slay the father and continue to live with the king—what would you do?

Among the men, three groups immediately emerge: a large group of father slayers, a large group of king killers, and a third group that is a mixture of those who refuse to do either, those who do both, those who turn the sword on themselves, and those who devise a unique solution. Many of the men would prefer to discuss the options than admit to a choice.

As a story is told, the storyteller inside each listener sends up images to meet the words. A story is taken in by matching the words with scenes instantaneously produced in the imagination of the listener. The psychic response to the choice offered the son is swift and unhampered by conventions or morality. Something in the psyche responds to the story's tough language, and images and feelings deep inside leap at the choice the way the son leaps at the opportunity to go off on an adventure with the father. If the ego does not edit the image that leaps up and if the imagination is not censored by the inner counselors, a man will see which way the sword swings for him at that time. Sometimes he gets merely a vague sense of which *direction* the sword cuts; then he must follow that trajectory in order to find the image of who was slain this time.

I say "this time" because it is a largely preconscious response that the story elicits. Each time we hear the story, our response could be different. In the imagination, in the inner world of emotional images and landscapes, the father and the king have been slain over and over. They're used to it. They even recover and keep agreeing to these excursions to the clearing. As the story indicates, they have no choice but to do what they do; choice, in this case, lies solely with the son. The son has to make this choice over and over as if each slaying needs repetition in order for him to get the message that he is the son of his father and the son of a king.

For some of the men in the third group, the rational arguments against patricide and murder leapt to the fore so quickly as the story was told that they were not able to observe their deeper responses. These men are simply stuck in the literal meaning of the story. As the discussion of symbolic slaying goes on, many in the third group hear some other man say exactly what they feel about their father or precisely what they think about a mentor, teacher, or boss. Then they move over to the father killers or the king killers.

The groups are like camps set up outside the village. The men in each camp will talk to each other first about why they have chosen that group; then the three camps will come together, and each camp will report back to the community at large.

In the camp of the father killers, everyone takes a turn telling his story of being wounded by the father. Some men seemed to have no choice when faced with the dilemma. As soon as they felt the sword, the decision was made, and it was off with the father's head. Now that chorus launches into a long litany of exact descriptions of the father as seen through a son's eyes. Their choice was clear-cut and full of anger: He struck me with the ax and left me for dead; now it's my turn to strike back. He left me when I was three years old, no explanation, no return; if he did come back now, I'd take his head off. He beat me every day for twelve years, and I've slain him a hundred times in my mind. For what he did to my mother, I'd kill him if he ever came back. He didn't ever strike me, but he didn't ever protect me from anything; now he needs to feel that. He preferred my brothers and rejected everything I brought him; let's see if he'll reject this sword. He drank himself into a stupor, and I hate that head and that cursed mouth. He called me a sissy and had to outdo me at everything. His work meant more to him than anything I ever did; with the sword and the blessing of the king, I can finally cut through his rage. Nothing is forgotten. Long-buried memories rise up like the son in the story returning to consciousness.

Mixed with the anger and rage are tears and voices that trail off into sadness. The pool of sorrow grows along with the rage. Men who are less enraged but no less determined join the chorus: killing the father means continuing forward; not killing him would mean regression. Going back would mean agreeing to be struck again. Going back would mean accepting that I was his property, a slave to his anger. I've gotten everything I can from going back home so many times; it's time to move on. If I don't strike him down, he'll come into everything I'll do. He'll keep claiming me as his boy; I'm finished with that. He disowned me because I'm gay, and I almost killed myself; I could kill him for that. When I accepted the secret, I killed my father; this is just the ritual completion. If I killed the king, I'd lose all that I've struggled for. Killing the king would mean killing my spiritual life. The king is big enough to give me the sword and the right to choose; my father is always trying to drag me back to his condition.

On the other side, the king killers can't wait to speak. Blood is thicker than water, they say. If my father didn't truly love me, he would have taken the gold and left me with the king. Throughout everything, I just wanted to hear my father's love for me; I forgive him for the ax. No matter what has happened, I couldn't kill my father. If I killed my father, I would die as well. That my father stopped what he was doing to come find me is all I need in order to go to him. Now that I have a sword, I don't need to fear my father. All the king offers is material wealth; my father's love is greater than that. If he wasn't sorry, he would never have come after me. My father is natural; the king is a tyrant who rules by force and lies. The king can't be trusted; he's willing to lie and say I'm his dead son. The king is simply a false father; he'll use me for his own purposes. The king has caused all the killing; now it's his turn to die. I had a mentor who led me on and then stole my ideas for himself; this king will misuse the son in the same way. There was a lesson to be learned from the father, but the king just causes pain. If his own ministers don't believe him, how can I trust the king? I had to keep the lie to protect myself; now I'm ready to be with my father. There are plenty of bad leaders in the world, but I only have one father.

In the camp of the king killers, there's much discussion of these false-father kings. A man says, "It's easy to understand how I could wind up standing in a crowd in a lonely village in Oregon waiting for a guru in a Rolls Royce to drive by. If you can only imagine how desperately I needed to be seen by a noble eye! And any more than a glance would have been too much." Another man was betrayed in the inner sanctum of academia by his mentor. Several men with business careers throw in stories of betrayals by chief executives. An ex-army officer who volunteered for Vietnam cuts through the talking with a piercing scream about the betrayal that sticks in his heart like a sword. He bewails having led and directed troops of men to their deaths only to find that there was no point to it.

In the camp of the king killers, there's no lack of heads that can roll. Any hundred men can tell a hundred stories of betrayal. Eventually, the discussion moves to the lack of leadership in the culture, to the refusal of the leadership to admit the secret that everyone holds a spark of royalty. There is a collective realization that the false kings of

American politics and industry have not only ignored the nobility in men but actually allowed it to die. In the camp of the king killers, the question becomes: When all the illusory kings are cut down and the inner illusions are put to the sword, will there be anything left of the son's capacity to trust another king, or even another man?

Meanwhile, the third camp keeps dividing into smaller groups. One subgroup contains the refuseniks: I just won't do it. The story tricked me into this position; I refuse to handle the sword. I break the sword in pieces and walk away. I bury the sword in the ground. I take the sword and go to another village. I leave the sword with them and take all the horses so they can't follow. I refuse to be forced to decide. I'm going to a new village; they can come if they want.

This group wants to settle the dilemma without the sword. They see the sword as the cause of the trouble. They seem to be refusing to *be* the sword or take the sword from the king. They are also refusing to look at death. In the psyche, refusing to commit means refusing to let something die.

Opposite the refuseniks is a small group of men who wield the sword quickly and slay both father and king. They are willing to do this again and again. The members of this group feel a reluctance to relinquish the sword. This place is too hot, the sword is held too tightly, there's no scabbard in sight. Anyone could lose his head in this group. These men have risen right out of the flames of the forge and been thrown into the clearing without cooling or anointing. There are Vietnam veterans in this group. They were pulled out of Asian jungles, aflame with the fires of napalm, and thrown right into the streets and back roads of America. They're still burning with betrayal from both sides—from the fathers who led them to the war and from the king who left them in the flames too long and then turned away when they came back on fire. In this group are black men who feel on fire every day in the streets of big cities; many people pretend not to see their fire until they burn their own neighborhoods, making the forge visible to both fathers and would-be kings. Also in this group are men who were beaten at home and "rehabilitated" in prison—or else were so severely burned in their father's hut that they carry their own prison around with them, and when they come out, they come out swinging. Heads of families, heads of state, heads of corporations, any head that flies will cool the fires imprisoned in their own heads temporarily. Not too many questions here. There's a silent call for water to cool things down.

Another group would shatter the sword, break it up, and get rid of it. Something has happened to these men to make things brittle. When the test comes, it is too shattering; everything breaks into pieces. Some in this group were thrown from the horse before they even reached the clearing; the test was over before it started. All the pieces of their story need to be gathered together. They sit outside the chief's hut and tell it to each other.

Some of them say they'll just go on to the next village, or they'll start their own village. The father and king are flawed characters, and both their villages are failures, so these men will simply start over someplace new. They are the masters of manifest destiny; they are the real estate developers of the male psyche. There's always the next village, the next big idea, the next relationship, the next job, the next invention of their personality. They deny their ancestors and claim that they can avoid the weaknesses of the chief by founding a village where people won't suffer. At this point they don't realize that the rat, the father, and the king will appear in the next village as well.

Across from them is the quietest group. One gets the sense that its members should be approached gently. They are truly sad. This is no game at all. When given the sword by the king, they were clear that they would have to use it on themselves. It is hard for them to explain why this would be the best way: I'd wound myself and see who would offer to die so I don't kill myself. I'd kill myself rather than decide, rather than continue to suffer and see them suffer. If I was gone, there'd be nothing to fight over. I've been paralyzed since I heard the choices.

No matter how these men handle the sword, it always points back at them. Their attention to themselves is too sharp, too cutting; no matter what happens to them, they stay focused on their own complicity in the events. They are stunned by their position. As they work through the story, they feel that they are inside the horse or the slave girl, waiting. Several men have said it this way: "It's as if I'm inside the horse that is to be slain. If someone has to die, it will be me."

The first time I saw a man take this "suicidal position," I reacted to it literally. I took him at his word. I talked to him privately. He was in a lot of pain but could see the symbolic aspects of his position. He felt that he was the son still trying to be born into an active life. He felt that either the sword might cut him out of the horse where he felt trapped and ridden by the father and the king or the sword might slay him. He eventually agreed not to try suicide. He agreed to visit the camp of the father killers to see how they worked with their anger.

There is always more than one man who would solve the tension of the story through self-destruction. Once it is made clear that there is a camp for those under the sword, many stories of contemplated suicide come out. The men who turn anger on themselves have a lot to say to each other. Most men have felt suicidal at some point; it seems related to the feeling of being no one's son—neither the father's nor the king's. When there's no hope of being loved by the father or blessed by the king, a man begins cutting himself down.

Each of the camps can teach something about fathers and kings and the slayings that go on in the psyche. There isn't a "right answer," except to learn more about the wounds and emotions on the road of the two fathers. Without a place in the heart for a father a person feels cut off from a source of strength and protection in life. Without a sense of royal connection, a person cannot heal old wounds, fears making mistakes when opportunities appear. Men go back and forth between the villages, between the camps.

In the first camp, the father is cut down to human size, and the king rises as a figure of symbolic and spiritual value to the son. The second camp scrutinizes anything that pretends to be kingly and then cuts its way back to the love in the father's heart. Spending time in each camp is necessary. Each camp sharpens one edge of the sword. Camp three is focused on the sword itself.

Everyone winds up in the third camp eventually. Some start out there, trying to avoid the sword or wielding it in a rage in all directions. Eventually, the men begin to focus on a tempered sword, one that fits the hand and spirit of each individual. Like the sword in the stone that was waiting for the future king, there is a sword for each man that will release when his hand touches it just so.

There are many metaphors for the shaping and making of a man from a boy. A man can be remade from the instructions of a spirit animal encountered through the ordeals and isolation of a vision quest. A man can be taken through a shamanic surgery where he is dismembered, cut to pieces, and put back together as a new person. The ground can open, swallow a man down, and force him to wander amongst ghosts and old bones until he finds a song to build a life around. There are many ways and most people go through more than one style of being remade. In this story the wound of the son gets put through fire and comes out as a sword. A fire is released in the son by the rough ax blow of his father, and this is converted into a sword that is smelted in the king's village. At the end the king gives him an actual sword. This represents the sword that the son has become; the sword is his temperament that will be tested on father and king. They are the fathers of his temperament, of his wounds and blessings.

The father by mistake and the king by intention have made the fire burning in the son into a metaphorical sword, and father and king must face this before the son can choose a direction for his life. The scene represents the inner temperament of a man, an emotional situation between fathers and sons, and a cultural condition as well. The anger and pain in the wounds of the sons either turn inward and destroy them or break out and become a threat to others. If the fathers and elders of a culture don't meet the sons on the grounds of their wounds and tempers, everyone is in danger of feeling the sword. The core of grandness in the sons, the spark of royalty, won't be released without drawing out the fire that surrounds it.

The ability of a man to discriminate between one thing and another is affected by his temperament. The sword metaphor combines the capacity to judge with the ability to feel. In the sword, thinking and feeling come together and the capacity to slay is tempered with the feeling to protect. What's being made is the sword that will cut through the invisible umbilical cord that ties father and son together, that ties the child to the family and keeps him dependent on it. The son is being remade, his spirit and temperament are being forged, and the longings in his soul are being released. The grand expectations within the son that caused him to throw the rat away find fulfillment in the sword. The son's sense of risk, excitement, expectation, and desire forms the fires that smelt the sword. The dangers that he presents to the world must be faced by father and king. When the father and king wait before the son, who alone has the sword, the son is taking part in a ritual, an initiation, that can move the son to a third place. The son becomes the sword being honed between the stones of father and king. The son's spirit gets refined through the craft of tempering.

The making of the sword involves the tempering of the blade. The blade goes from fire to oil or fire to water, which heat and cool it to balance its temper between strength and flexibility. Too much fire and the sword is brittle; too much cool water and the metals won't marry, the sword won't be able to hold an edge. In the early imagination, the metal of the sword and the mettle of the man were identical.

Among the Celts and Africans, the sword was cooled at least once in the blood of the man who would carry it, since his fortune and character were being forged in the sword. Water from a sacred well or stream was also used. Or the sword was dipped in oil, as in the rites of baptism when initiates are anointed with chrism, or holy oil. In old Europe the name for the forger of swords and men was smith, swordsmith. The hammering and forging of men was a mystical craft. As in alchemy, the smith assisted in the transformation of base ore into tempered metal. In Africa this craft was practiced at the same time as in Europe. In Africa the forge of the smith was imagined to be inside a lion or leopard; thus, the sword was made inside the king of the land. There's a reference to this image in our story when the chief is called "King Lion, he who causes fear." And at one time the mention of King Lion would have announced the craft of the other-inner-underworld, where people are smelted in the fires of their souls and tempered and reshaped. Also, a scabbard was carefully made, for the sword without a scabbard is unfinished.

The sword that has been forged in the hut of the lion king is partly the sword of courage that can expose the son's woundedness and partly the sword that can sharpen his ability to distinguish between the father's curse and the king's blessing. The king has blessed the same place that the father cursed. The father bit the son's head off; the king anoints his head. Where the father can't help but open a wound, the king is able to place a blessing. One source of the word *bless* comes from the French, *blessure*, which means wound. One of the responsibilities of those who would rule, lead, or mentor becomes learning to see into the wounded area of the hunter's son and spot the blessed streak that suffered the wound.

In the camp of the father killers, it begins to dawn on the men that the king gives the sword to the son knowing that it may be his own head that rolls. The king gives the sword of discrimination to this son who stands between a father by blood and wounding and a father by blood and secret blessing. This story must be repeated a number of times; the father's head must be taken off over and over until his ability to wound the son has been taken away. The king's head must roll again and again until the area of blessing becomes recognizable through the pains of disappointment and betrayal. When the story is heard over and over, more of the awakened son gets revealed. He gets more and more familiar with the sword of consciousness and more knowledgeable about the wound that is also the place of blessing.

This story says that the images of father and king must be separated from each other and that every son is given a sword with which to make this cut. Rather, every son *is* a sword for making these cuts. The story also participates in the old idea that a man is not born but made, forged from the blows of his family and the hammering of the kings that temper him. Over and over a son reenters the hearth of his father's village and the forge of the lion king. Each time the entry is as a son. If things go well, then each time a little more of the man emerges.

This story of father and son begins with the rat and ends with the rat: "Off with the rat's head!!" The rat is the symbol of determined and changeable life that can enter and leave through any opening, that can digest shells and coverings, that can survive the greatest disasters. The rat leaves ships before they sink; when it leaves a house, that house will soon fall. In Egypt, the rat was a god that could destroy from below but that also had the wisdom to know which way to go in times of trouble. The rat was invoked for both survival and great success. In India, the elephant-headed god Ganesh, lord of wisdom, prosperity, and successful endeavors, is always seen riding on or accompanied by a rat; thus, great accomplishments remain connected to the lowly intuitions of survival.

The rat of survival and the elephant god of grandness work together. This story is ruled by the rat and guided by the rat. The rat is more than the next meal. The son's survival and growth depend on more than food. The symbolic, imaginal, and spiritual realms of the boy must survive as well. The blessings and gifts of grandness and royalty are essential elements of survival for the son. At the end of the story, when the rat reappears, it's as if the rat rests on the head of father or king, whoever receives the blow of the sword. Sometimes the son must take the head off the father in order to survive. Sometimes he must take off the head of a king in order to move closer to his father and find survival there.

The rat represents surviving in both the literal daily world and surviving in the grand world of spirit and emotion. In the beginning of the story, the rat replaced the son in the eyes of the father. When they arrived at the fire, the father saw more rat than he saw son, and that's part of the wounding of the son. It's a psychological blow when the father sees the rat as more important than the son. It's an ax blow that stuns the son's world. Yet it awakens something in him and marks the spot where his grandness was not satisfied and was not blessed. It begins the questioning from deep within the son; how could the rat be more important than the son who follows in his father's footsteps so carefully and so expectantly? How could the father's job or career be more important? How could money or a bottle of liquor or someone else's problems or love be more important?

The son is looking for an exact blessing that welcomes the grand part of him into life, that anoints something in him that works like a gift. The giftedness in the son keeps rising up to receive a blessing whenever it senses that circumstances might provide it. The gifted area has come into the world with the son. It doesn't derive only from the father; it may even be contrary to the ideas of the father and the mother. It hides beyond the usual sight of the parents. The gift of the child may even be opposed to the expectations and wishes of his family.

The arrival of the rat forces the differences between the father and son to be seen, and the differences are as great as those between an elephant and a rat. The father can lay blessings and curses on his child. It's clear that he has the power to do so because certain things he does are never forgotten, and because he is looked to with awe and fear. The child will seek the blessing of this awesome figure, but the father can rarely see the seeking of his child. The father at these times of seeking is in a state of human limitation. The father cannot give exactly what the son looks for. Usually the father cannot see who the son is trying to become. The father can only see the grandness of the son when the king is present, or in some secret way he cannot quite get into words. The father has to have the security of his own "psychic village" in order to walk to the village of his son's grandness. If the father's grandness has never been blessed, that's a very difficult, maybe impossible, walk.

The grandness in the son provokes wild emotions in the father. And the son, in seeking a blessing, receives a curse. Much later the willingness of the father to give may become visible to the son. If the father truly was generous and was able to love the child, the son may see it later. But at some point there will be a rat between father and son. The area in the son that seeks blessing cannot help but offer itself to the father. It is a place of such openness that it allows the blow to come far inside. The father can do or say several things that could be taken as a severe blow. One of them will reach all the way into the soul of the son and open a wound in the area that seeks to be blessed. The wound drives the son away, secretly seeking a blessing.

The father and son each see and hold the rat differently. They are in different worlds. What the father passes to the son becomes changed as soon as the son handles it. This is the quantum physics of the relationship between father and son. If children were simply satisfied with what the parents offered to them, they would remain children forever. It's not simply that parents don't try to give enough to the child, rather it's that whatever the parents give is never enough for the child. The child has a destiny outside the imagination of the parents. The child has an origin that is not simply made of the understanding of its parents. There is a mysterious occurrence when the child is born. It's stunning to the son to realize that his own father doesn't see the shape of his expectations, doesn't see the grandness in him and doesn't feel the delicate uncertainty with which he walks into life. The father and son are both shocked by the great longing they feel for each other and the way that they clash when they come close to each other. Between fathers and sons, a long distance grows easily, silences spread from something small to something wide and seemingly unending. Something mysterious connects them and something awkward and painful drives them apart.

On the road of the fathers, the task of the son is first of all to survive. Following that, to learn to use the sword that is his inheritance from the kingly father to make the distinctions between the mysteries and the wounds in the father's world. True to its nature, the dilemma story ends with a question. There are always questions about fathers and questions for fathers. Sons are always in quest of something and fathers are always in question. The rat returns to its hole and father and son take another path.

CHAPTER 5

SPIRIT FATHERS

.

W<small>E EXPECT FATHERS</small> to give the direct stuff of love and admiration, information and knowledge. Fathers expect to be able to teach and give the son all they know and feel. Neither of these things happens as we expect. Just when the father is trying to communicate some esoteric or favorite point, the son can't hear it, already knows it, knows it better. Or the son tries to learn something, wants to be close to the father by receiving something from him and to see his father's eyes light up as they look at him—but he asks the wrong question, does the wrong thing, and it all goes away or blows up. Why? Why are the father and son so close yet so often knocking each other far apart?

There is a deep and mysterious connection between father and son that precedes even the birth of the son. There is a strange resonance that fathers and sons feel and have such difficulty converting into words. How many sons have waited years to hear the father's love put into words? How many fathers have anguished over how to express their love, only to find deeper silence? How often has the son started out to give sweet words to the father and found bitterness coming out of his mouth instead? Although father and son can suddenly be enclosed by a feeling of closeness, even of identification, it is hard to speak of these feelings and harder still to act on them.

As a boy, there were several times when I could slip right up to my father, could slip within his spirit. When my father would strum a guitar and sing, I could get right next to him. He only knew four chords, and he sang quietly, but his spirit opened up and I could feel it. When he was watching a good boxing match, then, too, I could see into him. As he got inside the fighters, I got inside him. I learned that he, too, was fighting, though he never said what it was that he fought. When he was dressing for a wedding or a celebration where there would be music and dance, I could see something different about him. The air around him was different, and I wanted to be next to him. I could actually slip within the air around him, if I moved quietly. If I said something or asked for something, this special atmosphere would go away just as suddenly, as if the edges in the words broke some silent sound being shared. Inside that closeness, I loved him easily; what's more, I *knew* him. Within that fragile, permeable space next to him, I think that I was reacquiring the knowledge of his spirit that I'd had before birth. Quietly, I was following the tracks, hunting with his spirit in the music and in the fighting.

I've heard many men speak tearfully of how it felt to be next to their fathers, and then shake their heads at the unspokenness of what passed between them. I've heard men of different races, of wildly different roots, ask the same question: why such pain and silence between father and son? Why such sweet sorrow when the silence breaks? Li-Young Lee has captured this feeling in his poem, "A Story," when the father finally breaks through the great silence between him and his son:

> . . . *Are you a god,*
> *the man screams, that I sit mute before you?*
> *Am I a god that I should never disappoint?*

These questions ring in the great silence that descends on generation after generation. But often the questions raised in one story are answered in another. This second story of father and son reaches far back into each of them.

THE SWEETNESS OF LIFE

Once many years ago, there was a great hunter who knew all the secrets of the bush and its inhabitants. When his wife told him she was pregnant, he knew that this would be his firstborn son. With the help of magic formulas, he lured the unborn boy out of the womb and took him hunting in the bush. He taught his son all his knowledge of the bush: which berries were edible, which flowers poisonous. He taught him about animals and birds, how they walk and fly, where they hide and when. When they came back, the hunter's wife was asleep, and he conjured the boy back into the womb; she didn't seem to notice.

The embryo was not taken out, no physical removal took place; the hunter, by means of his magical power, controlled the spirit of his unborn son. It was this spirit that accompanied him on his hunt, while the body went on growing in the womb. In this way, the spirit learned effortlessly while wandering the bush. Perhaps the spirit was really the hunter's father, about to be reborn as his son.

When the days were fulfilled for the son to be born, the women of the village assembled to sing songs in praise of the firstborn. And such a big baby! After a day or two, he could speak, and he refused his mother's milk, saying he craved meat, like all men of his rank. The third day he began to creep; the next day he stood up, and after five days he could walk and run. He was grown up.

So the day after that, the son went hunting with his father, this time in the flesh. They heard the honey bird sing, and the father knew it would lead them to a tree where the bees had honey. They found it; the father told the son to receive the honeycombs as he took them from the bee's hive and put them in the calabash. "But don't lick your fingers, for it is very bitter," he said. The father wanted to control the honey himself, but he forgot that the son knew as much about the forest as he did. By the time the father climbed down, the son had eaten the honey.

The father was enraged. He decided to test the son's power. He knew the language of animals. He called the big beasts, the elephants, the buffalo, the lions. They all came charging at the son. The son did not blink. He took up a tree trunk and knocked all the animals to the ground. The father did not blink. He said, "Not badly done. Now I would like a fire to roast all this meat. There's smoke on the horizon. That must be a village. Go get a burning log, while I guard our meat."

The son went off toward the smoke. There was a village, but the villagers were big cannibal people, whose great noses always wished to smell delicious human meat. The son ran back as soon as he saw this tribe. But it was too late; a cannibal child had smelled him and seen him. The cannibal people all came running after him.

The son came running into the clearing, shouting, "Father, climb a tree and hide, monsters are coming after me!" The father thought, "He is a boy, after all. What have I to fear in this forest?" The son managed to climb the tree unnoticed. But the cannibal people fell on the father before he could move. They feasted on him, every bit of him, enjoying it and licking their lips. Then they helped themselves to the pile of elephants, buffalo, and lions. When they were absolutely full, they returned to their village. There, they drank all the beer they had been brewing and settled down to a long satisfied sleep, as was their custom.

The son climbed down and followed them to the village. Once they were snoring away inside their huts, he tied shut the doors and set fire to them. They all died in the flames.

Nearby, the son found men and women prisoners who were being fattened for consumption by the cannibal tribe. He released them all. They made him their king. He married one of the women he had saved. They built new huts. The queen became pregnant. The new king knew it would be his firstborn son. He lured the unborn son out of the womb and took him hunting in the bush. He taught his son all he knew of the bush.

When I first read this story, I was struck by the directness of the image of father and son exploring the bush together before the birth of the son. While the mother and son sleep and rest in their mutual ocean, the spirit of the son grows in contact with the spirit of the father in their mutual forest. Father and son know each other separate from the womb of the mother, in a way that the mother is not aware of and in a way that becomes more mysterious to all of them as the son grows up out of the womb. The womb world of the mother and the world of the body are not involved in that knowing between father and son. The story says that there's a possible sweetness between father and son, a full sharing of the knowledge of life, but there's great trouble sharing it once they are in separate, grown bodies.

Most cultures say that there's a connection between the child and the parents before the child is born. Some say that the spirit of the child picks the parents to whom it will be born. Some say that the spirit child picks its mother when she is near water; others say that the spirit child enters the father when he is out hunting and then goes from the father to the mother. Some cultures say that each child is the spirit of a grandparent or ancestor trying to be born again to his or her own children.

Because our modern culture wishes to specify a moment when life begins and a moment when life ends, the spirit of life becomes imprisoned by biology and sociology. Life becomes history denying mystery and literal reality denying spirit and soul. As a result, every problem the child has must be traced back to the actual mother, the actual father, and to literal events. This puts a great weight on each parent and also narrows the ways in which the child can imagine getting out of the troubles that will inevitably appear. Older cultures believe that each child is born into a long story, a story that started well before the child begins his or her life and that will go on long after that life is over. The tree of the family has roots that go deep into the earth and branches that reach high into the sky; the tree's life is much longer and greater than that of any one child. The relationship between father and son grows as a branch on the family tree, coming from somewhere, growing along together, and one day dividing as well. Father and son are of the same roots but they are headed in different directions.

"The Sweetness of Life" says that father and son are close because their spirits have already been together under inspired circumstances of learning, examining, and passing specific knowledge of the family tree and the Tree of Life from one to the other. A modern imagining of this can be found in the transfer of DNA from father to child and then the flooding of the fetus with hormonal knowledge that converts body and brain to male shapes.

The story telescopes the childhood of the son down to a few symbolic days: for the first two days he didn't speak, then he spoke and refused milk, after five days he could walk and run and was ready to go hunting. This story is ruled by the honey bird, a spirit bird that brings messages and reinforces the point of the story. Father and son can hunt in spirit form before the son fully enters this world, and father and son can hear the song of the honey bird and its promise of sweet reward. But, when they reach the tree and the father, son, and honey are embodied and present together the trouble begins.

The son in the rat's story threw away what little the father handed him, while the son in this story eats everything the father gathers. All or nothing, that's how it stands between father and son, over and over. The magic of the father that drew the son's spirit into a delightful learning of animals and trees now turns on the son in a raging charge of those same animals. The father becomes enraged and the son outraged. The son defends himself with a tree, and later finds protection in a tree, as many a son has done. Father and son are destroying each other and most of their surroundings.

The chorus of men has also followed the honey bird, and they begin to gather around the tree and comment on the exchange of honey between the father and the son. The first man says, "Well, the father was teaching the son. He was saying 'Be patient, wait, hold onto things. Carry it all back to the village.' The son shouldn't have taken all the honey and shouldn't have eaten it at once. The father was trying to teach him how to use things in this world."

Another man chimes in, "If he was trying to teach him about honey, why did he say it was bitter? I think the father wanted all the honey for himself." Another says, "No. The father was trying to instruct the son and instill discipline in him."

A man says, "It's the typical setup between father and son. They are in a vertical relationship. The father takes the sweet things in life and the son is stuck below suffering the whims of the father." "It's the lie that got me," says another man. "My father lied to me about everything, the whole story of his life in the family was lies." Another man says, "The father simply can't tell the truth to the son, even when he desires to speak a truth to the son, it somehow comes out as his truth, often a bitter truth, and not something that the son can gather in readily."

Another says that his sympathy goes with the father, that all the sweetness in life has become bitter for him. Everything has been cared for and carried back to the village; everyone has been provided for. Meantime, the father's life has become more and more bitter and all he can foresee is some kind of cancer and death.

Another man says, "I felt the suffering of a father who realizes that he can't give the son what the son needs in life. He's supposed to know everything and be able to give it to the son. When he can't, he's frustrated and angry."

"No. The father's rage is simply that anger when he sees how full of sweet honey the son is, how full of promise and potential in life, whereas the father himself has tasted the bitter side and knows his own limitations and opportunities that have passed by and not been tasted." A father echoes this, saying, "My primary feeling toward my own son is jealousy. I see him able to taste sweet things in life that I never tasted in my childhood. For me the whole house was dark and bitter."

A man speaks from a torn place in himself: "When I stay in the position of the father, I feel like restraining the son. But if I move to the place of the son, I feel like indulging in the sweetness of honey." Another man says, "I'm jealous of that son because he did eat the honey. I wish I would have had the nerve to eat the honey despite what my father had said. Instead I think I became like my father so early that I've never tasted the honey. I'm still looking for it."

"It was the word 'control' that got me, because my father controlled everything that I did. He had my entire life planned, not only as I was living it, but into the future. It took me years and years to find my way back to that tree and get a small taste of some sweetness in my own life that was not handed to me and forced down my throat by my father."

Another man says, "Because my father's attitude toward life was so bitter I felt that I would have to steal any sweetness that I would ever taste. And so, I've tasted sweetness but never felt that I had the right to it. And even what has tasted sweet has had an aftertaste that carried the bitterness of my father's life in it." "My father would answer every question and respond to every problem with some big idea, some platitude, some statement of principle or belief that would obliterate my own ideas and my feelings. My father, hiding behind principles and reminding me of the needs of other people, left me feeling bitter and empty." Yet another says, "The problem in my house was scarcity. My father always acted as if we were about to enter a famine. Nothing could be enjoyed, or wasted, or fully experienced because there was never enough. And it's true that sometimes there wasn't even enough food, but the feeling that scarcity was coming from every direction put a bitter taste in everyone's mouth."

Part of the bitterness that the father lives with is the difficulty that he has in passing what he knows of the sweetness and beauty and desires of his own life to his son. The father is caught in the upper part of the tree, in the upper structure of the patriarch, and he gets caught in the sense of rules, limits, and restrictions that begin to awaken as soon as he becomes a father. Most men, when they are first fathers and while the child is small and not speaking, make serious commitments not to act like their own fathers. Then, to the surprise of the new father, he suddenly acts in the way that his own father acted. Becoming a father stirs up the family father spirits, and the extremes of fathering awaken.

Even the old titans, the ancient, exaggerated forces of the "great father" stir from their dusky abodes. Human fathers often get caught in the broad sweeping patterns of ancient, titanic deities. As tensions and confusions begin to rise up between father and son, the father will get pulled to an extreme that seems out of proportion, inhuman. Especially at those critical points in the child's life when something is beginning or being born out of them and needs protection or blessing, the father seems to get possessed by a denying spirit. One father will move through the lives of his children like a mysterious cloud pattern they can't hold onto; another will storm, shout, snap, and stomp through their lives so that they can't get away from him. The Greeks named the gods of these extremes Ouranos and Kronos; the Romans called them Jupiter and Saturn. We tend to refer to them as the "absent father" and the "devouring father."

Ouranos/Jupiter, the absent father, leaves a gap between himself and his son that keeps the son feeling abandoned and overexposed. It's as if this father is always escaping the son's grasp in cloudy answers, disappearing behind abstract principles, or hiding behind the black-and-white veil of the newspaper. The airiness of the Ouranos father denies the son, denies the body of the son, denies the embodiment of the father-son emotional world. The son feels incapable of reaching a father who can disappear into endless outside projects, or is a minister who occasionally descends from the pulpit but can effect an escape into God's laws whenever the son comes too close. This capacity for denial is developed in part so that the father can deny that he needs to speak to or even answer the requests and questions of the son. The Ouranos father repeatedly sends the son to the mother, pushes the son back into the mother or into matter. "Go ask your mother" is a classic move that allows the father to float away. The disappearing father keeps climbing up the tree away from the son. He abdicates his ambiguous role as human father and often won't hand down sweetness or bitterness. Instead he leaves the son bound up in himself, with only clouds and silence. Where the son expects him to be, he isn't. The son can't get the recognition of the father and must seek all acknowledgment from mother, with whom he can become overinvolved. If the father is always distant, the potentials and possibilities of the son recede. If the father is frequently holier than thou, or higher than thou, the son sinks into the cavities of earth, into depressions, caves, and graves.

Saturn/Kronos pulls the human father the other way, toward active oppression, dominance, and devouring. Kronos sees in his son, in his children, his own wounding and downfall. The child is not avoided; rather, as the son climbs toward the father, or toward any sweetness in life, Saturn sees a threat to himself, snatches the child, and devours it.

Saturn is easiest to see in a father who rages, beats, and strikes at his children, or strikes at whatever tries to come out of the child. Any effort on the part of the son, to be close or to be seen, can call out the rage of Kronos rather than the admiring attention the son seeks. If the father refrains from raging and attacking the children, he can hold the Kronos position by pouring acidic waves of bitterness, cynicism, and sarcasm down the tree of life. Whatever the child brings out to show his father is quickly washed in an acid bath that burns away the attempts of the child to advance or move forward in life. The Kronos father devours with teeth of rage, with rules that restrict and bind, and sarcasm that chews up the enthusiasm of the child. He is Saturn with his rings around everyone, and Saturn the old lecher with his hands in everything. He is Kronos as time ticking away throughout the house, as Father Time who cuts eternity into sound bites with his sickle, and he stands by every doorway as the Grim Reaper. He takes the sweetness of life and turns it into bitter nights. Sharon Olds has written extensively about the devouring presence that can possess a father mysteriously. This is from her poem "Saturn":

> He lay on the couch night after night,
> mouth open, the darkness of the room
> filling his mouth, and no one knew
> my father was eating his children. He seemed to
> rest so quietly, vast body
> inert on the sofa, big hand
> fallen away from the glass.
> What could be more passive than a man
> passed out every night—and yet as he lay
> on his back, snoring, our lives slowly
> disappeared down the hole of his life.

The son of a Kronos father can become like the edge of a blade always ready to face disaster, overly alert, his teeth clenched for an attack that could come at any moment. Or, he gets sadly frozen before the overly watchful eyes of a paranoid god who sees everything new as a threat to his position. The Kronos father must be accounted for, his whereabouts must be known. He is a constant force that dominates and possesses. The son of a Kronos father must expend his time and energy in order to avoid being eaten by his father's rages, sarcasms, and addictions time after time. The son can become stuck, paralyzed by the excess emotions loose in the house. The father that demands decisiveness can clench the son in indecision—the son feels damned if he does, damned if he doesn't.

A father of either type can block the movement of the son not only toward the sweet things in life, but also toward the ancestral roots of the tree. Often, the father obstructs the tree that is trying to grow in the life of the son, and the son must move through this bitterness with the father in order to grow into a greater life. The taste of bitterness that so many fathers and sons have shared often closes their mouths to each other. The fathers don't speak to the sons, and the sons don't say anything to the fathers. How often it's heard that a man hasn't spoken to his father in so many years and a father hasn't found a way to communicate to the son since such a day when some dramatic event happened and he lost his temper or cursed that son.

In the story the inability of the father and son to speak to each other becomes the attempted killing of one or the other. The rage of the father draws first the thundering herds, then cannibals out of the nearby village, as if the father becomes a devouring force that will eat the son, and the son has to meet him practically with an equally devouring force or else be swallowed up. The father becomes the cannibal people. The father becomes Saturn eating his children, and the child, the son, has to respond with something clever or something strong in order to avoid being swallowed and nibbled down altogether. The son moves to a distant village and starts his own life, trying not to think of the bitterness with the father. Then, one day he learns his wife is pregnant, and the story starts over again.

When the son becomes a father, will he get caught in the rages and bitterness of his own father and one day find himself doing exactly what he said he would never do? Or, does he avoid that trap altogether only to become a disappearing father who climbs up the tree and just keeps going? Does he rise above the pain and confusion of the raging father only to leave behind a son who can't touch or reach his father? There are many fathers who escape becoming a devouring spirit only to find themselves as distant and remote as a sky god. There are many sons standing at the foot of the tree of life with an absence of both what is sweet and what is bitter, not sure what to do, not sure whose son they are, not sure what road to take.

Left on their own to deal with these complications and difficulties, father and son almost always convert the tree of life to a cross. There's very little question about whether father and son will cross each other during the growing of the son. It's inevitable. The question becomes: Will the father and son ever share some sweetness? In the story the son becomes a father, and there's an implication that when he becomes one there's another chance. He may, from the position of fathering, be able to see into his own father. But he may just as likely get caught in the bitterness of being a father. Sometimes it's the bitterness of life that gets shared first between father and son, and only if they stay at the tasting of things together can they get to the sweetness.

The story represents not just a personal problem but a cultural one as well. And it is a spiritual problem that exists between generations. The spirits of the father and son are tangled up and must be untangled. Parent and child need relief from each other. Because the troubles between father and son create so much opposition of spirits and so much rage and bitterness, many cultures seek a third place to turn. Often, the son turns to his grandfather for this relief.

The grandfather is the father with a certain amount of grandeur and grandness. The son can see this, and the grandfather may see a grand quality in his grandson as well. An old proverb says that a grandfather and grandson can be friends because they share a common enemy: the father. The son and the father have all of the conflict we've seen between them, but there are unresolved issues between father and grandfather as well. The male lineage in any given family is trying to work something out in this world. Grandfather, father, and son will each work on the same issues but from differing angles. The angle of the grandson is closer to that of the grandfather, or perhaps it is more visible and tolerable to him. The angles of father and son clash.

In some cultures the grandfather and grandson refer to each other as brothers. They are spirit brothers; they share a spirit the way brothers do. Neither the grandfather nor the grandson will ever completely understand the father, they share that also. The grandfather is at one extreme of life, the grandson at the other, and the father is somewhere between them. The grandfather is learning to let go, the grandson is learning to pick things up, and the father is usually trying to hold on. Many cultures offer sympathy to fathers and mothers, for they are always stuck in the middle, shaking their heads.

The tree with the honey is a universal symbol of life but also of initiation. The tree combines masculine and feminine characteristics, and different cultural groups will initiate boys and initiate girls at this tree. Grandfathers and grandsons meet at the roots of the tree. The grandson prepares to climb up into life's bittersweet branches and the grandfather prepares to join the ancestors below. What passes between them has mythic and spiritual value. A grandfather can release the grandness of a son to soar above the trees and can give him a mythic ground to return to. Even after death a grandfather can guide the spirit of a grandson. The grandfather can see which way the grandson's spirit is trying to go; he can lay the ground for the grandson's initiation. If there is no direct family grandfather, another elder can take the role of grandfathering the son.

Typically, fathers do not initiate sons directly. The father, if he's up in the tree of initiation, can be blocking the son from going forward. The ambivalence between the father and son gets in the way of the mystery the son is trying to taste. In traditional initiatory cultures, the son is initiated into the sweet and harsh things of life by men who are not as deeply and disturbingly connected to the son as the father. It's the uncles, the mother's brothers, who can give sweetness more directly to the son. Even unrelated older males initiate the sons, for they have even less trouble and less need to deliver bitterness to the son. Then, when returning from initiation periods, the son will re-meet the father on the ground of adult men. They will then have a chance to speak to each other, as we say, "man to man." Often sweetness can come back into the relationship then, for they each carry their own bitter things and their own dreams of sweetness. Amongst the Masai, a son must find a honey tree and gather the honey to make the beer, so that everyone can drink some sweetness after his initiation.

One of the purposes of initiation is to put a small death between father and son, a death that ends whatever bitterness they share and also puts a limit to whatever sweetness was between them, so that on the other side of that small death they may meet each other as men and re-find the roots of the tree of the honey bird. Without initiation and something that moves father and son away from the cross that they bear together, it often takes the impending death of the father before their voices can be found again. Often that moment is missed and many men walk in the bitterness of never having said what they wanted to say to their fathers before actual death separates them.

When the father and son do find a way to share the sweetness of life there is something magical about it. The spiritual connection that existed between the hunter and his unborn son appears again, when father and son can share their sense of wonder at life. If they have moments of companionship together, those moments are magical and sweet, and without them life seems bitter indeed.

Several things must happen to keep father and son from stirring up all the cannibal people. If the father has handed a mess of bitterness to the son he must, at some point, admit this and state it to the son. A son is always a little confused about how much of this bitterness was his fault for wanting so much sweetness and how much of it was his father's weakness in giving bitter when sweet was desired. Often the father has to make the first move and say, "You know on this occasion when this and that happened, something sweet could have been there, but I was caught in my own bitterness, and so I gave the bitterness to you." Sometimes, to their surprise, when the son realizes the truth of what happened he releases a herd of elephant and lion anger at the father, and the father has to avoid being completely trampled by the son. For if there's a rage in the father that could kill, there's also a rage in the son that could kill. At that point, the job of the father becomes to avoid being pulled back into his own rage. The rage of the son needs to be heard, not matched. The father might have to feel like a grandfather listening to a grandson who needs to release frustration and pain. Someone once said, "The job of the young ones is to kill their parents. The job of the parents is to not retaliate."

It's probable that with regard to the sweetness of life, the father and son must return to the tree many times and make many attempts to pass the sweetness from one to the other. If the mistakes of the son are not taken too seriously, and if the bitterness of the father is not considered too poisonous, eventually, despite the splattering of honey on the ground, there may be enough sweetness left to pass between the two. If it happens, the son will have a much greater spirit for living into life, and there will be an increase in his capacity to learn things quickly. As a matter of fact he will encounter many things that he seems to know already. And when he's feeling the strength of the branches of the spirit living in his life, he can turn back and see his father and see his humanness and suffering as a man. An old saying says, "Initiation makes the parents more human." The more a person gets initiated into the sweetness and bitterness of his or her own life, the less god-like and more human the parents appear.

Besides, there is no end to initiating; the end of one stage is also the beginning of another. While the son looks back to see the source of his life in the humanness of his father and the mysterious spirits of the family, he sees the womb of his mother again, this time from the outside. He realizes he came from the mother as well. The Tree of Life stands at the initiation place of both boys and girls, both masculine and feminine. Soon he'll have to go looking for that tree again. The next time he will find it in the territory of the mothers on the ground of the feminine area of the forest. The end of one story is also the beginning of another.

2

Moving the Mother

*I am She who accomplishes without cease and
without end the transformation of all.... I am both
She who thou namest Death, and She who thou namest Life!*

THÉODORE DE BANVILLE

THE BOY AND THE HALF-GIANTESS

There was once a certain boy, a king's son, who said that he was going out to see what was in the world. So he started off and wandered on and on through a broad forest. Eventually, he came to a clearing and saw a large lake. He walked all the way around the shore of the lake and saw no footprints but his own. Then he reached into the lake and took a handful of water and drank it down. He took another handful of water and gave it to his dog. His dog! What dog? His dog. He decided to see who else drank at that lake. So he climbed a tree and sat in the branches, and his dog lay down at the base of the tree. He stayed in the tree and gazed across the surface of the lake.

After a time, the boy saw something coming over the horizon. He squinted his eyes and peered down as the shape came closer. Soon he could see it was a half-giantess coming his way. She came right to the shore of the lake. She lay down and began to drink the water and didn't stop until she had pulled all the water of the lake and every bit of moisture from the sand in the lake bed. Then the half-giantess began to weep, saying that her thirst was not quenched. She lamented that there was not enough to drink, that she would never quench her thirst because someone had stolen her water. She wept on and on; only after a long time did she calm herself down. Then she rose and strode away.

Soon the half-giantess reached her hut. She made a fire and set a huge cauldron over it. She brought out bags of corn and poured them into the water that was heating in the cauldron. She put in wheat, rice, and bags of barley. She poured in beans and peas and other seeds. As this mess began to cook into a porridge, the half-giantess caught two bulls and threw them into the cauldron. Next, she caught chickens and other small animals that ran or flew by, and finally she added a rat to season the soup.

Meanwhile, the boy had climbed down from the tree by the lake and wandered over to the house of the half-giantess. By this time, the half-giantess had just finished cooking. She went into her house to dress for dinner. The boy saw a tree near the cauldron of soup. He climbed the tree and reached down to pick some meat from the soup with his spear. His spear! What spear? His spear. He picked up a chunk of meat, and tearing it in half, he ate one piece and threw the other down to his dog who lay at the foot of the tree.

Soon, the half-giantess came out of her house all dressed for dinner. She sat down at the cauldron and began to eat, and she didn't stop until she had cleaned the pot of all the grain and had devoured every piece of meat and every bone. She didn't stop until she had licked the entire cauldron clean. Then she began to howl and scream and curse and yell. She said that someone had stolen her porridge, someone had taken her meat. She fumed and cursed, shouted and screamed that there would be no end to her hunger, that her very food had been taken from her lips. She carried on in full fury until the middle of the night; then she calmed herself and went into the house.

The boy climbed quickly down. He called his dog and began to run. He didn't stop, or pause, or look back until he had run all the way back to his parents' village. When he arrived, he went to his father and said, "Father, now I have seen what is in the world."

CHAPTER 6

THE BOY AND THE HALF-GIANTESS

THE SON WE followed in Part One walked right into a blow from the father—that is, right into his disappointments with the father and right into the tense territory between fathers and sons. In this story, we follow a son who seems younger, as though the path of the story is taking us back toward birth as the son steps into the territory of the mother—not of his mother exactly, but of the Great Mother. Most old stories and most old cultures carry the sense of a feminine deity, a great being or composite of beings that keep giving life to the world. She can take many forms and delights in doing so. Because of her involvement in every form of life she is often called the Great Mother. Sometimes her territory is all of nature, and then she's called Mother Nature. Sometimes her territory is called the Land of Mothers or the Land of Women, or else the Land of Memory. "Men's work" has been a series of paths uncovering and discovering areas of the psyche. The pattern that emerges is one of working into the territory of the masculine before stepping into the territory of the feminine. Even when a man feels driven to do this work by the difficulties he has with the feminine in himself or by the problems he experiences in relationships with women, he almost always begins by dealing with the masculine before he can take a path into the territory of the Great Mother.

In walking the path behind the father to seek a blessing, the son finds a curse. Here, walking into the realm of the mother to see what there is in the world, the son steps into a spellbound area where little tastes cause big trouble and he can only see half of what's before him. When I tell stories about mothers to groups of men, we all seem to fall under a spell ourselves. The atmosphere in the room becomes heavy; sometimes the room even starts to spin. Thoughts become murky and unclear. We seem to be pulled back toward a watery womb. We can no longer remember what we started out to look for. At the beginning of the story, we feel alert and full grown, but after a while we seem to become smaller and smaller until we are left standing awestruck and confused before a vague and looming aspect of the "mother."

This territory feels different from that of the father and son. Usually the blow from the father can be named, stated in a single sentence that carries the shape of the blow like a curse on the son's head. The weight of it knocks the son down and puts him on the dark road looking for another village. Here the son heads into the bigness of the world during daylight and finds surprise after surprise. He's specifically not following the footsteps where his father hunted into life; that's one way we know he's stepping into the realm of "mother." And yet not only are there no footsteps of the father, there are no footsteps at all, even by the lake where there should be! And instead of being handed a rat, a dog suddenly appears: "What dog? His dog."

He has entered the territory of the Great Mother, where his inner sense of mother, his little mother inside, meets the mother of all things. On the father's track the son got a blow he had to carry and work through, but this son encounters his wound in the mother world as a spell, what I call entering a spell or falling under a spell. The entry of the son into the world of the fathers began with a wound, and he will experience a wounded, incomplete sense of himself when he enters the territory of the mothers. Instead of finding the exact psychic and physical place where the father's ax struck, this son finds himself in a location he can't understand or can only half comprehend. The son sees both more and less of what he expected to find in the world. Some things appear to belong to him, but other aspects of the territory are only half of what they should be, as if they are shrouded in a mist that will suddenly reveal something else. The son becomes surprised, curious, watchful, confused, wary, fearful, awed. He says nothing, hides in trees, and finally runs out of the area. He has to climb the trees to see what's happening down below. In the terms of the psyche, below and behind can be the same—he's looking inside himself and back in his life.

The son sees overwhelming displays of sorrow and rage that both intrigue him and scare him. No one asks him questions, no one explains anything. It is not until he is out of the area that he is able to speak about it. The story ends and leaves us with many questions. What does the father say? What does the father's culture say? Does the father know this territory? Was he able to stay in it longer than the son, or does he avoid it and not speak of it? Does the father say, "Well that's how your mother is, that's how women are, that's how the 'other half' lives"? Is the father under the same spell, or is he able to dispel some of the fear of the son?

These same questions will arise at the men's retreats when these stories are being told: Are the men going to suffer their own confusions and overwhelming emotions, or are they going to band together by demonizing women "out there"? Are the men going to go down to the half-made world of the feminine within and behind, or will they blame emotional troubles on actual women "out there"? Are the spells from the mother-world going to be undone a little and missing parts of the feminine seen, or will there be an increase of hatred and fear towards literal mothers and women?

At the retreats there is usually one spoken agreement and one unspoken rule, both of which help to avoid the tendency to literalize life. The spoken agreement is, no physical violence. If the wounds of those gathered are to be re-opened and the troubles of the culture are to be met straight on, then physical violence has to be removed as a possible result or solution. In other words, the retreat seeks a different solution from the usual one in our culture. The unspoken rule is that proceedings will begin with poetry and be carried along by stories. That underlying rule turns out to be as important as the agreement to no physical violence. When there's no physical violence, the affects of powerful, eruptive emotions emerge in images instead of simply physical acts. We find that the force of emotion that can deliver a blow like the hunter's ax can also flood a person with passion that touches something grand within and with compassion that touches those without.

The presence of poetic metaphor and mythic stories can break the spell of literalism that restricts the world of the feminine to the personal mother and to actual women. If there are only men present and they relate to the feminine beings in the stories, then troubles with those beings exist in the men, not simply in women. The tendency to literalize the feminine in the psyche as actual women is one source of men's tremendous fear of women and the recurrent violence toward them. When men turn to the inner feminine, however, they run the risk of activating the spells around the wounded feminine inside, which can reduce them to spellbound boys. The half-giantess represents an answer to both problems: She can't be literalized because she's only half visible and her disturbing incompleteness keeps everyone awake. She also represents the way the modern world can't grasp the full powers of the feminine forces in people or in life.

There's a third aspect of the retreats that disperses the tendency to literalize and concretize opinions and beliefs. The places for the retreats are camps in remote parts of forests, so that the events take place within nature. The retreats are "held" by the trees and waters and earth around them, and they have the sense of uncovering and discovering that the boy in the story enters when he sets off into the world of lakes and trees. Each retreat starts like a new story, another foray into the unknown world. Despite the fact that the troubles are the same old ones that people have had over and over, there are no footprints around the lake and surprises turn up like the dog in the story.

Ahead lie the blessings of the feminine realms and positive images of the beautiful princesses and noble queens who reign there. But before we reach those stories, we need to enter a more archaic part of the psyche where some half-truths must be faced. The son must experience an intense shock in order to dislodge his assumptions about women, about the mother, and about the feminine world.

When the son followed his father, he expected his father to see the royal core in him and to have it blessed. Instead, he got devoured, knocked down, and abandoned. Similarly, the son in this story encounters a half-giantess, an ancient, mysterious image of the Great Mother when she appears as devouring and negative. The half-giantess has relatives throughout the world of myths, from Grendel's mother in the Beowulf epic, to the Hindus' black Kali who devours everything and everyone gleefully, to the old hag who keeps the cauldron, to the ogress at the bottom of the water, the mistress of beasts, and the queen of the underworld.

Psychologically, the story stirs the mother complex, in which the archetypal Great Mother overlaps with and gets confused with the human mother as she was experienced by her child. The half-giantess is the mother who knows right away what the boy is doing, whether he is dipping into the cookie jar, into the waters of sorrow, or into the brew that is currently cooking in the psyche. This is the image of the Great Mother who holds on and smothers, who can consume a child's feelings and still feel unfulfilled. Leaving home, as the son does in the story, always activates the mother complex, with its mixture of spells and charms.

When men enter into the dream-like story of the boy and the half-giantess, they find themselves drawn to one of two camps. At one of them, there is a lake, where no animals come to drink. At the other, there is a cauldron in which all the animals are being cooked. Each camp has a tree: one overlooks the lake of the half-giantess; the other overlooks her cauldron and its boiling waters. If you had to choose, to which tree would you go? To which tree do you feel closer right now? Which half-giantess are you drawn to—the one who wails for the loss of water or the one who rages for the loss of food? The one whose sense of loss causes sorrow or the one whose sense of loss causes rage?

The first time I told the story, I was pulled to the camp with the burning cauldron where the half-giantess was howling and raging. My own voice became full of her rage at the boy who had taken some meat from the stew. While I was in the camp of the angry giantess, I realized that in my family I had been given permission to be angry, even enraged. But feeling sad was another story.

I could argue with my mother and my father and withstand them by stepping into a state of anger. Getting angry protected and fed my spirit, which was anchored in anger. The story of this anger goes way back. When my mother begins to tell stories about my early childhood she'll inevitably reach the place where she has to leave me at the top of some dark stairs and I throw a fit. It's a good story. She'll tell it in front of me as if I'm not there, or directly to me. We both disappear into that story. Unless I'm really distracted I learn something each time I hear it. I know now that it's my mother mythologizing my birth and early years. Every mother does this because there's a mythos in the beginning of anything. One reason mothers tell stories as if their children aren't present is because mother and child are caught in a spell that is somehow approached in those stories. The stories are not exactly the truth, nor are they just made up; rather, they are pieces of myth and fact mingled together. They are markers on the path that leads back to the womb and draw us closer to the spell that envelops mother and child.

In my childhood, the "top of the stairs" was a landing several floors up in the apartment building where we lived. It was during the war, and my father was gone. I had two sisters, one a year older and one newborn. My mother couldn't carry us all down the stairs at once by herself, and I was too small to climb down the stairs alone. When she had to leave the apartment, she would sit me at the top of the stairs and carry my two sisters down to the street. There she set up the carriage, put my baby sister into it, then left my older sister to watch the infant while she climbed the stairs to get me, by then wailing, screaming, howling, throwing a tantrum. This happened over and over. Sometimes it awakened, disturbed, and involved the neighbors. No matter—I screamed and howled every time. My baby sister would often be crying in the carriage as well. My other sister was watching an infant she wasn't tall enough to see. My mother was rushing up and down the flights of stairs. Neighbors were watching, complaining, slamming doors. She's doing all she can do, but it's never enough to remove the howling and crying.

In a sense, this story is my mother's version of how I fit into the family. It's not the only version; still, it reveals many family themes and personal styles. It's like one of those dilemma stories in which someone has to get a fox, a chicken, and a hound across a river. There's only room for one person and one animal in the boat. How do you do it? How do you cross back and forth without allowing one animal to get eaten by another? How do you distribute the capacities, tendencies, and emotions of each child and make it to the other side? In our family, the distribution was clear: baby sister cries in the carriage, big sister holds onto the carriage and her emotions, brother howls the frustration and rage of the family, mother tries to run between the two scenes as quickly as she can. Eventually, everyone settles down. I see half of the giant emotions from the top of the dark stairwell; my sisters see another half down in the street. Father is out of the scene.

There are of course practical reasons for my mother's solution to the dilemma. The baby had to be carried down and protected in the carriage. The oldest child would be the best guardian—at least she would be able to stand the longest and to speak if necessary. That means that I had to be the one who was left behind and left out. Or are there other meanings to this solution? Does it mean that I was like my father, left out of the feminine trio at the base of the stairs? Was I a reminder of my father and his comings and goings, how he had left her with three babies and three flights of stairs? Or are men and therefore boys better able to cope on their own? Or is there something else beyond all of this?

There is something else. My mother says that she knew I would be a storm of a child. She tells it like a prophecy. The night she went into labor was a dark, stormy night in the middle of winter. My father was gone. There was thunder and lightning, unusual for that time of the year in New York. She was scared, worried about my father, about how she would handle another child, about the raging storm. Later, it all made some kind of sense when I would get angry, frustrated, enraged. It made sense that I, rather than one of my sisters, should sit in the rage at the head of the stairs. Does this mean that there was a fury in my mother during the pregnancy, during the labor, during birth and my infancy? Was this fury connected to the war going on? To the father being gone? Is the fury hers, or mine, or someone else's? Or is this story simply a way to justify her actions? These are questions we ask from the top of the stairs or the top of a tree.

A family has to allow a child some emotion, or the child won't live at all. But the parents can't afford to allow the full range of emotions to a child—not if they live in the same house with that child and are afraid of experiencing those emotions in themselves; not when certain displays of emotion were forbidden in their childhood homes; not when those feelings are a painful reminder of how often a child has to feel its way through life. Inevitably, taboos and prohibitions become established in the family hut that restrict some of the basic human emotions and actions, creating a protective space around a boiling cauldron of rage and disappointment.

As I told the story and found myself drawn to the boiling cauldron and the half-giantess's rage, it occurred to me that I had been prohibited access to the emotion of sorrow; I had been prohibited access to the lake where the giantess lay down and wept for the loss of two drops of water. I could come and go around the boiling cauldron, examining and entering into the rituals of rage, but the lake was prohibited. There were no footprints around the lake. The ground was swept clean. The stillness and lack of traffic said, "Keep away, walk on tiptoes, this is off limits to you." In fact, in my family, I was to pretend that this area didn't even exist. For me, going into the land without footprints was like walking directly into a stinging wind, for when I faced grief, I was unable to see a way forward or a way out. Trying to face these emotions alone and against the winds of prohibition was an overwhelming task. In another family, the "Do Not Enter" sign prohibits access to the cauldron of anger. In those families, when something goes wrong, well, it's just too bad; we're all sorry, but there's nothing more to say. Getting angry will only make it worse, they say.

Both the lake and the cauldron are sources of the Water of Life; they are entryways to the great waters of the psyche. These depths can be entered through the lake of sorrow or through the boiling waters of anger. Every family has plenty to be angry about and plenty to be grief-stricken about. These are two of the great seas of emotion, two of the places where men get lost and then found. They are two of the great areas for human action, for healing and change, two places where the family enacts its rituals of prohibition, inhibition, and exhibition. Entering these areas activates the "emotional bodies" of the men and stimulates the spells connected to them.

Emotionally, a person can only be in one of these landscapes at any given time. Thus, when these scenes in the story are painted in broad strokes, in great washes of emotion, they provide an opening through which each man can discover where he is at the moment and where he was permitted or prohibited to go as a child.

At the lake there is loneliness. There's the waiting for the approach of the half-giantess. There's the question of why no animals have come. There's the outpouring of tears and the long complaints. There's the shadow of the rocks and pebbles spread across the lake bed while the son waits for the half-giantess to go calmly on her way. There's an empty lake bed to be viewed after the half-giantess has left, the sadness of fish floundering on the bottom.

Over at the cauldron there is fire and heat; animals appear and are torn apart. There is a spear and a house. There is a sense of change and things firing off. The time there feels full of events, even if they are disastrous and fearful. There can be even the appearance of the half-giantess dressed up for dinner creating some sense of bizarre celebration. And an opportunity for escape appears; the chance to run straight away from the whole thing.

The territory around each tree has an elemental atmosphere of emotions that can function like a spell. At each of these trees, the boy's unformed psyche must confront the mysteries of the world. Some things are much too full, and others are only part of what they should be. What kind of world has the son entered? He has wandered into a forest where every drop of water belongs to a half-made giantess. He set off to see the world, and now the world offers him a look at halfness. He has found the area where careful account is kept of all the elements in nature, where everything that happens is noticed, where the slightest thing taken becomes of greater importance than all that was left alone. His open-eyed, innocent foray into the world has led him to a halfworld where emotions run to extremes and bodies can be half of what they should be. This first try at seeing the world shows him a side of life that he would not choose to see.

Children love to climb trees. It's thrilling and scary and gets them above things that are usually looming over them. It moves them closer to God in heaven, or to the goddess Nut who is the heavens, or to Venus, or to Mars, or to the stars. They climb nearer to what they imagine watches from "up there." From the tops of trees, they can see things that cannot be seen from below; they can be birds looking down on the earth. They can see to the bottom of the lake or watch the sky reflected on the surface of the water. They can get above the atmosphere of Mother's disappointments. They can get away from what weights them down. They can rise above the circumstances of their families.

Part of the tree is for talking with God, with a deity of some kind. Part of the tree means being held by nature in ways that the family cannot hold. Some boys take to climbing trees frequently both because they have inclinations to talk to God and because there's such disorder on the ground floor inhabited by the family. In urban life, climbing the tree can mean retreating into a bedroom and not coming out except for absolute necessities. It can mean getting out of reach by going to secret places, in fact or in imagination. A tree house can be a perch that allows a boy to be near home yet out of reach. Right in the backyard he can drift with the clouds, keep secret things, and be looking down on the family. In cities, rooftops can serve the same purposes, to get away and to get above. The imagination soars and the problems of daily life don't have to be faced, but they can be looked down on. The family tree becomes the World Tree.

For some men, it is obvious that the first tree in the story stands in the yard of a family that cannot allow the son access to the lake. For some reason, the boy has to learn that taking even a little of the Water of Life will be more than someone in the family can stand. One man says it straight out: "If I were to take from the water, I would have broken my mother's heart. She had already had so much trouble and grief that even a little trouble on my part would have been unbearable." Another man says, "I was there, too. In my case, I couldn't cry without my mother beginning to tell the story of her own troubles. How could I do this or that to her after all she had done for me? Any attempt to drink my own sorrows would provoke such an outpouring that I'd have to get into the tree to avoid being swamped by my mother's overflowing." "All I can recall is the bone-dry earth at the bottom of the lake. It was as if my mother had dried up. There was no capacity to give or flow into things. Everything was held back, dried up. The house was like an emotional desert. The message I got was not to mention anything about the loneliness all around, not to mention the lack of footprints around the house. I didn't invite anyone over, and I wasn't allowed to have a dog."

Some men say that the lake holds the tears of the mother, that she drinks the water up and then weeps it back when the lake is dry. From this image flows a discussion of the mother's sorrow and the grief in men. A man says that from as early as he can remember, he would sit in the kitchen with his mother. She would tell stories of how life had dealt her this or that blow. She'd weep. He would be overwhelmed by her sadness. His father was one of her disappointments, and she wept for what he had done and what he hadn't accomplished. As he speaks to the other men, this son realizes that he has been drinking his mother's tears, that the two sips taken from the lake contain his view of the world and his view of his father, seen through the salt tears of his mother's eyes. He, however, couldn't cry. He sees his own sadness as distant and small, as if he were watching himself from the top of the tree. Now, sitting by the tree with other men, he can see that he has always been an observer of life.

Another man tells of his mother being ill throughout his childhood. He always had to tiptoe around the house and could only go near her at certain times. There was nothing either of them could do to change this. It made the whole house solemn and quiet. Life became walking carefully around the lake and not drinking at all because death could come at any time. Taking even a sip could precipitate her death. For him, the half-giantess was lying on her side at the water's edge. The missing half was death. When his mother died, he didn't grieve because he had always been awaiting her death. Now he begins to grieve for the boy at the water's edge and the mother who could never mother and the dog he could never have.

His story brings up talk of the dog who suddenly appeared in the tale, and the dog leads to talk of isolation: "The dog was the thing that got to me. If I hadn't had a dog, I would have had nothing. My only friend in the whole place was my dog. I shared more with my dog than anyone in my family. He'd always sit right at my feet." Another voice says, "I wish I'd had a dog. My whole childhood was so solitary. I still feel like I'm walking around the lake and that there are no footprints, not even my own. My mother died when I was small, and I've never even cried about her death. It's as if the lake dried up when she died, and I'm left with this empty lake inside me."

Other stories of climbing the tree emerge. "I think that I just decided to stay in the tree. I've never come down. I took a look at my mother's inability to handle the little things missing from life and decided to stay in the tree. I live my entire life in the treetops. I refuse to come down and deal with any losses; it's not worth it. I don't want to wind up falling apart over things that can't be undone." "I had to be the man of the family. I had to pull myself up and watch from the tree, but I'd better not say a word about how I felt. I now have a great capacity to rise above my own pain." "I watched my mother drink herself to death, watched helplessly. It made me afraid of life, and I've never entered life any further. I'd never follow the half-giantess. When people get angry, I head for the trees."

Over at the cauldron, it's a different scene. Men are talking about mothers who raged and howled. Some men are saying that they stayed in the tree out of absolute fear for their lives. A man says, "I saw my brother go into the stew, and I didn't want to follow. I tiptoed everywhere, and when it got hot, I'd head straight for my room." Another man says, "The whole scene at the cauldron reminded me of waiting for dinner at our house, with everyone sitting on their hands. No one could touch anything until my father got there. If you dared to, you'd get whacked with the spoon." "Dinner was when my mother and father would fight, and we'd be quiet as mice because we didn't want to get blamed for whatever it was." "My mother would always find something wrong. Sometimes I didn't know what I'd done—or sometimes I hadn't done whatever it was; I had just been nearby. Then I'd get beaten. As soon as I could, I got out of there. Ran away. Never looked back." "What got me was the simple, matter-of-fact way the half-giantess caught and cooked animals. My mother can still devastate me with the most matter-of-fact statements, just tossed at me or my wife. I'm always too stunned to do anything."

Another man says, "I thought you said the boy was *in* the cauldron when he got the meat! I saw the boy and the dog in the cauldron, in the stew. Because I became part of my mother's wrath. I've cooked in her wrath. I'm always afraid that I'll disappear in my own rage. I have no sympathy for myself. All my compassion goes to animals, like the dog." "The only way I could be nourished was to steal, to find moments of calm and steal what I could." "I had to trick attention and nourishment from my mother; I got it in spite of her." "I had a tremendous fear of taking anything. I could never take the last piece of toast, the last cookie. I couldn't be selfish. I had to wait and see if anything was left over. I learned not to want, to take what I was given, to wait. Now the only way I can ask for something is to get enraged and make huge demands."

Other voices speak. "I was afraid that the dog would bark. I felt like a boy again and could barely control my fears. What if the dog barks? We'll both be eaten. To me, the two bulls were my father and me; we were eaten up. We couldn't argue with my mother, no way. I didn't listen to the rest of the story. I climbed higher up the tree." "I spaced out as soon as the boy went near the cauldron. I've always felt half present. I started to space out, to go out of my body—I've done this ever since I was a kid." "It was exactly the opposite for me. I'm looking at the stew boiling, and then I feel it boiling inside me. I'm starting to get angry just looking at the stew. I'm getting angry now, talking about it. I get angry hearing other men's stories. I get angry if someone near me is angry." "I was simply frozen in the tree. I wanted to run, but I couldn't. I just stayed right there because I felt so guilty for taking the meat. I just stayed there because it was my fault. I shouldn't ever have taken anything."

Near the cauldron, the feelings are rendered into many parts. These men followed the half-giantess for a variety of reasons; they all knew that there was danger, but they followed her anyway. There's a lot of anger and fear in this camp. There's the feeling that potential nourishment is nearby, but to get it you must face danger. It's dangerous because you could be eaten—or beaten—instead of fed. One man says he could always tell when things were heating up at home; he could smell it. That's what the cauldron represented for him. He could smell the storm brewing, and the question was where to hide.

Being near Mother was an all-or-nothing condition; he would either be given treats, or he would be the next thing devoured.

Another man says, "At the cauldron, it's difficult to remain conscious of who I am. That's what comes out: I get obliterated by my mother's rage rising up in me, and I'm gone. I don't even recall what happened, and for days I feel empty and don't know who I am. It's not the 'her' back there; it's the 'her' in me. That version of her is always there, and it can blow up to the size of a Cyclops at any time. And when I hear that she's dressing for dinner, I can't stand it. How many times did this happen when I was a kid? The exact feeling: I'm waiting; I know what's coming. What's the sense of running? I can't get away. I'm just stuck in the anticipation of the trouble coming. I hate it. The anticipation eats me up! Whatever it is, get it over with. All right, all right, I did it! Whatever you say. I can't stand hearing about it over and over. Get it over with! It's her questions that are tearing me apart. I can't answer those questions. How do I know why I did it? I can't answer."

Another voice speaks. "In my house, everything was supposed to be perfect; we were supposed to have the 'perfect meal,' but it never was. How could it have been a perfect meal? Looking back, I don't even know if my father really wanted a perfect meal. My mother says that's the only reason things went wrong. But he sat there so stiff. I think he was scared, too—too scared to do anything. So it was just easiest for everyone if I got torn apart for some little thing; then he could sit still, and she could rave about how it *could* have been the perfect Christmas, or birthday, or whatever."

Still another man says, "The spear was what I focused on: I was trying to put the spear in carefully and take just the right amount of attention or stuff from the kitchen, from the world. But my mother always thought I took too much. She'd ask me, Aren't you ever satisfied? What do you think I had as a kid? Who do you think you are? Does everybody owe you everything? So now, whenever I want something, I have to go through this endless list of questions from inside. Am I doing this because I'm selfish? Shouldn't I be able to do without this? Isn't there a cheaper way? It's as if any desire on my part is going to unravel the world, which is so fragile that if I take one more piece out of it, it will fall apart. The trouble now is when a woman asks me what I want from the relationship—do I want children? do I want anything?—I can't stand it. Either I shut down, or I blow up. Either I begin to rage and boil and just explode, attacking everything, ready to tear up the relationship, or I just get away from it. I don't care. I won't care. It doesn't matter to me. I'm outta here. I'm gone. If this is what it's all about, if this is all it is, I'm outta here. If this is what the world is, I'm gone."

By the time each man has spoken the atmosphere will be filled with spells. The lake and the cauldron are big spellbound areas that people continually wander into, find themselves caught in, and can't explain how they got there. While alone and under the spell it is very difficult to learn anything about it. After the spell disappears there is a strong inclination to avoid the area where the half-giantess was found. The trouble is that each area provides missing emotional nourishment without which a life can become dry and starved. The half-giantess only appears where a person needs to go, and she always appears when an important area of life is approached.

CHAPTER 7

THE SPELL

ONCE AGAIN THE men who have entered into the story have divided into camps based on shared feelings and shared images. These two groups are, to begin with, encampments outside the house of the mother. The men are meeting within the emotional atmosphere that every son feels when he is near the mother. He feels it when he runs to the mother's body as a child, but he feels it when he approaches the mother as a grown man. It's as if at birth the child has an invisible aura around it that doesn't wash off with the afterbirth. It's as if he's born with a caul that is not visible but through which things must travel to get to him. If a man is "hard to get to," he's still firmly within this caul. I'm calling this atmosphere or emotional covering a spell, a tendency to get caught in a mood or an emotional storm. The spell increases near the mother, but it travels with the son, catching up with him sooner or later whenever he stops long enough.

One of the great difficulties for sons who try to work on their troubles with the mother is that the beginnings of these troubles are preverbal. Similarly, the mother has trouble hearing about the son's issues with her because she knows him in this preverbal way as well.

Mother and child have a long unspoken relationship. They once participated in everything together. The thinnest membrane separated them and it was permeable. The mother knows the child from the inside out. Until the mother's "water broke," the child grew on the inland sea of its mother.

Each child has absorbed the mother from her bloodstream, from the conditions of her internal lake bed, from her dreams, from her plans for the birth that develop consciously and unconsciously as the child grows within her. Even while the mother-to-be is not aware of her pregnancy, the embryo is going through its most explosive stages of growth, and the fetus, with its transparent skin, is absorbing everything in an extended feast of subjectivity. The child grows from a single cell to great complexity inside the biological, psychological, and mythological systems of the mother. The pregnant mother becomes unusually absorbent as well, and the psychic atmospheres of the family and even of the surrounding culture are taken into the womb world. The child is being made from the choices and habits of the mother and from the culture that surrounds her. The inner lake in which the fetus grows is fed by the stream of the mother's diet, her relationships, and her imaginal life.

This process of interpretation is what I call "mythobiology"—mythologizing bits of biology. The embryo is embedded in the biology of the mother's womb, but it also floats upon the waves of feeling passing through the womb. It grows in an otherworldly state that can only be understood through myth. Each person is a child of the biological womb, of the psychic weather, and of the mythic ocean. In all three ways, it is part of "Mother."

As the mother inflates with the child, her imagination heats up, and her emotions become more specific and more changeable. The fetus inside rocks in an ocean that receives the moods of the mother like calms and storms at sea. Mothers know this; that's why they tell stories with such authority about how the birth of the child reveals the child's nature. The mother knows the climate within which the child has grown from one cell to millions. For both mother and child, the complex involvement with the mother begins before the child's birth, as the embryo moves from the simplest, most compact condition to the great distinction of an infant.

The unconditional love of the mother, like the mother complex, is also preverbal; it, too, begins before the child's birth. For everything that happens to the mother passes unconditionally through the cell walls to the child in the womb; this sharing comprises the mother's unconditional love. It provides the child with its first view of the world and its first experiences of love.

Birth marks the first separation of the two and the beginning of the end of their completely shared world. When the son isn't walking the road of the father, he is seeking to complete the world that ended with the breaking of his mother's water. In "The Sweetness of Life," the father's spirit took the son's spirit out of the womb and went hunting in the bush, showing the son the father's way of knowing the world of animals and plants. What they learned together changed, however, when the son entered the world of flesh and bones. When the father and son sought sweet nourishment at the honey tree, they clashed. But the son's spirit in the womb also receives images and information from the magical body-making of the mother. The son becomes acquainted with the inner rhythms of life while sharing the inner rhythms of the mother. The merged state of mother and fetus is so thorough that all embryos appear female for the first six weeks in the womb. A shock occurs in the womb when the rapid release of hormones causes the appearance of the male embryo. There are further shocks awaiting mother and son after the womb time, and a great shock awaits the son when he enters the world on his own. For the rest of his life shocks will accompany meaningful changes.

There's an old idea, shared by many cultures, that the pain and struggles of the birth and separation from the mother cause the newborn to forget what happened in the womb, forget where it came from, and forget who it is in spirit. The shock of coming out into the world causes it to lose all the knowledge of itself that it held just hours before. The child lands on an island of life after birth much as a passenger lands after a shipwreck. Everything must be relearned; this land is different enough that what is poison and what is nourishing must be rediscovered. From this point of view, life can be a series of encounters that shock the self into remembering who it is—and, indeed, this is one way to define "initiation." In initiations people remember who they are and who they are trying to become. To remember who he is and what he knows, the son requires shocks like the one that occurs in his mother's womb when he becomes male. The half-giantess represents one of those shocking encounters that makes the son begin to remember and to emotionally awaken.

As a symbol, the half-giantess draws attention to the spell of the son. Her very appearance states that he only knows half of the story, half of his life and of nature. She considers his attention to details very important. Psychologically, the half-giantess shows him that he is emotionally half-formed. Ecologically, she demonstrates that every little thing remains connected to every other thing, even little sips alter the balance at the end of the day. Mythologically, the half-giantess says that leaving the area of the mother means stepping into the great womb of the world where the emotional and psychic fullness before birth must be rediscovered.

Someone once asked, Does the half-giantess put you under a spell or help break the spell by shocking you awake? The half-giantess loves those kind of either/or questions. They're easy for her to answer and she always answers the same way: yes. The half-giantess is an image of the incompleteness of mother in the consciousness of the son.

She appears at the places where the personal mother, the inner feminine of the son, and the Great Mother of the world all meet. Where the actual mother couldn't give what the son needed or wanted, the "inner mother" of the son forms a spell of wishes, demands, broken emotions, and fantasies. Where the personal mother "fails" to satisfy the huge expectations of the child, the Great Mother settles in like a spell.

The half-giantess is half personal mother, half "inner mother," half Great Mother. Three halves make her whole. That's her style of math and humor and intentional shocking of logic.

If the half-giantess feels ignored and mistreated she'll enter a person, a relationship, a village, and spread an emotional spell as far as she can. The less she is looked at, the bigger she grows, though she always maintains her halfness. In her territory, whatever is denied, avoided, and not looked at holds the energy for meaningful change. Change comes from the unfinished areas, not from pretensions of wholeness. Her halfness calls for completion. The half-giantess is a force for emotional awakening and change. When attention is given to what she's pointing at, she calms down, rearranges herself, gets dressed for a nice meal.

The images in stories draw out distinct and personal details from each listener, so that each person sees their own half-giantess. When I ask men and women at events what the half-giantess looks like, there are as many different pictures as there were of the wound given by the father in the story of the hunter and his son. She's been seen as only the left half of a huge body; as a body whose right side is gigantic and whose left side is tiny; as a Cyclops; as just the top half of a body or as only the lower half. She's been seen as half the size of what a giant should be; as a huge woman cut diagonally in half, one half of her appearing in a vague mist; as a big woman with only one breast; as just the front half with no back or as just the back, always turned away. These are images of the unfinished "emotional body" of the viewer. They are ways of catching sight of a person's inner life as a body.

Some people are activated only in the lower half of the body, and they have to channel most emotions and imaginations by stepping on someone, walking away, or having sex. Other people start their emotional lives in the upper chest and move straight up from there. A cyclops can only do things, see things, feel things in one way. An inner emotional mother with only one breast runs dry, runs out of emotional nourishment. Only seeing the back of the giantess is an ongoing affront to the emotional life of the individual.

Some people's descriptions are similar to those of hags and giants in folklore throughout the world. Usually, halfness is a code for primeval, for half-beings belong to a race that existed before humans. There is usually no explanation of how they became half instead of whole. In many parts of Africa, they wait at the border between the village and the bush, and they prey on the irreverent and unknowing.

In Ireland they were known as the Fomorians—giant men and women with one arm, one leg, and one eye apiece. They inhabited the land when humans arrived, and the humans had to pay tribute to them with grain and sheep and drink. Of course, the Fomorians, like the half-giantess in our story, made a big porridge out of these gifts. They claimed ownership of everything and were always ready to go to war, so they had to be paid off or else they would raise a loud complaint and make trouble. The humans eventually defeated them through magic and tricks, but they also intermarried with them, and their characteristics appear in their descendants. In fact, there is some trace of them in everyone.

The halfness of the half-giantess stands for the unfinished emotional world of the child and the incompleteness of even the best mothering by the human mother, who stands at the place where one world meets another. During her pregnancy with the son, the mother expands with the spirit of the Great Mother while the son races through stages of growth inside her. As a child, the boy cannot separate the Great Mother from the human mother. Being near the mother activates the feelings he has toward the Great Mother. In the vicinity of the mother's womb, he feels that he is at the shore of the endless ocean of the Great Mother, the goddess of water. For years he feels close to wholeness when close to the mother, held near her womb, or sleeping by her as he used to do. Each of their senses of where the other begins and leaves off is distorted. He feels entitled to drink from her pools as he did automatically in umbilical times. She feels that he should understand her feelings and respect them as she sees fit because she gave to him the very pulsing of her organs while he grew in her. She feels that he is a part of a story growing out of her. He can easily feel that his story is completely entangled in hers and caught in a spell.

MOTHER AND SON

She goes on with her story,
this woman whose twelve-year-old son
has drifted into the party;
her mind is still with the guests.
But her flesh has claimed possession of his.

She pushes his hair back from his eyes,
curls a lock of it around her finger,
while continuing to entertain us
with her wit. The touch of her hand
embarrasses him, but only a little;
he shrugs slightly, that is all.
Now she smiles at him
as if conscious of his presence
for the first time.
It's a loving smile, of course,
but not altogether a friendly one:
there's a pride in that smile
and a sense of power,
even a hint of cruelty. She's a normal parent.

She pinches his earlobe now, plays with the buttons
on his shirt, talking with us all the while.
He wriggles for an instant, and then
surrenders, half-gracefully, to her caresses.

They both know she's the stronger,
that she'll be the stronger for a while yet,
that he couldn't break away from her
even if he could make up his mind
that it's what he wants.

ALDEN NOWLAN

Someone once said, "What's been wounded by the masculine must be healed by the masculine. What's been wounded by the feminine must be healed by the feminine." One reason to come face-to-face with the wounding fathers and wounding mother figures is to begin a learning and healing process. The wounds from the mother often take the form of spells that come over mother and son when they come near one another, especially if this drawing near is done unconsciously. Some rituals of initiation are intended to break that spell. Until the spell is broken, the child's imagination, so tied to the mother's, forms extreme fantasies of life events, images that are more tied to the primeval than to the everyday world.

While the father's curse often has a verbal component, the mother has a profound preverbal effect. It's hard to put our feelings about her into words, and she can make our heads spin like a dizzy spell. In the territory of the mother, we struggle with moods and spells in order to find the creativity and emotional wholeness they obscure. On the other side of the spell are inspirations from an area needing attention and a deep humor and satisfaction about life.

A spell may appear as a mood that comes over a man without warning. Unless a man works on making his emotional life more conscious and unless he commits to involvement in ongoing relationships, he may never become aware of the emotional patterns, the spells, that he wanders through over and over again. A man may become a regular visitor to the cauldron of the half-giantess. When circumstances in the outside world become difficult and the pressure starts to rise, the cauldron begins to heat up and steam. As the man moves around the house, his wife and children can feel that he's "in a mood." At first, his mood is as faintly perceptible as a fine mist or as heat waves rising from the surface of things. Only later when the cauldron boils over does the man become aware that he has been hauling sacks of grain, stoking a fire, and even dressing for the occasion.

The man in his mood can become the half-giantess. She doesn't mind; she doesn't scruple over gender. She's happy just to put on her dinner clothes and get a good rave going. There's such a clearing of the air after the rampage that she may go off whistling to herself, all settled down, ready for a good sleep. After the half-giantess calms down, the man may feel like the boy in the tree. He may want to get away and not talk about what happened.

Another man may avoid relationships altogether in order not to attract the attention of the half-giantess. If he stays away from the emotional areas within, he may slip past the giantess unnoticed. If he doesn't take any sips, spear any meat, or try to take any emotional nourishment, he just might be able to get by.

But let's say that one day he decides to see what is out in the world, and he sees a woman coming along. She's beautiful; he sees her as something whole. They fall in love; they live together. He says, at least to himself, "She's all I want and all I need to be happy." Other people say she's his "better half," and he agrees. But it doesn't work out; things go wrong. He finds her too demanding and tires of trying to satisfy her needs in the relationship. She feels he's too distant, except when he wants comfort or sex. They begin to have territories where they can easily set each other off into familiar disappointments or familiar rage.

If he's a young man, he's really in trouble. How could he have been so wrong? he wonders. He feels caught, trapped. He didn't see the other half of her or of this relationship. He didn't see what was coming. She's either just like his mother in certain ways and he has had enough of that, or she's not at all like Mom, she can't compare at all, she's not half good enough.

Either way, there's something missing: understanding, freedom, respect, faithfulness, support, erotic love, common interests, patience, passion—something. And this missing part becomes everything. In the words "Something is missing in our relationship!" you can hear the footsteps of the half-giantess. The man becomes less and less able to talk about what he is feeling, and there are fewer things they can do that will bring back the sense of completeness with which they started. He begins to withdraw from her and from the "them" of the relationship. Soon, she says that if it weren't for her, they'd never speak at all. He's always behind a newspaper, a book, a sales report. Or he's always in front of a TV, a ball game, or a machine that needs attention. There's less intimacy, less gentle talk, less touch, less revealing of one to the other. Soon enough they're on opposite sides of a lake of sorrow or on opposite sides of a cauldron that's in a constant simmer, ready to boil over. They've entered the territory of the half-giantess without knowing it. But something in each of their psyches knows it because he's spending his time in the tree house and she feels like a monster when he looks at her.

Whatever actual words she says, they work like a chant that stirs the spell, that repeats in his head, "It's all your fault." This is a mantra of the half-giantess: "It's all your fault, it's the faults in you that ruin everything, and they are all your own fault!" No matter what his partner may actually be saying, he's hearing this in the tone of her voice. He's seeing a huge woman, and as she becomes more exact about what the trouble is, he feels more like a drop in a lake, about to drown or dissolve.

The half-giantess has come out of her house inside the man and is now intercepting anything that comes toward him, cutting it in half. The more rational and calm his partner's statements are, the more they fill him with grief, rage, and helplessness, for the half-giantess makes these statements sound like impossible demands. If this situation goes on long enough, he will begin to see the half-giantess in the face of his wife or partner. Soon he feels that he's going to be smothered in the gushing of her emotions or torn apart like a bull at the cauldron.

Relative size is blown out of all proportion by the half-giantess. This is the meaning of her vast sorrow over the two drops of water in the story. The man feels that his emotion can never be as big and as dangerous as hers. His partner has become mixed up with the prever-bal mother who was so large and could be overpowering. An outside observer might see a scared, endangered woman; the man sees a terri-fying giantess.

If he has never dealt with this half-giantess inside, he won't be able to talk about her. He may be so devastated when he realizes that he has disturbed the waters that he can't speak. Or the half-giantess may obliterate his attempts to speak with a flood of tears or a howling rage. He feels diminished; his feelings for himself are reduced. What we think of as "him" is reduced to an adolescent in a struggle to hold onto his gender identity. He's a boy who feels that his growing integrity and independence are threatened; then he's an infant who feels his bodily well-being is in danger, and finally he's an embryo in fear of annihilation. Through the course of an argument, a man may be many different psychological ages. If the core areas of his complex involvement with the mother are approached, he may "lose it" altogether—lose the various integrities of age and self-awareness. When he loses it, he may become a giant, a giantess, a cauldron boiling with the poison of a time when he missed out on something he needed, or a dog that will bite and tear as if pursued by a raging giant.

If a man doesn't have an image of what the threatening feminine already inside him looks like, then he can project the image onto any woman. Since the half-giantess insists on being attended to, she makes sure that men see her acting in women. A man may claim never to see this half of the feminine. Such a man can't see any wrong a woman can do; he's avoiding the lake and the cauldron. Women will either find him dry and unappetizing, too easily treed, or will knock him over with a spoon. There are good reasons why fairy tales and myths are inhabited by hags and witches and their spells. Taking little sips of the world activates the spells already in the man. It's not that the fairy tales are antiwomen; it's that looking through a fairy tale, you can glimpse the emotional spells around people as they approach the lake of life.

If a man refuses to look back into his childhood at the times when he set off responses in his mother that were way out of proportion, then he's still running, like the boy at the end of the story. He may be running to father, clinging to principles, organizations, and abstractions that will keep the lake and the cauldron at a distance. Or he may be staying up in a tree, trying to remain above all that mess in the psyche. But the half-giantess is always waiting. Whenever someone wants to discover what lies within, or wants to explore the psychic landscape, the half-giantess will demand some attention. Men face a choice between living a lonely life in the treetops or getting down into the disappointments, sorrows, and rages of life. If the half-giantess is faced, eventually she settles down. And if she is given little offerings that acknowledge that she's there, then she settles down sooner.

Telling her unfinished story is an offering to her, and we'll come back to her story later. Meantime, the son has returned to the father, saying he has seen what's in the world and implying that he's seen enough. And yet, once an initiatory stepping out occurs it can't stop. At least in the psyche, once separation begins everything inside prepares for meaningful change. There's no real turning back once begun. If the son stops now his head will really spin; and the psyche will spin its wheels expecting to follow the change that was begun. The son must enter the territory of the great feminine forces again.

CHAPTER 8

THE LIZARD IN THE FIRE

THE LIZARD IN THE FIRE

A father told his son, "If you ever sleep with a maiden, you will die." Then the father hid his son in the bush. He let the boy grow up in the forest.

One day a maiden came into the bush. She saw the son. The boy saw her. The maiden said, "You live so alone here. I'll come each day to visit you."

The youth said, "My father told me I would die if I ever lie side by side with a maiden, as if a sword would go through my heart."

The maiden said, "In that case, I'll not come again, for it is not my wish that you should die."

The young man said, "No. Please come again. I beg of you, please come anyway!"

The maiden said, "Good, then. I will come back, and if you die, maybe you will come to life again."

The next day the maiden came again. The youth and the maiden lay together. What happened? The youth died; he died. Just as the father said, he died.

What did the father do? What did the mother do? They wept.

What did the maiden do? She ran deep into the forest to the old hunter of the bush and told the hunter the whole story. The hunter said, "Why, that is no problem. All we need is a lizard and a fire."

The hunter went to get a lizard. The youth was brought to the village. Wood was gathered and piled high. The fire was lit. The people of the village all gathered round. When the flames were great, the lizard was set in the fire. The hunter said, "Now, here is the situation we are in: If the lizard burns on the funeral pyre, the young man will stay dead. But if someone pulls the lizard from the fire, the young man will return to life again."

The father tried to pull the lizard from the fire, but the flames were huge and hot, and he was driven back. The mother went forward, but she, too, was driven back by the raging flames.

The maiden? She jumped right into the center of the fire, pulled out the lizard, and brought it back alive. The young man? Well, he sprang back to life.

The hunter said, "Now, here is the situation: The young man is back in life again. If he kills the lizard, the mother will die. But if he doesn't kill the lizard, the maiden will die." Kill the lizard, and the youth and the young woman will live. But the mother will die. Don't kill the lizard, and the mother and son will live on, but the maiden will die. The question is this: What would you do? What would *you* do?

Once again the son has returned from the forest after an encounter with the feminine. Instead of running back to his father, as he did after visiting the half-giantess, he is carried home as a corpse. In the previous story he barely makes it back alive, this time he comes back dead. Will he die completely or will he, through dying a little, enter life more fully? Or will someone else die?

In this story, a whole community gathers around the burning issue of who goes into the fire and who gets to stay in life. The future of the whole village is involved. An old saying goes, "In initiation, everyone suffers." The fires through which young men and young women must pass have an affect on everyone. It is also said that if youths don't pass through such a fire, they will burn the whole village down. So the question at the end of the story must be faced: What would you do?

I've told this story many times, to groups of men alone, to whole villages of women and men, to people of all colors and ages. When I tell it, the story itself acts like a fire thrown into the center of the room. Everyone who answers the burning question adds to the fire because each answer sparks others to disagree. Everyone faces each other across the fire. The discussion of the story becomes a ritual of disagreement. The conflicts inherent in the audience come to the surface, and the fire of disagreement makes the audience into a community. This time the community chorus includes women and men.

One man says, "No problem. I'd kill the lizard." Silence. A woman says, "That means killing the mother. Why doesn't the boy's father die? He started all the trouble in the first place."

A young woman says, "If the lizard doesn't die, the maiden will die, and there'll be no one to carry on the tribe." A young man adds, "She's the only one who went into the fire for him; he has to kill the lizard for her."

Another woman laments, "I've already leapt into the fires for several men and come out scarred and burned and it didn't change them at all." A man answers, "It's all or nothing. If the son doesn't kill the lizard, anyone who gets close to him will get burned over and over."

Someone else protests, "Why does there have to be killing at all? Why can't everyone just live his or her own life, each doing his or her own thing?" Someone answers, "Doing your own thing can mean not doing anything, and not doing anything means the young woman dies.

That's not right. She's the one who has risked the most. You can't suddenly say people are on their own! That's a cop-out."

Another voice pipes up: "I'd kill the old hunter. He's behind the whole setup. Who says killing the lizard will save the maiden? What if he then says, 'Now, here's the situation.' I'd kill him." A woman says, "I agree. It's another patriarchal story: the father tells the son that the maiden is bad, and the old, male patriarch says the answer to everything is to kill the mother. It's the same old story. Blame women. We need new stories that don't solve all problems by killing women and animals. Kill the old patriarch."

Now I jump into the fire to defend the story. "What new stories? All stories are 'old stories'—it's how people see into them that changes. If you make a new story, you make another dilemma. Besides, the story is more complicated than it looks. . . ."

"Wait a minute!" Another woman is on her feet. "Who says the hunter was an old man? I thought she was an old woman who knew where to find the right kind of lizard and knew just what the situation required. Why couldn't it be a wise old woman hunter?" Another argument breaks out: did he say the old hunter was a man or a woman? Everyone looks at the storyteller.

What did I say? I don't know. I was just telling the story. It's not memorized and recited word for word. The story is part remembered and part created every time it is told. The two aspects of memory and making go on together, like two streams rushing into the tongue, each carrying words that become one river as they go over the cliff of the lip. So I don't know what I said this time.

One of the women speaks again: "He didn't say him or her; all he said was the old hunter. It could be either a woman or a man."

Yeah, I knew that.

Storytelling is designed to provoke emotional reactions in the listener, and these reactions awaken images that the listener must try to capture. The story comes to life through emotions and memories so that the two aspects of remembering and making continue in the listeners. This story prompts people to take a stand at some definitive place around the communal hearth and then add to the fire.

At the fire created by this story, women and men take a variety of positions; they don't simply polarize. The young men present tend to group together; they feel that the lizard has to die, for each of them wants to be with the young woman. Still, one young man says he doesn't want to kill the lizard because his mother is his only parent.

She has raised all the children by herself; it doesn't seem right for her to die, even if it means that he has to lose something. This young man's comments bring a lot of sadness into the room. The fire cools down a bit.

Now we are taking another look at the mother, but this time we look at her with sympathy for her work. Eventually, an older woman says she feels that the lizard has to be sacrificed. She has a son and knows she has to let him go. Killing the lizard sacrifices her role as mother so that the son can reenter life on his own. A lot of people agree.

This story dramatizes what I call "moving the mother." In order to enter the scene in the village and get a "felt sense" of where the story is going we must shift from seeing the mother as a literal woman to looking at her role as mother. A woman may take on several roles in life, may wear several cloaks, and mother is one of them. This story approaches a ritual moment in the life of family and community when roles must change for the good of all, and it provokes a discussion about the role of the mother in relation to the son and daughter of the village.

The story asks: will the son live only as a part of the mother or in relationship to the young woman? He cannot do both at the same time. The son moves between mother and maiden, between boy and young man. What is it that needs to be said and ritualized in order for the son to be able to see the young woman for who she is and not simply hang his mother expectations, disappointments, and demands on her? The story says that a lizard must die and people must pass their love through a fire, or the young man and young woman will not be able to sustain the gaze into each other's eyes. Unless everyone goes near the fire and then changes their position, the spells of childhood may dominate and divide the young people.

This is the lizard's story, it goes into the fire first and shows everyone that the fire doesn't kill completely. At first, the lizard represents the son. While the son appears dead, the lizard sits in the fire. The lizard is a symbol of where the son is: He's on fire. If someone can get the lizard out, the son will live among the people again. But if his relationship to his family remains as before, the young woman will die. If he doesn't take the lizard out of the center of his life, he won't see the maiden as a source of life for him, and some hope in the community and the future will die. If they can't see each other eye to eye, the lizard will live. Then the mother will always be the same mother to him, and the fire will burn through the village. For lack of sacrifice, the village will die.

Without rituals that show how mother and child walk together to a certain line and then separate, the psyches of mother and of child will continue to share a psychic skin. The story says that the line must be drawn by the community and that a lizard must die to mark the spot; otherwise, everyone will go back to living as before. If this happens, then something will be dead in the son, and the young woman will fade into the mother. The father? He will not see the courage of the maiden and will contribute to the endless childhood of the son.

In order to move the mother, there must be a place to which she can go. There also needs to be a community to witness the movements of mother, daughter, father, and son. There needs to be an old hunter and a willing lizard. But if she can't move to another position of authority and caring, the mother clings and holds on. She is used to taking the temperature of her child; she even takes her own temperature from the child. It's not just the son who must go into the fire and then come back in a new skin. It's not just the maiden who must leap into the fire and step out into a new garment. The mother, too, must go through the fire and come out to pick up a new cloak. The mother must move some of her affection from her child to the art of nourishing culture; otherwise, what was life-giving can turn cold-blooded and cling to the life it once nourished. For the mother, the cloak on the other side of the fire is that worn by the wise old woman in stories. If a village doesn't offer its mothers such a cloak, the mother gets stuck in a literal position.

Modern cultures have a continual problem seeing the mother as something other than the literal, biological woman who gave birth and/or raised a child. The mother herself can tend to literalize life. The mother is involved in the literal birthing and growing of the child. The symbol of mother is actualized in the life of a woman. Therefore the mother tends to literalize, and "mother" tends to be seen literally. One of the spells that must be broken open is the spell that holds a woman as mother captured in literal terms.

The phrase used in initiation literature is *separating from the mother.* It's more than distancing from the mother; it's more like cutting the ties with mother temporarily. The psyche tends to see it as a killing or slaying, as we saw in the story with the father and the horses and the slave girls. In this story, before the "death" of the mother is considered, the son has already died. What happened out in the bush put the son into some form of death. Now it's necessary for the mother to enter some form of death. Because the son only suffers a small death, he now reenters life in a bigger, fuller way. The same type of change has to be accomplished for the mother. In modern societies there are increasing difficulties when these changes are attempted. The stages of life after physical motherhood tend to be vague and devoid of meaning. There is a lack of active, respected images of where the mother goes when she dies to her motherhood. Our image of motherhood is not broad enough, and the cloak of mother gets stuck at the place where the birth mother meets an image of death. This causes a cultural spell to form around and within the mother, the son, the daughter, and the lizard.

In order to break the spells that keep each person in roles he or she is outgrowing or passing beyond, each requires a new position to enter. For the mother to release the child, as child, she must move on to another full role. For instance, when a culture has a position of old wise woman or worldly crone, a woman can move from the stage of mothering children to the stage of mothering culture and caring for the community. She can find her place at the well of wisdom and the cauldron of inspiration. Women can attend the wombs of culture where the mother can mix living experience with the wisdom of inspiration. Mother becomes grand-mother. She moves from giving literal milk to actual children to dispensing "milk wisdom" to all her children.

The image of mother is all-encompassing, extending across life from before birth to after death, from the origins of life in the teeming ocean to burial in Mother Earth. There is both a birth mother and a death mother. Traditionally, a midwife used to attend birth and death, washing and covering the new children coming into life and washing and covering the dead for their return to the ancestors. She was the wife of their birth and of their death. She stood for the Great Mother who is three times a wife, three times a mother: at birth, during life, and at death. In this ancient image, womb and tomb are connected, each a source of wisdom. When a culture avoids and denies death, it loses the wisdom of this darker womb. Making death biological only, makes birth biological mostly, and diminishes the birth mother, the death mother, and the roles a woman can fulfill.

Troubles with moving the mother come from our images at each end of life, birth and death. When birth is not seen as a community event, as well as a family and personal event, the value of "mother" is reduced. When the role of mother is confined to the personal and practical, a whole area of wisdom diminishes and spells multiply. When the image of the Great Mother as the womb of life and the tomb at death gets condensed into a literal mother, then the personal mother becomes the focus of unreal expectations, fears, and disappointments. When the death mother is denied and avoided, the human mother tends to be seen as deadly. More than that, the fear of the death mother becomes a fear of women in general and, specifically, a fear of women acting in a strong way.

Without the sense that there are stages and roles after motherhood, mother becomes a place of stuckness and getting spellbound. Women can become afraid to enter it and afraid to leave it. Without the promise of other meaningful cloaks to wear, some women continue to mother, in the most literal way, children who have grown into adults themselves. When this happens, the spell between literal mother and children continues to the end of life.

The fires of initiation intend to break the momentum of this pattern. They break the spell of the inner mother within the son; they make a break for the mother with regard to that particular child; and they eventually mark an end for the mother with regard to childbearing and child rearing in general. There are two unusual and marked characteristics of human mothers: First, the period of mothering, nourishing, and tending to a child is greater, longer, more extended, and more involved than in almost any other animal; and second, a woman's period of childbearing comes to an explicit end with menopause. On the one hand, the role of mother is extended tremendously among human beings, and on the other hand, it comes to a distinct end, which is not the case with other species. So from the point of view of the mother standing at this fire in the midst of the community, there comes a time when she moves to another position both because the son or daughter is moving to a new position and therefore the mother must shift and because the voice of Mother Nature makes that statement.

And if the mother can't move, then why should the maiden leap into the fire? For if the maiden can't move from the fire to a new position in the eyes of the son, why should she risk herself to keep him connected to life? And if the maiden won't make the leap of faith for the youth, why should he disobey his father? Why should he die by becoming really close to her? And if the son is not going to go far enough into his life to taste death, why should he face the issue of death at all? Why should he ever grow up? On the other hand, if the community doesn't care enough to watch his struggles with life, why should he care about the life or death of anyone else? If his life doesn't count, how can the love of the maiden have value?

When the father withholds his attempts at advising and protecting, the son finds struggles with life and death on his own. Even if there are no tears from the mother and father, the fire will still occur, but the ritual for which it is intended will be aborted. If there are no old hunters available, there will be no willing lizards, and the fire will reach everyone. Instead of little symbolic deaths, young people will help towns and cities burn, and old people will cling to ways that lack dignity and they will refuse the cloak of dark wisdom.

Clothes, cloaks, and skins are being exchanged at the lizard's fire. In the process, the main characters must become nakedly human, and they must be burned a little, scarred a little, in order to learn who they must become. No great change can occur, no birth, without something dying. The lizard moves from the waters of birth to the fire of death, and everyone watching sees something of himself or herself dying in the fire and something else coming out of the flames. Change is the essence of initiation. Cultures that have lizard clans say that lizards are the ancestors of all the land animals and that lizards who shed their tails became the first people. Thus, in the fires of initiation, each person touches these ancestors again, and touching our beginnings allows things to begin anew.

In the story, there are many little sacrifices that make the fire. The father's authority over the son and over the maiden gets sacrificed, for they both disobey him. The idea that the mother or father can save the son from the fires of life perishes. If the son kills the lizard, then he sacrifices his old attachment to the mother. The son's image of himself as completely independent and never needing help— that, too, is sacrificed. When the maiden leaps into the center of the fire, the idea that a young woman must be helpless burns away. The sense that a woman's role is only to mother goes up in smoke. By the end, everyone has lost some skin, and the lizard's old bones have been warmed.

The heat of conflict and the burning fires of change that are occurring in the village warm the blood of the lizard. There is an intense, dynamic exchange between people and symbols that releases emotions and ideas and increases life energy. In one sense, the lizard represents the cold-bloodedness and clinging of everyone involved being made visible and then heated in the fires of community conflict and change.

A symbol is a mystery that directs attention to insights and change. Lizards and snakes are brothers and sisters. Both shed skins, shed previous appearances, and seem to pass from life to death and back again. Lizards live on a branch of the tree of animals that extends all the way back to dinosaurs in prehistory and to dragons in mythology. Lizards were among the reptiles that moved out of the Great Mother ocean and found ways to live on land. Like all good symbols, lizards live between one thing and another, between fish and mammal, between crocodile and snake. People describe lizards as fish on land, snakes with legs, little crocodiles, miniature dinosaurs.

Lizards move every way possible, including swimming and flying from tree to tree. Their ability to cling defies gravity. Grab the tail of some lizards, and they will leave it with you. What is in your hand will wriggle and seem alive for a while. Meantime the lizard itself has gotten away and grown another tail. This is similar to how symbols and stories work: They leave a piece of living information with anyone who catches them. Everyone who pays attention to the story walks away from the fire with a piece of the lizard. For a while it burns with life and warms spirit and soul. Then it grows cold again. Another lizard must be found.

After the story, the mother of the son has moved and the son has survived another of life's fires. But, where does the mother in the son move? Where does the son go with his "inner mother"?

CHAPTER 9

BREAKING THE SPELL

We left the chorus of men divided into two camps back by the lake and by the cauldron of the half-giantess, and it's time to return to the spells they've been dealing with. The story of the half-giantess as well as the many tales of hags and witches and task-making queens are excursions toward the inner mother, the inner feminine, and the great mysteries of feminine figures in mythology. As we engage the images in stories, our relationship to women and the feminine becomes deliteralized and begins to move in psychological and mythological directions. In order for the son to move the inner mother, insights into the feminine symbols, and changes in emotional attitudes, are necessary. Basic emotions and attitudes have to be re-entered and re-experienced before going forward and breaking the spell.

The chorus of men is divided like the half-giantess herself, each camp dealing with a part of the emotional world. At the lake, the primary emotion is sorrow, with depression nearby when the lake becomes empty and dry. Over at the cauldron, there's anger and rage as the primary emotions, with excitement and fear stirred in, making a spinning excess of the emotional world. These aren't the only spells that get set in an individual or group, but they are two of the major areas of emotional life and learning, and two of the areas of great stuckness. Two old proverbs exemplify this. One says, Every increase of knowledge is an increase of sorrow. Another says, He who is never angry is unborn. The territories of sorrow and anger are places where things are born, increased, and buried. When they are not known, willingly entered and activated, a person's emotional body doesn't grow. The half-giantess wants every drop of sorrow and every bit of anger to be known.

In the half-giantess story, the son runs back to the place of the father and says, "Father, I've seen what's in the world." More clearly it might be said, "Father, I've seen what's in the world when I'm looking through the spell of my own emotions." When the son runs away from how he sees the world and speaks about it, he creates some distance, which can be a healthy viewpoint. If there isn't some place and someone to go to, to return to, and say that he's seen some of the emotional spell that can come over him, he will get emotionally stuck. Left on his own he will remain under a spell. There needs to be a place he can go where he can find an emotional and truthful response to his fear, a place where he can talk about the huge emotions that take over a person or take over a relationship.

It has become common for men to lack close male companions with whom they can share their emotional lives. This usually means that a man will pour all of his emotional issues into one relationship, or into his immediate family, and this can make that relationship a largely spellbound area. His own safety and the safety of his loved ones can be at risk because he has no place to experience the emotions, memories, and spells of confusion except at home. Or, he will try to avoid areas and situations that might provoke overwhelming emotional responses. Feeling stuck or restricted and spinning round and round the same issues are characteristics of the emotional spells that arise when the affected areas are approached.

Spells can be activated by a number of situations: intimacy, extended involvement with another person, beginnings, departures and separations, exhaustion, a change of life stages, or staying isolated. Any of these things can unconsciously stir the spells and capture a person before they are aware of it. Falling in love may activate the positive aspects of the spell at first, but as a relationship ensues, the spinning and stuck aspects of the spell will appear. Avoiding an ongoing relationship only means that the spell will unconsciously arise in the isolation that is created. But any of these situations can also become an opportunity for discovering and recognizing spells.

Within the spellbound area there are resources and nourishment, as shown by the lake and the cauldron of the half-giantess. But getting the full value of these emotional resources depends on how many times they are attempted, on learning the right approach, and on finding a safe distance for each occasion. Spells, emotions, and memories are bound together, and all are affected by distance. If the boy in the story stays away from the lake, doesn't taste any of life's water, and leaves no footprints, nothing happens. He doesn't get exposed to the howling sorrow of the half-giantess. Of course, the dog doesn't appear either, he gets nothing for his dryness, and lives alone. Too much distance and life gets stuck, nothing happens. At the other extreme, if he dives into the lake, he may disappear into the sorrow of the world, or get swallowed and live his life inside the half-giantess, never knowing how he affects others or how they might touch his grief. Not enough distance and the spells, emotions, and painful memories cover over everything.

As we heard from the men gathered at the trees, one way of dealing with the spell is to repress it, to deny that it exists and to push it down or away. But if a man denies the size or existence of the trouble, the half-giantess only grows bigger and the man only feels smaller, and it sets up a future, larger eruption of that emotion. Some men tend to withdraw into a depression that flattens out the landscape as it was after the half-giantess left. Another way some men deal with the spell is to express it excessively, to become addicted to it, or to run all of their life energy through the acting out or expression of that emotional spell. Some men enter the rage of the half-giantess, which usually leads to self-destruction or the battering of others.

Finding the right distance between a person and the powerful core of the events, emotions, and spells that affect him or her allows a person to withstand the overwhelming aspects and penetrate the spell.

Standing in the emotion means a practice of trying to learn aspects of the spell and to become aware of when the half-giantess is nearby before she takes over. Eventually it can be seen that the emotions being stirred up are beneficial or appropriate, and experiencing them can be nourishing to the psyche. The idea is not to become the emotion, to become like a storm pounding against the walls of the hut. By standing in the area of the emotion one can become aware of the huge motions of these feelings and learn how to settle down from them. Then if the emotions become excessive or overheated, if awareness begins to disappear, there's the possibility of getting out, of leaving before it gets to be too much.

The half-giantess demonstrates that the emotions cool, calm, and settle down. She then participates in things, including having dinner. That image shows how the hugeness of the emotions can be learned about. Eventually, a person can learn to feel the area of the spell and feel what it is trying to settle. Even in the story, the son and the dog were nourished before they retreated to the distance.

Breaking the spell releases energy for living and creative force. Getting through the blockage where the emotions are stuck makes not just that emotion but other emotions more available and more serviceable. Putting a limit on rage, finding a way of containing and releasing rage that otherwise enchants the psyche, makes energy available for the emotions of joy and sorrow. Getting past a blocked, flat, depressed, emotional landscape at the Lake of Sorrow releases some joy and makes anger available as well. Emotions are not isolated; breaking the spell around one emotion makes all the emotions more available. In other words, the boy enters a more complete, or whole, emotional life by his visits to the two areas, and this is part of what the half-giantess demands.

The spell forms around an area that's important to the life of that person. If a man is missing a sense of belonging to life, he may find it within the spellbound area. A sense of inner purpose that keeps getting lost may be hidden there. Just as the father's curse fell on the area where the son was seeking blessing, the mother's spell falls on an area where the son can find something charmed, a giftedness, an inspired area of inheritance. If he avoids dealing with the spellbound area, he also avoids learning something of the charm and the grace and even of the fate that are in his life. For these spells always fall into areas of fate. By fate I don't mean some part of one's future that is concretely determined, but that spells fall into areas that reach to a great depth, that open to the inner world and reveal the moving waters of an individual psyche. When a man breaks open the spell to some degree, his ability to see grace in the world and his ability to receive grace from the world increases.

The boy in the story takes two tastes of each place and finds himself in great trouble. And for him it's appropriate to taste these things and leave. It's a good thing to learn to know when one has had enough—enough anger, enough sorrow, enough fear, enough distortion, and enough conflict in one's life, in a relationship, even in one's community. Finding a place of retreat, a place where these things can be spoken about and reflected on, cools down the psyche. But there's another step as well, and we'll have to go into another story to see it. I call this step "taking the third sip at life," or "taking the third taste that leads to the grace within the spell."

One of the secrets of breaking the spell is going further into it. In the terms of the half-giantess story, going further means taking a third sip, or a third taste of the spellbound area. Another way to see it is finding the third part of the giantess. She doesn't appear whole by putting two halves together but by finding her third aspect. In her mathematics, there are three halves, for the great feminine always occurs in triplicate, the triple Goddess. The great feminine is seen in three-foldedness: the three phases of the moon, the three stages of a woman's life—the young woman, the mature woman and mother, and the old crone. She's seen through the three cloaks of those stages. She's also seen in the three Muses, the three Graces, the three Fates, and in the way most things in stories are repeated three times.

What the half-giantess points toward, stomps the ground for, howls about, is completion through the third part of the feminine. In order to see the third part more clearly, we'll have to look into another story. In Celtic mythology, the old goddess and queen is called Cerridwen. In the stories of Cerridwen, the lake and cauldron of the half-giantess come together, for Cerridwen lives within a lake and there she keeps a cauldron in which she brews three drops of inspiration. Those three drops allow whoever tastes them to know everything there is to know about their life: their origins in the past, their emotions and intelligence in the present, and the direction their life is going in the future.

In order to go to the third place, to go beyond the two sips that the boy took, a person has to enter Cerridwen's lake. From there, Cerridwen goes round collecting each herb, each blossom, and each root needed to cook the milk of inspiration in the cauldron. She collects each item at just the right moment in its cycle, based on the phases of the moon, on the surging and sinking of the waters of the earth and the plants that grow from it. At the end of a year's worth of collecting and stirring and simmering, there will be three drops of inspiration, three droplets of the milk of wisdom, made through the combination of water and fire in the cauldron of the Great Mother. Everything else in the cauldron will be poison that can cause death, so that the knowledge of life and the knowledge of death are mixed in the same cauldron. Seeking the milk of wisdom, the droplets of inspiration that can change a life forever, also means going near the dangers and the poisons of the cauldron. From this view we can see why spells are at once attractive and fearful.

A boy named Gwion Bach arrives to stir this cauldron for the year of making the drops of inspiration. Gwion is an orphan, or in the terms of our half-giantess story, he's a son who has stepped out to see what is in the world. He's away from the literal mother and father and has descended or been pulled into the waters of Cerridwen. However, the three drops are not intended for him. He's there as a worker, as someone laboring next to the spinning of the cauldron. The three drops are intended for a son of Cerridwen named Morfran, which means "utter darkness." He's a son of great darkness whom Cerridwen wishes to change through these drops of inspiration, to bring beauty to him, to bring knowledge into him, to make him seen and loved by others.

In this story we have a dark son and an orphaned son. In other words, the unseen, dark part of ourselves and the abandoned and lost part of ourselves are waiting at the cauldron for inspiration. Then, on the last day of the year of turning and spinning and laboring at the cauldron, when everything was ready for Morfran, three drops flew out and hit the thumb of Gwion. Instinctively, he stuck his burning thumb in his mouth and tasted all three drops. In that moment he knew everything there was to know about the past, the present, and his future.

Gwion saw that Cerridwen would fly into a rage at the loss of those three drops. He saw that she would howl and wail and try to devour him. He knew that he'd better flee and not appear as himself at all. The orphan became a hare and fled. Cerridwen arrived, and raged over the loss, then she turned herself into a greyhound and pursued the hare that Gwion had become. He leapt into a river and became a fish. She chased him in the river as an otter. He became a wren and she a hawk. He turned into a grain of wheat among thousands on the threshing floor. She became a black hen, found him out, and swallowed him. For nine months, she bore him inside. At birth, she was going to kill him for taking the drops, but he was of such beauty that she couldn't do it. She wrapped him in a leather bag and cast him on the mercy of the sea.

Eventually, Gwion was caught in a weir by a king's son fishing on the luckiest day of the year. When the boy returned to the surface from the depths of the sea, he had the gift of inspired speech. He had become a poet who could speak the truth. Upon his return, he received a new name: Taliesin, or "radiant brow," because his brow shone and his voice sang. In the Celtic lands, they say that all poets are descendants of Gwion, and to remain a poet, someone must practice speaking the truth. Since the truth that is spoken has been learned from the mixture of life and death, it has several sides to it. It's a truth that mixes dark with light; it is a truth that has emerged from spinning and turning within the spell of mother, man, and Great Mother.

Approaching the cauldron again and tasting all three drops can be seen as an elaborate and extended ritual that leads to a surprising knowledge of one's self. The heart of the ritual occurs when the orphan son suddenly meets an awakened and aware inner self. The three drops awaken something in him that eventually learns to speak in a surprising, poetic, prophetic way. But all around the moment of inspiration that deepens and heightens his powers of knowing and creating are elaborate rites of preparation and containing. On one side of the moment of inspiration, Cerridwen gathers all the fruits and roots of nature and Gwion heats and stirs the ingredients. In a story, a year, or "a year and a day" usually means whatever length of time passes while the pertinent ordeals are endured. So that the moment of inspiration and initiation into an awakened inner self occurs when everything comes ready, and after a long time of stirring just in that place that makes a person's head spin. Cerridwen demonstrates the piece by piece going to and leaving the core of the spell.

On the other side of the moment of inspiration, awakening, and change, there waits the series of shape changes leading to a rebirth. More time passes as the awareness gained condenses to a kernel of grain, which then grows again to become a new person. Gwion the orphan becomes Taliesin the found one, and after a "year" in the company of "Utter Darkness," he becomes the "Radiant Brow." The remaking of the son comes from nature on one side and inspired art on the other. Between the two, he tastes the drops that make him pregnant with himself and make him aware that he will have to live out this next life which was born in him and within nature and art.

Mysteries remain around this moment of radical change, for the mother's efforts don't reach the son for whom they are intended. It's the orphan, "nobody's son," who gets the inspiration. When the great change is about to occur, the son is separate and alone, or he feels separated and alone. And, it's an accident, a mistake. What happens appears to be both given and stolen. The inspiration belongs to the son, and it doesn't. He worked to get it, and it "just happened to him."

If he can't accept the burning that becomes both inspiring and the source of new fear, if he can't handle the suffering of change, he'll take up the blind eye of denial or sip the poison of blaming others. Going near the place of inspiration also means risking getting caught spinning in the spell or being poisoned rather than inspired.

A man in an event once said that his first drink of alcohol opened his psyche to things he had never seen before. With that first drink, his psyche soared; a great weight was lifted from him. He saw and felt more in that moment than he had in all his dull, dutiful life until that point. In order to stay near the inspired feeling, he became a drunk for thirty years, and he nearly died of alcohol poisoning. After several years of drying out, he could see with some clarity again. He could see that he had been drinking from a poisoned river of alcohol, and for thirty years he had been in a blind, drunken spell. He had stayed in the vicinity of the cauldron, but most of the time he had remained distant from true inspiration.

He had confused the spirit of inspiration with the spirit in the bottle. It is hard for us to believe that inspiration and knowledge lie within ourselves. It's hard to accept that we are children of a Great Mother, a mixture of careful gathering and simmering. It's also hard to accept that the raging and weeping half-giantess waits within us as well. Knowledge is painful; it burns and often reveals more than we wish to see of the conditions in the soul.

The moment of inspiration also can be a moment of initiation. Something will change; what happens depends on the son's willingness to see into himself and his ability to stay with fear and suffering. Standing in the moment of inspiration, and standing in the full heat of emotions, means seeing something genuine about one's self. The burning drops get past the daily self worn for the outside world. Gwion Bach is already an orphan when he agrees to stir the cauldron; thus, getting near the cauldron that could inspire means dropping the cloak of who we appear to be and putting on the orphan clothes we keep hidden inside. Tasting these drops that go all the way to the genuine self means changing—now.

All relationships are affected by the mother complex. It complicates how we see the world, how we enter the depths of our own souls, and how we enter relationships with people, especially with those who have a great capacity for love and generosity. What we make of "mother" as woman, as Great Mother, and as web of relationships will determine what we make of women, the world, and the intricacies of our hearts.

In cultures where there is no feminine deity, there is no mention of the idea that the mother who carries the child is herself being carried through pregnancy and labor by the spirit of the Great Mother. In such cultures, the human mother gets burdened with the expectation that she should "do it all," and she gets blamed when it "all goes wrong." Mother and son can remain connected throughout their lives by these huge expectations and their mutual disappointments, which act like a second umbilical cord to hold them together. Mother and son get caught in mutual inflations that lead to mutual blames and shames. If the son doesn't get a full taste of life, he feels poisoned; he begins to hate the mother and senses that he is the shameful son, the "utter darkness" in the eyes of people. His whole life becomes a mistake because he reminds the mother that all her effort and sacrifice turned to poison. Who hasn't seen a mother who sees only radiance in another woman's son and only a dark scavenger in her own? It's easy to have a wrong relationship to the spark of life that burns in the son's soul.

Each child needs to be warmed into life and held at the hearth of the mother. In traditional cultures, "mother" means whoever or whatever holds, touches, and nurses the child. At first, this is the actual body of the human mother. Then the child moves from the internal womb to the womblike arms of its mother. Eventually, the child grows too big for its human mother. It needs other mothers that will nurture other parts of itself. In most tribal cultures, nature becomes the body that holds and carries someone who has outgrown his or her mother's arms, and culture or artful living become the next womb. Thus, the inner mother moves to nature and to art. The human mother is relieved of having to carry and nourish one grown so big. The grown one is introduced to the Great Mother in nature and to the Mother of Inspiration, who presides over the well of memory and art.

There's a mystery at the core of the mother complex, and it will never open itself up to complete understanding. The mist rising from the cauldron ensures that no one will ever see clearly across the womb of events to know who did what exactly. Through the second birth in the oceans of Cerridwen, a man gains perspective on the first birth through the womb of his mother. If mother and son clash, those places will become openings to the ancient double-womb of Cerridwen. It's a double-womb because it combines the cycles of nature with the inspirations of memory and art.

Carrying the spell of the mother into nature can open the spell up and clear the air; the son can locate some ground that can give him sustenance which the human mother didn't have. The soul can find in nature the solace and scenes of deep sympathy that confirm the inner nature of the individual. Not just nature as pretty and predictably awe-inspiring, but nature in its complexity, in its capacity to put the beautiful near the ugly, the terrible next to the nourishing. Nature engaging the soul in suddenly complex situations of beauty and danger, as well as in times and places that settle the soul in newfound serenity. Nature revealing Herself in cycles so old that they can hold any grief and wash any wound we carry. Nature throwing us into circumstances that draw out qualities that are kept hidden from us because we are spellbound, physically and psychologically. Nature as the source of all medicines, as the pharmacopoeia that offers salves to the ways in which we've been burned in our attempts to taste our own lives. Nature opening our eye to the mysteries of beauty, giving the visions of "natural beauty" as gifts, freeing up the capacity for beauty in us and the capacity to see beauty in others.

The price of the gifts of nature involves giving up the heroic eye and accepting the cycles of birth and death. The beauty in nature is married to sorrow, and no heroics can remove the sorrow without destroying the beauty.

Following the other spirit of the mother, that of the Great Mother of Inspiration and Culture, takes us into the area of intuitive knowledge and prophetic sight that culminates in the poetic speech of Taliesin. Part of the art lies is in accepting what is trying to come out.

Everyone is an artist, not because of equal talents, but because there's a cauldron inside each of us. The heat of initiation boils the water down to the drops of inspiration. This cauldron will give inspiration when it's ready and has been stirred enough. The inspiration still requires a series of births and devourings, a series of encounters with the Great Mother and her appetite for changing forms and shapes before the inner voice can speak out artfully and confidently.

The water Gwion floats on is known as the ocean of memory, the ocean of Nmemosyne, Great Mother of Memory and Mother of the Muses. When the emotional spells are broken through, the songs and arts of the muses can be heard speaking and singing. Behind the painful memories that can block change lies the great ocean of memory from which ideas and inventions are born. The inner mother moves toward the deep tides of the soul and the inspirations of art and ritual. The son learns ways of being reborn from the Belly of Memory. He learns how he can participate in the artful making and workings of his own soul, and the ways of making culture. From the place of inspiration, culture equals nature; they are each eyes for seeing the world.

This series of encounters, either through nature or art, means that the son must also look at the darkness that is part of the mother. And he must at least momentarily see this darkness as part of the divine feminine, or he will ascribe that darkness to "Mom" and to other women. Part of the cultural oppression of women derives from the cultural denial of the divinity of the feminine. As the womb of increase and birth, as the old woman of wisdom, and as the voracious tomb that accepts all life into the realm of death, the feminine will always remain a mystery. But when the full extension of this mystery, from the underworld of burial to the ripened fruits suspended in the blue sky, is not acknowledged, then women are forced to carry the weight of all our projections about the feminine.

Allowing the powers of the great feminine back into conscious awareness in Western cultures involves remaking rituals that embrace nature and art. It also means facing death and once again seeing the mother as both womb and tomb. When we do this, fear and grief flood from the dark well of memories into the light of day. Finding the Water of Life requires tasting the waters of grief and death. Moving the mother means not only moving our huge projections off women but it also means facing the titanic aspects of the feminine. Ritual and art provide ways of entering and leaving areas of emotion and memories that could otherwise be overwhelming. Contemporary struggles over the value of ecology and the meaning of art are also conflicts about the place of Mother Earth and the Mother of Inspiration in the estimations of people. The rituals of the territory of the mothers seem to begin with relearning the cycles of nature and reconnecting art to personal and public rituals of maintenance and change.

As has been said, separation evokes the psychic ground of initiation, and this is one reason men's retreats are held in nature. But this separation also provides the distance necessary for men to stand in their emotions, to penetrate the spell, and to explore the emotional and psychic territory of the feminine and the masculine.

In tribal initiations the group of initiates becomes a family for each other. He who was held in the family and in the family spells was temporarily held in the group of initiates. This allowed the emotional world to be dealt with in new and unusual ways. Even now a group of men can often handle the rage that neither family nor spouse could face without some personal danger. Rage that would be dangerous to express toward an elderly or ailing parent can be usefully displayed in one of these events. Anger that is inappropriate to direct toward a child can go toward another man who is similar in size and able to handle the emotions and the threat of violence. A man can learn the inappropriateness of his rage, and can, by making mistakes that do not cause bodily harm to someone, see the size of his anger and have it modified by other men. On the other side, men are capable of opening the door of sorrow for another man, who on his own cannot find the door, or finding it, cannot bring himself to open it out of fear that he will disappear into the lake of grief. And a man stuck in some depressed place can often be spurred out of it by the playfulness of other men, by a direct challenge, or by the sudden feeling that, in these unusual circumstances, he might allow himself to feel, at least a little bit, what he wouldn't allow in daily circumstances.

Penetrating spells and opening wombs of memory usually requires finding people who can help and methods that can provoke and contain the emotions. The daily home has its spells of comfort and of spinning. People tend to do the same things over and over. Home includes the habits that we step into when we come near it. Sometimes the only way to break those spells is to get away from home. Parents are often surprised that their children, when stepping out into the world to go to school or to some other endeavor, are seen as more capable or more brilliant than they are at home. There is another home, the home where the soul dwells, and often it's under the unusual circumstances we encounter when we're at some distance from our regular home, regular work, regular relationships that the soul drops into the dwelling of its deep home.

Part of the time at conferences is spent in direct contact with nature, next to a lake or in the midst of a forest of great, towering, old trees. And that closeness to nature with no focus other than the internal movements of the soul has its own restorative qualities. Nature is the mother of renewal. Simply being near trees while in an aware state can renew parts of a person's life. When the distractions are minimized and the feelings and emotional life are maximized, the sense of immediate mystery in the natural world becomes visible and palpable again. Even those born and raised in the center of the city begin to feel like children of nature; they begin to feel nature as the mother that holds one's ideas, one's exclamations, and one's outpourings of emotions with utter sympathy. By dwelling soulfully in a place, a person can become reoriented to his or her center.

Pieces of one's self that have been lost and missing, or stunned into silence, can return, either through finding some acceptance in the grounds of nature or through stirring some memories in the grounds of the psyche. One way the wholeness of the half-giantess is found is through this combination of the wonder and complexity of nature brought together with the surprising fountains of memory and inspiration within. It takes some effort, some luck, and some grace for those things to come together. But those moments become the swelling of the soul that allows a person to return to regular life with a renewed sense of self and a renewed purpose and a renewed appreciation for family, spouse, and loved ones.

We need the regenerative aspects of both the feminine and masculine territories of the psyche and of myth. Initiations in each territory allow us to locate and heal the inevitable wounds of life. What has been wounded in the feminine gets suffered and healed through the feminine; what has been wounded in the masculine gets suffered and healed in the masculine. The spells of mother release inspirations and healing in the territory of the Great Mother, and the curses of father become blessings in the roads of the spirit fathers. Facing and entering the wounded areas becomes the core of each initiation. Through the troubles and wounds, tastes of the sweet honey of life can be found as well as the milk of inspiration. Both the mother and the father need to be moved so that women and men can see each other anew.

The son's movements in the stories that begin Parts One and Two reflect the differences between the way men tend to work on their issues with the father and the mother. The first son tries to enter his father's world, tries to get close to the spirit of his father. In doing so, he triggers the father's rage, and must then set off on his own with a new awareness of his wounds. He winds up, sword in hand, making fine distinctions between fathers and kings.

The second son leaves home alone to see what is in the world. When he leaves the father and looks into the world to see where he fits, he encounters his spellbound visions of the mother. In a sense, he's moving away from the mother, moving from the mothered world of the boy to the big world at large. He winds up encountering the mother carried within himself, and he is faced with the choice of examining or not his relationship to the basic elements of life and death, all the aspects of the Great Mother.

Moving the father and moving the mother lead into different areas of the psyche, into different mythic territories, and they involve different tasks. Initially, the son moves toward his father and finds a wound, and he moves away from his mother and finds a wound. The initiation of the son into his life as a man involves gaining a vision of his father as a man living his own life, a vision that distinguishes the father from images of kings and titanic gods who cannot really be reached. But the son's initiation also involves gaining a vision of himself in relation to the Great Mother, the great cycles of the earth, and to the creative forces of the great feminine energies that touch his soul. With this vision, he can begin to see his mother as a woman in the midst of her own life. Thus, initiation makes everyone more human.

Throughout the rest of the stories in the book, we will be alternating between the territories of the masculine and the feminine and tasting the fires and waters of the cauldron of death and rebirth. The parents will reappear in various forms, and figures that die in one story will return in another. From a taste of inspiration at the cauldron, it's time to turn to the masculine depths of the son.

3

Ceremonies of Innocence

I went out to the hazel wood,
Because a fire was in my head.

WILLIAM BUTLER YEATS

CHAPTER 10

RECOVERING THE BOY,
UNCOVERING THE MAN

Up to this point, the stories we have followed have led us into dilemmas and onto paths that ended in questions. They have been stories of incomplete initiations, adventures that haven't reached a conclusion. They have also been stories that were painted on a small canvas, that focused on one individual who moves within a small and well-defined space. With the next story, the Celtic tale of Conn-Eda, we step into a big story, one that aims at a distant destination and winds all the way there. It carries the mythic tones and trappings, the spells and ordeals—in particular, the sense of wonder—of the old Celtic myths. Celtic stories insist on the presence of the other, under-world and reveal it through images such as talking birds and cities under the waves. These images are part of the European and human heritage; they lie in the depths of memory as certainly as the paintings in prehistoric caves wait in the ground.

Fairy tales are woven like intricate tribal carpets. The images are spun of strong old threads of imagination. Like carpets they are made to survive. They can provide warmth and bring joy to the aesthetic senses;

they can be used to cover holes in the flooring; they can be walked on or meditated upon. There's an old idea that dynamic memories are woven into tribal carpets, set in the chords of old songs, and placed in the scenes of old stories. Tapestries, songs, and stories that hold the old images don't wear out but disappear and often reappear carrying a greater value than before.

Stories like "Conn-Eda" were used to teach the grammar of symbolic language, the crucial elements of basic rituals, and the aspects of initiation. Bardic storytellers were itinerant teachers who carried their stories from place to place, reweaving the old threads and spreading them out where people could step into the fabric of memory and renewal. Tales were told in gatherings at fires and hearths, at times of crisis, on holy days. Irish tales were grouped around stages of life and transitions. They were classified according to their ritual aspects and were told both at planned transitions and when crises erupted unexpectedly. There were stories for conceptions and births, violent deaths and voyages, courtships, cattle raids, and adventures. The story of Conn-Eda represents an initiatory adventure.

The adventure is here divided into four parts that reflect stages of initiation, followed by a fifth chapter that looks at similar aspects in modern life. Initiation can be described in three stages: separation, trials and ordeals, and a return or reunification. The return at the end of the trials presupposes an original unity that can be separated from. Initially, that unity consists of a child bonded to parents and a family wrapped in a caring community. Since that unity can't be assumed in modern life, I've added a preliminary discussion of union with mother and father.

At retreats, I tell a story like this story over several days, a part each day. The sense of each part sinks into the psyche of the listener overnight. The images ride through the ears of the listeners on waves of sound and winds of change. The stirrings caused by the sound of the story continue long after the telling. Hearing the stories makes them move; the sound goes past the listener's everyday ear into the depths of the psychic waters, where personal and ancient memories are stirred. Stories of this kind are not aimed at the front of the mind or the surface of the lake of the psyche. They aim at the back of the mind and the depths of the soul. They aim to awaken the parts of the psyche that yearn for change, to inflame memories of struggle, and to fan the fires of unfinished issues in a person and in a culture.

CONN-EDA

Once upon a time, or below a time, in the time that was no time, that is our time or not, there was in Ireland a king named Conn Mor. He was powerful but just and good, and he was passionately loved by the people. Conn's wife was the good Queen Eda, equally loved and esteemed for her grace and wisdom. She was the counterpart to the king, and he was the counterpart to her. Whatever quality was lacking in one was found in abundance in the other. It was clear that heaven approved of the royal couple, for the earth produced exuberant crops, trees gave ninefold their usual fruit, waters teemed with choice fish, bees made heaps of honey, and cows yielded such an abundance of rich milk that it rained in torrents on the fields and filled the furrows and ditches. In short, no one lacked for anything, and the people were happy.

Conn Mor and Queen Eda were blessed with an only son. Druids foretold at his birth that he would inherit the good qualities of both parents, so he was named Conn-Eda. As the young prince grew, he manifested an admirable beauty, a ready strength, noble bearing, and a bright mind. He was the idol of his family and the boast of the people. For a time, things were perfect. But perfection is rare on this earth, and when it does occur, it does not last. Good Queen Eda came down with a sudden, severe illness, and she died, plunging the king, the son, and the people into sorrow and mourning for a year and a day. The crops began to decline, there seemed to be fewer fine trees, and people began to suffer lack and loss.

After the mourning period, Conn Mor yielded to the advice of his counselors and took to wife the daughter of the archdruid. The new queen appeared to walk in the footsteps of good Queen Eda, until in the course of time, having had sons of her own, she perceived that Conn-Eda would always be the favorite of the king and the darling of the people and that her sons would be excluded. This excited in her a jealousy and hatred for Conn-Eda, and she resolved to effect his exile or death.

She began by circulating evil reports about the prince. But as Conn-Eda was above suspicion, the king just laughed at the weakness of the queen, the people supported the prince, and the prince himself bore his trials with the utmost patience. He always repaid her malicious acts toward him with benevolent ones toward her. Soon, her enmity knew no bounds, and she consulted a hen wife, an old hag who was known to be a witch.

"I cannot help you until I receive a reward," said the hen wife.

"What reward?" asked the impatient queen.

"That you fill the cavity I make with my arm with wool and the hole I bore with red wheat," said the old one.

"Granted," said the queen.

The hen wife stood in the doorway of her hut and bent her arm to form a circle with her side. Then she directed that the wool be stuffed through her arm into the hut, and she wouldn't let them stop until the house was full. Next she got on the roof of her brother's house, drilled a hole in it with her distaff, and directed that the red wheat be poured in until her brother's house was full. When these things had been done, the storage bins of the realm were much depleted of wool and wheat.

"Now," said the queen, "tell me how to accomplish my purpose."

"Take this chess set and invite the prince to play with you. Propose that the winner can impose any condition on the soul of the loser. Because of the set's enchantment, you will win the first game. When you do, order the prince to go into permanent exile or to procure for you, within a year and a day, the three golden apples that grow in the garden of Lough Erne, as well as the great black steed and the extraordinary hound called Samer.

All are in the possession of the king who lives in the castle below the surface of the waters of Lough Erne. They are so precious, hard to find, and well guarded that Conn-Eda can never attain them of his own power, and he will die if he attempts it."

The queen lost no time inviting Conn-Eda to play. He agreed that the winner could place conditions binding on the soul of the loser. The queen won the first game as was foretold. But she was so determined to have the prince completely in her power that she offered to play another game. Conn-Eda won the second game. The queen announced her condition first: "Go right now into permanent exile, or procure for me within a year and a day the golden apples that grow in the garden of Lough Erne, the great black steed, and the supernatural hound of the king of Lough Erne."

After he heard that, it was Conn-Eda's turn. "I bind you to sit on the pinnacle of that tower until my return," he said, "and to take no nourishment except what red wheat you can spear with the point of your bodkin. If I don't return, you are free in a year and a day."

The story of Conn-Eda begins in abundance and great unity. Mother, father, and child are perfect together, and the world reflects the unity and fullness of the family. The child inherits the good qualities of both mother and father, and the prophecies at his birth are promising. But perfection is temporary; it never lasts. The beautiful queen, the esteemed mother of the prince and the realm, dies. This plunges everyone into a year and a day of sorrow. The perfections of the realm begin to slip away. The king's counselors demand a new queen. That queen brings more sons into the royal house, and she involves the old hen wife as well. The abundance of the realm shifts from the castle of the king and queen to the huts of the old hag. What started as the perfect couple and their child begins breaking apart and breaking down.

The "good mother" dies and the bad mother steps in, and she opens the door for the "old hag of the world." The birth mother is followed by the death mother and behind them waits the old spell mother. At first the realm bursts with life and love, then the shadow of death falls over everything. Then it's time for the game of life and death to begin. The perfect son of the perfect mother has entered a descent, a fall from the grace he inherited to a grace he may reach on his own. From the moment death enters the upperworld abundance begins to disappear. The world of the prince changes from abundant garden and complete unity to the empty world of exile and the wasteland, and the place abundance must be sought lies below the waters of Lake Erne. Either the prince must turn to face death and seek to restore abundance from below or the upperworld will continue its decline and he will become a permanent exile.

This part of the story reflects the universal human saga of the fall from grace, when the abundance of sweet milk and honey flowing through the garden of Eden dries up, and the child of life is driven out. The garden and the fall from it are mythic inheritances in each human being. Everyone inherits a sense of the garden of peace and fullness, everyone inherits an awareness of the fall from grace, and everyone inherits the wasteland. I've conducted what I like to call "mythosociological" surveys, and of all the people willing to listen to stories of this kind, 100 percent have had the experience of being in exile. I have yet to find someone who doesn't know what it means to be in exile, to be banished from the "sense of home." In that sense, everyone is homeless, and a part of the soul is always trying to find a home. The exile knows that he or she has had a home and that somewhere still there waits a home for the soul. The garden of Eden is the soul's reminiscence about the sense of home. The garden of abundance includes the perfect mother and father, and not only does each parent appear full of fine qualities but the omissions in one find completion in the other. It is a seamless world of three-way perfection—mother, father, and child amidst abundance and mutual adoration. The flow of goodness is witnessed by heaven, earth, and all the people.

The garden of abundance is an imaginal landscape; it's a magic circle of nourishment, loving attention, and protection. The human child grows in a dependent state longer than the young of any other species. Nurturing the soul, spirit, body, and mind of the human child requires the attention of both kinds of parents and their complimentary gifts. If there occurs a serious lack of nourishment, of love or protection, the garden walls break too soon and the child falls from grace before receiving enough nourishment. If the child becomes exposed to he harshness of the outer world while still heavily dependent on the nourishment and adoration of the family, it suffers wounds to its very essence. Much of modern psychology has been a study of and an attempt to repair the original garden.

If a child is exposed to the harsh winds outside the garden before the self can gather its own protections and incorporate love into self-esteem, the self can be rubbed raw and torn apart. If a person was not in the garden long enough and they already feel torn and separated in life, throwing them into initiatory circumstances only deepens existing wounds that haven't healed. Before they can benefit from the stripping and radical reorganization that initiation attempts, they must recover from infant and childhood woundings. For them a return to the garden of unity and abundance must precede a separation that attends a brush with death, or such a "little death" will become a big death. It's as if they carry too much death from early stages of life to brush death again. Before the year and a day of mourning, the garden must teem with love and life. Returning to the garden of childhood can soothe and cover the raw wounds, and it can also be a preparation for a big change ahead.

Stories of initiation often begin with the sense that the initiate has been held in a garden of care and given a taste of plenty. Fairy tales frequently begin with a prince or princess to indicate that the initiate has been treated royally, has walked in the garden before the inevitable separation or fall begins. In this context, the modern recovery movement is an attempt to go back and re-cover the child, to ritually embrace the child as part of a community. The re-covery awakens the sense of abundance and the personal and cultural unity described at the beginning of the story of Conn-Eda.

Once the sense of full life appears, however, the shadow of death will reappear. The garden will one day grow dark, the good queen mother will pass away; the sense of loss spreads at her passing. Grief grows abundantly, darkness descends, the wasteland begins. On his own, the king cannot sustain the garden or the unity of the people. The new queen cannot possibly fill the shoes of the perfect queen mother who came before. Once the wall of perfection cracks, all mistakes become visible. As W. B. Yeats put it, "things fall apart; the center cannot hold and everywhere the ceremony of innocence is drowned." What will happen to the prince of great qualities when the garden where the ceremony of innocence occurred disappears?

Because this is a story of initiation, Conn-Eda must experience a loss of innocence, a fall from grace. But this won't happen easily, naturally, developmentally. It must happen through shocks. The loss of his perfect mother doesn't reach to his sense of self, for he already carries her perfection within himself. We can see his unbroken innocence and perfection in the way he sees and treats the malicious acts of the new queen. And the year and a day of grieving that puts a shadow over the entire realm doesn't make him aware of the shadowy aspects in himself and others. Only when he faces exile or certain death does he begin to move away from the innocence of his youth.

From behind the first queen mother comes the second one. She has a different face than the one who beamed affection down at him and saw all the good qualities in him. The second queen has other children, other sons, and an interest in their welfare. He is not the apple of her eye; he is no longer the only apple in the garden. It's easy to see how this scene is repeated whenever a new baby comes into a family, and the child who basked before in the glow of mother's loving eyes falls into the shadow of the new child. Some say that as soon as the mother turns her light away, the child sees the dark queen. Fairy tales contain many evil queens because children are trying to reconcile the image of the perfect mother-queen, who gives her love abundantly, with that of the terrifying mother who turns away. Fairy tales allow the child to carry these images separately. But the day comes when the child must face this split that preserves the world of innocence and realize that the mother of life and the mother of death are carried inside as well.

Conn-Eda's innocence sets the stage for his initiation. When the queen spreads rumors about him, he is benign to her; indeed, he not only turns the other cheek but he repays her with kindness. This kindness drives the new queen further into the land of shadows and from behind her comes the hen wife, the old hag of the world. By holding on to his innocence, the prince provokes an appetite like that of the half-giantess. The hen wife insists that great quantities of wood and grain be pushed through small openings. The requests she makes drain the storehouses of the realm. Now the garden of abundance is being reduced to a wasteland. The loss that began with the death of the queen continues. Once the perfect mother dies, the prince will have to encounter the Great Mother, who rules his destiny. Once the wall of the garden breaks, the son is on his way to an initiation through which he will break the spell of innocence and face death and loss in his own life.

Men's retreats are not initiations, but the stories told provoke memories of crucial crossroads, which arouse the emotions that were felt at those crossroads. When I tell the story of Conn-Eda at men's retreats, I usually stop at the point where each listener must choose to be exiled for life or to go after the golden apples and find certain death. Many men pick the dangerous quest; it's more heroic to follow that path, and this appeals to most of the men. But everyone is also familiar with the choice of exile. Strangely, it's harder to turn to that road. The quest may be dangerous, but it also offers glittering rewards. Exile seems more forbidding.

A third group doesn't want to do either. They don't accept the choices. Some won't even play the game of chess because it is rigged. One of these men says, "Fuck you. I'm not doing either. I'm tired of being forced into bad choices. I'm not going. Fuck you." Several others join him. They form a "fuck you" group. They are truly angry; they don't want to be in exile, and they don't want to face another impossible task. They won't move from the center of the road.

Their refusal to choose makes the choices more distinct and important. They express pain that is not stated in the story; they insist on being heard. Eventually, their anger dissipates, and after the anger goes, they start to feel alone and vulnerable. Behind the "fuck you" is a sadness and a wariness. It becomes clear that the angry refusal itself eventually leads to a lonely exile. Not accepting the game, refusing to choose, is a temporary position. It's the game of life, of life and death, that's being offered. There's really no way out; not playing, not joining, insisting that it's all rigged and unfair, eventually becomes a form of exile. The brush with death can be delayed but not avoided, defiance can't remain innocent forever.

A man says, "I'm going for the gold. It's the only choice, get the goods and come back a hero. He'll be better than before. These stories always turn out that way. Besides, exile isn't a choice, it's nowhere."

Another says, "Listen, I've always been in exile. There never was a time of plenty, not for me. There never will be such a thing. I'm not playing because my whole life is a kind of exile." Another says, "I'm in the garden and I'm not getting out. It will cost me too much to step out. One step out and it will never be the same. I'm not going. I won't risk losing everything I have. I know this garden. I'm keeping it, even if everyone else has to die."

Another voice comes from a group of men who sit off the road. "I can't choose. I'm stuck. I'll wind up going along wherever the story goes, but I can't choose. It's too heavy to make my own fate." Another says, "I can't make a real choice, at the last minute I'll just go one way or the other, but I'm afraid to look at it until then."

In the language of the story, when Conn-Eda agrees to play the game that may put conditions on his soul, he takes the first step in the process of initiation. This process tends to be both voluntary and involuntary. At first he doesn't know what he's getting into; eventually he's laying down conditions of the soul as well. Initiation is always more than one bargained for. People who go through it often say, "Had I known what I was getting into, I would not have gone." And initiation depends, at least in part, on a desire in the initiate for greater knowledge, feeling, and spiritual depth. Initiation cannot be forced on someone, nor can it be faked. The body can be pushed and dragged, but the soul cannot. It may begin as an accident, a surprise, or an unfair event, but if lasting change occurs, the whole self must get involved.

Initiation strips away what a person has and who he or she has been. It involves, first of all, losing everything or giving away all that one has in order to become no one before becoming someone again. Cultures that practice initiation rites have previous ceremonies and experiences that wrap the initiate carefully into the society. Before a person's initiation, the subject feels known and secure within his or her family and gender identity. They have a sense of their community and a connection to the otherworld of spirits and ancestors. You don't initiate someone who is nobody. You can't strip away what isn't there. If someone feels already stripped bare to the world, he or she may in fact be in the midst of an initiatory experience. But if someone refuses to enter into a life stage or necessary transition, he or she may need first to reconnect with or relocate something that has been lost. The person may have to go back before stepping out. Some people are in the middle of initiatory events and don't know it; others need to find some sense of unity and inner abundance before they move out into the world at all.

For others the separation that begins the initiation may come at the right time but go in the wrong direction. The destination is not clear at the beginning. A group of youths enter an initiatory road together, but at the crossroads they go in different directions. They may share a series of events that mark each of them for life, but the marks are deeply individual. In tribal initiations, as in stories like Conn-Eda, the first steps of initiation are clearly marked. In the modern world, they are rarely as clear and often go unnoticed as initiatory.

Entering the modern world is like stepping into an initiation already under way. It's like stepping into the middle of a ritual in full swing. Loss and pain are everywhere. Images of death prevail, and boundaries are dissolving in all directions. Such deep disorientation and intensity are characteristics of initiatory ordeals. Most of us have become so used to disorientation that we have begun to feel at home in this sense of being lost. When the borders of countries the world over change daily and the value of currencies and of food swings up and down rapidly, the middle stage of initiation—the ordeals—becomes our daily environment. In front of us there appears to be nowhere to go or return to—if, in fact, we do survive—while behind there seems to be something missing that should have been there, for we need to have something definite from which we can separate.

In other words, we need to have a place to come from, a home that we are leaving, and a place to go to, our next home. Many modern people have had no home to begin with—that is, no home in which the soul could dwell while it became acquainted with this earth. Thus, for many people, the first step they must take is actually back toward childhood. This first step must be taken before looking at initiation can proceed. Considering initiation in the modern world often begins with a return rather than forging ahead.

In Conn-Eda's story, he hears the conditions of the game with ears that expect that he will win. He's an innocent and has been in the garden with the good mother. He has survived the shadows cast by the dark queen, but now that queen has become an emissary for the old spell mother. He accepts the game of being exiled or finding a home in himself, the game of seeking his own resources rather than receiving the abundance of the garden.

Like most young men, Conn-Eda is in deep before he knows it; his life is on the line before he understands the nature of the game. Like most young men, he probably thought he would simply win; he didn't know how much loss the world could offer. There's no fixed time in stories. There's no telling how long it will take for a man to accept the conditions on his soul and to learn about loss. But the spell, the enchantment, always has limits that become more clear when the conditions are accepted. Once out of the garden everything has limits, especially innocence. Initiation makes a life more immediate and meaningful; it shifts one's awareness from dreamy possibilities to the limits of the present.

The first step away from innocence and into the separation that awaits Conn-Eda occurs when he accepts the conditions on his soul and places some on the queen. Accepting the conditions means everything else stops for him. The upperworld stops; he's out of the garden. He doesn't return the trouble thrown at him with smiles and innocence; he accepts the nature of the game. If he's to lose everything and descend in exile, she'll have to do without nourishment and be exposed to the air and the weather above. For now, he has enough trouble. The prince has already moved away from innocence, but where does he turn when he turns away from family and his first home?

CHAPTER 11

THE DRUID'S HUT

Now Conn-Eda was troubled in mind, for he was ignorant of what steps to take. He wandered about until he thought of an old druid whom he considered a friend and a knowledgeable man. The druid asked the cause of the depression in the youth's spirit. Conn-Eda told him his entire history with the new queen and the chess game and the laying of conditions on the soul, and he asked for help. The druid set before Conn-Eda the oldest of wines and the freshest of foods. The old man said that the morning was wiser than the evening. In the morning, he would go to his "green place" and consider the situation of the prince.

The next day, the druid said, "My son, you are under an almost impossible *geis*, or condition, intended only for your destruction. No one could have advised the queen except the Hag of Beara, the greatest druidess in all of Ireland and sister to the king of Lough Erne. It is not in my power to interfere on your behalf. But if you can find the ancient bird with human speech, it may help you in this matter. That bird is difficult to find for it alights in the forest for only three days in a year. It is difficult to approach, but knows all things past, present, and future. I don't have much help to give you in your search but if you take the little shaggy horse out back and let the reins drop, the horse may lead you. And if you present the ancient bird with this precious stone, it may tell you how to find the treasures you seek."

The fall of the prince is both a descent and an education. His mother has died, his father has been absent since the trouble began, and he doesn't know which way to turn. The story weaves aspects of initiation into the fabric of the narrative: Life is interrupted, stopped, or turned aside in some way that can't be denied or covered up. A youth's actual mother and father acting in their typical ways cannot help the situation, or their help is more hindrance than assistance. He suffers a serious disorientation that separates his life from others.

Conn-Eda remembers an old druid and goes to him. He has an instinct to seek help, and once he accepts that he is ignorant, he turns to someone with knowledge of these matters. He makes another move away from innocence: He doesn't wait for something to come to him because he's well-intentioned or a "good boy." He goes looking for help, moving him further away from his first home. In initiatory terms, a part or period of childhood has ended, for the area that he enters seems forbidding to the child's eye. Whoever goes this way won't see things as they did as a child. For the druid doesn't ease the problem, rather he confirms that the *geis*, the conditions on the prince's soul, are intended for his destruction.

The druid plays the role of a mentor for the prince. He welcomes Conn-Eda and listens to him. He feeds him, slows him down, and hears the condition he's in. The druid has the ability to hear the nature of the problem weighing on Conn-Eda's soul. He doesn't reduce it to something else or diminish the size of the trouble or take on the prince's problem. In the design of the story, the queen goes to the edge of town and gets advice and spell-making materials from the old hag. It's as if the old spell mother says, Here's the test for that son of life: Let him deal with exile or enter the waters of life in a way that forces him to be broken down and remade again. Once the son has accepted this condition, he has to find a druid's place on the other edge of things where he can be seen as one separated out and torn by life-and-death issues. There he receives some advice and tools for breaking the spells of childhood and enduring the conditions on his soul.

The druid takes care with the prince, but he doesn't become a savior. He helps, but in a limited way. The mentor is not simply a replacement for the missing father or the lost mother. He or she nourishes, comforts, and advises—but within limits. Conn-Eda is not treated as a child. The druid gives Conn-Eda a small stone, a shaggy horse, and some difficult advice. He looks into the spirit of the young man and acknowledges the seriousness of the trouble and the limits of his help. It's more important that the druid act as an elder than that he be significantly older. It's more important that the mentor be familiar with exile and be able to recognize the appearance of the great themes of life and death. The druid's hut is anywhere the youth can get reoriented without losing touch with his own spirit. The druid is any person or figure that comes to mind when the youth knows he's in trouble.

Ultimately the druid is connected to the spirit in the young man; he has an eye for and an interest in the prince's spirit. Their ceremonial meal is a statement that he is willing and able to nourish the exiled prince. The druid deepens the awareness of danger that Conn-Eda already feels. Then he says that the morning is wiser than the evening. They each have to sleep on the troubling questions, and the druid must consult his deities—he doesn't answer right away. When he does answer, it can't be a simple formula: An initiation involves the usual stages but also the specific conditions of the initiate.

It would be encouraging for everyone if druid huts like the one in the story were set outside of towns or at the edges of neighborhoods and barrios. Then people in need of some advice—some food for the soul and some sense of direction—might go there and be seen and heard. This is what education actually should be. The word *education* means to lead someone out, to draw something out of someone. At the hut of the druid, the prince's spirit begins to be led out and given guidance. Education takes place when the spirit and soul are engaged and involved. In initiatory moments the student can't hide feelings, needs, and desires. The initiate can be seen through and seen into. The fact that tribal initiates are usually naked can be seen as symbolic: The initiate's soul is temporarily exposed and naked to the eye of a mentor or elder. That type of seeing, listening and sorting out of soul conditions happens to Conn-Eda in the druid's hut.

Stories display the mythic backdrops and ideal images that are the psychic inheritance of people. The individual soul expects to be seen into and heard out while in these conditions. Frequently the expectation goes unfulfilled, as listening to the stories of mature people and observing the conditions for young people makes clear. More often than not, the separation that triggers the dynamics of initiation is not taken seriously enough by family and community, and any sorting of soul conditions is haphazard. Unless the separation becomes clear and the conditions of the soul are perceived, the subsequent ordeals seem chaotic and meaningless or simply punishing.

The dynamics of initiation may be seen as affecting three main groups of people: those who are experiencing changes of life stages and/or are unexpectedly thrown into circumstances of separation and disorientation, those who are looking back and uncovering memories and emotions connected to breaks and radical changes earlier in life, and those who are experiencing ordeals but are not ready to undergo change.

The first group includes all young people who usually undergo both stage-of-life changes that may be perceived as such and dangerous brushes with death that are rarely perceived as initiatory. From this perspective, any event that causes severe separation, disorientation, and a sense of death or near death is initiatory. Whether others judge the events as positive or negative, legal or illegal, right or wrong, does not matter. The conditions of the soul and the permanent change trying to occur are what matters. In modern societies the druid's hut might have to be fabricated on the spot—in a neighbor's home, a police station, a therapist's office, or a hospital. Those in the midst of ordeals may have to be met wherever they are undergoing the ordeals.

People in the second group are reviewing events that happened in the past. When their lives get stuck or they feel out of touch with a sense of inner meaning and outer purpose, they can search through their biography and memories and find those pieces of radical change that make them who they truly are. Initiation events are often buried in the shadowy areas of the psyche, and when they are ignored they drain a person's capacity to change in life. The times of radical change in a person's life require return visits, especially at transitions through other stages of life.

The third viewpoint comes from those who were abandoned in infancy or were so severely abused in childhood that they are looking for the garden, not the opening of the road to initiation. They are not strongly enough connected to their deep self, to their family and to the human family, to be able to suffer the rigors of initiatory stripping. They need to be embraced in the "sense of home," and their psyche needs to be contained and healed before any initiatory moves occur. Once they are secure in this sense of self, perhaps some of the abuse experiences could be seen as also having initiatory aspects.

A person can find him or herself in these positions over and over. When a life change is under way, one of the first steps is finding the appropriate viewpoint. An attempt to withstand the ordeals of life and the winds of fate could be destructive when a return to the garden is required to cover a wound that has been open since childhood. The reverse is also true—seeking perfect, parental solace when the horse of change is waiting to be ridden makes a person more infantile. The druid's hut is a symbol of the space needed for working out an appropriate orientation. At a men's conference, all three orientations may be going on at the same time, and an initiation story can allow all three to move the way they must.

The druid and the druid's hut can be pieced together from bits of memories. The druid is partly inside the man and partly made of other people. Inside every man waits the capacity to be a wise old man, a mentor, a druid who knows the purpose of his spirit. A disturbance of the spirit awakens the druid inside and beckons to druids outside. Our memories include occasions when the disturbance in our spirit was so evident that someone spoke to it and gave us something. Often, as we search our memories for these occasions, we are looking for something huge because our emotion at the time was huge, but what was offered or found was often quite small. The true size of it may only be revealed when it has been carried long enough and far enough. If we look for the huts of druids within our memory, we must look for the small things that were given. Partly, the mentor in the story teaches that there is no great gift that's going to solve everything. We look for a big emotion, but a small gift can reveal a druid hut that was hidden for a long time.

When I was a sophomore in high school, I became disappointed with the nature of school and troubled by the limits of education it offered. I was attending a Catholic boys' school; the instructors were Brothers. In a sense, the situation resembled a druid hut. The Brothers were older men in black religious garments who were there to teach; their role was partly spiritual and partly practical. We went there to learn, and at times the depressions in our spirits were more than apparent. But our teachers tended to expound doctrine, established ideas, and fixed beliefs. Within me was a spirit desperate to be led out. Going off to high school was just enough separation to raise expectations in the soul. I felt it and so did my classmates. By sophomore year, the trouble and expectations alive in the soul had not been recognized, and there was growing disappointment. There was a scramble for what to do with the unmet expectations.

In my case, I joined the troublemakers. There was an unspoken division in school between the good boys who studied, were "smart," and obeyed rules and the bad guys who didn't obey rules and were therefore apparently ignorant and couldn't study. The students knew that this separation was too simple, but blurry distinctions were forced into harsh ones by the commitment of the teachers to discipline.

At first, I was among the top students scholastically, but I also tended to be among the most disruptive. It seemed to me that being a good student meant having only school spirit, not personal spirit, and remaining blind to aspects of the school that were destructive, including some harsh and abusive teachers.

Defiance became our way of manifesting spirit within such restrictions. As our sophomore year wore on, a group of us formed around this spirit of defiance. We defied the system; we practiced penetrating the inadequacies and weaknesses of the teachers. Those who depended completely on control for order, we provoked out of control. Those who really did not care to be there, we left their class. Several in our group were always failing tests, so we worked at ways of cheating in order to get everyone in the group to pass. Several times we were caught. More discipline was brought to bear on us, and attempts were made to break up the group. We weren't asked questions that might have opened up our disappointments and frustrations. We were separated into different classes. We were warned over and over, but the warnings did not disturb us as deeply as the conditions we already felt in our souls.

Eventually, the school threatened several members of our group with expulsion. But was I to be included? The fact that I was a disciplinary problem with decent grades broke through some of the lines that were usually used to divide good and bad, smart and ignorant.

While I waited to hear if I was to be expelled, a little druid moment occurred. One of our teachers was a Brother who had come from Cuba to teach in New York. He didn't speak English well, and he was a mixture of races in a mostly white school. But the most outstanding thing about him was that he was strangely impassioned. He had a spirit that could not be smothered in the religious habit. He was easy to provoke and to make fun of. We imitated his speech; we mocked his great lips. We provoked his passion so that the lesson of the day would be forgotten while he erupted into a mix of English and Spanish and howling sounds that were both terrifying and entertaining. We treated him badly. We assumed that he didn't care for us either.

While it was being decided who would be put out of the school, this Brother took me out into the hall. This ceremony usually meant the placing of more restrictions, such as detention or even physical punishment. I was scared, but I was also angry and wanted to direct the force of anger somewhere. I was thinking, "If he touches me . . ." I didn't know what I would do, but I was ready to explode with the violence of my feelings.

In fact, I was ready for anything but what actually occurred. For this strange Brother spoke to me about the condition of my soul. He perceived that part of me wanted to study and learn and part of me could not resist the spiritual expression of the defiant group. He saw my true interest in spirit and my attempts to hold onto the spirit through defiance. He saw the exile going on in me and the exile that I was heading for. Now that I look back on it, it is clear that he, too, was an exile—exiled from his own language, from his land, exiled in the impassioned intensity of his emotional life. Somehow the exile in him spoke to the exile in me. It was no great thing. It was no remedy for the troubles of life, but he gave me little pieces of advice that temporarily ended the exile.

I don't remember exactly what he said, for he had trouble getting the words out. We were both fuming. But he mentioned loyalty. He recognized the loyalty we had in our troubled, troublemaking group, and he said something about loyalty to myself and to learning. He said the point wasn't to learn what was being taught but to learn how to learn. I was stunned. He was actually talking to me, right into me, not down to me. He was talking to the loyalties in me, and he was challenging me. He broke the rules in speaking to me that way. He said I was to be called before the board of teachers who were to decide who would be put out of school. The vote was close in my case simply because of some high grades. He said with a few days of good behavior on my part, he could convince the board to keep me in school.

I don't know if I agreed with him or not, but it was the passion of his expression, his willingness to break the rules in giving me information, and his apparent interest in my welfare that made me pay attention; made me, in fact, thankful; perhaps made me decide to stay in school; more importantly, made me decide that my interest in studies was genuine even if the classes I attended were not.

For this piece of the druid hut, for that stone, for that bit of advice, I have to thank that Brother. I have to acknowledge that through him suddenly the word *Brother* took on an expanded meaning. At least momentarily, it meant a true teacher, it meant one interested in the spirit and passion of life. It also meant Cubano, and African. It stood for a spirit willing to speak directly to the trouble. That small stone, that bit of giving, dropped past the defiant barriers that I was putting up, and held in the memory, it continued to grow inside me. Since that day, I've turned that stone, that piece of the druid's hut, over and over in my mind and heart.

The importance of being genuinely seen and heard can't be overestimated. One of the ways that the soul grows is by being seen and recognized. If a man has never been recognized at the soul level, he won't know who he is in times of crisis and he will feel inauthentic more often than not. If a man has never been heard, he'll have great difficulty listening to others. One of the things that can happen during a men's retreat is that the men who tell their stories can feel heard, just as Conn-Eda is heard by the druid. Some men come to these retreats because they are clinging to an innocence that must fall; others have been brutalized by life and need to renew their innocence so that they can hear more than the bitter tones of cynicism that dominate the wasteland. Some need relief from an exile that has lasted too long, and others need the encouragement to move on.

In their responses to the mythic stories and as they tell their personal stories, men say surprising things, but you sometimes have to listen hard to hear them. The first piece of learning in this sudden community of men becomes opening the ears to the stories of others. It is encouraging to hear a painfully familiar theme spoken out from another man's life and startling to hear how different another's life can be. Often the inner story seems in great contrast to the outer man. Listening can be the fastest way of learning respect for what a man might carry inside. As the African proverb says: A man is like a pepper, until you've tasted what's inside you don't know how hot it is.

The stories tend to go in one of two directions, either toward recovery or toward initiation. For some people going back to relocate their childhood and recover what was laid bare becomes essential for living. They can't risk anything new without remaking themselves. They were thrown into a fire way too soon. They're severely burned and platitudes about "pulling yourself together" and "getting it together" deny how wounded they continually feel. To the deeply betrayed child, initiation is another form of abuse. To the abandoned child who has not been admitted back into life, separation is not new but ever-present. These men tell stories about wounds and losses that occurred in childhood and that are a revisiting of that child. Often, the story will be preceded by a description of the family and how it operated, so that the wound to the child can be understood in its original context. Or else the story will just drop out as if a child were present telling it. Either way, the scenes that we enter are those of childhood and family life.

The other type of story sounds different and has to do with events that include wars, divorces, prisons, mental breakdowns, deaths, betrayals, addictions, and diseases. These are of a different order; they have to be listened to differently; they come into the ear with a different shape. The age of the speaker doesn't seem to matter as much as the age of the one inside who is remembering and telling the story. It isn't whether it happened to the man when he *was* a child, but whether it happened to him when he was *as* a child.

One of the differences between the two types of stories is complicity. Genuine stories of loss and helplessness in childhood will lack the complicity of the child, or the speaker will put so much responsibility for the events on himself that this can be seen as covering up for a thorough helplessness. In other words, the complicity is absent or overly present. The speaker knows that it isn't his fault, or he is making it so much his own fault that we know it isn't and can tell him so.

The other stories are told with some sense that the teller was somehow an accomplice to the events. He entered a situation looking for something, trying for something, and couldn't extricate himself from it completely. He is in some gray area between doing and being done to. His story has to be heard differently; there are resonances of harmony and discord. If there was terror, there was also some sense of beauty. If there was great sorrow, it is held with firmness, embedded in his voice in a way that says, "I'm not asking you to take this from me. It's mine to tell about." Even the finality of a lost limb is told with a voice that holds the limb, the cut, and the loss together. These aren't stories of simple oppressions, of weights dropped on a child before he could get out of the way. They are stories of going into the weight of a loss, going into the mouth of a wound, dwelling in the break of an event long enough to become complicated with it. The weight of this is distributed throughout the man. The story lives in him. These are the stories of who he is and the terms on which he has to be heard. He is telling who he was, not just what happened to him.

These stories remake him. Try to take away the pain, sorrow, wonder, or fondness in it and you will take a part of him. Besides, he won't let you. He isn't offering it to be taken away, he is offering it to be opened again. It operates in him as a gift and as a womb because things keep coming out of it when it is opened. It keeps him in life; his life is partly hidden in it. The courage and care that goes into opening those wounds are gifts that are encouraging to anyone who can hear. Hearing those wounds speaking makes life more bearable and feeds the soul.

The telling of personal stories gets enhanced when kept in proximity to traditional "fairy tales." The themes of life and loss are contained in traditional stories, and surrounding a group with mythic stories stirs the life themes of the listeners. The point of the personal story isn't simply biography—"I am what these people and events make me to be." Rather, it is retelling episodes to stir up the important themes of a life, to separate from the surface details and find an emotional orientation. The inner pressure to reveal painful stories and express confusions is human and healthy. Relief can be immediate. If something has been risked in the telling, if it isn't rehearsed and edited, you can see relief flood the body of the speaker after the telling. Some genuine seed has been found inside that has grown into feelings and words, that has grown from being heard.

Moreover, the personal story needs to be told because it is partly a communal story. It partly belongs to the community and makes or remakes the community. Stories reduce feelings of isolation and hopelessness. Genuine stories make communities more genuine; false and self-serving stories drain the soul of a group and a culture. The retreats I'm referring to are rituals for developing and refining the ears for hearing stories and for nourishing the roots of community. The ear for myth hears into the personal stories as well as into the fairy stories.

I have seen standing in the same room and talking by turns men who were abused in childhood and those who were initiated by similar forces. Both felt unseen and unrecognized by their communities and by the culture. Both seemed to be standing in similar psychic pain. But, one group was turned back toward childhood with their eyes looking toward birth and the other group seemed to be turned the other way looking at something different. That got me interested in the image of the turning of a person's head from the issues of childhood to breaks and radical events that cause the reorganization of the psyche toward a possible destination in life. Initiation rites were used to interrupt a person's life and arrest their vision, to stop their habitual ways of seeing life and their place in it. Then the aspects of bigger life, bigger emotional, spiritual, sexual, and imaginal life were entered. Death was introduced as an aspect of life and of change. The turning of the head included glimpses of death and destiny.

One reason for the study of initiation lies in learning to separate psychic threads, distinguishing between those that are leading back to unfinished pieces of childhood and those that can pull one across the threshold to greater life. If too many threads of life tie someone back to childhood, dragging them over the threshold and through the fires of initiation can be cruel and dangerous. The initiate is always scared, but usually healthy, eager, cared for by someone, and desiring initiation. That desire is different from the need of a child to be loved, reassured, and taken to the bosom of family and culture.

Initiation makes a crossroad between childhood and the rest of life. At this turn one leaves childhood behind, and any return to it will go back through this point in the road. Childhood will live forever, just as a child imagines it, forever and ever and ever. But it will be in the area of the forest that lies behind this sign in the road. The sign represents the marks and scars of initiations. The head of the initiate turns away from childhood, away from the child that he was, and whenever he looks back again, he will see it differently because he will be changed in some defining way. Initiation dislodges the parents from their position of dominance over and support under the child. The initiate learns that there are other levels of support in life and that life can end. If the initiation is thorough, the individual gets exposed to underlying resources inside himself and to a layer of purpose and destiny, born of struggles, that remains inside. The initiate learns that something has been carrying him besides his parents.

The druid's hut stands at the crossroads where life turns from one direction to another. Conn-Eda has to discover whether there lives an abundance of life in himself or if the experience of abundant life can only be received from his mother and father. If Conn-Eda doesn't enter the hut and speak of the conditions on his soul, the darkness within him will grow. If he does enter the hut, he'll have to learn to see life another way. Either way, his life has changed forever. The possibility of greater life has awakened in him; there's no turning back. As Goethe says:

THE HOLY LONGING

Tell a wise person, or else keep silent.
Because the massman will mock it right away.
I praise what is truly alive,
what longs to be burned to death.

In the calm water of the love-nights,
where you were begotten, where you have begotten,
a strange feeling comes over you
when you see the silent candle burning.

Now you are no longer caught
in the obsession with darkness,
and a desire for higher love-making
sweeps you upward.

Distance does not make you falter,
now, arriving in magic, flying,
and finally, insane for the light,
you are the butterfly and you are gone.

And so long as you haven't experienced
this: to die and so to grow,
you are only a troubled guest
on the dark earth.

GOETHE (TRANSLATED BY ROBERT BLY)

CHAPTER 12

THE LAND BELOW THE WATERS

Conn-Eda thanked the druid, mounted the shaggy little horse, and set out. He let the reins hang loose, as he had been instructed, so that the animal could choose its own path.

After some difficulty, they reached the hiding place of the bird with human speech at just the right time. There in the dark forest stood the ancient bird. Conn-Eda placed the stone near the bird and asked how he could accomplish his task. The great bird took the jewel, flew to an inaccessible rock, and addressed the prince in a loud croaking voice: "Remove the stone from under your right foot, take the ball of iron and the cup you find there, mount your horse, cast the ball before you, follow it, and your horse will tell you all you need to know." Having said this, the bird with human speech flew out of sight.

Conn-Eda took the ball and cup, mounted the horse, and cast the ball before him. The ball rolled and the horse followed until they reached the shore of Lough Erne, where the ball disappeared into the water. Suddenly, the little horse spoke: "Put your hand in my ear, take out the small bottle of all-heal and the little basket you find there, and remount with speed, for here your difficulties begin."

Conn-Eda did what he was told, and they quickly descended into the waters of Lough Erne. The prince was amazed that the water was as the atmosphere above; they neither drowned nor suffocated. Where he expected to swallow water and lack for air, he found he could still breathe. They had entered the otherworld. Now he saw the ball rolling before them, and Conn-Eda clung to his little steed.

They came upon a river there, a water among waters, guarded by three frightful serpents. A loud hissing filled the ears of the prince as he looked into the serpents' great yawning mouths with their formidable fangs. The horse spoke again: "Open the basket and cast a piece of the meat you find there into the mouth of each serpent; then hold on. If you cast accurately, I'll get us past them; if not, we are lost."

Conn-Eda cast the meat unerringly, and the little horse made a prodigious leap past the serpents and over the river. Once on the other side, the horse asked if the prince was still mounted, and the prince replied that it had taken only half his strength to stay on. The little horse commended him and said that while one danger was over, two remained.

Again, they followed the ball until they came to a great mountain that filled the landscape and flamed with fire in all directions. "Prepare yourself for another leap," said the horse, and he sprang from the earth and flew like an arrow through the flames and over the mountain. "Are you still alive, Conn-Eda, son of Mor?"

"Just alive, and nothing more," Conn-Eda said, "for I am greatly scorched."

"You are a man of destiny," said the horse. "There is hope that we will overcome the last test."

The horse carried the ailing prince to a cool valley and told him to apply the all-heal from the bottle to his wounds. The all-heal soothed the wounds of the prince and healed the burns. In the green glade, the prince recovered his health and strength until he was better than before. Then he saw the iron ball rolling into a broad plain. The prince mounted the little horse and they followed it down.

Dropping the reins means letting go, not being in charge, submitting to change. For Conn-Eda, dropping the reins also means dropping down, descending into the waters of uncertainty and entering the stage of ordeals. Once Conn-Eda accepts that he has lost the first chess game, he begins to drop. Admitting that he is in trouble is another part of the fall, and asking for help drops him further. The druid then puts him on a little shaggy horse, an unwanted horse kept behind the hut. Little horses like this often inhabit fairy stories. They are lame or hobbled, they don't go full speed, or they go the wrong way. They are the only horse left in the stable after all the warriors have mounted up and ridden away. They're the overlooked, left-behind, unwanted horses that wait until we're ready to drop down to them, then they carry us to the trials of fire and water that await us.

During initiation someone or something other than our usual "self" takes charge. The "ego," the usual ruler of the person, must submit to some other force or authority and lets things go. All of the awareness and attention a person has will be needed to endure the ordeals. So, there is a loosening of personal identity that allows hidden, undeveloped, even denied aspects of the self to appear. The executive functions of the ego and of the lord of the castle won't get Conn-Eda to the lake. Unless he allows the horse to lead, he may wander forever in exile on the surface of his life. On the other hand, dropping the reins means facing ordeals on a lowly animal.

The little shaggy horse appears when all Conn-Eda's princely coverings come off and all his high expectations fall away. It's tough for a prince used to giving directions and accustomed to being held in high esteem to let go, to drop down and let something below him lead. The higher one is regarded by others, the harder it is to drop down. The more responsible you feel, the harder it can be to give responsibility over to another. The more you are seen as in charge, the harder it is to stop charging ahead and simply follow along. Of course, the hardest thing to let go of is one's high and fixed opinion of oneself.

The first trial of the prince is whether he can let go of his fixed opinions of himself. Even if a man has been a son-in-exile most of his life, his fixed description of himself as a dark prince or a bad person will have to loosen or he won't feel the horse below him. Initiation is a process of uncovering who a person has been and discovering the little horse waiting to carry him further into life than he would go on his own. When a son gets on the little shaggy steed he begins moving toward events he has never faced before, and he will have to accept what he has always regarded as below him to survive.

The shaggy little horse waits as the undeveloped, unkempt, uncared for aspects of the prince's "self." In a sense the horse has been there all along, already headed somewhere, just waiting for the reins to drop, waiting until the prince moves toward the ordeals life has arranged for him. It turns out that the horse has an appointment with the ancient bird who knows where both horse and rider must go.

The little, unkempt horse is a deeper inheritance than the son's rank of prince, his position in the family, or his standing in the community. The shaggy horse comes out from behind the stable when all other opinions don't matter because the issues of life and death have to be faced. A man only learns the shape and qualities of that unwanted horse when he has accepted some sense of being alone and exiled, when a druid figure points to it, or when the opinions of others and his own self-judgments are diminished by the onrush of events.

Dropping the reins means learning to trust the inner horse whether its qualities are judged good or bad, bright or dark, by others. When I've asked men to describe their inner horse, each is different, and the qualities one man sees as most important another sees as least desirable. It's clear that the horse can not be made of a person's best features because it has looked shaggy and undesirable until now. Dropping the reins means trusting that something carries a person through life, something usually not seen and generally not valued. Unless a man can trust that shaggy-horse self, he can't trust "himself" and he can't trust others. Unless he "lets go," he can't trust, and if he can't trust, he won't be able to breathe under the waters of life.

Getting off the high horse of controlling oneself or others, of being in charge, of knowing where one is going, can be very difficult for men. How many wrong turns does it take, for example, before a man will ask for directions? Stopping the search, admitting to being lost, getting out of the car, and asking someone else the way usually comes as a last resort. Since finding the way without help is a form of succeeding, asking for directions seems a kind of defeat. It means accepting disorientation and admitting that we don't know where we are. Feeling disoriented and exposed triggers all the instincts that say the situation has turned dangerous and that we are vulnerable and afraid of falling prey.

Men usually learn about trusting themselves and others while within groups of boys and men. The shaggy horse within gets seen by friends and the occasional mentor. Under circumstances of trouble and tribulation, friends see what "he is made of," how you can trust him to be. Within groups, under pressure, men learn to feel the horse within and learn to trust it. The sense of seeing the hidden horse carrying a person is often the basis of friendship. Often friends can "pick up where they left off" after years of separation because their inner horses recognize each other and resume a conversation unaffected by superficial changes. But, the inner horses notice changes that mark the soul of the friend. Initiatory circumstances make brothers of the inner horses of men and connect those horses regardless of the high or low positions of the men in regular life.

Throughout life, entering a group of men can awaken the inner horse of a man, and it usually awakens as shaggy and feeling "out of it." As it wakes up, old feelings stir. Fears and phobias, issues of trust and distrust, instincts to join the herd or to flee, and instincts to lead the pack or follow another's lead, arise. Gatherings of adult men out in the forest working with questions of spirit and soul causes the inner horse to become very alert.

I like to tell proverbs at the beginning of events. Many proverbs are teachings about orientations and disorientations. One of my favorite paraphrases is a statement by an archaeologist who was lost: "It is better to wander without a guide in uncharted land than to follow a map made by tourists." Indeed, men's retreats usually begin by our entering uncharted land. We don't know where we're going until we get there. At the start, we haven't found the little shaggy horse, and even when we do, there's a struggle over letting the reins drop. Everyone is afraid at the beginning; you can feel it. In fact, if you don't feel the fear, you're not feeling anything else either.

Entering a group of men whose direction hasn't been determined beforehand raises instinctive animal fears. Anything could happen. We all know that groups of men are capable of violence, so one fear is that someone might die. The next fear that occurs to each of us is that it might be me. Among men, instinctive fears and the possibilities of violence increase during times of disorientation. Disoriented men are scared and dangerous, especially toward each other. Still, a serious change of direction can't occur without disorientation. Disorientation precedes any new orientation.

For a group of men to travel together into the unknown, they must develop a sense of trust, without driving the fear too far away. The process feels similar to getting on the little horse and letting go of the reins. The fears don't disappear right away, because they involve issues of inner trust and trust of others. Besides, fear can be a sort of guide to where the ordeals begin. The catchall word for the fears among men is *homophobia:* fear or dread of what is similar or the same as I am. Since American culture has a dread-love relationship to sex, homophobia usually means fear of love with those of the same gender. But it has many other phobias inherent in it. There are fears of being physically harmed or dominated by another man; fears of being intellectually dominated and spiritually damaged or misled. There are fears of the bodies of other men, fears of the spirits of other men, and fears of the souls of other men. At the bottom lies a fear that something in other men may be the same as something hidden in me, a shadowy something that I barely know of myself. At that level, homophobia is a fear of men based on not knowing my true self and fear of what may be hidden within me. It's not only a fear of the sexuality of other men, but also of the power, intelligence, emotions, and spirit of others based on what I still don't know about myself. Usually those who differ from me sexually, racially, and by physical type are the first and unwilling carriers of my inherent phobias. Excessive fears and extreme dread of trusting others comes from a lack of trust in myself and a blindness about who I am and of the nature of my inner horse.

Sometimes at the retreats, we try to build trust directly by doing trust exercises. These exercises reflect another aspect of dropping the reins, for when we allow the horse to see where to go, we are in a sense allowing ourselves to be blind. The inner horse can awaken when we accept blindness about where our lives are going, thereby deepening trust in ourselves and others.

Fifty men stand in a clearing in the woods and blindfold themselves. Then they wait to be led away. Fifty men who can see approach, and each chooses a blind man randomly, instinctively. They lead the blind men off, each pair going its own way. The blind man doesn't know who leads him, and the men never speak to each other. They never know because the whole exercise is conducted in silence. Later, the blind and the sighted switch places, and the sighted men choose new partners. Everyone gets a chance to be led by an unseen leader, and everyone leads a vulnerable man who can't see. It's a beautiful thing to observe, pairs of men moving with incredible care all over the landscape—a small man leading a large man, a timid man being led faster and further than he would choose to go on his own.

It starts out simply, each pair working out silent communications and getting used to each other. Gradually, it becomes very complicated and adventurous. The blind men run at full speed, galloping like horses led along by the vision of other horses. The blind men climb trees, go up and down steep hills; some erupt in dance steps they never see themselves execute. Some go too far; little accidents and jokes are played out. Some become intricately involved in touching the bark of trees, blades of grass. The whole area gets explored in great and careful detail. Fears are replaced with surprisingly deep feelings of trust and care. The whole place feels more known than it ever could be through one pair of eyes. When it's over, there are many gentle feelings to describe and a great deal of laughter; both bring tears to the eyes.

The experience has to be talked about. Each man has trusted another, but since the guide who shared this strange, intimate adventure is never known, he could be any man at all. There is no way to know for certain the color, size, ethnicity, education, or status of the guide. Even in homogeneous groups, the exercise tends to broaden trust beyond the limits of the group. Trusting one man opens up the possibility of trusting any man, and of gaining more trust in the inner man as well.

The experience of being blind brings up all the fearful feelings associated with letting go and dropping down. Men talk of feeling incredibly vulnerable and alone while waiting to be chosen. Some know that they were among the last picked, and they felt as they had when they were not picked for games at school or for dances. All felt great relief at the touch that indicated they had been chosen. The stages of letting go that followed are described in beautiful detail. For some, being led gave them an exuberant feeling of freedom that they didn't want to end. The gratefulness toward most of the guides is wonderfully deep.

During this exercise, the men are encouraged to walk right up to the edge of where they are comfortable together and to keep pushing the edge. Some go too far. But, there are others who watch and interfere if there's physical danger. All of this happens in silence. The bodies learn to communicate. What starts out clumsy and scared becomes subtle and exhilarating. Most men find leading more difficult and painful than being blind. While leading a surprising weight is felt. Watching out for obstacles and learning the blind man's rhythm and styles of movement turn out to be heavy work.

Being blindfolded opens the inner eyes and forces a man to see his life differently. It allows him to see that something carries him through life and makes it possible for him to trust his life more deeply. Allowing himself to be led shows him that something guides his life, leading him toward his fate, possibly toward a destiny as well.

Conn-Eda is like a blind man being led by the little horse until he sees the bird with human speech. He passes the little stone to the bird and receives an iron ball and instructions to follow the ball and listen. It turns out that the ball was right below his foot. He was standing on it but didn't see it. The weight that will take him to the edge of the lake and down into the waters of his life was right there, below his usual stance. He drops his reins even further. Now the trust that he has developed for the horse needs to expand; like each of us, he needs to trust that his inner life is real and has weight and leads somewhere necessary. Conn-Eda drops further and further into his own life. In the same way, the process of initiation gives weight to a life and makes it necessary to follow where that weight pulls us.

One of the universal methods of beginning rites of initiation is to blindfold the initiates. Blinding them tells them that they can no longer see the way they saw before. They must begin to see in some other way. This also symbolizes the fact that initiates always enter the ritual blindly. If they knew where the path of initiation was going, they wouldn't follow it because initiation means losing everything. The blindfolded initiate is often painted white, as if he had joined the spirits of the dead. In order for the initiation to occur, it's as if everything must die for a moment. The initiate goes blindly walking through the death of his childhood or of some former state that comes to an end.

The eyes of a child see everything, whether joy or sorrow, as continuing forever. But being blindfolded convinces the body and the imagination of the blinded person that he will not live forever, that someday the world he usually sees will go dark. Because blindfolding raises the dark vision of death this practice occurs widely throughout history and throughout cultures. The initiate's eyes turn inward and begin to see his wounds differently. Death is the universal image of the breaking apart and ending of things, and wounds are like small deaths, marking the small breaks in life. Initiation leaves its own clear wound as well as increasing the initiate's capacity to have insight into wounds. The ritual performances of tribal groups are the elaboration of the steps that the psyche requires to feel and know that this person has changed and that in changing himself he has changed the group. In initiation, everything and everyone changes, but no one can see exactly which changes will occur. In initiation, everyone goes a little blind.

Once Conn-Eda has dropped the reins, the shaggy horse becomes the guide of the story and the vehicle that carries him through the ordeals. From here on, the story can be seen as a series of stations or tableaux that the prince and horse arrive at, as if each of the blindfolded men were led to a place where they see or hear something mysterious. Each man will interpret what he sees and hears through his own life; even when initiations are done in groups, the effect of the rites are different for each person.

The first station on the road of ordeals and trials occurs when the prince and horse arrive at the resting place of the ancient bird who knows all things. When the story says that the bird can only be seen for three days in a year and at a certain place in the forest, that can be seen as referring to annual initiation rites. The three days are mythical days that describe the period when initiations are under way and everything else stops. Often those days were not on the calendar and were therefore missing and mysterious periods. Whatever happened on those days was difficult to describe in terms of normal time and space.

The ancient bird represents the spirit world, sudden insight, knowledge of future and past, flights of imagination and visions. It speaks to the prince before the horse speaks to him; it opens his ears through its speech of past, present, and future. It opens the otherworld to him and confirms both the direction he has taken and the danger he is in.

In exchange for the stone from the druid, the ancient bird confirms the spirit of Conn-Eda and reveals to him the iron ball. Conn-Eda is being instructed by the ancient bird in another way of seeing and hearing—Conn-Eda is told that he should listen to the horse in all matters. The ball is a sign that he must follow the course of these events. In order to survive underwater and through fire, Conn-Eda must see with inner eyes and use the gifts in the horse's ears.

The fact that the tools needed are in the ear of the little horse, added to the fact that Conn-Eda is instructed to listen to the horse in all things, points out that this initiation is about hearing the world in a new way. The abundance that disappeared in the world behind and above reappears in the ear of the horse. Though the eyes tend to dominate modern culture and the activities of men, the horse points to the metaphoric wealth of the ear. Inside the ear are the drum, the anvil, and the stirrup to ride this horse of hearing things in a different way.

Of course, the iron ball rolls with gravity into the waters of the lake and keeps rolling and descending. The iron ball's steady descent pulls the opposite way of the sudden moves, the appearance and disappearance, of the bird that speaks. Where the bird speaks and takes flight, the ball silently pulls downward into waters heavier than air. Within the water there will be fire and flights, so that the leaps of the visionary spirit are drenched in the emotional world below. The initiation of the prince combines the confirmation of his spirit with immersions in the emotional realm of the soul. The ancient bird blesses his endeavor and directs him downward as if to tell him that life can't be made only of flights and visions.

Initiations open up the world this way, through sudden flashes, visitations, and insights. A person gets foreknowledge of events or everything happens at just the right time. Knowledge arrives with wings, from an eerie voice croaking somewhere inside or in a dream. But, integrating the effects and meanings of the flights of spirit takes a lifetime; and initiations move by way of both spirit and soul, fire and water, flights of confirmation and descents full of doubts.

Strange events are occurring both to the prince and within him. All he knew has been left far behind, and even his ways of knowing have been altered. Hearing a bird speak and following a ball that rolls through forest, fire, and water are expressions of something big and deep trying to happen to him. Taking instruction from a horse and taking a basket and a bottle from the horse's ear require a relinquishing of the rational mind. The language of the story indicates that what happens here is strange beyond normal seeing and speaking. These are not just signs of the other/underworld, they are proof that he has entered it fully and that the rules of the realm where past, present, and future meet now dominate.

The only way to communicate what happens when a man stands next to the waters of his own life is through metaphor. Entering into the depths of the psyche can be overwhelming and dangerous. Rites of initiation intentionally put people at the edge, where they must sink or swim with the capacities and resources they carry within themselves. When there are no prepared rites, the psyche of a person will take any significant interruption of the daily world and throw a person into the realm of ordeals and trials. Then the person better mount whatever horse is waiting. The horse is the way of moving through the depths. At the edge, he will either learn from the horse or he may never know what carries him through life.

The changes that occur during initiation take place deep within the initiate. They cannot be explained or described in a simplistic or literal way. The inner and outer worlds are opened up, and what the person hears and sees defies definition. The emotional, imaginal, and spiritual worlds are heated up and cooled down, and only metaphors can carry the sense of mystery and change.

In ritual initiations, there is always a secret part of the rite. Part of the secret is that what happens occurs so distinctly to each individual and has so much mystery in it that it cannot be spoken of adequately. But also, the practice of secrecy helps keep the psyche alert to this change that has occurred inside. An old idea states that the soul grows around secrets. The mysterious secret core that makes a man who he is can never quite be said. Metaphors are fashioned to evoke these mysteries of change. Thus, the conditions the second queen places on Conn-Eda's soul provide the grain of sand that penetrates the oyster shell and irritates the oyster. It causes both continuing irritation and the formation of a pearl. But even when the shell of an initiation cracks open and the pearl can be seen, there's no explanation for what has happened, for it happened in that mysterious, hidden place inside.

The next tableaux occurs when the ball rolls into the waters of Loch Erne and disappears, and the little horse stops at the edge where the land meets the water, where one thing turns into another. That's a place of radical change through descent, through immersion and submersion in the inner, underworld of emotions, of personal and mythic memory. The surprise to Conn-Eda is that he can breathe, that he can manage in this new atmosphere. Water is heavier than air; thus, he has entered into the weight of his life, but the big surprise is that he can tolerate being there and that he has an anatomy for living in that atmosphere. Many a man's heart is full of grief, as if he has held back and blocked up a lake of tears. After years of not weeping, he fears that he will drown if the dam breaks.

After many years of not crying, I felt that I would suffocate and drown any time I approached my own sorrow, or anyone else's sorrow, or the sorrow of the world. Since I couldn't live in my own sorrow, I couldn't touch anyone else's. I was surprised to discover how many men feel the same way. The idea that men don't have feelings is deeply wrong. More often, men don't have a way of immersing themselves in those feelings. The story explains that often what is needed is a horse, a trusted animal who can carry one into these depths of emotion.

For a man to discover that he can breathe underwater, the wall around his heart must be broken open without breaking his spirit. Part of the functions of initiations for youths was to open their hearts to sorrow and release the fire of their spirit. Both water and fire need to come out. Before birth, an eruption of testosterone changes the embryo into a male. At puberty, another eruption increases testosterone thirty times over. Testosterone can inhibit weeping. Thus, there is a complicated relationship among the water elements in a man—that is, among testosterone, sweat, and tears. Often it's easier for a man to offer sweat or blood instead of tears. The flood of aggression and sexual drive at puberty occurs at the expense of the tear ducts. A complicated operation is needed to open the ducts of the eyes and the heart after puberty seals them off. Initiation matches changes in the body with changes in the soul.

Men who gather at this part of the story take many points of view with regard to this edge between land and water. One man says, "I didn't want to go any further. The whole idea of going into the water immediately rose in my chest like a welling up of tears uncried for many years." Another man says, "I felt the same thing, but I felt stuck. I felt that I couldn't go that next step into the water." And another man says, "I felt similarly, but when the horse said 'take from my ear the bottle of all-heal,' I was encouraged to go on. I felt that if I was carrying something that could heal I also might be able to descend into those waters."

The next man says, "I didn't even hear about the all-heal. All I felt was that going that close to the water would make the incredible amount of tears that I've been carrying all my adult life try to come out, and I've been sitting here holding them back ever since." Right next to him, the man says: "I was relieved to let go and slip right into the waters. I never cried at my mother's funeral and I've been weeping here and don't want to stop."

Often the tears of one man will pull the whole group into the waters—a descent into what matters in each person's life. The story has been dropping all the way from the garden at the beginning, and here it descends rapidly. One man is right on the edge, the next plunges in, and the whole event changes shape and feeling. That's the way of the story and of the psyche.

The scene at the edge of the lake depicts an event that changes one's consciousness. But in order to be able to go into the lake, several things have to happen. First of all, Conn-Eda doesn't feel alone. If a man is disconnected from what carries him, from his horse-sense, it's unlikely that he will go into the lake. But when he does he must remember not to just plunge in without carrying some food to pay off the guardians of the otherworld. He also may not go on if there isn't a promise of healing. Instinctively, a man knows that entering the deep waters of his life can "burn" him and heal him. Some of each will occur. The elaborate rituals of initiation are set up to balance the fear of change with the sense that the things needed are at hand.

The next tableaux is reached when the horse stops because they are approaching a river running within the lake, a water within the waters. They smell a terrible stench coming from the fire-breathing serpents. When placing themselves in this story, men tend to gather along either bank of the river, and a few seem to be in the river itself.

One man says, "I was delighted to be able to take the three pieces of meat and accurately throw one into the mouth of each dragon. It's something I've never been able to do in my life. But in the story I felt the exhilaration of hitting something accurately, with no time to spare and no wasted effort." Another man says, "I'm in the same place but without the same luck. I feel that earlier in my life I had opportunities, and if I had just been more skillful, more accurate, if I had cast the pieces more carefully, I wouldn't be facing my second divorce as I am now. For me, the three fire-breathing dragons are painful marriages that ended in fires. And as I look into the mouth of the last one, I seriously doubt that I'm going to make it past this river. I think that my story stops right here."

Another man says, "I'm before that. To me the three fire-breathing dragons eat up my whole life. One is my marriage, the second my two children, and the third my job. To me they seem like mouths asking and asking, and I give them more and more and more. But I feel empty and stuck on that side of the river, and listening to the story I realize if I could just cast a little bit of meat to each one rather than imagine I must feed them endlessly, I may be able to get by and go on. I'm getting more and more angry as I wait here."

A younger man speaks and says, "Listening to all the disasters in the world and hearing about relationships that end in all this brokenness, I don't even want to leap. I don't even want to look at those dragons. I'm discouraged. I don't even want to sit on the horse."

And the next man speaks and says, "And I'm landed on the other side of the river and answering the question of the horse when he says 'are you still there?' I say yes and it only took half my strength, and I'm completely surprised to find myself at a place in life where I feel more grounded and more settled and still have a great amount of energy left and feel like it's time for me to move on and to deal with more issues in myself and in my life."

In the story, the iron ball rolls on, pulling the horse and the prince further into this landscape of the underworld. The next tableaux they arrive at is the mountain of fire. As most men know, below the surface waters of their feelings stands a great flaming mountain that is difficult to cross, and most men who manage it are only barely alive afterward. The anger that is in each man seems capable of destroying everything, including the self. Some men push that volcanic mountain so deep inside that it doesn't appear to be there. But, they dream of beasts in basements, of killers loose in the streets, of worldwide catastrophes. Or they have a heart attack. This mountain of hot feeling inside a man must be faced, or it will destroy something. As they prepare to leap over this mountain, the horse advises the prince to hold on tightly, for the horse knows that if they reach the other side Conn-Eda may become a man not just with a fate but with a destiny.

The men who gather at the mountain gather on both sides. One man says, "The mountain is before me, and it's in the form of a serious illness. I found out that I have cancer, and I don't expect that I will live through it. It's bigger than I am and no doubt it will burn me up and destroy me. But it seems that I have to make the leap anyway and go through radiation and other treatments. Mostly I'm sitting here feeling that I can't move any further because of the size of the fire in front of me." The next man says, "I'm in the same place and I've been stuck here for twenty-five years. For me, leaping past the dragons was going to Vietnam and getting out alive. But now, and for twenty-five years, I've been looking at the burning mountain, which somehow is the dead bodies of those that I served with who didn't come back. They are before me like a mountain of fire. Every time I try to do something to move my life along I can't get over the mountain because I feel that I would have to carry them with me." After they speak, the weight of the water that surrounds everyone in the story can be felt.

After a while, another man speaks. "I did make the leap over the mountain, and now I'm just on the other side, clinging to the horse, and the horse is asking if I'm all right and I'm not quite sure. After years of drug and alcohol addiction, I almost burned myself to ashes. And now that I'm clean of that, I'm on the other side of that mountain but barely alive. What got me was the prince saying, 'yes,' he was there but barely alive."

"I'm there too," says another man, "right with those words, 'barely alive,' but not because I'm burned up, but because I think I've been burned out. I'm fifty-five years old, and I've had my career and been successful, leapt over mountains, piled things up, and raised my children. But if someone asked me where I was right now, I'd say I'm barely alive. I'm glad to be where I am, but I also am not able to go on. I don't understand what I've done. I'm disoriented again, at my age."

The last station or tableaux in this part of the story is the green glade. This is the place of healing where the horse tells the prince to pour the all-heal on himself and his burns, which are washed away, leaving his skin renewed. It's a cool, green place where the psyche can settle and cool down from the heat of the ordeals that have preceded.

In contemporary times, there are usually very few men at this part of the story. Once, out of a hundred men, there were two. One was a young man and the other was an "elder." The elder said he was there because he had reached a place where he could finally let go of all the striving and all the trying and let some healing come into his life. He had begun to take care of himself, had begun to see himself as someone worth caring for, and had let various things bless him. He was also counting his blessings.

The younger man was surprised to be there. He was about to get married, and when he heard the story it connected to his plan to be married in a meadow, on a hill. The image of standing among friends and family, in the cool green of the meadow, drew him there. Now, he realized that the wedding was a healing of some sort. It was a cool place, a place of beauty and promise that he was headed for. Suddenly he felt a joy about going to this wedding, since for years he had been fearing that he would never marry. Everyone was surprised to hear of the wedding scene after the burning mountain, but everyone also felt the sense of promise it brought. If a man has no knowledge that the horse can carry him both into and out of trouble, he may avoid the troubled areas that can lead to healing. And without the occasional glade of cooling and healing and making new skin, the ordeals of life won't make any sense. Without an awareness of the original conditions placed on the soul, ordeals are simply painful occasions instead of sufferings carrying the soul toward a destination.

Conn-Eda barely reached the green glade to receive the anointing with all-heal. The psyche recognizes that some ordeals seem to take everything out of us and give us the actual or at least the felt sense that we almost didn't make it. In the glade, a man will feel there is a reason he is alive, because he was almost claimed by death. The feeling of surviving a near-death experience can open the healing places and cause the inner horse to hope. It can be a long time or a short time in the healing glade, but soon enough the iron ball rolls across the plain and we follow.

These stations of fire and water, of burning and healing, are places that a person returns to over and over, to learn more about them, to feel more fully, to learn what has happened in his or her life. I would say it's only by revisiting these places that a person grows to be an elder and gleans some wisdom. It's only from knowledge gained in the burning fires and the healing waters that a person gains the ability to pull others through those fires and to help them not drown in the waters of their own lives. In that sense, initiation is not linear and direct, but it winds around in paths that keep coming back to the same river with its dragons and back to the same mountain with fire in all directions. The tempering of a person is ongoing. And one of the keys to healing comes from being aware of when the psyche needs heat and when the psyche needs cooling and quiet.

In tribal life the ordeals are condensed into rites of passage. Since the tribe returns to the same rituals each time a group of youths comes of age, the meaning of the ordeals is continually revisited. An old saying says that initiation never ends. When the rites are ongoing a man goes from being pulled through the emotions and spiritual ordeals the first time to preparing the rites and helping to pull others through later. He keeps reliving his own initiation and adding to it the events and emotions currently in his life. He keeps working, pulling himself and getting pulled through the ordeals; he keeps shaping the meaning of his life. If a man doesn't take his inner life seriously, his outer life will lack meaning. If a man can't feel a purpose for his life, he will lack courage at critical times and lack commitment when it counts. If a man can't find the glades of healing, he'll get consumed in the mountain's fire.

The series of scenes in this section of the story represent an ideal progression of ordeals. At each station on the route something is said to the prince: Follow the ball, listen to the horse; take the tools from my ear; mount up for here your difficulties begin; if you cast accurately you'll get there, if not you're lost; perhaps you are a man of destiny; apply the oil, you may pass the last test.

Each ordeal involves advice, some tools or talismans, a test, and a further confirmation. The elements of old rites are barely hidden in the narrative. Each scene seems like a site from which the elements of old rites could be excavated and uncovered. But mytho-archaeology isn't the whole point. Also being shown are basic elements of how the psyche views traumatic and piercing life experiences. The point isn't simply to rediscover how initiation was actually done by certain tribes or ancestors. Nor is this an expedition to reinvent or steal existing tribal rites and insert them wherever there is trouble and pain. It's more about entering into the initiatory style of perceiving, suffering, and healing the conditions of the soul.

The complicated scenes in the story show the elaborate way the inner soul sees experiences in the outer world. The descent through the emotions stirs ancient ways of touching and seeing the web of the world. So much happens underwater or in fire because the relationships in the realms of initiation are in constant flux. This realm inspires, regulates, and resonates change. It breathes, acts out, and smells like change. There are no exact formulas for handling radical change, and no assurances or insurance policies that guarantee certain results. Finding the shaggy horse doesn't begin a fixed ceremony that produces certain abundance at the other end. The horse first speaks when the "difficulties begin," then he warns that failing the first test means being lost (not simply losing, but *being lost*). The result of diving into the waters of change can mean being lost for a long time, or losing the sense of meaning in life. All along the way there are questions, and in these lie the meaning of the word quest. Even after the mountain of fire and the healing glade, the shaggy horse only concedes that now there is some hope.

In cultures that don't have ritual initiations, events that are felt and experienced like the stations in the story occur randomly and in any order. From the point of view of the psyche, time is a fluid element that can flow in any direction, and though the sequence of events may add up to a complete ritual process, the experiences can occur in any order. Working within a story gives a certain order to the experiences in an individual's life, and it can help reveal hidden meaning in those events. By physically laying out the "stations" of a story in the room where the story is being told, men can choose or be pulled to the scene that reflects a similar ordeal in their past or that they are undergoing presently. Some men even pick places that are approaches to an ordeal, because they know they are preparing for a trial that is soon coming.

CHAPTER 13

BOUND FOR THE SACRED

The horse and rider followed the rolling ball until they entered a broad field, where they could see across the plain a great city surrounded by walls. The only entrance was guarded by two towers that shot flames randomly, burning anything that passed between them. They saw the iron ball roll between the towers and disappear into the shining city.

"Stop here," said the horse. "Take from my ear the small knife, and with it kill and flay me. Then wrap yourself in my skin, and you can pass through that gate unscathed. Once through, you can cross back and forth at your pleasure, entering and leaving as you wish. All I ask in return is that once inside the gates, you remember your little horse, come back, and drive away the birds of prey about my carcass. And if any drop of that all-heal may remain, pour it on my flesh. Then if you can, dig a pit and bury my remains."

The prince was shocked! He said that he would never sacrifice friendship for personal gain. He said that what the horse asked went against his bearing as a man, his ethics as a prince, and his feelings as a friend. It went against all he believed in. Besides, how could he part with the one who had helped him through such great difficulties? The prince said he would rather face death itself than dishonor their friendship.

"Forget all that," said the horse. "Unless you follow my advice in this as you have before, we may both perish completely and never meet again. Besides, there are fates worse than death."

Reluctantly, the prince took the knife from the ear of his little horse, and with faltering hand, he pointed it at the horse's throat. His eyes were blind with tears. The dagger, as if compelled by druidic power, leapt to the horse's throat. Before Conn-Eda knew it, the deed was done, and the horse fell at his feet. The prince fell, too, and wept until he lost consciousness. When he recovered, with many misgivings, he flayed the skin off the horse. In the derangement of the moment, he covered himself with the skin and stumbled toward the flaming gate of the magnificent city. In this demented state, he passed through the flames unmolested.

Inside was a shining city, and the prince stood in a busy marketplace, filled with wonders and wealth. But Conn-Eda saw no charm there. As he stood in his daze, the last request of his faithful companion forced itself upon him and compelled him to return. He found an appalling scene, for birds of prey were tearing and devouring the flesh of the little horse. The prince chased them off and poured the all-heal on the body of the shaggy steed.

No sooner had the all-heal touched the inanimate flesh than it changed before his eyes and assumed the form of a noble young man. Conn-Eda, awestruck, reached out and amid tears of joy and wonder embraced this fantastic brother. Then, the marvelous youth spoke: "You are the best sight my eyes have seen, and I am most fortunate for having met you. Behold your shaggy steed, changed to my natural state!" He explained that he was brother to the king of the magnificent city, that the druid had enchanted him but had been forced to give him up by the honest request of the prince, that he could not recover his natural state until the prince had performed the deep sacrifice. He also said that the hag of Beara was his sister and that she had not wished to destroy Conn-Eda, for she could have done that in a stroke. Rather, she wished to free the prince from future dangers and rescue him from his relentless enemies.

Together the young men entered the magnificent city and were received with great joy by the king of Lough Erne. The powerful black steed, the hound of supernatural powers, and the three golden apples were bestowed on Conn-Eda, and a joyful feast began. When the year and a day approached its end, Conn-Eda passed out through the flaming towers, over the mountain of fire, and past the three huge serpents. He was not harmed, and his passage was swift on the great black steed.

Finally, the prince came in sight of his father's realm. The queen was still on the pinnacle, but she was joyful now because she was sure that this was the last day of her imprisonment. She was full of hope that the prince would not appear and that she would be done with him forever. Then she saw a movement on the horizon; she squinted her eyes, and after a moment she could make out a shape approaching. She looked as hard as she could. The shape grew into three shapes. Soon she could not deny that they were the prince astride the black steed, with the magnificent hound beside him. She raged in grief and anger, cast herself down off the pinnacle, and disappeared into the ground.

Conn-Eda was welcomed by his father, who had mourned his son as lost forever. The prince planted the golden apples in the garden, and instantly they produced a tree bearing similar fruit. These golden apples seemed to draw on all the splendor of the world below, for soon the earth produced exuberant crops and the trees gave ninefold their usual fruit. The waters teemed with choice fish, the beehives overflowed with honey, and the cows yielded such an abundance of rich milk that it rained in torrents on the fields and filled the furrows and ditches of the earth. No one lacked for anything. Conn-Eda succeeded his father; his reign was long and prosperous, and even now the western province of Ireland is called Connacht after him.

When I've told this story, the part that causes the greatest uproar comes where the prince slays the little horse and envelops himself in the torn skin. This is the last ordeal in the story, and it is what the story has been leading to, for after it occurs everything changes. There is no way to adequately explain or define what happens in this moment. It is a sacrifice surrounded in mystery, ambiguity, and irrationality. The story says so directly. A conflict occurs between the horse and the prince, followed by a mysterious act—the knife moves as if by "druidic force." After the sacrifice follows unconsciousness, dementia, weeping, and stumbling about, and during this period everything changes. This is the story's way of describing the mystery and ambiguity at the core of all deep ritual.

Arguments break out about what happens at this point, about what the story says and about what it all means. The first time I told it and the time came for everyone to go to a place in the story from which they wanted to work, there was a huge surge, a crowd trampling its way into this place in the story. More than half of the men present wanted to be in the spot where the horse was slain. It took a long time to hear the reason why each man was there. The reasons were complicated and in opposition to each other. The story seemed to create a whirlwind of chaos and confusion that swirled around the body of the shaggy horse.

The shock of the prince was also felt in the room. Men take very distinct positions inside details of this scene, and a turmoil of emotions takes place. A man says, "I couldn't do it, couldn't carry it through. It's wrong. The horse has done everything faithfully. I can't do it." This makes another man angry, who replies, "Your fondness for the horse doesn't go far enough, for the horse itself is saying you have followed its advice until now, and if you don't follow this advice, you will cause a fate worse than death. It's not your fondness for the horse stopping you; it's your fondness for counting on the horse and not wanting to be alone."

These men are reenacting the conflict between the prince and the horse. It doesn't matter that everyone has heard the rest of the story and knows that the horse changes into a prince. What matters is how each man felt and imagined the sacrifice. What does a modern person do with a scene where someone must slay and flay what has been carrying them through trial after trial? The fondness for the horse is genuine and the demand for sacrifice is as unmistakenly present as the knife.

Another man says that he stands at the place where he flayed the horse. For him, this represents tearing off a marriage that has lasted fourteen years and now is over. Hearing this part of the story, he realizes that he is also peeling the skin off his own life. No one argues with him, because of the torn feelings carried in his voice. Everyone begins to recall times that they had to pull away from something or someone loved and depended on. A man tears out the words he had said while burying his dead child. A man says he is the knife trying to cut through the darkness in himself. He says it with such a cutting tone that no one argues or asks what darkness it might be. But it causes the next man to recall how he had set out one night to end his life, and he was on the point of doing it when through his tears and anguish there burst a desire to live. He has never understood that but never forgotten the moment. Then, another man says he is the horse cut open and flayed. He has just been through a heart surgery and still feels the cut of the knife and the dismembered feelings that leave him in constant fear of his life.

In the story, Conn-Eda has to act in a way contrary to his knowledge of himself, contrary to what he has been told by others about himself and about living. He must go against what he believes he should do, beyond what he thinks he can do. What occurs comes from somewhere deep in himself, and he winds up inside the horse, within the skin of what has carried him to this point. Rather than being carried through the castle gates as a "prince" might expect, he's down on his own feet, unaware of what he is doing, stumbling, blind, and wrapped in torn skin and shadows.

This is a place of mystery. Some people can speak out some sense of it and some cannot. Who can say what mystery is within a person? Who can say what it feels like to be that person, wrapped in that life? All of the ideas and beliefs the prince has about what life ought to be won't get him through the fiery gates ahead. Some very painful cut will have to be made if the prince is to get to the place of inner resources, for the little horse cautions that there are fates worse than death. For each person this will appear different. Whatever a person's horse is, it has carried him or her that far and knows intimately the ordeals of his or her life and has no concern for what others might think or feel. In order to pass through the gates, a person must open up and get inside the torn and painful body of longing that would rather die than keep from living out life fully.

If the story started in the field before these gates, no one watching would say that this is the perfect child of the perfect parents. No one in the upperworld would see in the demented, suffering, bloodied appearance of Conn-Eda the beloved prince of the realm. At this point in the story everything is reversed, upside down, or turning around. Even after Conn-Eda passes through the gates and enters the realm, teeming with the sights of life, he no longer has eyes for the treasures he started out seeking.

From the time when the horse offers the knife to the prince, everything begins turning. Instead of saying "hold on" when faced with danger, the horse is saying "let go," not just of the reins but of everything he holds dear. For the first time, the prince argues and tries to refuse the advice of the horse. From the same place that the healing oil came, there comes a knife. The act of flaying the little horse and having the prince wrap himself in the hide creates a realignment of everything, most especially of the sources of abundant life and abundant death.

In terms of the inner world of a person, it is the emotional life that turns around. It could be said that in this moment the prince is no longer "himself." He's become his own shadow, or the other side of who he has been. The upper and lower parts of his psyche turn. If a person is carried by anger, he or she has to walk in sorrow. If a person is making his or her way through grief, he or she will have to break out of it. If fear drives everything along, courage will be required, and if doubt covers everything, faith will have to be entered. If the prince cannot do this, he will never pass the gates of the city, and he will meet a fate worse than death. If he is always the upright son of righteousness, he must wear a darker skin. If he carries an image of himself as dark and mean-spirited, he will have to tear it off and stumble into generosity.

In the skin of the new emotions and unfamiliar attitudes, Conn-Eda passes through the fire unscathed, and now events reverse again. Instead of exploring the realm and receiving gifts for himself, the prince returns to the field with the all-heal and renews the skin of the horse. This shifts the relationship between death and life and releases the sources of abundance deep in the earth below the lake. The alignment of the lowerworld and the upperworld is remade. Out of the chaos and suffering and the rites of burying comes an inner brother, the image of the new inner life. The spell of the inner brother is broken.

One of the surprises in the story comes when the radical change occurs and what comes out of the slain body of the little horse is another young man. Cutting through the enchantment reveals an inner brother, one related to all the otherworld figures and connected to the treasures. Often in fairy tales, what comes at the time of deep change is a princess. The prince and the princess embrace, and the world is made whole again by bringing the feminine and the masculine together in a new way. But ours is a different story, and it points at another type of wholeness, at another type of healing.

Conn-Eda is the brother born in the upperworld, and the prince from within the horse is the brother in the inner, other, underworld. This image reflects the idea that every man has a brother deep in the psyche who needs to be uncovered. The story says that the uncovering feels like being slain, exposed, and torn apart. There seems to be barely enough healing capacity to make the change, and there is a burial grave ready if the attempt to reach this part of the self doesn't work. Carl Jung called this other brother the shadow, the hidden aspect of the psyche that appears as the same sex as the individual and that needs to be learned from and learned about. Jung also said that the shadow is everything that we are not conscious of at the moment. In other words, this shadow brother keeps being remade as our awareness changes. The rest of life is spent attending to mysteries that open through the sacrifice of the shaggy horse.

The initiation in the story forms a relationship between Conn-Eda and this changing, surprising shadow brother, for Conn-Eda agrees to go back to the kingdom in Lough Erne regularly. Now both his inner world and the otherworld have become real. The otherworld becomes a place he can relate to and from which he can carry things back and forth. Because Conn-Eda releases his inner brother from the spell he was under, abundance returns to both worlds. Initiation heals wounds in this world and breaks spells in the otherworld. Abundance returns when the trouble in each world receives attention and healing. It is an old Celtic idea that at times of initiation and seasonal change the two worlds open to each other. Then there are opportunities for healing in both realms, but the dangers of dying increase as well.

One of the healings carried in this story is the image of an inner brother who lives under the waters and can lead to the resources of the underworld. One of the roles of initiation is to connect the initiates through these inner brothers, who at first appear shaggy and unwanted but through shared ordeals help deepen the gender of the initiates. Before a man can feel the abundance of life, he must experience a deepening of his gender and a deepening sense of himself.

When Conn-Eda returns, he rides a great black steed, accompanied by a supernatural hound, and carrying three golden apples. It's as if the son of the hunter from the story in Part One has answered the question of whether he is the son of a king or not; the ritual of the slaying of the horses has also been deepened. And, instead of the boy and dog running back to the father's house in fear of the half-giantess and the world, that son is returning with a connection to the dog that is deeper than natural. Like the son in "The Lizard in the Fire," Conn-Eda has returned from the fire to life and brought abundance with him. He has survived his brush with death and increased all of life. Now he has a way of going back and forth between the world below and that above.

The story of Conn-Eda places abundance at the beginning and at the end. At each end of the story, there's abundant life surging through the realm and everyone has their fill. At the beginning, this abundance represents a ceremony of innocence, a festival of fullness with an innocent child as the focal point. The growth of the child results from the best gifts of mother and father. At the end, another ceremony of abundance occurs as the flow of life returns to the rivers and trees, people and animals.

In the beginning, the child is born and abundance surrounds everyone until the good mother dies. Then everyone and everything falls into grief. At the end of the story, the queen plunges into the earth as the prince reenters with the horse, dog, and golden apples. Abundance follows the flaying of the horse and death of the queen. Thus, in the beginning, abundance precedes death, and at the end, abundance follows death. In the middle, the relationship between life and death is radically altered. The ceremony of abundance at the end is not created in innocence but with an increased knowledge of death. The son has seen the world from below and seen darkly into himself.

It should be noted that the queen is not a woman who dies for the sake of the prince or the kingdom. The story is not a literal program for the destruction of horses, women, or feminine power, and seeing the queen on the pinnacle as an actual woman misses the point. But also, to focus on the queen ignores the more powerful feminine force of the hen wife, the old hag of the world who arranges the chess game. But even the old hag is not bent on the destruction of the prince or the queen or on keeping the realm a wasteland. The story represents a radical reorganization of the prince's sense of himself, and it points to the necessity for immersion in the ambiguities and conflicts within before it is possible to have fruitful powers without.

Ritual initiations lay the groundwork and set the stations in life that will be revisited over and over. As this story says, perfection is always temporary, as is wholeness, and points of balance are just that—points between periods of imbalance. In the psyche all deaths are small deaths. The old hag will be back in another guise; there will be more horses and more queens and more ordeals. The initiatory events in people's lives reach extreme areas of their character and leave traces that can be rediscovered and learned from again.

But even in modern societies without evident rites of passage, if we review our lives with an eye for initiation, we can find artifacts that might be pieces of an initiation that was trying to be enacted. We can comb the surface of our lives, looking for fragments that stick out of the dirt, looking for things off the beaten path. And we can hunt for wounds and scars and extreme behaviors that mark the separations that tried to open and broaden our lives. The eye that searches for initiation sees things ceremonially and ritually. It is always looking for the iron ball to follow. It will return to areas of memory and emotion where the ball was lost.

There is no certain ceremony that changes a boy into a man or without which a boy cannot achieve manhood. The boy in a man's psyche may see it that way, however, and say, "I was waiting by the edge of the village to be taken away from my family and childhood. But no one came and carried me into the ecstasies and ordeals of initiation." He expects that it will be a big deal, that it will be evident and direct. If nothing like that happens, he concludes that there was no initiation, that he missed it, and that the opportunity is gone. Because life didn't change dramatically back then, it can't change now, and he will remain a boy forever. I've heard exactly that from many men who appear outwardly successful and even mature, but who clearly state that they left their sense of inner longing somewhere in the past.

The psyche expects rites of passage that deepen the imagination, open the spiritual eyes, and expand emotional capacities. The inner life expects to be led out, to move from physical growth to sexual activity and learning of love, from naïveté to psychological savvy, from innocence to knowledge of life and death. When the expected rites of passage don't occur, anything that makes a break from childhood and opens other ways of seeing and feeling can become a substitute. Anything that contains fire, that tears at life and stirs the shadows, becomes a substitute rite of passage. If parents and everyday culture didn't perceive it as appropriate or meaningful at the time, all the better. They weren't supposed to see it or participate anyway.

So it is not that the boy within missed the "initiation." Rather, at the time it wasn't seen as an initiation. Perhaps there was an accident, an illness, or a big mistake; rules or bones or hearts were broken. Things were never the same again and people never saw each other the same way. There was an outbreak of passion, foolishness, or violence. There was a mental breakdown or an emotional collapse. Perhaps the event was overlooked, mistaken for a crime, or considered something the boy would outgrow instead of something he'd grow into. As a result, the event receded and was covered with layers of disappointment, cynicism, shame, or blame.

But somewhere in those events lie the first cuts of the knife that lifted the skin of childhood. Somewhere in them are the visions that opened the imagination to genuine terror and genuine beauty, if only for a second. Somewhere are the words that carried wisdom through the ear of the child to the heart of the man. Somewhere there was a touch that revealed the passionate intensity of a body capable of love and generating life. And somewhere a fire was lit that could erupt in a rage or burn in protection of someone. Neither the boy's expectations nor the pieces of initiation disappear completely. They lie hidden in the psyche of the adult, waiting to be uncovered. They automatically stir from hiding when new breaks in life are encountered.

The eye that searches for initiation can spot pieces of events from these breaks in life and fit them together to meet the deep expectation of an initiation that will open us to life and death. The eye hunting for initiatory pieces can see into divorces, wars, imprisonment, psychic breakdowns, sudden departures, depressions, and funerals and begin to collect the artifacts that can be reworked into ceremonies and identified as the scars that mark the meaning of a life. This eye sees with imagination; it sees the images trying to emerge from the events that have already marked us in an unforgettable way.

A tragedy becomes completely tragic if we remain blind to the part of ourselves that the tragedy makes sacred. An old saying is that the afflicted are sacred and that sacred space smells bad. A life trying to change wraps itself in afflictions; it smells and looks as bad as the flayed, shaggy hide of the little horse. A psyche trying to change will pour through any wound or break, whether it's physical, mental, emotional, moral, legal, or spiritual. The tragic events and the glorious epiphanies in our lives offer opportunities for us to learn most accurately who we are and how to nurture our souls. The shocking nature of these events doesn't completely disappear; it remains in the memories we carry and points to a deeper ground that offers us instruction. Conn-Eda faces death several times over, suffers dementia, thinks he has taken the life of the one being that helped him, and believes he has violated all principles of honor and reason. Yet the horse seems to say that it is a fate worse than death not to risk entering life fully—shadows, chaos, blood, and all. Conn-Eda returns as a survivor of the underworld and as a witness of mysteries that defy description.

There is no single initiation that occurs once and gives us status for the rest of life. Initiation consists of the willingness to set out, to begin, to step into something with no certain outcome. Tribal initiations both bind and unbind aspects of a person's life. The initiate keeps being unmade and remade. Each of us has a core of spirit and soul that can tolerate the unmaking and grow into a new form. Bonds are temporarily undone, and the rebinding realigns essential elements of the life of an individual and a group. It is everyone's affair, but the core remains individual and mysterious. The core events are between the individual and the mysterious forces of life. Initiation is a way of effecting deep change that is inherently dangerous. Undoing the threads that bind individuals and groups in order to get more life into both attracts danger at the points of undoing and remaking. The danger can't be predicted exactly. The risk is always death, but only a brush with death can allow more life to enter.

CHAPTER 14

CONDITIONS ON THE SOUL

IF THESE OLD stories are tapestries that show images of tribal rites and memories, what have they to do with people living in a modern world that operates without such rituals? Since the conditions of modern life are so drastically different from the ways of ancient cultures, what value has the study of initiation to everyday life? If there is a value, is it strictly personal or only for a few?

First, other than the imprints from the family during childhood, initiatory events are what make a person who they are and open the ground for growth after childhood. This is as true now as it was in ancient cultures. But also, I believe that events that mark an individual permanently happen within the larger, sweeping events of a culture, and these indelibly imprint a generation. Once a person has separated from the family they enter the waters of the culture and become a member of a group caught in certain waves of events, in conditions of the soul placed by the larger forces of society. By the time an individual reaches shore again from these two journeys, he or she is changed forever, personally and collectively, even if unaware of it in initiatory terms.

The generation, the community, and the culture-at-large are the next family for the individual. However, when people aren't initiated into specific relationships within the larger culture, they don't feel as responsible for the conditions of their generation, those that preceded them or those that follow. Through the phases of separation, ordeals, and return, the generations are made both related and distinct. When each generation handles life-marking events apart, the result is an excess of self-interest, hostility, and resentment among everyone.

The popular term for the relationship between generations is "the gap," as if the only thing that connects one generation to another is separation or distance. Initiation makes a connection across that gap; it creates communication between the lives of one generation and the lives of the next. Besides tempering the character of the individual, initiation attempts, on a cultural level, to make bridges from one generation to the next so that people can go back and forth across the bridge and exchange necessary information. The generation gap can also be seen, in initiatory terms, as the opening that is called separation. The space between is not supposed to remain empty. The generations are not supposed to seal themselves off from one another. Rather, the generations in succession are fated to move through the stages of life together. To find and maintain a sense of continuity and community, they have to step into the fire and waters that tend to flame and flow in the gap between them.

The larger events that sweep a person away from their family and into the waters of life are often named, so that we can identify ourselves as part of the Lost Generation, the Depression Generation, the World War Generation, Generation X. If those titles are seen as images of ordeals, you get the sense that each generation is carried by the sweep of waves of change. Within every sweep, through the ordeals that are presented to a whole group, each individual has his or her own twistings and turnings. Another way to say it is that there are individual games of chess that put conditions on the soul, and there are larger games that bring many people to the board.

One of the problems today is the increasing alienation of young people during and after periods of ordeal, which is intensified because there are generation gaps without generation bridges. When there is no community waiting to welcome, acknowledge, and close the life breaks of youth, the separations and ordeals tend to continue. They may quiet down, they may submerge, they may be repressed, and they may cause people to be depressed, but they continue. In that sense, I feel that the extreme separations and ordeals that began in the 1960s still continue in the 1990s. The tearing open of the culture through the Vietnam War, the Civil Rights Movement, the Women's Movement, and the Cold War has not yet ended. These serious divisions, which affect our culture's understanding of life and death, continue to divide. Thirty years later, the same issues press on the next generation. The issues of the current generation are the children of the issues of the previous generation.

In the context of these gaps and separations, unfinished ordeals and unwitnessed returns, I feel it necessary to tell part of a personal story. Within it are some of the pieces of ordeal and much of a stage of separation that I experienced. Although it is a story of individual separation and wandering in exile, it rests uneasily within a cultural separation, which I feel is a generation's experience that still seeks a proper conclusion before other gaps can be bridged.

By the time I sat down and accepted the game of chance from the hands of fate, I already had opinions and questions about the Vietnam War. Everybody did, everyone was questioning and arguing about the purpose of the war and the intentions behind it. It was a questionable war. In the midst of the questionings, I received a draft notice. This was before "the lottery," which named and made clear that this was a game of chance being played by a whole generation. It was before numbers were issued to all the eligible young men, who then, willing or unwilling, found themselves sitting at the table of the game of life and death. It was before it was clear that the chess board was spread across the country, though the luck of the draw was already affecting most of the people of three generations.

The draft notice was like a message from the chess game saying, "Check. Your move." It was saying, "You may not have known it, but you have been part of a game in progress, and it's now your move." This type of message, one that places conditions on the soul, requires a response. One response is permanent exile; another is to go for the gold whether it means a little death or a big death. There are others responses, and each marks a person for the rest of his or her life. That's how people spoke of it, and that is how it felt to those involved. Some were "deferred," which says that the game of life or death will occur at another time, probably on some other ground and under some other conditions on the soul.

Once I received my notice, I was required to respond within a certain period of time. I wrote a letter to the draft board saying that I objected to the war. If they had a war some other time, that they were willing to declare as a war, and that had purposes I could understand and to which I could commit, they could send me another notice. As far as this war went, I wasn't ready to kill other people and expose myself to death for unstated, unclear purposes. In effect, I was trying to say, I understand that conditions can drop on my soul, that ordeals have to be faced, but I didn't ask for this game. I'll wait for the next game. I was also saying, I've got an arrogant, intelligent horse that's above this.

The draft board didn't accept my objection. They sent forms that detailed the nature of "conscientious objection" and the rules under which it could be sought. My objection at that time was very specific and didn't seem to fit. It wasn't that all wars were wrong and I wouldn't show up for any of them, but this was not a declared war and it was an unwise war. I had already worked through to the realization that I would defend my family and friends against violent attack. I had seen the dynamics of battle in gang fights, and I had an appreciation for the feelings of tribal turf and the loyalties that underlie them. But I had also seen the pointless harm that resulted and the tendencies to get mad with battle; I had seen a bullet from a "zip gun" turn in mid-air, return, and strike its owner.

I considered the various options for a way out of the war. I couldn't object on religious grounds because I was currently struggling to separate from the religious ideas I had been raised with. The inconsistencies of the church were what were most evident to me. So, my conscience would not let me take refuge in the church I was trying to step away from. Eventually, the pacifist option intrigued me. This seemed like a whole personal philosophy that I could learn. So I tried to adopt it.

My friends and I hung out at a certain bar. It was 1964, and the war was often a main topic of conversation. Some of the guys would return to the bar on leave from the Marines and bring their new Marine buddies. Other guys were waiting to be drafted or planning to sign up. The bar owner was a surly man, unfriendly to strangers and young people. He would sing "Waltzing Matilda" when he was drunk and lead the older men to reminisce about World War II. If you wore a military uniform into the bar, you were not treated as a stranger and people would buy you drinks.

One evening, sitting at the bar, I told my friends that I had decided I was a pacifist. A big argument started about pacifism versus cowardice; another raged over whether someone could object to a specific war. Some said that either all wars were wrong or you answered the call to any war. Not only was I the only pacifist in the bar, but no one there really believed that I was a pacifist either. I wasn't sure if I believed it or not myself.

In the midst of the arguments, a friend of mine asked me to step outside. I went first, and he followed. I turned to ask him what he wanted to talk about and found myself lying on my back on the ground. He had punched me in the mouth and knocked me down. He said, "If you're a pacifist, you'll stay there." I was already getting up and saying "What are you hitting me for?" when he hit me again. He repeated, "If you're a pacifist, you'll just stay there." I got up quickly, and before he could hit me again, I hit him. That stopped him from knocking me to the ground, but it gave me a new problem: I could no longer argue that I was a pacifist.

I wrote back to the draft board restating my position: I wasn't objecting on general religious grounds, and I wasn't objecting on the grounds of pacifism. I objected that this was not a just war, that it was not a wise war, and that it was not even a declared war. Their response was a new set of options: either I appeared for induction or I would be subject to arrest and would go to jail.

As the date of my induction approached, I increasingly felt that I was burning with this question of whether to go to the war or not. Most of the guys I knew had signed up or said they were eager to show up and do great damage when it came their turn. Like most families at the time, mine was influenced by World War II and felt that when the call to war came, you went in service of your country, as my father and uncles had done. I only knew a few people who were opposed to the war—a couple of younger guys in the neighborhood and a folksinger I had worked with on a delivery truck. Mostly, I was alone.

So I walked many nights along the streets, trying to reach a decision. What should I do with these conditions: exile myself to Canada, go ahead and play the game, or simply say no? The feeling of "no" was the strongest, but I didn't know what the no was. Was it no more excuses, go there and fight? Was it no more time for growing up, go and face death now? Was it no way of getting away from the opinions of friends and family? Was it no way to live in this country but you must go somewhere else? Was it no way to avoid jail? Or was it no way to say "no" when called outside to fight?

Eventually, the day came and I went to my induction appointment with the questions still unanswered. I was walking forward, but the voice inside was still saying no. Inside I was still picking up one position and laying it down for another. Everyone else that showed up seemed wrapped in a similar shroud of silence. I guessed that they were examining the conditions set on their souls as well. We were inducted in the midst of our confusions, each standing there for reasons we couldn't have articulated, but we didn't have to. The induction was general, not specific. What we shared was a common age grouping, a common area of birth, and a date with fate or destiny.

So we all got on a train. It was before dawn on a midwinter morning, and it was cold. The train rumbled out of Whitehall Street in New York, banging through the sleeping city, and headed south. Eventually, there was an announcement that the train would stop for half an hour. We could get off and stretch our legs. Someone suggested that there was enough time to make it to a liquor store, and a bunch of us headed off to find one. Sure enough, there was one nearby.

We rushed in there like madmen, hoping either to put out the fire inside or to fire up some courage. I bought a pint of Irish whiskey, and soon, back on the train, there was a strange party going on. Bottles were being passed around, voices were growing louder, jokes were being told. We now looked like a bunch of young guys headed to a football camp or a game.

There was an African-American man sitting quietly by himself. I became curious about his continued silence. I went over, offered him a drink from my little bottle of whiskey, and asked why he was so quiet. He took a drink and handed me the bottle. He said he was planning how to get out. I said I had been thinking about that, too, but it seemed a little late now. The train was moving pretty fast. We didn't know where we were. It was too late to get out or get off. He said quietly, "I'm going to get out." I asked how he was going to do it. He said, "Two words." "What?" I replied. He said he was going to use two words. He didn't want to say any more about it except, "You'll see. I'll get out with two words." We had another drink of whiskey. The word whiskey, I remembered, is an adaptation of two old Gaelic words, *Ouishque-bagh*, which means "Water of Life." I wondered if it wasn't a question rather than a statement: Water of Life or Water of Death?

When the train reached the army camp, it was night again. As we ran toward the lights of the distant building, I stayed near the quiet man with the two words. We entered a brightly lit orientation center and sat stiffly in chairs. A sergeant stood up and began to tell us what was what. In the midst of our confusion and uncertainty, he was pretty impressive. His uniform was perfectly pressed, his posture erect. He had prepared this speech, and he boomed it out with a big voice and very little hesitation. He looked strong. He had golden stripes on his arm, and he was laying down the law. When he took a break, a captain stood up and explained that he was an officer and a priest. He talked to us of God and war. I was reminded of the conscientious objection forms as well as of my study of religious wars. I felt disoriented again.

Soon enough, the sergeant began to read the roll call. When each of us heard his name, he was to snap to attention and say, "Present, sir." A wave of nausea went over me. A voice in me wanted to say, "No, no, I won't jump to attention. No, I'm not present. No, sir. I'm here against my will, and against my better judgment. I'm here against everything that I know about living." I began to worry about what I would do when he called my name. Eventually, he did. I stood up slowly and nodded my head. The sergeant repeated my name more loudly. I knew he was insisting that I answer with, "Present, sir." I felt like I was back in grade school. Finally, I said, "Present." He went on to the next name, and I sat down.

When one name was called, no one answered. The sergeant read it again; no answer. Someone was sent to check the head count. After the full list was called, there was still no answer to that name. The sergeant asked if anyone knew whose name it was. I knew right away that it was the man with whom I had shared the whiskey, but I didn't say anything. He was sitting there quietly, just as he had been on the train. He was inside himself. Each time his name was said, he barely breathed, didn't flinch or move. Soon there were men in uniform going all over the room trying to figure out whose name it was and why there was no answer to it.

The men in uniform told us to look around and, if we saw someone near us who had not answered, to speak up. We hadn't even put on uniforms yet, but we were being asked to point out anyone who was different from us. It was a critical little event. As I learned later, this pressure to join the group would be applied every time someone was beginning to separate from the group. Sure enough, someone sitting nearby gestured toward the quiet black man. The sergeant came over, veins popping out of his neck, his body stiffly at attention, air puffed into his chest so that he seemed larger than he had before. He yelled at the man to stand up. The man just sat there. The sergeant yelled it louder. No answer. He insisted that the man stand up and answer to the name. Slowly, the quiet man stood up, and while every ear listened, he simply said, "Fuck you." Two words.

The sergeant was beside himself. He looked ready to blow up. He called for a captain—not the priest but another captain—who came and gave orders to the quiet man. Once more, this man slowly stood up and said his two words. Repeatedly, orders were given to him, and whenever he did answer, it was with the same two words: "Fuck you." He was roughly taken out of the room. There was one empty chair now among the group. The sergeant pulled himself together and returned to telling us what was what.

Now I realized that this man's quietness had been partly his way of concentrating so that he would be able to put everything into those two words. There had to be nothing in them that could be interpreted as hesitation, as holding back, as any tendency to agree to participate. His two words were the complete antidote to "Present, sir."

The next day we were ordered to the barbershops where we had our heads shaved. Then we were taken outside, lined up in ranks, and made to double-time in place. It was piercingly cold, and because of my hair being cut off, my new hat was bouncing around on my head. Just as I was adding up all these discomforts, I saw the quiet man, still in civilian clothes, walking between two armed soldiers. We were ordered back to our tents, while he was being taken in another direction. I broke ranks and ran to where he was. I had to know what had happened. He said, "Up until now I've only said two words. I'm on my way home. Good luck, man." I ran back to my position and double-timed along with the rest of the soldiers, but now I was not so cold.

I felt a lot of respect for the simplicity of his plan and for the way he stuck to it and achieved what he wanted; his success warmed me. He had acted out and spoken out beyond the ambiguity that I felt. He had said yes and said no. Showing up was accepting the conditions of the game, and refusing to go any further was setting his own conditions. To my eye he had converted the general conditions to his specific life and acted within himself. He knew himself better than I knew who I was.

I went through basic training and on to jungle training in Panama. The day came when our entire battalion was gathered in an outdoor amphitheater. An officer was showing maps and photos of Vietnam and describing how the Vietnamese would secure a hilltop, dig in, and aim various types of guns down the hill. Our mission in this example was to express our patriotism by running up the hill, knocking the "gooks" out of there, and taking over their positions. I asked a question: What was the value of that hill? He said that wasn't the point. I said it was a point to me; if we were going to be asked to risk our lives for that hill, I wanted to know the value of it. He said he was teaching military technique and strategy; our job was to follow orders when they were issued. I felt more conditions being laid on us. I tried another approach. I asked him if it was possible to call in firepower or planes and to take out the top of the hill with superior weaponry before we charged. He said, "Of course. The top could be blown off the hill, but that isn't the point." The point was that we were to follow orders.

Suddenly, an inner voice spoke. I stood up and said, "No. I wouldn't do it. It doesn't make any sense." A big commotion broke out. Other men spoke up, saying, "I'm not sure I would do it either. If there are other ways of taking this hill, why should everybody be risked this way?" Others argued, "An order is an order." Sergeants and officers began to run around shouting orders for everyone to be quiet. The captain teaching the class once again said that there would be an order given and everyone would charge up the hill together. That was what patriotism and loyalty to the unit were about. Once again, I said, "No, I won't do it." I was finally finding out what the "no" meant and what the voice was saying no to.

The next day I was called before the commander of my company and warned not to speak out again, and I was advised on the limits of my role as a soldier. I stated my position again: If I was given an order to do something as foolish as the example given in that class, I would say no. He decided not to give me any more orders at that time. I was left alone for a while. Then, someone decided that reverse-psychology might apply in this case: If I didn't want to follow blindly, I must want to lead. Suddenly, I was made a platoon leader.

The next training exercise was a war game where each company had an objective and each platoon a role in accomplishing the objective as well as a responsibility not to get captured by enemy platoons. Each platoon was given its assignment. Ours was to find and attack a certain hill that may be occupied by the enemy. Incredible! But it wasn't an intentional re-creation of my dispute over dying for an unnamed hill, it happened unconsciously. The assignments were random.

Actually, I would have respected a conscious attempt to find out if my objection was the same as a leader as it was as a follower. I would have admired a conscious test that turned an abstract objection into a concrete, albeit non-combat, game situation. The fact that the replica was unintended and unconscious made more clear that I was being asked to be unconscious of my own life and death. If they expected me to go up that hill unconsciously and die, well consciousness just might be in the other direction.

On the mission map there was a valley with a stream. I led the platoon to the stream, where we stayed cool and rested. When we returned late, I was relieved of my "command" and put on K.P., kitchen duties. For a while I washed a lot of dishes and did a great quantity of push-ups as sergeants and officers took turns giving me little orders and punishments. One day I was given an order and I simply said, "No." It came down to one word.

Soon after that I was given all kinds of foolish orders, and I found that I had no choice but to say no to them. As a series of orders and refusals ensued, I found my attention focused on one word: no. This led to a series of court-martials, which led to a series of punishments, which eventually led to military prison.

At the court-martial before I was sent to prison, I was allowed to speak in my own defense. Since I was confined to barracks, I had time to figure out what was happening within myself. I realized that I felt strongly that the war was not my war, and I wouldn't kill someone else to defend just myself. Then I saw that in the argument over taking the hill I had seen my own death. My reaction to assaulting the hill regardless of any considerations other than an order given was a glimpse of my own death on a nameless hill. Once I had seen my own death, I knew that if I continued in that direction I would die.

A part of me was standing in a fire, and when I realized what the fire was, there was no turning back. I could not change my mind, for my mind was already changed. Once I looked squarely at that death, I was finished with the doubts in my mind. I found myself saying, "No, I won't wear the uniform. No, I'm no longer part of this." At the court-martial, I had a chance to articulate what had been burning inside from the time I received the draft notice. Since the officer who was to offer my defense told me before the trial that the verdict and sentence had been settled at the officers' club, I was speaking for myself and to myself. That seemed appropriate in a strange way.

The military had difficulty accepting the finality of the no I was stating. What began as an exile from family and friends, from "the world," as everyone in the army called back home, led eventually to solitary confinement in a prison cell in Panama City. When I couldn't convince them with words, I used sign language. I became silent and refused food and clothing. I drank water only when I showered, and I was otherwise not present to them. After many weeks of refusing food, I was force-fed, and after weeks of that, I was released from the cell and eventually sent home to be discharged.

I was released from the prison, but not from the fire. When I had entered the cell I weighed 150 pounds; when I left I weighed 87 pounds. I was put on a plane flying from Panama back to the States. Everyone on the plane was military, some on leave from duty in Panama, most returning from Vietnam. I was handcuffed to two armed guards. They were Green Beret sergeants returning from their second tour of duty in Vietnam. Their job was to escort me back to the States and turn me over to authorities there. They were curious about my emaciated condition, so I told them some of my story. Their interpretation surprised me. They both felt that I was fighting my war while they were fighting theirs. They were the only people to whom I had spoken in almost a year who understood my position.

Theirs was a minority opinion. Many of those on the plane knew who I was and the nature of my protest. A sergeant from my company announced to the entire plane that I was a traitor escaping from real punishment. Many of those on board took turns coming over and cursing me. But the two who were guarding me announced that anyone who had anything to say to me would have to deal with them first. If anyone wanted to fight, they were ready. The plane quieted down. Then my guards told me about their experiences in battle, about firefights and the danger of being blown out like a flame on a candle. I told them of my feeling that I had been standing in a fire.

We talked in images of fire most of the way to the United States. They helped me see that from their point of view there was very little difference between their fire and mine. This helped to contain my fire; it protected me like a salve. From those two men I learned something about the role of "older brothers" in initiations by fire. I'll say more about this later in the book.

Eventually, I was released from the army and made my way home. It had been just over a year since I had left. My mother and father had written letters to gain my release. My brothers and sisters welcomed me home. When people asked why I had stopped eating in the prison, at first, I said, it was just an instinct to refuse food. If I ate like normal and dressed as usual, how could I say that I wasn't present? My position wasn't that I was leaving, but that I was gone. Not eating was a way to demonstrate that I wasn't there. Years later I read a newspaper story about political prisoners in Ireland who had gone on hunger strikes. Some had died of starvation while in solitary cells. This led me to research the act of refusing food, and I found out that it was an old tradition in Ireland—indeed, in all the old Celtic places. Traditionally, a citizen who is being forced by an authority to do something against his or her will fasts on the doorstep of the authority until the unjust and unequal use of power stops. Now I felt that my fast was not just a personal decision but was part of an old tradition that was known in my bones and had been activated by dire circumstances.

I'm not saying that my sense of justice should apply to everyone. But I am saying that the conditions on my soul insisted on being recognized. And I am saying that standing in this kind of fire, a fire that burns in the soul, connects the living individual to the fires of his or her ancestors. Ignoring such a fire can mean death to an individual, death to a generation, and deep wounds to the soul of a culture.

Years later, in a conference, there arose a heated discussion of the Vietnam War. There were many men of my generation present. As the discussion went on, men began to represent the various positions taken during the war. There were a number of veterans who had been in battle. There were some men who had left this country, gone to

Canada, and now had returned. There were men who had been conscientious objectors and had served as medics. One of these had served in combat; another had worked in hospitals. There were men who said they had used trickery to avoid going to war; with help from doctors, minor ailments had become major medical problems. One had feigned insanity; another, homosexuality. Each position involved some burning, some fire, some suffering. Their positions weren't equal, but each man needed to describe his burns.

The suffering of those who had been in battle was clear. In some men it was still smoking. When they spoke it was as if smoke was coming off their bodies from embers still burning inside them.

A man who had gone to Canada spoke about always thinking about the war and about men who died while he had gone away. Another said his exile had continued long after the war, when he found that he could live in civilization only half the time. The other half, he wandered and camped in forests and woods alone. Another vet told of paralyzing flashbacks and terrorizing nightmares and constant efforts to just keep from exploding. A man who had converted a minor ailment into a medical release told how that choice still burned in him, too. He needed to tell the men who had received literal wounds how he had made an imaginal wound his passport out of battle. Strangely enough, they had nothing but forgiveness for him. Their own wounds gave them sympathy for his imaginal wounds.

The ordeals and tempering of the men in that generation didn't happen only on battlefields. Men were scattered to different parts of the landscape. Everyone at the conference had parts waiting to return, and many were carrying memories and ghosts still waiting for a proper burial. Men are still waiting in hospitals, wandering the streets homeless, and pouring liquor on fires inside that won't go out.

That was one of the few occasions I've seen when the specific conditions of the soul had gathered again in one place, with no restrictions on speech and with an appropriate container to hold the various flames. The result was a lot of weeping and forgiving and some healing and some burying.

Men had gone into the flames of that war with certain attitudes and opinions, but they had often come out with quite different ones. Many of those who had entered into battle with a burning belief that they were saving the world or saving their country had come out burned. Some were still shocked from horrors they had seen, or from the contrast between the bizarre flames of battle and their return to a rejecting, disinterested culture. It healed and cooled them to hear that those who had not gone to war had also suffered and had held in their hearts some sense of great thankfulness to those who had gone despite the intense differences of opinion. Those who had not gone benefited greatly from hearing directly the suffering of those who had and from hearing their words of forgiveness. It was like finding the green glade after the burning mountain.

When looking at life with an eye for initiations, important events don't get "put behind" and out of sight. Rather, they are revisited as events that burned and might heal a generation and reconnect the individuals within it. When the fires of one generation are denied some "all-heal," they smolder in the psychic forest waiting for the next generation to try to leap through. When the troubled fires of one period are avoided, the shining city of inner resources sinks further down and the upperworld wasteland grows.

Because the fires of the last generation broke out everywhere very few have cooled, and most are still burning. The fires don't go out because people turn away. Those that were burning were thrown right back into homes and farms and cities, and many still burn. You could call it cultural posttraumatic stress syndrome or a generation standing in a fire. The fires are fed by all the unhealed separations of previous generations, and the flames flicker in modern cities and hiss from the mouths of urban gangs and reignite ethnic wars. The fires of war are ritual fires. Once they are set, they can only be put out by healing rituals of an equal intensity.

4

The Land of Fire

*You don't give a man a weapon
until you've taught him how to dance.*
CELTIC PROVERB

THE FIREBIRD

Once upon a time, not this time but another time, in a certain place, not in this place but another place where broad forests stood and many birds flew among the branches of ancient trees, there was a realm ruled by a mighty king. In the realm, there was a young hunter, and the hunter had a horse that was a horse of power. It was such a horse as belonged to the men of long ago, a swift horse with a broad chest, eyes like fire, and hoofs of iron. There are no such horses nowadays. They sleep deeply in the earth with the men who rode them, waiting for the time when the world has need of them again. Then, all the great horses will thunder up from under the ground, and the valiant men of old will leap from their graves. Those men of old will ride the horses of power, and with a swinging of clubs and a thundering of hoofs, they will sweep the earth clean of the enemies of God. At least, that's what my grandfather said, and his grandfather said it before him, and if they don't know, well, who does?

One day in the spring of the year, the young hunter was riding through the forest on his horse of power. The leaves were growing green in the sun, and there were little blue flowers under the trees. Squirrels ran in the branches, hares worked through the undergrowth, yet it was quiet. No birds sang. The young hunter listened for the birds, but the forest was silent except for the scratching of the four-footed beasts, the dropping of pine cones, and the heavy stamping of the horse of power.

"What has happened to the birds?" the young hunter mused aloud. He had scarcely uttered the words when he saw a big curved feather lying on the path before him. The feather was larger than that of a swan, longer than that of an eagle. It lay there glittering on the path like a flame of the sun, for it was a feather of gold. Then the youth knew why there was no singing in the forest; he knew that the firebird had flown that way, and the flame on the path was a feather from its burning breast.

Suddenly, the horse of power spoke and said, "Leave the flaming feather where it lies. If you take it, you will be sorry, for you will know trouble, and you will learn the meaning of fear."

The young hunter turned the matter over in his mind. Should he pick up the golden feather or not? He had no wish to learn fear, and who needs more trouble? But on the other hand, if he picked the feather up and presented it to the king, the king would be pleased and might reward and honor him, for no king had a feather from the burning breast of the firebird. The young hunter turned the decision this way and that. The more he thought, the more he desired to carry the feather to the king. He knelt to the ground, picked up the feather, remounted the horse, and galloped back through the green forest directly to the palace of the king.

The young hunter entered the great hall of the palace, walked its length, bowed before the king, and offered the feather as a gift. "Thank you," said the king, "a shining feather from the burning breast of the firebird is a thing of great wonder and value. But a single feather is not a fit gift for a king. The whole bird held here before me—that would be a fitting gift. Since you have found the feather of the firebird, you will be able to bring me the firebird itself. Either you present the whole bird here before me, or the edge of this sword will make a path between your head and your shoulders and your head will roll."

The young hunter bowed his head and went out weeping bitter tears, wiser now in the knowledge of what it meant to be afraid. The horse of power was waiting and asked why the youth was weeping. The hunter said he was required by the king to bring the whole firebird. Since no man could do that, he was weeping at the fate that awaited him—the certain loss of his head. The horse didn't console him, didn't offer to flee with him, didn't dismiss his fears.

"I told you so," said the horse. "I said if you took the feather you would learn fear. Well, grieve no more. The trouble is not now; the trouble lies before you. Go to the king and ask that a hundred sacks of maize be emptied and scattered in the open field near the palace. Ask him for three lengths of strong rope, and be ready at dawn."

The next day as the red of dawn burned the darkness from the sky, the young hunter rode out on the horse of power and came to the open field. He covered the ground with maize. In the center of the field stood a great oak tree with spreading boughs. The hunter hid himself in the branches of the tree, and the horse of power wandered loose in the field. The sun rose, the sky grew gold. Suddenly, there was a noise in the forest surrounding the field. The trees shook and swayed and seemed ready to fall. A violent wind blew. The sea piled itself into waves with crests of foam, and the firebird came flying from the other side of the world. Huge, golden, and flaming in the light of the sun it flew, and then dropped with open wings onto the field and began to eat the maize.

The horse of power wandered nearer and nearer the firebird as it ate. Suddenly, the horse stepped on one of its fiery wings and pressed it heavily to the ground. As the firebird struggled, the youth tied three ropes around the bird; he hefted it over his back and mounted the horse. In this fashion, the three rode to the palace of the king. The youth carried the great bird into the palace. The broad wings hung on either side of him like fiery shields. As he moved through the great hall, he left a trail of flaming feathers on the floor. The king gazed on the bird with delight, thanked the youth for his services, raised him to noble rank, and immediately charged him with another task.

"Since you have known how to bring me the firebird, you will know how to bring me the bride I have long desired. In the Land of Never, at the very edge of the world, where the red sun rises in flame from behind the blue sea, lives the beautiful Vasilisa. It is she whom I desire. If you bring her to me, I will reward you with silver and gold. If not, my sword will pass between your head and shoulders like a wind that tears through a forest taking off the tops of trees."

The young hunter walked out weeping bitter tears that fell to the floor of the great hall. He descended the steps and went to where the horse of power was waiting in the courtyard.

"Why do you weep now, master?" asked the horse.

"Because the king has ordered me to go to the Land of Never and bring back the beautiful Vasilisa, or he'll take off my head."

"Didn't I tell you that you would know trouble and learn fear? Well, weep no more; grieve not. The trouble is not now; the trouble lies before you. Go to the king and ask for a silver tent with a golden roof and all kinds of food and drink to take on the journey."

The youth asked, and the king gave him a silver tent with a gold embroidered roof, every kind of wine, and the tastiest of foods. The youth mounted the horse of power, and they rode many days and many nights. They came at last to the edge of the world, where the red sun rises in flame from behind the deep sea.

The young hunter looked out on the blue sea, and there he saw the beautiful Vasilisa floating in a silver boat with golden oars. The youth let the horse loose to wander and feed on green grass. As for himself, he pitched the silver tent with the golden roof at the edge of the world where the shore met the water. He set out a great variety of food and drink, dressed himself in the finest clothes, and sat down to wait for the beautiful Vasilisa.

Vasilisa spied the embroidered tent where it stood in the sand between the green grass and the blue sea, and she admired it. She came to the shore in her silver boat. From there, she could see scenes from old stories embroidered on the sides of the tent. She saw the open door of the tent and, within it, the hunter, who sat silently in the center of the scene.

Vasilisa left her boat and her blue sea and went to door of the tent and looked inside. The hunter welcomed her and offered her old wine and fine foods. She accepted, and they ate and talked and toasted each other. The wine was heavy and foreign to her, and her eyes closed as if the night itself had perched upon them. She fell into a deep sleep. Quickly, the youth folded the tent, lifted the beautiful Vasilisa, and mounted the horse of power. She lay as light as a feather in his arms and was not awakened by the thundering of the iron hoofs on the ground as the three of them rode back to the palace of the king.

The youth carried Vasilisa to the king, and the joy of the king was great. He thanked the hunter, rewarded him with silver and gold, and raised him in rank. Then Vasilisa awoke, discovered that she was far from the blue sea, and began to weep and grieve. The king tried to comfort her, telling her of their forthcoming marriage that would make her queen. But his efforts were in vain, for she longed to be in her boat on the blue sea. The king insisted on the marriage. She finally said, "In the middle of the deep sea there lies a great stone, and hidden under that stone are my wedding clothes. Unless I wear those garments, I will marry no one at all. Let him who brought me here return to that land, and find the gown." The king ordered the youth to go at once, saying that if he brought the garments back, he would be rewarded; if not, his head would roll toward the sea.

The young hunter walked out weeping as before, and again the horse, who was waiting for him, asked the cause of the grieving. "The king has ordered me to return to the edge of the world and retrieve Vasilisa's wedding garments from beneath a great stone at the very bottom of the sea. I'll surely die attempting it, and if I don't die from that, my head will roll from his sword. But there is new trouble as well. Even if I should manage to bring the wedding clothes, I'll be helping the king marry the beautiful Vasilisa, and I'd rather die than see that!"

"I told you," said the horse of power, "if you picked up that flaming feather, you would learn fear and find trouble. Well, grieve not. The trouble is not yet; the trouble lies before you. Now mount up and we'll go back."

After a short time or a long time, they arrived at the edge of the world and stopped at the shore of the sea. The horse of power saw a huge crab crawling on the sand at the edge of the sea. The horse approached the crab, then suddenly stepped on it with its heavy hoof. The crab cried out, "Don't give me death; but give me life, and I will do whatever you ask."

The horse said, "In the middle of the deep sea under a great stone lies the wedding gown of the beautiful Vasilisa. Bring that gown to us."

The crab called in a voice heard over the wide sea. The sea became agitated, and from all directions came crustaceans of all forms and sizes. The shore became covered with the crabs and lobsters who gathered together. The old crab was the chief among the crustaceans, and he directed them to move the stone at the bottom of the sea and bring up the wedding gown. The horde of crustaceans returned to the sea. After a time, the water was disturbed again, and out of it came thousands of crustaceans carrying the gold casket that contained the wedding gown.

The horse of power carried the young hunter, and the hunter carried the casket and gown just as he had carried Vasilisa and the firebird. Soon they arrived at the palace, and the hunter once more walked the length of the great hall.

But now Vasilisa refused to marry the king unless the young hunter was put to bathe in rapidly boiling water. The king ordered some servants to gather wood and make a great fire, then to place a large cauldron on the fire and attend it until the water boiled fully, and then to throw the young hunter into the cauldron. The rest of the servants were busy preparing the palace for the royal wedding. A great feast was prepared as all the people of the realm gathered.

Everything was ready at once: The water in the cauldron came to a seething boil just as the wedding feast was all prepared. The hunter said to himself, "Now this is trouble. Why did I ever pick up the flaming feather of the firebird? Why did I not heed my horse?" Remembering the horse of power, he said to the king, "Presently I shall die in the heat of the fire. I only request that I may see my horse once more before my death." The king granted his last wish.

Once again the young hunter left the palace weeping tears that fell to the ground of the great hall. He descended the steps to where the horse was waiting in the courtyard. "Why do you weep now?" asked the horse.

"I weep because the king has ordered that I be boiled to death in a cauldron already heated and ready. I weep because you and I will never more see the green trees pass above us and the ground disappearing beneath our feet as we race between earth and sky."

"Fear not, weep not," said the horse. "When they take you to the cauldron, do not hesitate; rather, run forward and leap into the water yourself!"

The hunter ascended the stairs and entered the hall. When the servants came for him, he ran forward and leapt into the seething cauldron. Twice he disappeared under the boiling waters, and then he leapt out of the cauldron. All stood amazed at the sight, for not only had the youth survived but he was now more handsome than before, and he was imbued with a beautiful glow.

The king thought it a miracle, and seeing the beauty of the hunter, he wanted to bathe in the boiling cauldron himself. He plunged into the seething water and was boiled to death in a moment. Afterward he was buried. The wedding feast was all ready. The people were all gathered. The great hall was prepared for the wedding of a queen and a king. So, the beautiful Vasilisa celebrated the wedding feast with the hunter. They became the rulers of the realm and long lived in love and accord.

CHAPTER 15

THE BURNING FEATHER

W<small>E</small> <small>ENTER THIS</small> story on the thundering hooves of a horse of power, as if the prince from the last story has become the hunter in this one. The black steed that rushed up from below the lake now charges into the land of fire, carrying the hunter to his meeting with the burning feather. He has entered a part of the forest where fire is the primary image and initiation moves through burning and risk, through danger and beauty, through passion and confusion. Two of the functions of initiation are to expose a man to the extremities of his emotions and to help him find his purpose in life. Without purpose, a part of the soul turns bitter. Without passion, the spirit of a man withers.

In this realm, a single feather can ignite a purpose that lives throughout a person's life. But it's also the realm where going one step too far can mean being burned to death. In the land of the firebird, passions, great imaginations, ambitions, and fires of love can break out but they can also break a person down. In order to survive, a man must learn ways of moving raw passions into forms that can contain the heat yet keep his heart open. The images and themes in this section leap like flames across cultures, across time periods, and from the edges to the center of the realm.

Once there is enough fire in the hunter's head, the feather is all that is needed to awaken the burning figures inherited in the human psyche. Kings are made and unmade, the most beautiful woman in the world begins to approach, and the great spirits of nature and dreams stir.

It's clear in this Russian tale that finding the burning feather represents a visitation of a great spirit. Nature is hushed; the realm of the king has nothing as valuable as a feather from the burning bird. Everything—both nature and culture—stops at the flight of the firebird. There are echoes here of the Holy Ghost; of the magical Simurgh, bird of the ancient East; and of the Phoenix that repeatedly rises from fire and ashes. But unlike a tribal group that might unite around such a soaring symbol, a modern gathering of men will be sent in different directions by the shining feathers of the firebird.

Each man expects that someday he will break out of whatever limits bind him, that one day there will be an outbreak of the spirit inside him. This spirit needs to be seen, and the power of it experienced. In other words, the psyche of a man expects to experience an initiation by fire. It expects that one day his whole life will break open, that one day a great opportunity will fall like a golden feather before him. Then he will be needed, he will be desired, and the purpose of his life will become clear to him. He will be faced with a choice in which he must go one way or the other.

This expectation lies not only in each individual man's psyche but also in the psyche of each generation. Each generation expects that there will be some burning issues that it will have to face, struggle with, fight over. As an individual or a generation matures, a fire builds, an awareness of burning questions grows. Both individuals and groups await the flaming feather that will send them charging after the firebird.

But seeking the answers to the burning questions, as the horse of power points out, becomes a task full of trouble and fear. Picking up the burning feather is a symbol for risk taking. The young hunter is willing to risk trouble and great fear in order to touch the gold of the feather that has fallen to him. Telling a man who feels a desire burning in himself that he is heading toward risks will not deter him. Hearing of the risks can stimulate the desire even further, because the desire is actually to be initiated through surviving risks of death. This desire for risk is a beauty and a danger in men, a failing and a strength, a dread and an expectation. Men are willing to risk burning up in a fire of desire, in a flame of error or destruction, in order to not miss the opportunity to handle a golden, burning feather. Deep down, every young man knows that only through risk can he open his heart. There, a fire is already burning, and its beauty and light can sustain the community, or it can become a raging fire that consumes the youth, anyone near him, an entire culture, the earth itself. The fire must be acknowledged and the risk accepted in each individual and each generation if both individual and culture are to thrive. Each generation enters the fires of change; denying or avoiding the risk of it increases the fire faced by the next generation.

When the young hunter rides out on the horse of power, he is driven forward by the expectation that a break in his life, an opening, will occur, but he doesn't know when or how. When it does the whole forest becomes still as a church, as if all are watching the golden feather drop from the heart of the mythical bird into the heart of the hunter, like a spark of destiny falling into his life. This ceremony will change him, stop him, burn away who he has been, and open him to a mystery of which he sees, in the feather, only one part. For a moment he is in a sacred condition, and that is enough to change the direction of his life.

Telling the story of the firebird to a group of men is like tossing the golden feather directly into the middle of the group. For each man, the flaming feather represents something going on in his life at that moment, or it reminds him of a past time when gold and fire fell before him. There are many surprises as each man describes what the feather means for him; we learn something of the passions and the purposes in each man's life. Some men jump up to tell their story, just as they must have jumped to pick up the feather. Others recall backing away from the feather and becoming as cautious as the advice of the horse ever since.

One man says that the feather was the moment when he realized, at nine years old, that he would be a writer. Another says that the first time he made love, his world opened up, expanded; everything broke apart, and he saw the depths of himself. That was the feather for him. The next man says that he had never held a flaming feather in his hand until he picked up divorce papers and found himself searching for a king who could tell him that his life still had meaning. Another man says that the golden moment occurred when he decided to have children; that moment began a series of changes that have caused him great joy as well as great trouble, for the decision forced him to open his heart and his life. A man speaks with certainty about the flaming feather in his life, when he began to play music as a teenager and joined a pickup band that took soaring flight, turning out gold records and allowing the group to live like kings. They were one of the hottest bands in the world, and they flew on the wings of a firebird until one of them burned up in the flames and died. This man survived the soaring flight but spent years trying to discover the purpose and value of it.

A big surprise comes in discovering how many of those who came of age in the 1960s and 1970s see the feather as drugs. A man tells of trying a "little line of cocaine, light as a feather," which became a burning habit; that first hour on the drug was like the "high-flying bird," but it led him into the hell of addiction for ten years.

The golden, burning feather is a symbolic piece of the heart of the firebird that causes a man's life to heat up and pulls him in a certain direction. Men can't necessarily understand each other's image of the golden feather. Each sees a part of the firebird, and the feathers are entry passes to diverse realms, ruled by different kings. But whatever vision, feeling, or action they are related to, they all cause a fire to break out in the life of a man. This fire may be anything from a vocation that calls him in a certain direction to a seemingly small choice, like snorting a line of coke, that has bigger and bigger consequences. Some are huge feathers from the beginning, and others start as little tail feathers that grow. Some see the feather as golden and shimmering; others see the burning aspects of it. Some men have picked up everything they've seen that could be a feather; others need to be reassured that their memory of an event actually involved something golden. Some are standing with the feather in hand, and others need to reach way back to find one almost lost in the debris of their life. The feathers drop into breaks in a life, either sudden breaks or the anticipated changes of life stages. Just as picking up the feather intensifies and changes the young hunter's life forever, so these turning points that the feather represents inevitably increase the burning in a man's life and make a clear break with his past.

Getting to the imaginal, emotional, spiritual heart of a person requires something extreme. Thousands of years ago our ancestors knew this was necessary. Elaborate rites were developed to connect the fires in the hearts of youth to ancient images that would sustain and unite the tribe. The hunter in the story has happened on one of those rites, carried there by a horse like those of his forefathers. He might as well have entered the deep caves of Lascaux and the heart of the imagination of the ancient tribe. There, in the solitary depths, in absolute stillness, lights would have suddenly flared, and he would have been confronted with images of soaring animals, birdmen, chases, dances, matings. The forms marked on the walls within the earth evoke the ancient images in the youth's own heart.

Initiations in the land of fire are as extravagant as the human heart, which has always carried mysteries and passions of love and of hate. Everything in such an initiation rite is extreme, at the farthest remove from the ordinary or normal. Ancient tribal cultures etched essential and mysterious images into high, treacherous cliffs and hid them in caves deep in the earth. The effort it takes to get to them heats the heart and keeps away the faint-hearted and simply curious. Paintings and carvings on cave walls and bold cliffs are so extreme that they have survived the passing of ages and the rise and fall of cultures. You can see the same instinct at work where young people paint and carve hearts that name their loves in difficult to reach and dangerous places. And, when the effort isn't made to lead youth to the heart of the tribe, you can see the angry messages in graffiti on other walls.

It was extreme to go so deep into the earth, and extreme care went into the theatrics of producing the sudden light, flooding with fire the "other world" depicted on the walls. A sense of the elaborate relationships between light and dark, life and death, art and ritual appears also in structures like New Grange. It was built so carefully that the light of the sun at the reach of the Winter Solstice pours through a hole and travels up a walkway to flood the ancient sanctuary with the first light of a new year and light up ancient designs on the walls. All at once the sun speaks from its point of farthest decline directly to the heart of people waiting in the dark, which is both tomb and womb.

There is no explanation for this event even now. It's a heart mystery, but it connects the inner expectations of people with the extreme motions of the earth and sun. Something extreme must occur in order to deepen one's connection to life, warmth, and beauty. Each youth looks for that extreme occurrence and will drive horses and cars full of horsepower as fast as possible to break through to that place. They will explore the depths of the earth and fall into great depressions in order to enter that cave. They will climb trees, mountains, and break sound and light barriers in order to touch one feather of the firebird in its flight. They will fall disastrously into the depths of love and lose all contact with the everyday world in order to feel the darkness that can only be lit by their fire.

Initiation by fire attempts to open paths to beauty through the risk of increased passions. Youths attempt to get beyond the limits of their own family and childhood and to overcome the inertia that stands like a wall at the border between boy and man. Within the young male, nature lets loose a series of eruptions that increases his physical size in spurts of growth, that throws his behaviors into extremes of aggression and passivity, and that opens his imaginal life into dreams and visions of flying and falling. He heats up as biological, emotional, and spiritual flames sear him from inside. He is driven to seek an outer experience that will match his inner heat and turmoil. If he doesn't get connected to the mysteries, to the warmth and beauty at the heart of the culture, he may burn with rage and injustice, or turn cold with resentment and depression.

The experience he seeks will push or pull him beyond what he knows, till he finds himself in an ambiguous, marginal area. Usually, a feather is a light thing, its hollow core filled with air and wind, but when a burning feather comes into a young man's life, it has the impact of an arrow, penetrating the youth and separating him from all he has known. When he reaches for that golden, burning feather, a crack in the world opens before him. Should he step in?

In this land of fire, the first step is not to "grow up" and take more responsibility. Rather, the point is to open up, take off, break out, and feel the feathers of the heart burn with flight. Two forces meet at the point of the feather: the charging passions of the hunter breaking out and a piece of burning spirit falling in. What happens next can lift a person's spirits or leave him in ashes. Usually, he can hear some voice nearby warning him that picking up that feather, that aspiration, that career, that lover, that ambition, that gift, that draft notice, that weapon, that train ticket, that money will only increase his trouble and increase fear. Usually, the warnings confirm his attraction to the feather.

In the story, the decision of the hunter is a clear one. He knows of the king and the soaring firebird and of the connection between the two. In many initiation rites, events are arranged so that the initiate begins to feel impassioned and expectant. The initiation may be a quest for a spirit vision or the practice of dances; it may be austerities and meditations that precipitate a breakthrough of spirit. There may be herbs, drugs, strange foods, or the lack of food used to break past the initiate's usual sense of self. Or, a person may be thrown into a competition or struggle that forces him to reach deeper, get smarter, or try harder than "ever before." The results include the flooding of the initiate with sensations, feelings, dreams, visions, knowing voices confirming that he or she is blessed with luck, courage, wisdom, strength, love, or magic. The results are then acknowledged by a chief, a king or a queen, a spiritual old man or wise woman. This fixes the blessing in the heart of the initiate and sets him on the road of learning to live with that piece of spirit, that beginning vision, that way of making or loving.

For a modern person, many of the ritual preparations, encouragements, admonishments, and acknowledgments won't be there. Extreme events will happen but not in the context of a ritual. There will be life-defining episodes, but the events won't open and close like a ritual. It may close too soon to reveal its secret or stay open so long that it burns too much.

The feather magnifies the self and reveals the life trying to live its way into the world, which until then may have only been seen in small glimpses. There is something particular around which each inner life takes shape. Inner legends and tales grow around the courage that one displayed at certain times, which seemed to rise from some well inside. Or, it may have been insights that came just when everyone else was stuck; or strength arrived that seemed superhuman; sublime nuances of feeling became a song whispered in a lovely ear; or persistent effort persevered through small steps painfully taken, alone, against all odds.

In these moments, the mundane becomes mysterious. Everything falls into place, or some unusual capacity breaks through. It can be as simple as a youth hitting the winning basket. He may not even be a great athlete, and he may have a limited career, but for one moment he rose in the air and released the ball at just the right time, making a basket as the buzzer went off, and everyone saw it and was drawn to their feet—a golden moment occurred. Something broke out of him, and some collected attention fell on him. He goes on and lives his life in this or that career, but frequently he reads the news accounts of games and watches tournaments where the conditions occur again, and he re-visions that golden moment.

Once, I heard a man tell, with exquisite detail, the intricacies of kicking a soccer ball into a net to win a game. He said he was completely aware of everything that happened within that moment—how his body lifted off the ground and then turned in mid-air, pivoting so that his foot could meet the ball, which was flying toward him. He felt, and could almost see, the little bones and ligatures of his leg align themselves to change his direction, meet the ball, and drive it toward the goal. But he could also see, through peripheral vision, the place of everyone on the field, and beyond that, he could see his father sitting in the stands. He could recall the feeling that was imbued in him in that moment, and as he spoke of it, you could feel it in the room as well. The ball went into the net, and of course, he's never forgotten it, nor could he separate it from the eyes of his father and his teammates. But strangely enough, it was the end of his soccer career. To him, the gold in the moment was the deep awareness and knowledge of his body. Neither his father nor teammates could understand why he didn't continue to play. He struggled with his own understanding for years. Finally, he began to study physical therapies and learned that the golden moment had been a glimpse of his vocation to study and work with the intricate movements of bodies.

I heard a man tell of his childhood where he was beaten almost every day by his mother and father. He described the incredible torment of knowing the beating was coming, knowing that the only attention he was going to get was through the distortion of this beating. But then, strangely, he found himself on the other side. Because he had been so beaten, his way of acting was misshapen, and his emotional scars drew people's attention. His schoolmates began to taunt and beat him as well, as if he carried a mark they could see. But somewhere in the midst of this, he struck out in a blind, crazy rage. To his surprise, this caught everyone's attention. In the red frenzy of the moment, he saw the fear in everyone's eyes and felt the effect of the power of his rage. Unfortunately for those around him, these burning moments only occurred when he was pounding on them, but within himself, he felt like he was getting the golden attention he desired. Eventually, he wound up in jail and lived mostly the dark, or shadow side, of that fire.

Such moments can be golden, holy, or just burning. If the flame of the burning feather, if the golden light of attention, does not move toward the symbolic, it necessarily moves toward the shadow. If it does not move toward the greater sense of the fire of life, it necessarily moves toward the greater sense of the fire of death. The light of this inner fire must be seen, momentarily at least, to move further into life. On the other hand, if the fire is set too strongly, burns too hot, burns too continuously, then the person can be burned to ashes, can be taken out of life like the blowing out of a candle. Ritual initiations are an attempt to ensure that the fire is seen, contained, and moved to the symbolic realm.

Finding the feather makes the youth momentarily whole, or holy. The feather connects the divine bird to a spark of the divine in the youth. In touching the feather, he touches the *numen*, the spirit in himself and in the world. Mana—holy heat—has fallen on him. In common figures of speech, spirit is often identified with heat and fire. When the spirit has hold of or has entered someone, he or she is said to be *on fire* with it. Visions are *burned* into the soul of man. In ancient India, *tapas* was inner heat, a creative sweating caused by a communication from the spirit world. This infusion of spirit and heat from the firebird, then, has put the young hunter in a sacred condition. His imagination turns toward the king of the realm. He wants to be at the center; he wants to be seen as the one holding the golden feather. He rushes there full of enthusiasm, and the center of the word *enthusiasm* is "theus," or god.

When the horse of power speaks, it does not say, "Don't pick up the feather," although some listeners always hear the story that way. Rather, what the horse says is ambiguous. It warns that the feather is spiritually hot, glowing with mana, dangerous with taboo. Part of the danger in the holy moment, when the hunter picks up the feather, is the fact that the feather, the firebird, and the king are all ambiguous. That which is taboo can heal and make whole, but it can also burn and destroy. The feather is both gold and burning. The visit of the firebird can lead to a fuller life or to the end of life. The king may provide honor and rewards, or he may cut off the young hunter's head. The only way to negotiate these ambiguities is through some knowledge of the inner drive to encounter a sacred fire and the great symbols of life. If a youth comes upon this feather without a connection to the horse of power, without knowing a king, he will burn up. Anything that shines like gold, burns like fire, and causes a respectful silence to fall will appear to him to be a sacred power. Hordes of men have confused the power they feel in holding a gun or a needle or a bottle with the sacred power they seek.

As we saw in Part One, there is an old idea that a person's genius comes into the world with him or her at the time of birth. Through the struggles of birth and the early years of life, a person's connection to his or her genius is overshadowed and forgotten. Another purpose of an initiation by fire is to begin the struggle with one's own genius. Picking up the golden feather represents a moment when we break through to that place of genius. But reconnecting with our genius means an increase in fear and sorrow, as well as joy. It increases both the fire in a life and the trouble. All of the passions heat up as the interest in risk, danger, beauty, and spirit increases.

There are two parts to the rediscovery of the place of genius. In one, we sense the golden light of the flame in ourselves; in the other, someone else must see the flame in us. Both are necessary for the fire to grow. When both occur there is an outbreak of spirit that changes the course of our lives. If neither of these things happen, we may die, either literally or inside. If others see the flame in us but we don't recognize it, we will burn just for them and eventually burn out. If the flame cannot find a life-enhancing way to be seen by others, then it will burn a line toward death in order to be noticed before it goes out. Just like any fire, the flame of genius can light the way and warm the room, go out from lack of attention, or burn everything to ashes.

The first time we touch the flash of our own genius we may survive by luck; after that, we must learn how to contain and handle it or we will burn ourselves and others. It's also necessary to learn where the flame is trying to lead us. In the Arabian story of "Aladdin and the Lamp," the genie, or genius, is suddenly released. It has been bottled up too long and knows it. Genius has expectations and intentions; it has a destination. The genie explains that at first he was ready to thank and serve whoever released him, but as time passed, he grew angry and vowed to destroy whoever set him free, raining destruction on the world. Aladdin has to learn quickly how to trick the genie back into the lamp, how to bargain with him and contain him. Genius comes from an ancient, fiery place in the soul, and to handle it, Aladdin has to know his own wants, wishes, and desires.

In a European version of this story, "The Spirit in the Bottle," the genie is found in a tiny bottle at the root of a great oak tree. A young man finds it while wandering away from where his father works cutting wood. He's hunting for birds' nests, looking in the tops of trees, when he hears a tiny voice coming from the roots of a huge, ominous oak. In this story, there is no horse to warn of the danger and trouble to come, so the youth opens the bottle, and the spirit rushes out and describes how he will crush every bone in the body of whoever has released him from his prison. Like Aladdin, the youth tricks the genie back into the bottle by pretending he doesn't believe that something so huge could come from something so small. To get out again, the spirit offers the youth a cloth that can turn anything it touches to silver and, with its other side, heal any wound. The youth accepts the cloth, and the spirit goes his way. The youth saves his father from poverty and goes on to become a great healer. Thus, the spirit that would crush whoever goes near it and set fire to the world also has the capacity to give abundance and heal any wound. But ignoring it, throwing it away, bottling it up too tight, makes it murderous.

One way or another, when a youth desires change and picks up a burning feather or rubs the lamp, he lets genius loose. For doing so, the youth gets exposed to two great dangers and two shining gifts. The gifts are the capacities to turn mundane things to riches and to heal wounds. The dangers are getting caught in the ancient rage of the spirit or concretizing the spirit into an addictive "high" of any type. There are no guarantees, no insurance plans, and no turning back once we touch the place of genius. We need tricks and special skills in order to handle our genius. Trouble, fear, and the heat of passions are the signs that we've come near it. And if it has been a long time since we were in touch with that flame, then the trouble and fear will be great, perhaps even overwhelming.

In the story of the firebird, the young hunter enters a "holy moment," with the burning feather in his hand and the horse of power to carry and advise him, but he needs acknowledgment or confirmation of the feather and a direction to go in. Being infused with the sacred also means to be in holy trouble, and like someone returning from a vision quest, he needs another to help him hold the vision. For these things, he turns to the king. Initiation by fire cannot be strictly internal. The king needs to confirm that the feather truly fell from the firebird's burning breast. Without the king, the youth would not know where to take the feather, which way to direct this genius fire. The king represents the center of the psyche and the culture. In story terms, picking up the feather at the edge awakens the king at the center.

If we stand at the end of this story and look back, we can see that the key figures are drawn to the center from extreme edges and remote areas. The horse of power has its origins underground with those horses of old, as well as under the lake in the previous story of Conn-Eda. We enter the story riding this extreme, old horse at some remote place in the forest. The firebird flies out of the sky at the edge of the world where the sun rises and then gets carried to the center, first as a feather and later in its entirety. The firebird also represents the sense of the holy extremes of spirit, beauty, and danger. And the beautiful Vasilisa must be found at the farthest edge of the sea, and her magical gown must be brought from its deepest place. All these things begin at some extreme edge and are carried to the center of the realm.

By looking at the end of the story, we can see that the purpose of all the fires and ordeals is the making of a new king and queen. And for the realm to be renewed in this way, the young hunter must go to the edges where the images of power, spirit, beauty, and love are scattered. Culturally, this means that whatever youth find in their wanderings at the edges of life, in their experiments with spirits and emotional powers, has to be brought to the center if youth are to survive their desires and if the realm is to be renewed. Some burning desire in the hunter led him to the feather, but there's no such thing as a little bit of desire; admitting that the heart of a person can inflame with spiritual meaning means nothing less than changing a whole life. Some resources held at the center are needed at the edges, and out beyond the borders of normalcy are the inspirations and beauty lacking at the center. The young hunter and his horse of power are what connect the firebird and the king, bringing the edge and the center together, the great forest and the great hall. The king and the youth need each other.

When the hunter enters the hall of the king, he has entered a rite of passage that will send him back and forth between the king and the horse. He will be torn by desire and power, by contraries and dualities of the spirit. The young hunter will go back and forth between these two poles of authority, these two types of role models, and these two innate authorities in himself.

From the king comes desires, demands, and threats of death if the hunter doesn't rise to fulfill the king's longings. The king has a sword that can bless or kill, storehouses of valuable foods, tools and currencies, but he lacks the mobility, recklessness, and passionate nature of the hunter. The king knows what he desires and what the realm lacks, but he cannot move from the center to satisfy either. The king's demand for a much greater exposure to the firebird is also a demand that the youth embrace his genius fully.

The king can be threatening, coercive, insatiable, domineering, and tyrannical. The king is the opposite of the horse and the immediate source of the trouble and fear that the horse warns and prophecies about. From the horse comes advice that limits the emotions stirred up by the king and strategies to keep the young hunter from losing his head altogether.

The course of this adventure, the size of the events, and the regulation of the heat are out of the hands of the hunter. The horse and king are also the two poles of the mentor: One brought him to the feather, the other pushes him beyond it. The reorganization of the psyche of the man will take place in the comings and goings between these two poles. The mentor, like the feather and the firebird, can bless and burn the hunter. Horse and king are two types of resources opened by finding the feather. One is demanding and dominating, extreme with desire; the other is patient, supportive, knowledgeable about limits, and intelligent in ways that exactly match the requirements of the tasks at hand.

The king and the horse can also be seen as two aspects of the elders of the tribe trying to be uncovered, and they can be seen as two directions that the hunter's spirit must travel. The king sits in the place of expanding desire, and the horse holds the place of deepening skills and using resources. They can also be seen as the hot and the cool poles of his psyche. The king keeps firing up the hunter with ambition and driving him to further extremes, and the horse sets limits. The king represents excesses and risks of all kinds, and the horse awakens every instinct for survival.

The king makes it all or nothing, "Either bring me the entire bird, the whole thing, or your head will come off." But the horse says, "Let's take one step at a time. The trouble is not now anyway." The king says, "It's either now or never." But the horse says, "Don't burn yourself out over this because there's more trouble coming." The king inflates the hunter and turns the heat of his inner fires up, and the horse brings him to the ground again. The effect of the king is to make the possibilities of accomplishment and failure monumental, while the horse deflates the effect of both. Whenever the hunter gets too hot, the tears of frustration and of sorrow begin to fall from his eyes. That's when he turns and descends to the horse. The horse converts the demands and threats of the king into requests for help and resources.

The king gives orders and the horse gives a sense of order. The king says, "Do it," and the horse helps him understand how to do it. The king is the seat of authority, but the horse has the intelligent strategies to accomplish everything that the king desires. The king is the genius in the hunter, fully blown up and in charge of everything. And the horse is a companion of genius with technical awareness, limitations, expertise at the tasks, and the ability to keep to the purpose. The king has material resources and certain types of riches, but he doesn't have the ability to touch the great things of the spirit except through the hunter. The hunter can't handle these great burning aspects of the spirit without being in contact with the horse, which grounds everything to the earth and keeps supplying encouragement, support, and strategies to find the way.

Strangely enough, the king longs for something just as much as the hunter. In some way, they must long for the same thing. What is commonly called "hero worship," or looking for a "role model," is also looking for a king who can value the golden feather burning in the heart of a youth. The importance of a role model is not that he or she models normal social behavior but that he or she has seen the firebird, has touched gold and handled fire. The role model is the king of some world the youth desires to enter. The king is an ambiguous, bright, and threatening figure between the hunter and the firebird.

The horse, the cooling, strategic aspect of the mentor, can be embodied by another person who has a soothing, supporting, encouraging effect on the psyche of the hunter. Often when people are in the fires of difficulty, they imagine or dream of an older or more experienced person who could handle the difficulty. Or they wish they could act like a certain person, or ask them for help. The person who enters their imagination represents the pole of the horse of power and a capacity they need to develop in order to fulfill their desires and find inner authority. The hunter can't stay with the king and get the strategy, support, and help that he needs. He must go to the horse, who cools things down and lays in a plan and gives him the feeling and timing for asking for help. The horse part of this polarity feels as if it has been through this before and gleaned knowledge from the experience— it hasn't just sat in the place of the king and simply burned brightly with the glow of the firebird. The horse carries the sense that the whole situation and the whole psyche needs to be regulated and moderated.

There's a huge anger toward men with authority in this culture. There's a known history of the lack of blessing the spirits of young men and young women and a wariness toward anyone in a position to be demanding. This has resulted in an excess of passion in some and a lack of it in others. The image of the king sitting there, issuing demand after demand, holding the sword over the head of anyone seeking a blessing is much more familiar than the helpful horse. When men speak from this part of the story, the anger and wariness speak first.

"Wait a minute," says one man. "I'm angry at this king that demands one thing after another and won't do it for himself. I'm tired of being told what to do by one boss after another." Another says, "I've walked back and forth through the halls of academia looking for one person in authority that would say, 'This is a genuine feather that you're carrying in your attempts to write a dissertation.' Instead, I've had mentors and instructors take the burning ideas right out of my papers and use them for their own purposes." Another man says, "All I've ever learned is that you can't trust people in authority. Besides, I don't need any big ideas, I need a job." And the next man says, "I don't need any more success at work. What I want to know is what happens to the passion for life? Where does it go? Can it be found again?"

The most common experience of kingly authority at the various centers of culture is the experience of it as dark, tyrannical, and even potentially cannibalistic. At best, the image of the king has become one of an ambiguous figure who may have authority for the wrong reason, will misuse it, may have great resources but probably got them in the wrong way, may be capable of generosity but wants something painful in return, and is not willing to suffer his own pain in order to get those things that he desires. The harmony in a chorus of modern men, even in a chorus of modern men and women, comes from the shared knowledge of the darker side of the ambiguous king figures.

Initiations in the land of fire require both the threat of the extreme king and the reassurance and reserve of the horse. The job of the hunter in these adventures is to stay in touch with the feather, to survive in the midst of the flames, to hope on his way to the throne and despair on his way back to the horse. He is in the middle, like a flame burning between the two poles of the mentor. He becomes a display of the heart of the firebird. Once the burning golden feather has been picked up the king awakens, and whether it is the worst of times or the best of times, there will be trouble and fear.

CHAPTER 16

LITIMA: THE INNER HEAT

THE GUIDE THROUGHOUT this story is the horse of many powers, who can see trouble coming and provide strategies to meet each ordeal the hunter encounters. The horse also helps contain the torrent of emotions released each time the hunter finds himself in impossible situations at the margins of life. In the end, these ordeals by fire increase the hunter's capacity to trust the horse and himself. Standing ourselves on the margin as the next millennium approaches, we can learn from old cultures that value these experiences. If we study the last of the traditional initiations that are occurring even today, we may recognize in the separations and alienations in our own communities rites of passage trying to be seen.

The willingness, desire, courage, and recklessness that are part of seeking the firebird are aspects of what the Gisu people in Uganda call Litima. To them, Litima is the violent emotion peculiar to the masculine part of things that is the source of quarrels, ruthless competition, possessiveness, power-driveness, and brutality and that is also the source of independence, courage, upstandingness, and meaningful ideals. Litima names and describes the willful emotional force that fuels the process of becoming an individual. It is the source of the desire for initiation and of the aggression necessary to undergo radical change. But Litima is ambiguous; like the burning feather, it has two sides. The source of independence and high ideals can also be the source of ruthlessness and brutality.

The inner force that expects to be initiated is powerful and undetermined, masculine in tone, and eruptive in style. In the story, the firebird represents just such an ambiguous eruption. When it comes, the waves crash, the very trees shake and tremble. There's violence about. Everything else falls to silence. Similarly, societies that attend to the initiation of youth provide rituals that require that everything else come to a halt. Questions hang in the air: Will this generation of youth find a connection to spiritual meaning and beauty that can lift the flames of Litima to the high emotions and ideals that keep the light at the center of the tribe burning? Or, will they be a generation of possessive, power-driven people? When the questions are not seriously entered, the eruptive inner forces move toward physical violence, possessiveness, and brutality.

Young men and women need help in order to open themselves to adulthood. The raw passions and ideals of youth need expression and attention if they are to grow toward the skills and wisdom of elders. Although radical change can occur at any time in a person's life, the force and desire for it necessarily occurs in youth. Cultures that provide initiations offer a ritual for awakening the spirit of each initiate and letting his or her emotions flow; they give the Litima a channel through which it can be expressed. These cultures know that the fire in each youth, the emotional body of each, must be seen, tested, and educated. As we saw earlier, to educate means to lead out, to educe, to elicit, or even to extract something. Litima is that something—both the capacity to erupt in violence and the capacity to courageously defend others, both the aggression that breaks things and the force that builds and protects.

Litima names a spirit characteristic of youth as well as periods of dramatic change. It is volatile, asocial, and mobile. It disrupts, makes friction, throws sparks, blows smoke. Litima intensifies everything, and the fires of Litima light up the hidden, shadow areas of the individual, family, and society. The red and black colors often worn during an initiation by fire seem to say that the road is made of flames and shadows, fire and ashes, tears and smoke.

This warning might as well have been inscribed on the care-instruction tags inside our gang jackets when we were kids in New York. My first jacket had to have the perfect combination of brightness and darkness, and I went from store to store looking for a coat that would display what my friends and I felt. We were ten to twelve years old. We had stripped-down bikes made from the used parts of other people's bicycles. We swooped through the neighborhood day and night, arms extended like wings, feet pedaling like mad, trying to catch up to our own spirits. If we had the same jackets, we would be part of the same bird and the same spirit even when we were apart. As soon as I saw the jacket, I knew I had found what we were looking for. One side was orange-red satin, smooth and shiny; it reflected light like fire. The other side was completely black, a dense fabric that absorbed light and reflected nothing. Even its black buttons were dull. You could disappear into that darkness. It was perfect. We each struggled to buy one. We wrapped ourselves in them and flew through the neighborhood day and night, sometimes red and sometimes black.

Later, we learned to walk slowly up to the corner, as if there was nothing going on within us. On the corner, Litima would accumulate around us like an atmosphere. The amount of Litima in the air would increase noticeably when specific guys or certain combinations of guys showed up. If the group was large, the amount of Litima would multiply rapidly. The feel of it, the direction it would take, the intention that would form could be dictated by the heat of one member, by an accidental occurrence, or even by a single word.

If there was "nothin' doin'," or only a few of us showed up, our Litima might turn us into an a cappella singing group, and we would look for a subway or hallway to serve as a resonating chamber. We would get lost then in the harmonies and dissonances of the songs and the little dreams they evoked, singing our way through the images and emotions in one song after another. Love songs expressed our interest in union as well as the loss and longing we already felt. The early songs of rock and roll and bluesy jazz allowed us to sing out our inner conflicts and rebellion. We made harmonies of our conflicts, and we made conflicts where there were dull, predictable harmonies.

We wanted to be seen by the people passing by: We were posing, we were singing in public, we were dressed to draw attention. But we also felt very separate from the mundane march of life through the subway and the streets. We were outside it, at the crossroads, on the edge. We became heated and volatile if questioned, yet we needed to get something out of us and into the air. Hanging out on the corner was like being on the edge of the village; singing in the subway was a way to visit the underworld; and roaming the streets was an internal as well as external experiment with Litima.

If we had worn red cloth, or had painted intricate, black patterns on our limbs and woven feathers into our hair, if we had been half-leaning on tall spears, half-standing on one leg like the Gisu initiates in Uganda, we would have looked even more how we felt. The feathers and painted designs would have expressed our affinity with the firebird's song and flight. Leaning on the spears would have shown our willingness to defend or fight: One hand was committed to the song; one was ready to protect the longing of the singers or accept any challenge that came along. Without knowing it, we stood like the youthful warriors of the Red Branch in Ireland, who set themselves up along the borders of a province. When a stranger came along, they would offer him a choice: Would you have a poem or a battle? For youth, it can go either way—burst into song or burst into battle. The beauty of the song and the edge of the sword exist in the same territory—the borderland of Litima. All the old tribes knew it, knew that the arts of life had to precede the skills of battle.

The corner on which we stood was the crossroads of song and battle. The dark stairs leading to the underground train were also irresistible, for there, between the ear-tearing, mind-wrenching passage of subway trains, we sang harmonies, bringing a kind of light to that underworld. Without knowing why, we found and made ambiguous asocial places in which to display ourselves. We were finding the edges of our culture, finding the marginal areas within the landscape of the city. This is the inevitable task of youth as they stand on the border of adulthood.

Our other job was to be ready for anything; readiness and edginess were all we had. We were strangely dependent on a surprise, an accident, or a sudden inspiration in order to move. If nothing moved us, we simply hung out, like a crew on a becalmed ship waiting for a wind to rise. It was as though we were waiting for the arrival of the firebird or instructions from a king.

Then, into the gathering at the corner would come a member who was angry at a parent, a cop, a store owner, or some rival, and this would ignite everyone's anger. The corner would turn red with activity. Boasting, cursing, threatening would erupt. We would push each other physically and emotionally like a football team before a game. The corner would heat up; lethargy would turn to frenetic dance. The outcome might be a simple dance of anger that overthrew garbage cans or broke some windows, or it could become a fight within the group or a battle with outsiders.

Our outer cool was a covering for an ongoing inner dance of constantly changing emotions and sudden crises of the spirit. In our case, eruption into dance, song, challenges, and fights were random events that overtook us. Many traditions of initiation prepare the ground for crises of the spirit and develop dances that display the emotions and spirits moving through the youths. These dances take place at the center of the community and at the edges of it. Feathers and fire and leaping into the air are common elements of the displays. During the leaping dances, all other activities stop as people of all ages prepare food and drink to feed and encourage the dancers. The initiates dance for longer and longer periods, leaping higher and higher and falling into ecstasies and exhaustion. The steps from childhood to adulthood are danced; the motions, emotions, and spirits of the youth are indulged and encouraged similarly to those of infants.

What modern society tries to dismiss as a stage out of which youth will grow automatically is actually a crucible in which the future of the culture gets forged. Adolescence is a return to the womb— not the physical womb of the mother but the womb of culture and of nature. The transitional period called adolescence is spent wandering inside the psyche of the culture and the mysteries of nature. Adolescents are always absorbing whatever the culture is digesting, especially its inner concerns and attitudes toward the nature of the world and of people. The word *adolescence* derives from *ado*, adult, and *lescere*, to nourish. The *adolescere* group are the next adults being nourished by the psychological, emotional, sexual, and spiritual foods of the culture.

The adult is the being who grows out of this second birth in each human life. If the culture doesn't stop for the crisis inherent in youth, the youths will become adults who are not ready for the crises they are about to encounter. If the deep conflicts of youth are ignored and left unresolved, the new adults will be unable to solve deep conflicts in the culture. If the adults feel they were not nourished, their elders will be ignored, and forgotten.

Hanging out on the corner or the edge of town, seeking the extreme where beauty and danger meet, pushing everything to the edge—these are all part of the impulse of youth to reach the margins of individual and cultural life and to dance in the fires of change. Left on their own, they will still find the questions burning within a culture and find ways of altering consciousness, but that is not the same as going to the edge and returning to the heart of the community with something valued and valuable. Take away the nourishment of a community, which sees beauty and value in the extreme dances of the initiates, and youth appear to be wasting time. Replace a sense of experimentation, in which youth learn about human nature and the unifying images of spirit and myth, with fear of change, and the corner becomes simply dangerous.

On "our corner" everything in life got dealt with in some fashion. But the edges of legality, morality, sexuality, and spirituality were approached and crossed randomly. Life-altering events and attitudes were neither focused through ritual nor guided by those who had consciously crossed the same borders. Where the accidental knowledge of the group ended, fear and ignorance took over. Idealized sentiments in our songs of love could be kept separate from our actual treatment of girls. Our displays of loyalty to each other could be proven by attacking anyone different: anyone too gay or even too straight, people who talked differently or had different colored skin or just different colored jackets. Our internal conflicts were pushed out onto other people and attacked out there. We had to act out and emote or we became depressed, but our actions lacked the focus brought by the intentions and shapes of rituals.

Looking back at those days on the corner, I can see that the conflicts we were acting out were in the culture as well. We absorbed and expressed back the sexual, racial, and class conflicts that were waiting in the shadows of the culture. If you hang on the corner long enough, you can see every conflict in a culture go by. If you stay there too long, angers and resentments get out of control. The marginal period can easily become a marginal life.

In tribal cultures, these "marginal ones" would be in the bush or in the wilderness, like the Maasai and Samburu initiates in Africa, or like the Fianna, who used to roam the wilds of Ireland for half the year, or like Australian aborigines, who went on "walkabout," wandering out, crossing borders, seeking the edges of consciousness. Each feature of nature was also part of a mythic story, so that they walked nature and myth at once. This ritual touched the old ones on the way to finding the next self of the initiate. In these cultures, the separation from ordinary activities, from families, and from the previous stage of life was literal and mythical. It was lived out, carried out, worn on the body, made evident to everyone.

The instinct and inspiration to separate, decorate, and be seen in the extremes and margins of life occurs to all modern youth, but the shaping containers of nature, myth, and elders usually do not. Displays of long hair or baldness, earrings, tattoos, strange clothing or nakedness are typical initiatory styles that arise spontaneously in youth. Although the roots of the displays are in ancient symbols and universal emotions, they often become random codes or even fashion statements in modern societies. Earrings are used universally to mark the shift of attention and feelings in both girls and boys. The ring pierces and decorates the organ of hearing to indicate that the holder is beginning to hear in a new way. The ear gets extended toward wisdom and beauty and pierced in a little rite of wounding. Later, the entire head and body are marked, decorated, and treated differently to indicate the sweeping changes occurring inside. What occurs randomly among modern youth was often turned toward art within ritual cultures.

The initiation of groups of youth, called Morani, in eastern Africa provides an excellent example of complicated and elaborate initiation rituals. The ritual camps are set up for several months each year, and the rites of passage take many years to reach completion. Similar to rites in ancient Europe and the Americas, many of the displays focus on the heads of the initiates. They cut their hair and enter a period of darkness and loss. When the new hair grows, it is colored red and covered with feathers. As the initiates heat up within, they take on the image of fire and birds. Eventually, they become moving works of art, dancing symbols of the spirit of the tribe. They move from loss through fire toward beauty, and eventually to a coolness that prepares the way to becoming elders.

Among the Maasai, the first steps are a stripping away wherein the youth give away all their possessions, ornaments, and toys. The hair on their heads is shaved off and replaced with ashes. They leave the village, join the band of initiates, and wrap themselves with black cloth. These actions strip away the hair and covering of childhood an envelop the youth in the black cloth of emptiness and darkness befor entering the red fires of initiation.

A double ritual is enacted. Because the search for a new identit must begin with the loss of the previous identity, the initiate is, o the one hand, emptying himself of childhood in order to open himsel to manhood; he is making room for the next stage of life. On the othe hand, the culture is also stripping him of his identity as a child. I other words, the youth both lets go of the previous stage of life an has it taken from him. He participates in giving it away, and he suffer the loss of it. Moving the youth to the edge of life where the radica changes can occur is accomplished by both individual and group; thi makes the process real and complete and reduces its dangers. When a initiation ritual is viewed from the outside, it can appear that th elders are dragging the youth to the edge. But as we see in modern life where adults minimize their involvement in the fires of youth, th youth head for the margins of life anyway. Without the support an assistance of the group, youths easily come to believe that the radica change trying to occur is leading them to their death. After all, in th depths of the psyche, change and death look similar.

The red and black cloths of Maasai initiation rites are emblem of the heating and cooling of the psyche, the flights and falls, th heights of hope and depths of despair. Psychologically, the period o youth is naturally manic and naturally depressive. Because their live are being remade, they are being pulled to the extremes. One extrem is the heat of battle where life can be made and destroyed; the other i the emptiness and endless reach of solitude. Both require courage t face. On his own, a youth can easily soar into an excess of flight or fall into inertia. In modern societies, it is only when a youth display an excess of one or the other that his or her predicament will finall draw the attention and concern of adults.

If a contemporary youth began to give away his possessions, fo example, we might see it as a sign of potential suicide. Yet in an ini tiatory culture, this is not a signal of quitting life altogether; rather, i marks the beginning of a ritual departure, a "small death" that wil increase the youth's life. By refusing to acknowledge a youth's driv to the edges of life and need for childhood to die away, a youth ca easily mistake the need for childhood to die with the coming of actua death. It is the elders' responsibility to demonstrate to youth the dif ferences between the "little deaths" and the "big death" that wait at the border between this world and the otherworld.

A youth who empties the child-world of himself leaves it for the children who remain. If he gives to those that are coming behind, then a link between generations begins to be made. Now, it seems more common for men to hold onto childhood toys and keep remnants of boyhood as if trying to stay in that realm. Perhaps the rest of life seems empty and meaningless, and we had better drag along all we can from the past or we'll be left with nothing. We carry snapshots of ourselves, albums full of pictures, as if to prove that we were part of a family and that we are "somebody." Some parents keep the toys and trophies of their children as if trying to maintain a shrine to the child that was. Such behavior seems to say that the only soul is the child-soul and that it must be sustained or all life will end. It seems to say that losing the child will not lead to finding the man or woman but to losing life itself. The idea that the death of childhood is the same as death itself seems embedded in our culture. The culture cannot open itself fully to the marginal life of adolescence because it won't relinquish the pristine dreams of childhood. It tries to hold onto the "imaginal child" even as more and more of its real children become brutal and brutalized.

In the tradition of the Maasai, the dark period ends with a ritual circumcision that removes the last covering of childhood and opens the stage of heating and reddening the psyche. This growing towards red begins with hunting for birds. The Morani must hunt and capture a multitude of birds for a broad headdress that makes a bird's nest of the initiate's head. Birds of all colors and habits are sought. The seeking itself makes the youth imitate the wide wanderings of birds. Lovebirds, songbirds, and water birds are hunted, as if to replicate the intense and diverse flights of imagination, beauty, wonder, distance, and spiritual delicacy of the early stages of initiation. Feathers from three dozen birds may be used in a headdress that is then worn while dancing before the tribe. The Morani become birdlike or bird-headed, like similar images depicted in cave paintings on all continents. They join Horus of Egypt, the shamans of Siberia, the feathered braves of the American plains, and the hunter in the story when he is enveloped by the firebird.

The birds' nests they wear on their heads are another symbol of their rebirth. During this time they cannot touch weapons, and no one can attack them. They are vulnerable, like birds in a nest. Even enemies of the tribe can see and respect that. And they are imbued with spirit. Harming them is spiritually dangerous to the one who would harm.

This is a temporary nest in which the psyche of the initiate broods on the elements of Litima: the ferocity required for hunting, the artistry essential to singing, and the gentleness required for loving and healing. At this point, the initiate is a small bird, gathering the force necessary to begin the fights, flights, and long dances of the confirmed initiate. He enters the nest from which his new life of greater capacities for aggression and loving will emerge. Later, when he is confirmed and wrapped in red, he will become like someone turned inside out.

Imagine if modern youths were wearing these self-made crowns, if their heads were adorned outside with what was going on inside—or if adults learned to recognize youths' spiked hairdos and Cardinal baseball caps in all their symbolic fullness. Then, both initiate and adult could learn about the actual and potential being inside the nest. It would be evident that the youth had left the parents' nest and was in his own makeshift, temporary nest. The brilliance of the Maasai tradition is evident: Inside the nest will grow the new hair of the confirmed initiate and the dreams, ideas, and ambitions that will be the songs of his adult life. The Morani are not only wearing their hearts on their sleeves but also their psyches on the top of their heads. Their inner emotions and spirit are ex-posed through their appearance, movements, and songs. In terms of our story they are moving through the great hall toward the king. They are dancing within the firebird and dropping flaming feathers on the ground as they dance.

The nesting stage precedes the immersion into a decade or more that will be spent "reddening" the psyche. When the nest comes off, the head is blessed by elders using water mixed with honey or milk, and then encased in a thick paint of red ocher. Red becomes the dominant color. The hair is braided, plaited into dreadlocks, and turned red like the burning feathers of the firebird. Many rituals are worked up for these initiates, and the youths perform leaping dances that grow longer and longer in duration. During the dances, they spend more and more time in the air; in a sense, they are flying. And they are heating up; they are growing toward red. The message to any onlooker is that this psyche is on fire.

As the reddening increases, quarrels and displays of competition occur. Fights break out among the initiates, often in front of the uninitiated girls of the tribe. Actually, the girls encourage the fighting; they egg it on. This series of spontaneous fights exposes the aggressions and even brutalities of the youth. Older initiates, confirmed warriors, monitor the goings-on so that the initiates don't seriously injure others or themselves.

The eruptive, aggressive behavior of the young males is carefully observed for its brutal and artful qualities, just as modern people observe sports heroes. The ritual attention we give to a specialized group of performers is, among the Maasai, given to the entire group of youthful initiates in order to learn the strengths and faults of their individual characters and of their generation. Eventually, they will be the tribal elders. Since they are writing the story of the tribe's future, everyone wants to read it and see who the authors are.

In contemporary societies, we pretend that this behavior should not happen, in spite of overwhelming evidence that it is happening, has always happened, and will happen again. Adults pretend to be innocent, and they unnecessarily blame all youth, of both genders, for the turmoil of their emotions, desires, and impulsive actions. The adults repress their memories of those disturbances, and the youth rebel or hide their own turmoil; instead of rituals of connectedness and separation, there is increasing alienation.

We see this stage in the story of the firebird when the hunter, following the advice of the horse, goes out before dawn, climbs a tree, waits with a rope, captures the firebird, and enters it. He does this with a combination of force and stealth. The horse leads him to the firebird and helps him both trick and capture the bird. The implication is that the great fires of imagination and spirit inside the hunter must be tricked and captured. But as the Gisu say, this Litima, this inner heat, this fire of imagination, this spirit of idealism and beauty, can also become brutality and tyrannical aggression. In other words, an essential part of the passage through the erupted emotions includes surviving angers and rages and learning to keep the spirit but not to the point of brutality.

During the reddening of the psyche in the lives of the Morani they describe themselves as emotionally volatile. They make no attempt to hide or control their feelings. Whatever emotion arises in them, they pour out into the environment. And they resist being restrained while doing this. They say that they are angry and want to assert themselves as individuals and as a group.

They often wander about free from responsibility. They raid other people's cattle, they steal food for their feasts, and they fight among themselves publicly. They dress flamboyantly and paint their bodies with dramatic designs in order to attract the attention of both the elders and the young women. They are promiscuous with young women their age, and they fight among themselves to impress them. They avoid all commitments so that they can wander and dance and engage in their conflicts. They sing whenever people look at them, make up songs, and decorate each other as if they were moving art projects. They are not just irresponsible and unawares, however; they do the heavy work of the tribe and protect the herds and villages.

What the Morani say clearly, the story only hints at. When the Morani say that they are angry and drawing attention to themselves through their emotional volatility, they are talking about the eruptions of anger, rage, and even frenzy that must be passed through to reach the beauty inside them. Presently, the modern nation-states forming in Africa treat the attempts to continue the traditions of initiation as damaging displays of irresponsibility, immorality, and illegality. But in these ritual reddenings, the borders and limits of everyday culture need to be broken so that the individual finds himself in some deeper place beyond.

Too strong a restriction on the extreme aggressions of youth also restricts their imagination and spiritual capacities. Not allowing the outbreak of the fires of youth narrows their ambitions. In fact, when the aggressions, even the brutality, of the young men of a culture are not accepted, then those aggressions are eventually directed outward toward another group. Aggressions that are not educated, led out, ritually continued, and directed can only erupt inappropriately or burn internally under layers of suppression or doses of numbing.

Since a part of initiation by fire involves stepping beyond the family and cultural norms to reveal the inner nature of the initiate, blocking that step can create criminal and deviant behavior out of natural inner needs. Asocial and even antisocial tendencies that could be openings to a genuine self lead to permanent exile and negative initiations that harm both individuals and society. In contemporary cultures, there is no assumption that boys can walk through a fire and reach an inner sense of beauty and spiritual worth. Yet, the capacity of youth and men to erupt in aggression, rage, and violence is in daily evidence. The concept of Litima says that in order to get to the part of the flame that burns with beauty and idealism, the part of the flame that has the capacity for brutality and rage must be risked as well.

In order to move this concept along, I want to tell another personal story where I caught a glimpse of this connection, of how blind, brutal rage moves toward an underlying beauty that can rise from the ashes of rage.

CHAPTER 17

THOSE WHO ARE BURNING

THE CONCEPT OF Litima and the images of the burning feather and the firebird are ways of showing the expectation men have that they will experience eruptions of spirit. Automobile makers, insurance agents, weapons manufacturers, cigarette companies, and many others predict and count on the willingness of men to play with fire. Because the need to move through fire is so essential it occurs both literally and symbolically in our lives.

Young men repeatedly answer the call to go to war and toward their possible death because the call looks like a shining feather from a firebird. The language of the call to war always invokes the expectations of a passage through fire, of being seen as golden, of being blessed by kings and loved by women. Although for some the call to battle leads to greater life, increasingly wars make actual death rather than "little deaths" more likely. In "modern wars," like that in Vietnam, everyone may agree that something is burning and feathers may drop in front of many, but each person interprets the meaning of the feathers differently.

During that war, some men charged directly onto the battlefield and were consumed, literally, in the fires there—in flamethrowers, in Agent Orange, in firefights, even in the "friendly fire" of bombs and napalm from the planes that flew overhead like birds of fire. Others went through those fires and came out—maybe barely alive, maybe half burned, many still on fire—but just surviving. Others picked the feather up and headed in some other direction, toward Canada or into hiding. Others took fire against the war, channeling the flames into protests. Some of these wound up in court and in prison. Each feather opened up a whole realm and a struggle with fire and burning questions.

My burning question eventually led to the military prison in Panama, where my education in Litima and fire continued behind the prison walls.

I arrived on a Saturday at midmorning, during the time when everyone was allowed out in the yard. There was a basketball court. I love basketball, so I immediately went out to play. I was dribbling the ball downcourt, looking for a teammate to pass to, and thinking that prison wasn't as bad as I'd expected, when suddenly everything went dark. I found myself lying on the concrete looking up at the biggest, blackest man in the place, who was asking if I wanted more. He had blindsided me, and he had also knocked the fantasy that this wasn't so bad right out of my mind. This was his yard—I could fight him for it, or I could accept it. I wouldn't have had a chance in a fight with him, so I said, "I just wanted to play ball." He walked away. I got up. If the horse of power had been there, he would have said, "Don't weep too much. The trouble is not now; the trouble is before you." The trouble I was to experience was the fire that was burning in the walls of that prison.

There are several ways to view a prison. In one sense, a prison is a place to keep people who are a danger to themselves and to others. Looked at another way, a prison is a place to store people who are experimenting with or caught in the margins of a culture. But seen from the inside, a prison is also an underworld, a world unto itself. The blindside punch reminded me that this was a stripped-down, bare-facts, raw world. On the way in, I had to strip down completely, bend over, and expose all orifices of my body to the prison guards. From then on, every time I left and reentered the prison cells, I had to go through the same procedure, just as all the prisoners did. There were practical reasons for this daily routine, but it was also a ritual reminder of who had the power. It was a ritual humiliation that distinguished the guards from the prisoners. It was a reminder that you had given up the most fundamental human rights. In a strange way, you were stripped down to who you were essentially. In a prison, if you have something to hide, it must be well hidden.

About thirty of us lived in a large cell with perimeter walls that reached to a high ceiling. We slept on metal platforms suspended from a cluster of low walls in the middle of the windowless room. There were few private areas and no private possessions. We were exposed to each other and to the guards. During the night, a guard would come through every half hour to make sure everyone was asleep. There was a rhythm to the guard's coming down the hall, opening the cell block door, walking all through the cell with his flashlight, and leaving out the opposite gate. And there was a period of quiet and dark just after each visit. Then, everything that could happen would happen before he returned. In the twenty minutes or so when the cell wasn't under observation, the men would work feverishly. Often, the focus of this activity was the building of a fire.

As I was to learn, the setting of this fire was one of the main rites of the place. After a guard had walked through the cell, the prisoners scrambled to gather enough paper and matches to make a fire. The paper was piled up as far as a man's arm could reach into the hallway outside the steel bars at the entrance to the cell block. Matches were lit and tossed out until the fire started. Then, everyone would hide and watch and listen. The guards would come running once they smelled smoke and saw the flames flickering against the wall in the hallway. They would immediately stamp out the fire, charge into the cell block, throw the lights on, and act as if they were going to catch someone with a burning match in his hand. We would all pretend we were sleeping innocently on our bunks. It was a kind of game. The fire was set in the same place every time, just as far as the longest arm could reach out of the cell.

The matches and paper were part of the very limited economy of the prison. If you were caught setting the fire or breaking some other rule, you would lose smoking privileges, and you could lose writing privileges, pens, and papers. These were the very things that were used to make the fire. Setting these fires was part of the ongoing power struggle in the prison. For the guards knew that the fires would be set, and they knew that these fires couldn't burn down the concrete and steel prison. Yet they still had to run down and put them out. In doing so, they were humiliated and frustrated. But the prisoners were momentarily freed from powerlessness and the daily humiliation of the inspection of their bodies.

This ritual provided drama that relieved the intense boredom of being in jail. But the drama had a symbolic meaning. Setting a fire was a symbolic statement that those who were locked up without rights and freedoms still had fire in them. Since the paper that was used was mostly letter-writing paper, the two discoveries that define human beings—fire and language—were brought together in a ritual of defiance. The group working together to set the fire by the cell door was essentially enacting a ritual that said, "We are human."

It turned out that at midnight a particular guard, who was despised by everyone in the cell, came on duty. The guard was a sadist; he was happy to guard those who were locked up. Even before I met him, it was clear from the way prisoners spoke that his habitual cruelty had affected the entire prison. Although we had many differences among ourselves, the sadistic guard was the most hated man in the place. In order to infuriate him, the fires were set on his watch more than on anyone else's. But I think his cruelty also intensified our need to make a statement that we were still human. Of course, setting the fire on his watch meant that he would once again exercise authority in some cruel way. He would find some contraband somewhere in the cell. Someone would get the blame and lose privileges, whether there was a genuine offense or not. There was a small war going on between the inmates and this guard.

As most wars do, the situation escalated. As the heat increased, some men in the cell began fighting with each other more, while others were planning how to get back at that guard. (Anyone who thinks that revenge is not a basic human emotion has never been in a prison.) Because of the frequent fires, more and more men lost smoking privileges until finally all of the cigarettes and matches were taken. This stopped the little fires in the hallway, but it increased the fires that were burning in the walls of the prison.

Everyone was used to getting up at least once a night to make the fire, so now we would all wake up and have twenty minutes with nothing to do. By this time, I had made some friends, and we began to gather to talk about an alternative to making the fire, partially to provide some variety and partially to regain smoking privileges. There were other groups in the general cell, as well, such as those who gathered around the big, black man who was the king of the yard and those who gathered around a Jewish man from New York who could some-how manage to smuggle drugs into the prison on a weekly basis. When these other groups found out that we were having a meeting, they were afraid that we were planning something against them, so they insisted on joining us. Very soon, what had started out as a small group gathered around one bunk became the entire thirty men gathered in a kind of congress.

The focus was clear: Could we find something to do other than set fires in the hallway? By considering this question, we had already begun doing it. Each night, at least twice, we would gather for twenty-minute sessions between the passage of the guards with their flash-lights. In the sessions, we would have an open discussion of what each man wanted to do. It was an odd congress. It was democratic and very human. The guards knew that something was going on, but they had no idea what it was. We had found a new form of power through secrecy. Because the guards did not know what we were doing, they were very interested in it. But if they were to come into the cell at times other than their appointed rounds, this would indicate that we had some power. So they stayed away. Still, each in his own way tried to pry or inquire. The one who broke the pattern was the sadistic guard. He would come in at odd times with his flashlight and catch us out of our bunks. This was a new form of humiliation. It made all of us feel like children. It made everyone enraged. The topic of the forums became what to do about that guard.

In a narrowly restricted world like that, the polarities of a given situation are quickly made clear. One faction within the general group wanted to kill the guard. They weren't joking. The feelings of humiliation, frustration, anger, hatred, and violence accumulated from childhood experiences right up through the most recent night of being investigated with flashlights had found a focal point. They felt if they could kill that guard, they would have a moment of freedom that would be worth the consequences. They would be free of the oppres-sor whom no doubt they actually felt deep inside themselves but who was also mirrored in the cruel eyes of this guard.

I was shocked. There was no question but that some of these men would do it. Several of the men were inside for assaulting other soldiers. One had assaulted an officer and another would occasionally take on all the guards. Another man had swallowed a handful of nuts and bolts so that he would have to be taken to a hospital for an opera-tion and in that way would get out of the prison for a while. He had been refused the operation, so he was sitting there with nuts and bolts in his intestines ready to do anything.

For several evenings, the faction that wanted to kill the guard discussed in great detail how to accomplish that. Meantime, another group was discussing how to acquire and bring into the cell appropriate weapons. Yet another group insisted that the only way to do it was to kick and punch him with fists and feet and not to use weapons. That way everyone could have a piece of the action. I argued for some alternative, like a lawyer presenting a capital punishment case before the crime was committed. I pointed out that no one in there had a term that was very long but that everyone would have a long sentence if they continued with the plan. I argued that removing that guard could just cause the arrival of another just as bad. I argued that it was wrong. I argued that it was as damaging to the soul of a man to kill as it was to the life of the man who was killed. They didn't listen.

Not only was I losing the argument, I was losing the respect of some of the men who were totally committed to the extremity of the idea. It was clear that if there wasn't some alternative to which everyone could agree, the congress would break into factions again. The primary faction would be those who would carry through the plot to kill the guard.

The only one who joined me in the arguments against the murder plot was a man from Puerto Rico who felt that it was morally wrong to do such a thing. He and I talked at length about what else could be done. He hit on the idea of planning a breakout from the prison, stealing a boat, and going to Puerto Rico. I asked if he knew how to sail to Puerto Rico, and he said it was somewhere north. With no more than that to go on, we proposed the plan that night to the rest of the group. Surprisingly, many of them were interested. It turned out that within the idea of killing the guard was a hidden desire for freedom.

Everyone began to argue about the possibility of actually breaking out of the prison. The walls were examined. Measurements of time and distance were calculated. For a while, part of the group wanted to break through the wall, and the other part still wanted to kill the guard. Eventually, everyone became intrigued with the idea of breaking out. A few of those most committed to the murder plot insisted that they would help with the escape plan only if the guard could be killed on the way out. That was as close to consensus as the group could come. So the new plan became breaking out of the prison all at once and disposing of the sadistic guard on the way out. The desire for freedom was not greater than the desire to punish the one who symbolized our lack of power and the cruelty of misused power. The only practical detail in the escape fantasy was the timing—the breakout had to occur on the watch of the cruel guard.

This was enough to start everyone busily working on different aspects of the project. The plan to kill the guard was put aside temporarily, and the nightly meetings began to revolve around the acquisition of materials that could be used to make a bomb that would blow out the side of the building and allow everyone to escape. Once the purpose was set and agreed upon, the ingenuity, dedication, and skills of the group became apparent. Men went to great lengths to acquire just those little bits of material that together with other small bits could fashion a bomb.

Everything had to be stolen while we were out on work details under the scrutiny of the guards. Since we were stripped and our orifices exposed and explored on every return to the prison, we could only bring in the elements of the bomb inside the cavities in our bodies. Once the group began to work on the plan, a whole new hierarchy of capacities became evident. Some men were capable of bringing large objects in without anyone detecting them; others struggled to contain small things. Once the implements were in the cell, they had to be carefully hidden or else everything would be ruined. Some of our evening sessions were spent with one man holding matches while another was taping something to a crack or on a ledge out of sight.

Eventually, many actual ingredients for a bomb were hidden throughout the general cell. Symbolically, you could say the cell was about to explode. I think everyone knew that as far as plans went, it wasn't a good one. But hiding pieces of a bomb throughout the walls of this big cell was an accurate symbolic statement of the fire that was already in there and the potential for the place to explode.

I don't know what would have happened if someone hadn't informed the authorities of the plan that was under way. But if at one extreme men can be sadistic and brutally cruel, then at another are those who are willing to betray. One of the men in the cell told the authorities about the bomb and the plan to blow out the prison wall. The authorities took this information very seriously. They immediately stood us all at attention out in the yard and began a thorough search of every square inch of the cell. It wasn't long before they found all the pieces. Then they began to determine where exactly to place the blame. While they were working on that, we were returned to the general cell having lost once again the privileges of smoking and of having matches and paper.

For a while, we were in there without the ability either to set fires in the hallway or to work on our plan for blowing out the wall. We also had the problem of a betrayer in the group. We now had to go about our meetings in a different way. Of course, each prisoner had ideas about who the traitor might be, mostly other guys whom that person didn't like. The murder-plot faction immediately switched its determination to kill the guard to a determination to kill the traitor as soon as we could figure out who it was. Actually, some of us already knew who it was. There was only one man in the cell whom we couldn't see clearly. He withheld something all the time. It didn't take much reflection to determine that he was the one. The question was what to do about it.

Someone had violated the unity of the group; now we needed to reestablish that unity. At one extreme, the solution was to kill him. After great arguments, long discussions, filibusters, and delays of all kinds, it was decided that he would be beaten but not killed. In a sense, it was a ritual beating. And as part of the rite, everyone had to give a blow; otherwise, the authorities would single some few out and put all the blame on them. At the appropriate time, the man was awakened, brought to the farthest corner of the cell, and each of the other men delivered a blow. He was then left there until the guard came through on the regular inspection. The traitor was found and taken out. He wasn't that seriously hurt, and he was now out of this cell—and our bizarre unity had been reestablished.

Meantime, the authorities and the guards were very disturbed, and they were, in turn, planning what they should do. Everyone sensed more trouble to come. As the horse of power said, "The trouble is not now; the trouble is before you." The faction that was most determined to kill the guard felt strengthened by the course of events. It was no longer possible to blow out the wall and escape, and it was possible that someone else could become a traitor. They felt the time to act on their plan was now. Those of us who had argued against it were in defeat. There was actually a lot of sadness about the whole situation.

Now I can see that the sadness came from this man revealing the plot to the authorities. The unity of the group was founded in the hope of escaping the humiliating aspects of prison, plus the focus of rage at the guard, and the surprising feelings of working together in secret. As crazy and as bound for its own destruction as the group seemed, the fact that someone would violate this unity caused a great sadness. And in the midst of this sadness, a new plan developed. If we couldn't explode the wall and get out, if we couldn't apply a force of fire to the situation, there was only one other way to go.

I don't recall how the idea struck or where it struck, but the idea arose to smuggle into the prison, using the same orifices that had been used to bring in pieces of the bomb, Magic Markers. In the course of the evening's meetings, it became clear that besides the violence that everyone felt toward the prison and those who guarded the walls, there was also a desire to express something in language. There were repeated orations to describe the cruelty of that one guard. There were elaborate descriptions of the feeling of being trapped inside those walls. There were reveries for lost times and lost freedoms. The idea now was to bring in markers and write on the walls the feelings that remained after the plots had failed.

The same men who had the capacity to bring in parts of the bomb now began bringing in markers of all kinds. It had to happen quickly before someone told the authorities that now we were piling up Magic Markers. And it had to happen quickly because it was certain that the authorities were planning some way to disrupt the momentum that had built up in the general cell. So we planned to do it as soon as we had enough markers to make a strong display of writing on the wall. Of course, we would have to do it in the twenty-minute periods between the inspection of the guards. We would also have to do it at night, in the dark. We also had to sustain enough good behavior to accumulate matches to make enough light to write by.

Just when we had accumulated enough markers, one of the guards let slip that there was going to be a general's inspection of the prison. The boat we had been planning to steal for the sail to Puerto Rico was the general's boat, which on occasion we were released to clean. The same general, it turned out, was coming the next day to conduct a formal inspection of the prison. The general, some top brass, and their staffs were arriving in the morning. That night, between the passing of the guards, each man began to write what they felt on the same wall we had planned to break through.

When we started, men were standing and writing at eye level. That level of the wall filled up quickly, and men began to crouch down and write below that. There was a consistency to what was being written. Mostly, it was "Fuck you," and "Fuck yours," and "Up yours," and "Up your mother," and "Suck mine," and "Eat this or that"—curses of some variety and great intensity. The writing was as furious as the curses. The legibility wasn't so good between the semi-darkness and the intensity of what was being said, but most of the words were familiar and had been seen on other walls at other times, so it was easy to read.

After a while, most of the ways of cursing people and things had been explored completely. The cursing had become elaborate—you could even say creative—in order to reach deep inside and capture the feeling. Images were beginning to come into the writing that were not typical of bathroom walls. By now, the lower levels of the wall had been completely covered. In order to continue writing, we had to reach up above our heads, and eventually one man would have to lift another man up. Everything was periodically interrupted by the guard coming through, when all of us would scramble to our beds and the whole place would become absolutely quiet, so the guard would not even think of looking at the wall.

Finally, men were standing on the shoulders of other men, writing with Magic Markers at the top of the wall. The men below were holding up matches to help the men above see what they were writing. As the words went up the wall, the cursing disappeared. Men began to write what they wanted or longed for. They began to write what it was that they missed and what was lost to them. Some began to thank people from their past or name a place outside that was symbolic to them. Others began to write verse. Spontaneous poetry that apparently was waiting below the curses began to be scripted on the upper wall. Some men were weeping, burning tears of frustration and tears of sorrow. Everyone was deeply quiet. Eventually, the markers were running out, words ran out, the matches burned out, everyone cleaned up quietly.

There was one more thing. We all knew that in the morning we would be receiving the grandest punishment the authorities could think up. We all knew that there would be an attempt to lay blame in this or that man's direction. We all knew that what had happened had come out of all of us and that it was surprising to all of us. It was something that we couldn't allow to be broken apart by the pettiness of punishment or by someone in the group weakening and betraying the others. So before the ink ran out, each man bent over, and another man wrote on his two cheeks the first two words that had been put on the wall: Fuck you!

In the morning when everyone went out for the ritual humiliation, the guards would see how we felt written on the backside of each man. In a sense, we were the wall walking. We were as solid as a wall, and we had found something beyond the shame and humiliation that we were expected to feel. Everyone went out, one by one, dropped his pants, bent over, and delivered a message to the guards. Since the general and his entourage were due to arrive in a short time, the guards preferred not to deal with this affront. They preferred to have everyone out of there immediately so that from the outside everything would look in proper order. They marched us out and stood us in the yard in ranks. By the time they went into the cell to see if everything was clean and orderly, it was too late. The general was on his way. There was no way to take all the words off the wall before he got there. The inspection of the general had to include the statements of the men from the general cell.

It was a long inspection. The general and his staff, the captain of the prison, and the prison guards had to read everything on the hundred-foot-long wall. It was too compelling to ignore. For just a moment, there was a reversal of the usual conditions. The authorities were reading the wall that had been filled with the feelings of the men in the prison, and they were held there by it. And the men from the general cell were standing outside breathing the air and knowing that they had expressed what needed to be expressed. We had achieved a moment of freedom.

Of course, we were all punished. Everyone lost smoking privileges and matches. I was placed in solitary confinement. I was moved deeper inside the walls, and I was moving deeper inside myself. But that didn't matter nearly as much as the image of the men standing on each others' shoulders and beginning to write poetry that they didn't even know they had in them. That's what I mean when I say that I believe there's a connection between violence, rage, and beauty. I had not seen all the markings of the underworld until I was part of that outpouring. Any tour of the underworld would be incomplete without that.

Since I never saw that wall again, it stays in my imagination as it was that last time, covered with writing that began in a furious rage and moved unevenly through sorrow into expressions of gratitude and affection, into shapes of poetry and prayers. This was the radical ritual that the little fires in the hall were burning toward: The defiant fires in the hallway eventually became the pieces of the firebomb that were hidden in the walls, and when the possibility of the bomb was taken away, the explosion that almost blew the wall out went inside the men and came out mixed with art.

Fate, luck, and circumstance caused the wall to be broken through in a surprising way. The wall was both in the prison and within our selves. The prison was part of a big war, and we were each in prison as a result of individual wars inside of ourselves. We each wound up writing from our individual fires of rage the anguish and torment of being within that war and being behind that wall. The explosion wound up coming out in the form of language, and the rite that resulted was one of complete reversal.

For a short period of time, positions were reversed and everyone had the opportunity to see and feel further than usual. The prisoners had found unity, expressed the full range of individual emotions, and made a group expression. The prisoners had left their insides on the inside wall while they stood in the morning air, not just standing at attention but standing full of attention. The guards were momentarily caught in their own game of humiliation and power as they watched the parade of asses talking back to them. The ritual humiliation was reversed, even to the point that the end of the body that usually can't speak was speaking with a collective voice.

Earlier, throughout the prison, preparations had been going on for the inspection of the general and his staff. Everything had been put in perfect order. Everything was cleaned beyond clean. This spit and polish and regimentation was a manic making of order, and the inspection was a display of hierarchy in the extreme. The general and his entourage were exact in their time of arrival, in their appearance, and their expectation was to be met with the same detailed sense of order and control. Instead, at the center of all the ceremonial ordering and hierarchy was this display of raw emotions and, amid the eruptions, the beginnings of art. The unity born of the emotions and confusions of the prisoners spoke from the wall to the shiny eyes of the medals and ribbons on the chests of the members of the general staff. The fact that something was communicated beyond the usual was clear from the fact that the officers didn't have the writing on the wall removed immediately. After the first passage along the wall, they returned and read it more carefully. Officially, they were outraged, but they also read certain parts of the wall again. I assume that those parts spoke directly to them and perhaps for them.

Litima is one of the concepts that has helped me understand this eruption at the wall. The inner fire that inevitably gets ignited within each person can burn things down or burn through to some expression waiting in the soul. The fire can become literal flames, explosiveness, or outbursts of uncontrollable rage. The fire can become fire power and bombing. Or, it can burn as some illumination in the dark. Each time this inner fire is approached, and each time someone picks up a burning feather, this dual possibility of the flame of Litima is lit.

Since then, I've seen this wall rise up in myself and exist like something I needed to break through again, or be there as something to cry against. I've seen that wall in broken walls covered with graffiti, screaming out from the broken bottles and broken dreams of city streets. And I've seen that wall spreading in the increasing number of buildings that require armed guards, the rapid growth of prisons, and the use of electronic searches at school entrances.

But, I've also seen the wall in the conferences that I keep describing. As men gather in a certain place, the wall is invisibly constructed. Everyone seems to bring some fire of rage, or outrage, and some sorrow trying to burn its way into language. To me, the wall goes all the way back to the ancestors writing in caves, the light being held by one person, while the stories of hunting game and hunting in the spirit were written on the walls. It seems as if the heat of emotions piles up and acts like a wall, sometimes holding things in prison too tightly, and sometimes becoming the walls on which the expressions of the heart are written. But I also see the ritual of writing in the dark by matchlight as being in touch with the firebird for a brief period.

As the Maasai and Gisu initiates say, they are angry, they wish to express themselves, and they wish to arrest the attention of the elders. For a brief period of time, and under adverse conditions, we arrested the attention of the authorities, and they responded as if they were compelled to read this language of fire. For a brief period, the firebird flew across that wall and even the eagles on the shoulders of the officers had to pause and attend to that burning flight. The point is not that everyone in a prison is burning with the inspiration of the firebird; the point is not that every contrary action and breaking of rules is an honoring of a great spirit. Some rages are so deep and go back so far in an individual or a family that they are fires that cannot reach a form of expression that is tolerable or beneficial to other people. But when the fire starts burning in an individual or in a group, there is an opportunity for everyone to go further than normal.

If the fire doesn't find a symbolic shape such as the firebird, it burns toward literal expressions of brutality. If the elders in a community don't recall, review, and carry some understanding of when this fire of Litima burned in them, they won't recognize it when they see it in others. The fire doesn't disappear. When the inner heat cannot burn toward a symbolic expression that speaks meaningfully to a community, it burns toward destruction. If kept inside, it burns toward an inner destruction, tearing down the body through drugs, alcohol, stress, or literal suicide. One great danger occurs when the fire is repressed, depressed, and compressed. The other great danger occurs when the fire burns out of control in a frenzy without the containment of art and symbolic images. In order to find the ways of containing the frenzy fires once they are ignited, we must turn toward water and the sea, which the king in the story demands and to which the horse of power guides willingly.

CHAPTER 18

COOLING THE FIRES

I F THE HUNTER never picked up the burning golden feather, he would have no entry into the land of fire. Once he does pick it up and bring it to the king, he faces death unless he finds the entire firebird. Then he will lose his head if he can't get away from the firebird and reach the beautiful Vasilisa at the edge of the great blue sea. One form of trouble is not getting far enough into the land of fire to be in the embrace of the firebird, and the next form of trouble is not being able to get out of the burning of the firebird. A person can't dwell within the firebird for very long, and every immersion in the fire requires some cooling in the waters of life, or the tempering of spirit and soul won't occur. The majority of the earth is water, the majority of the human body is water, even the land of fire requires the balance of water.

Although any form of fanaticism may qualify as being caught in a spirit or enveloped in a firebird, the warrior spirit is the most common image that describes being within something potentially berserk and capable of burning up a person. Most tribes and cultures have required their young men to enter warrior periods and warrior groups for protection and aggressions. It is one of the most fearsome appearances of human beings, and it is difficult to turn the heat of the burning warrior to another purpose. Cooling the warrior's fury, turning his heat toward beauty and intimacy, has always been a difficult task. When modern military groups release men who have been in battle or have been prepared to enter battle back into regular society without reducing the warrior fury burning in them, they violate old rules of humanity and turn the fire intended for their enemies on their own people. War is a state of frenzy subject to recurrent outbreak unless cooled and treated as an ongoing condition. The frenzy will rise again and again from the same place unless it is cooled repeatedly. In a person the cooling requires a reorienting of the psyche that is equal to the changes brought on by raising the inner heat.

There are descriptions of the reduction of the warrior frenzy in the myths of many lands. Stories that describe the great fire burning in the hearts of men often also describe how to cool the fires as well. These stories offer a vision of essential components for reducing the warrior and cooling the fury and fanaticism of inner heat.

In Irish mythology, the warrior spirit reaches its extreme in Cuchulain (pronounced "Coo-hoo-lin"), who leapt into frenzy while still a boy. He overheard a druid telling older lads that whoever took arms on that fortuitous day would die young but would win eternal fame as a warrior. Cuchulain went to the king and demanded arms. People tried to dissuade him, but he would not be turned from his purpose. He took a chariot and horses, spears and a sword, and headed for the borders where he might find a battle. Eventually, he encountered three brothers, enemies of his people from an ongoing feud. Each was a full-grown warrior. The first brother couldn't be wounded by the points or edges of any weapon, the second would never be defeated if he wasn't defeated by the first blow in a battle, and the third was swifter than a swallow crossing a sea. The young Cuchulain slew them each and all.

He turned his chariot toward home. On the way, he saw a flock of wild swans in flight; sixteen of them he stunned with his slingshot and brought them down alive. He tied them to his chariot with ropes and continued homeward. The wild swans flew above his chariot as it raced across the plain. He saw a herd of wild red deer that his horses could not overtake. Cuchulain leapt from the chariot and ran them down on foot. He caught two great stags and harnessed them to each side of his chariot and continued across the plains.

As he approached his own village a report was brought to the king: There is a solitary chariot approaching at great speed; wild white swans fly above it; great red stags run alongside its black horses; and it is bedecked with the bleeding heads of three enemies. The king knew it was Cuchulain in the throes of his battle frenzy and that he was a danger to the entire tribe. The women of the village went out to meet Cuchulain, and they went out naked to the waist, their breasts exposed to him. That caused the youth to slow down and lower his head, allowing the men to grab him and plunge him into a huge vat of cold water. The water boiled from the heat of his frenzy, and the vat burst apart. They plunged him into a second vat, and it, too, boiled up and burst. They put him into a third, and it came only to a simmer, then cooled down.

The fury of Cuchulain subsided, and he regained a normal aspect. He was then dressed in fine clothes and placed at the foot of the throne of the king, where he rested. Later he pursued Emer of the fine skin. Though she set riddles for him to solve and tasks for him to attempt, they eventually wed.

From the moment he hears of it, Cuchulain prefers to die a famous death than to avoid danger and die of old age. That's the nature of the spirit of the warrior, and it is very close to the ancient meaning of the Aztec word *macho*. The saying attributed to Native American braves, "Today is a good day to die," is another announcement of the presence of this spirit. But all the traditions that honored that spirit also valued it in other forms. The brave who says it's a good day to die distinguishes that day from others, and he often would not enter battle unless enveloped in the spirit frenzy. Irish warriors, like the knights of King Arthur, refused many challenges and battles when the warrior spirit was not present.

This story describes the reduction of the warrior through ritual methods in order to protect the people from his excess burning and return him to a human state. When Cuchulain arrives, he is on fire, his spirit extended from the soaring wild swans overhead to the jaws of the skulls hanging on his chariot. He must be cooled down, reduced, and returned to human condition for the safety of his community.

First, the women go before Cuchulain. In some versions, they are bare breasted; in others, they are completely naked—all of these old stories were written down by clerics who altered parts of them and omitted many details. When the story says that the women were bare breasted, it implies that Cuchulain is reminded of the breasts of his mother. Seeing all the breasts of the women of the tribe reminds him that he was once a human child who suckled at the breast of a woman. The white milk of the mother is used to cool the red glow of the gods of war. The version that says the women are naked connects to the ancient story of Gilgamesh, in which Enkidu, who ran wild with the wolves, was tamed before entry to the king's city by sleeping with a woman. One of the few powers strong enough to alter the course of battle fury is the love of a woman. The slogan "Make love not war" shows how one potent ritual can be substituted for another. The concept of "women who take the war out of men" connects to age-old methods of shifting the psyche from one inner realm to another. Water also dampens the flames of war.

As soon as the warrior's head drops from the position of fury the men of the tribe take hold of him and immerse him in water until he cools. Then he is placed near the king and dressed in fine clothes. Eventually, he seeks the hand of a woman famous for her beauty and wit.

There is no necessary order to these events. The immersions might have to happen first and the clothes from the king might need to cover and cool him before any women can be approached. In this story, the water was applied by older men who had experienced the same fires. For modern men, being contained in vats of water might be accomplished by being held by groups of men; these men can disperse some of the fire by drawing off the rage that is required for battle but is deadly to society. The battle frenzy gets talked out, washed with actual water, and settled by surrounding it with cool psyches. When the warrior is cool, he is returned to the center of the culture and dressed in fine clothes, like the hunter in the tent in "The Firebird."

The fury, going berserk, battle frenzy, are all ways of describing the inner fire when it burns in the direction of rage. Rage is a blind territory beyond the border of anger. In other words, there's a borderline between anger and rage. On the anger side of that line, the fire has eyes, for anger looks piercingly at its object. When a person is angry they often point their finger very specifically at what was said or done that stirred the anger. In order to be angry with someone, a quality of respect is also required. If respect is minimal or absent, contempt is a more likely emotion than anger. Although anger has a punishing tone when expressed, it generally has a point that seeks to continue feelings between those involved. When the point has been seen, the fire begins to diminish and the anger often dissipates.

Anger can maintain its focus, its point, up to a certain temperature that varies in each individual. When the heat goes beyond a certain borderline, the focus fragments and the eyes of anger turn into blind rage. It's as if the spear point of anger has been replaced with a fragmentation bomb; across that line, psyches begin to fragment and the fire takes over. The blindness comes from the loss of the point, the loss of personal awareness; the burning itself becomes dominant.

In another famous passage, Cuchulain's wrath and frenzy was described as a fearsome distortion that causes every part of him to shiver. His calves and feet turn in reverse position; one eye bulges out and one recedes into his skull. His hair becomes a tangle, and a jet of blood erupts straight up from his head and causes the atmosphere to fill with a red mist. In this condition he's difficult to defeat, but the same energy or rage that rises to defend the borders against enemies can blindly turn against his own home and people.

Most people would rather not cross that line. But, until people have crossed the line, they don't know where it lies. Another problem comes from the fact that anger protects people, and not going out to the borderline can leave a person unprotected. Healthy anger can work like the body's immune system. Anger senses when an invasion of personal territory begins and can raise a heat that stops the invasion. Anger offers the protection of heat and can be a light that clarifies the borders between and around people. Yet another problem comes from the fact that without anger the heat can drain out of a relationship. A relationship can end from having no borders or being all borders. Not having enough capacity and experience with personal anger can leave a person unprotected and can leave a coolness in all a person's relationships. When a relationship cools too much, you can guess that anger is not being expressed.

If anger too readily crosses to rage, the heat can destroy the respect necessary for sustaining the relationship. If a person continually goes across the line from anger into rage, or goes across so quickly that they are not aware of it, or people around them cannot bring their attention to it, then the personality begins to develop a habit of fragmentation. Then a small spark of anger quickly blinds the person. The cooling aspects of the psyche are lost immediately, and the person can't maintain self-respect or respect for others. Among warrior groups, stepping across the line becomes a discipline or practice. Discipline is practiced at that line so that a person can go close to the line and only when necessary go across. Only through crossing that line can the killing and maiming and wounding in war escalate so quickly. The same person who can be calm and helpful on this side of that line can quickly do great damage across that line. Crossing the line involves the entire community and deserves everyone's attention.

One of the aspects of initiations in the land of fire involves learning the borderlines of passion in each person's psyche. Often in tribal groups, when initiates were inclined toward the direction of the warrior, toward battle frenzy, and showed a tendency to leap over the line or to patrol its borders, they required special training. The capacity for anger and attraction to the borders of rage don't go away. Warrior initiations such as that described in the story of Cuchulain took advantage of one's capacity to enter the battle frenzy and, on the other hand, developed responsible techniques for limiting it, both for the benefit of the individual and of the community.

When the flames of anger don't burn consciously and don't mix with language or art to find expression, a person may become subject to sudden outbreaks of rage or subject to violent dreams. If awareness of those expressions is denied, a person can become cold and numb and subject to murderous or suicidal fantasies. Inverted hot rage can produce a heart attack, and cold rage becomes sadistic to others.

At the emotional borders between people, if someone feels angry and won't express it, the other people who share borders with them feel it. Anger is hot and mobile—if it can't get seen and heard through one person at the border, it crosses to the other. The person that feels the anger and doesn't move it to conscious expression is called passive-aggressive. They aren't non-aggressive, they are passive and aggressive; they are passive about their aggression. But, it leaks over their borders and increases the aggressive flames of the people they relate to and live near.

In the old parts of the psyche, there is an expectation that the land of rage will be visited and that the skills of anger will be learned. Everyone carries some sense of the archaic warrior spirit within them despite the lack of direct attention to it in modern life. In fact, the density of population in urban centers, the extended periods of work just to make a living, and the alienation caused by institutions increase rage while reducing opportunities to express anger, rage, and outrage.

The expression of anger and rage often gets confined to home. The capacity that can protect the home by temporarily entering the state of rage often becomes raging at home. The individual rage breaks out at home, and the tribal rage pours over the borders into the next neighborhood. The national rage is ready to explode anywhere, near or far.

On another occasion when Cuchulain went into a battle rage, he killed his own son. Neither one of them could stop the battle frenzy they were both trained in, and the result of the fight was the killing of the son. The rage of the father and his skills and experience were too much for the son to combat. The final image in the story shows Cuchulain standing in the ocean swinging his sword, still in the frenzy but now raging into the waves of the sea trying to cut through water with his sword. Finally, the huge, blind, burning fires of rage and revenge are matched by the endless, relentless, cooling waves of the sea. It's a knowledge come too late to avert the tragedy that occurs when men stay in the warrior fury too long.

The progression of the firebird story suggests that the fires of the spirit, the emotions heated by the contact with the firebird and the desires of the king, are leading somewhere. The great bird of spirit has been carried to the center of the realm, and the holy and emotional heat has dropped burning feathers everywhere. The next desire of the king at the center sends the hunter to a different extreme, not toward more fire of flight but to the sea in search for Vasilisa the beautiful. It turns out that the king has longed for the "most beautiful"; it turns out that the heated psyche longs for distant oceans, and the burning spirit turns toward soul. This desire for beauty takes the hunter to the edge of the known world, to where the wide, blue waters receive the red disk of the setting sun. In a sense, the firebird descends into the waters of the psyche, and a vision of beauty arises. The power and heat of the firebird generate a vision of the soul.

Once again the king desires something and requires the hunter to go to extremes, once again the hunter despairs and weeps his way to the horse. The horse points out other resources of the king the hunter needs; different tools and attitudes will be required. Some nourishing of the soul is about to occur, and the horse teaches the hunter that different powers are needed in this area of longing. This is the language of the soul and of the open heart, the language or longing for what it holds as most mysterious and beautiful. When the hunter saw the feather and his soul opened to that vision of soaring passion, he opened to life; now he cannot deny the language of the soul and its desire to expand into other extremes.

The image of the most beautiful woman in all the world riding in her silver vessel with her golden oars on the endless expanse of the blue ocean is also an image of the soul itself. What the soul wants and longs for is beauty to match its own. Beauty is the "other risk" of the psyche: In the order of events reflected in the story, the first risk of the psyche is the breaking out of the spirit, and the second is keeping the heart open to the expansiveness of the soul.

After burning within the firebird, the hunter finds himself waiting at the cool edge of the blue sea surrounded by foods and enclosed in silver. Now, in a sense, the lure for beauty is the hunter himself. Where before he remained hidden in the tree and the horse of power pinned the prey, now he waits inside the tent. What brings Vasilisa to him is the elaborate display of the embroidered tent, the fine foods and liquors, and the hunter himself dressed for the occasion. From his adventures of flight and fire, the hunter comes down to the ground and near the water. After his dance within the flaming wings of the firebird, the hunter sits within the reflective circle of the lunar tent.

In order to draw the soul's sense of beauty to him, the hunter must gather around him the ritual accoutrements of beauty. Here the horse reveals another kind of power—one that depends on slowness, elaboration, and waiting at the center. The hunter must set himself inside a story that can be interpreted from the outside. He is making a ritual of attraction, a display of reception. By being on the shore, he is "betwixt and between" the land and the sea, betwixt earth and water, and the soul attends all betwixt-and-between places: the evening when the light softens and lovers meet; the place between one heart and another; the territory between animal and spirit, between spirit and body. Thus, Vasilisa, as the embodiment of the soul, is drawn to the place of betwixt and between.

When I first told the story and saw the tent, as I was telling it, the tent was glowing as if softly lit from within. The silver sides were embroidered with scenes of gardens and people meeting, with the tree from which the hunter saw the firebird, with the bird coming behind it. The story doesn't say what is embroidered on the tent, but we know that he has completed the adventures with the firebird, has been seen and blessed by the king and raised in rank. He has found that which is golden and burning in himself and had it confirmed. That's the story he sits within. It's as if the soul sees the stories of his heart embroidered on the tent, and this is a signal that he is willing to enter the conversations of love, which consist of anecdotes of the heart. The hunter waits at the shore, within the stories he knows by heart.

Vasilisa comes from the sea drawn by the appearance of the hunter, who has wrapped himself in this fabric of art, and she now stands betwixt and between the otherworld where she wistfully floats and this inner world of his making. There is something else needed to draw her across the threshold. The hunter greets her kindly and invites her to taste the food and wines. Vasilisa enters, and they share the food, taste the wines, and toast one another. The wine has a strong effect on Vasilisa, and her eyelids become heavy as if the night itself is weighing them down. Soon she falls asleep, and the hunter lifts her onto the horse where she lies in his arms, light and curved as a feather. The feather became the entire bird of spirit, now the firebird is replaced by a gentle, wistful image of silver-gold beauty.

We know from the refrain of the horse that there's more trouble coming, but telling the story awakens a chorus of trouble and questions right here: What happened in the embroidered tent? Was Vasilisa misled and mistreated? Was she drugged with the wine? Are the king and the hunter treating Vasilisa as an object? Are they equally guilty of dominating and using her? What is going on?

Each man in the chorus must describe the image and the feeling associated for him with the scene of Vasilisa in the tent. Each must get out his story of what is going on between women and men, between him and his lover, between the masculine and feminine elements in his own soul. The value of mythic scenes is not that they distract us from "reality" but that they move current issues, feelings, and attitudes toward the wisdom in these stories. There is a deep, magnetic logic to these old tales that pull our current feelings up to consciousness, drawing our attention to ancient issues.

Some people get angry at the idea of the seduction and want to reject the tent scene or rewrite it so that there is no trickery, so that Vasilisa has a clear-cut choice. Some feel that choice becomes mystery, whether it's a woman and a man in the tent or a man awaiting his own soul. Some are angry at the conditions in society. Women are angry at men, and some men are angry that women are so angry at men. Clearly there is something wrong in the way women and men encounter each other in modern cultures, and it is getting worse, not better. The accumulation of suffering and harm among women is already unbearable, and the hatred and fear of men that results is undeniable.

The discussion has wandered back into the area of Litima. If young men are going to be initiated into this area of great spirit and fire, then that fire is going to be present when men go toward women. The heat from the firebird has poured over into this area, and the proximity of the ocean is not enough to cool the fires that have been ignited. You could say that this is the condition of our culture right now, that often the fire is ignited—at least the elemental fire of biological heat—but there isn't the cooling water to temper it or an embroidered tent to contain and protect both the young man and the young woman. At conferences, the current struggle for mutual respect between women and men breaks out just at the place where the old story presents falling into love and falling into the mutual life of the soul. The image of the tent that is intended to contain and protect the lovers actually forces everyone to experience the current conflict in our culture, which rages around the separation and union of women and men.

There are many causes for the mistreatment of women in modern culture. One cause is the distinct omission of community events that can illustrate the interrelatedness and interdependence of men and women, of feminine and masculine. Next to the concept of Litima and the attention to the masculine fires of emotion, the Gisu of Uganda place the importance of awakening feminine qualities and awareness in men. The Gisu value individuality and the development of independence, as we do in the West. But they know that opening the channels of Litima in men presents a danger to women. Thus, the initiation of men includes an initiation into the mysterious powers of the feminine and a distinct, non-sexual bonding with women. Kinship bonds are made between men and women, and the benefits of each gender are demonstrated to the other during crucial ritual events. These initiations involve a series of direct encounters with the emotions, the spirit, and the bodies of the young males. The intention is to bring the young men from boyhood games through the fires of

Litima into a complex relationship with past generations, the current society of women and men, and their own emotional and spiritual lives.

At a critical point in the initiation process, which eventually leads to circumcision, the male initiates wear women's adornments. In particular, they receive strings of beads that are made into girdles worn diagonally over the initiate's chest and thus over his heart. These bead girdles are like the ones that Gisu women wear over their wombs. It is said that these tokens of affection will give the young man strength to endure his initiation ordeals. The number of strings indicates the number of his female kin and their affection for him.

The beads are clearly associated with the intimate parts of a woman's body, as they are a decoration and honoring of the womb, ovum, and genitals of the women. They also represent the generativity, creativity, power, and sacredness of women. Worn by women, the beads wrap, cover, and draw attention to the womb of the tribe, source of all its people. The heart of the initiate, then, is shown to be like a womb that conceives and gives birth. The womb of the man is in his chest, in his heart. The girdle of beads is a symbol that combines rules of etiquette in sexual life, identification of the initiate with the women of his group, and ancient feminine images. The identification of the males with the women through these bead ornaments happens concretely, psychologically, and mythologically at once.

The beads come from two directions. Some women who confer the beads are initiated; they are of child-bearing status, or are mothers in the tribe. They are not the biological mothers of the initiates but rather the "ritual mothers" of this generation of men. As ritual mothers, they are conferring the strength of the feminine on the initiates. They are covering the initiates with the fruitfulness and power of their wombs. Some beads are also given by cousins and other female kin who become the initiates' "ritual sisters"—that is, they are part of the initiates' own generation. They provide the initiates with a sideways connection to women as they pass from boyhood into manhood.

The beads remind the women that they are the creative womb of the people, a source of the strength to endure, and each one a bead of beauty in the strand that goes all the way to the ancestors. The beads remind the men that a man is a boy whose heart has been opened through the eruptions of his spirit and the affections of "mothers" and "sisters." This process makes clear that more than "male strength" is necessary to complete the initiation into manhood, but he must have feminine strength and endurance as well. The initiates do not stand alone or in simple maleness. While the initiate loses some male skin in the circumcision, he gains the feminine strength in his heart.

Among the Gisu, to break the beads of a girl or woman is considered rape. The psychological state is made visible through the beads: It must only be the woman who removes the beads that decorate and protect both her virginity and fertility. Rape becomes the seizing and breaking of the girdle of a woman. And rape becomes a violation of a man's own initiation, of his own heart, for in the initiation he wore the girdle of women over his heart.

The initiates are eighteen to twenty-five years old. They receive the beads just as they are beginning the series of dances that leads to the public ritual of circumcision. They will be required to stand before all the tribe and not flinch as a demonstration of their ability to contain fear and maintain self-control. Days and days of dancing increase the inner heat of Litima before the circumcision. Receiving the ornaments from the women of the previous generation is critical for their entry to manhood. As the initiates stand before the older men and before the knife that cuts away the boyhood covering of their maleness, they stand also in the ornaments of their initiated "ritual mothers" and "ritual sisters." Thus, they are partially held in the protection and affection of their female supporters.

Among the Gisu, circumcision must be requested by the initiates. It is not done at birth; it is only accomplished with the young man's awareness and conscious preparation. The pain is anticipated, not denied. A stoic attitude is maintained, in marked contrast to the emotions stored by dancing.

The initiate stands before the tribe representing the ancestors, male and female; the living kin, female and male; and the masculine and feminine aspects of his own heart and soul. All of the elements of the group and individual are displayed in his appearance, in his dancing, and finally in his stoic stance during the circumcision. Part of the statement of the ritual is that he stands in and for the community; once his penis is uncovered before all, even that part of himself does not belong only to him. Moreover, his ability to withstand the ordeals of adulthood derive from a combination of intense emotionality and stoic containment. The ritual makes clear that he is made of the elements of male and female and must embody both to be in the community as a man.

The stoicism is not a simple repression of pain and numbing of emotions. The initiates are encouraged to express fully the range of emotions before and after the circumcision. Rather, the moment of stoicism marks the birth of the elder in the initiate. By demonstrating control of fear, anger, shame, and grief, he acts as elders act. In relation to the fires of Litima, he is "cool." "Coolness" is an essential quality of the elders. During this initiation process, the youth shows both fire and coolness, for he is initiated as both a fiery young man and an elder-to-be.

Modern psychology would describe this decoration of the youths as an expression of the "inner feminine." The initiate's "feminine aspects" and "anima" or soul are displayed in the eruptions of emotion engendered by dancing, drinking beer, and singing, and they are worn for all to see as ornaments. This is an extended display of "inside out"—the inner life worn on the outside, the heart worn on the sleeve. Although the women in the group have watched these boys grow up and know much about them, now the women must attend the death of the initiates' boyhood in order to learn the nature of the new men who will join the tribe and marry their daughters. The elder women brew the beer that fuels the dancing and the eruption of the emotions of the initiates. The women fuel the expression of the youths' emotions and also "cool" them with the beads across their hearts.

Meanwhile, the elder men ritually prepare the outside in order to include the village, the community, and the world itself in the initiatory events. They clean the ancestral groves, repair the shrines of the village, and make preparatory offerings in all directions. The elder men are making the outside world ready for the ritual birth of the next group of men, and they are demonstrating the spiritual attention and ritual care of the ancestors, the community, and the world as they know it. Thus, both the women and the men of the community acknowledge and engage the dual aspects of Litima.

Without rituals that bind men and women in a deep respect of the other, women are denied the capacity to know and the power to control their wombs and therefore their bodies, and men are denied the knowledge of their own hearts. One of the purposes of the pain of initiation is to allow the initiate to know pain in himself so he won't need to put others in pain in order to learn about it. Another purpose is to establish a compassionate relationship between the elder in a man's heart and the suffering of both genders.

In a sense, the hunter's new mission from the king is to convert the fire in him to a display and language of beauty, in order to attract the most beautiful and bring it to the center of the realm. These old stories are always heading for the most beautiful woman, and this does not refer to a beauty contest. The reference is to the beauty that rises up in the soul of a person who opens from the heart, the path felt when the heart of a person is open.

Vasilisa leaves the blue sea and comes to the ground where the hunter waits because he's been musing on the beauty in the world. She comes because he's cooling his fire. There's no sense of time in the story, so he may be sitting in the tent for years before she comes to him. He may go to the tent time and time and time again and find nothing present but his own struggles, his own burnings. If this is so, he won't see her and she won't come to him until he finds the center of himself and holds it long enough for his heart to open.

He can't have just a surface involvement with beauty. His interest must not be in seeing the results of a beauty contest. He also can't be wrapping himself in beauty made by other people; it must come from himself. He can't be sitting in the fears and worries of a boy who thinks that it might be the half-giantess coming. He must sit with a sense that what will come is of great beauty and that it will rise from the ocean, rise from the unconscious, rise from the sea of his soul. He must be sitting in some sense of meaning and knowledge of who he is in essence. And he must be in that spot long enough for her to reach him. If he's singing, he must be singing not for an audience or to achieve recognition or some level of accomplishment. He must be chanting in the state that wakes his deeper self.

In order for the hunter to sit in the tent long enough to attract the beauty of the soul, the intense passion that he has been living out and living through must be converted to compassion. If there was no passion to begin with, he wouldn't reach the place of compassion. But if there are only the raw passions of fire and heat, he will burn up before he reaches this place. Sitting in this tent of compassion means that he has found compassion for himself. One way in which he is central to the scene is in having compassion toward his own heart. Like the initiate with the womb beads, the compassion spreads to the point where it includes the feminine soul, and through her it spreads to include everyone in the tribe, just as the initiate is open and passionate and standing before everyone.

Vasilisa arrives because the hunter is wrapped in song or enrapt in contemplation. She approaches because he's meditating, and if he's meditating, then he's reached the same point as the great Tibetan ascetic Milarepa, who spent many years contemplating in a cave in the snow-peaks of the Himalayas. He had burned in a rage of revenge that caused him to kill many people; then he had burned in a holy fire of meditation that kept him warm and melted the snow in all directions. But he was facing a wall he could not break or burn through, though the enlightenment he sought was on the other side. Just at that moment when he felt he would never reach his goal, his sister and the woman he was once betrothed to brought him food and drink. Afterward, he broke through the wall, and he was sitting in the place he had been trying to reach all his life. In the case of the ascetic, "she" brings food to him, while the lover brings nourishment to "her." In each event there is a moment of radical change where the fiery spirit breaks through to another realm.

Someone once asked, "Is this, then, his sister, the sister of his soul? Is it his soul lover? Is it a muse? Is it the great mother of the ocean and of all memories?" And the answer is, yes.

The name of this woman must be different for each person who sees her. The beauty that she represents is the beauty that individual soul has been seeking. In the story that we're following, it's the beauty that has been prepared by the flight of the firebird. It's the beauty that has been awaiting, rolling, and coasting on the waves of the sea until the young hunter could pass the trials of fire and bring not the raw fire but the fire woven into the embroidery of art, which he has learned and converted into a nourishment that could feed others.

Someone once asked, "Is she a woman? Is she a part of him? Is she a goddess?" And the answer is, yes. For some find it in a woman, some find it in a place inside themselves, and some touch it in some event in great nature. Some find it in a man. Some find it in meditation and contemplation, and some find it riding in a ship on the sea. She is the beauty that's in the eye of the beholder. She is in the beauty that's in the eye of the lover. She is the wonder made up in the individual soul. She comes from the sea like the goddess Aphrodite, goddess of love. She comes from silver like the moon riding on the sea. And she also comes from the womb of his heart. Whatever she is to an individual, she is equal to the firebird, for she replaces the firebird in the place of desire. Whatever she may be to a given person, she is equal to the king, because she sits, eventually, next to the king. And she only arrives when the hunter sits central to the scene, when he sits within the tent and within what nourishes his soul.

If the king is a figure who can recognize a shining feather from the great spirit bird, then this is a queen who can recognize when a soul is singing. If the king is a king of desire who knows what's lacking in the center of the psyche or in the center of the realm, then this is the queen who is present when it's not lacking, who knows when the center has been found. And once the hunter has seen and held this beauty, he will no longer simply follow the demands and desires of the king who got him to this point. He will also follow the demands and desires of this queen who has appeared within him. Even though he is not yet king, he has already separated from the king who has directed his progress so far.

For a moment, the place where fire and water meet in the heart of the hunter opens fully. In that opening, the elder of the tribe, the king of the realm, the new ruler of the psyche, is born. The change is overwhelming and requires time and deepening to settle in. Neither Vasilisa nor the hunter are used to the strong wine of the heart. She loses consciousness or disappears from his consciousness. He returns to the old king. The horse has been waiting patiently and carries them both to the center of the realm.

CHAPTER 19

LEAPING INTO THE CAULDRON

W~HEN THE HUNTER~ returns to the center of the realm and carrie
Vasilisa into the hall, a series of reversals, replacements, separations
and reunions begins that culminates when the hunter and the kin
each leap into the cauldron. Previously, the hunter had danced throug
the hall enveloped in the flames and shining feathers of the firebird
Now he brings the woman of the sea, who is lamenting, grieving, an
protesting. Although the king continues to give orders and threate
death, the demands and desires of Vasilisa replace those of the kin
From the moment when the hunter becomes aware of the passion an
compassion in his own heart, a revolution begins that will overtur
the ruler of the realm.

Vasilisa laments the loss of her freedom to ride in her silver shi
and float on her ocean unbound and unrestricted. She will only marr
and cease her lament when her wedding gown has been brought from
the depths of the sea. She will be queen of the sea or queen of th
realm; she will ride in a silver boat with golden oars or wrap herself i
a gown of gold and silver. But she won't remain without symbols c
her sovereignty.

The gown is not a common wedding dress but one woven of silver and gold and found at the deepest part of the sea. When symbols of sovereignty are lost, they are often found in the lowest place. Sometimes in a story, a golden crown has been lost and fallen to the bottom of the lake. Sometimes a gold ring representing union was dropped and lies hidden below. The return of whatever has been missing can bring everything together for a moment. Just as the golden feather turned the hunter in a new direction, the gown is necessary to transform the realm.

The king could not move toward marriage until the firebird had been brought to him; similarly, Vasilisa says the queen is not present until the symbols of sovereignty are brought to her. The king desired gold and burning and an ascent that brought the firebird to the center of the realm; now Vasilisa requires a descent that will bring silver and water, as well as gold, from the deepest place of all.

If the king demanded one extreme, Vasilisa requires the other. So far the hunter has been a man made by fire. Can he also be made through water? He has become a man made by the sun; can he also embody the moon? He has worn his passions on the outside in the burning cloak of the firebird. He has gone directly into the fire and brought the radiant heat to the center of the great hall. Can he now move sideways like the crab, or must he always be ascending and going for the gold? Can he descend into the depths of the psyche? Can he learn the slowness of that deep water? Can he tolerate great pressure and hold his passions inside? Can he form a shell that will protect those on the outside from his otherwise-burning passions? Is his response to every dilemma going to be flaming up, taking flight, igniting the fires of war? Or can he find another way? Can he gather the garments cooled in the darkness of the ocean that are more akin to the thin shells of the crustaceans than to the fiery feathers of the soaring phoenix?

Ever since the hunter picked up the feather, he has been exposed to mysteries. Now he must explore yet another one. In the architecture of the story, the garment of fiery feathers must be matched by the silver and gold gown from the dark waters; the lowly crab must be seen as ruler of its realm just as the firebird rules above. The hunter must carry the sovereign gown of the queen to the court, just as the Gisu initiate must stand before his community wearing womb beads over his heart. In an initiation by fire, masculine and feminine are balanced at the extremes. The soaring of the firebird is balanced by the depth and stillness of the very bottom of the sea. Just as the king sends the hunter soaring after the firebird, the queen sends him to the depths of the sea and of himself.

For the realm to be remade through these tests of the spirit, the symbols of both masculinity and femininity must be brought to the center and made visible. After submitting to the demands of the king, the hunter must now submit to the demands of Vasilisa as the symbol of the great feminine in him, in the realm, and in nature. The horse, of course, cautions that this trouble is still not the greatest trouble, though it seems so at the time. As proof that the situation at the center has already changed, the horse doesn't advise the hunter to ask for any resources or aid from the king. For the first time since the hunter picked up the feather, the horse of power and the hunter ride off unencumbered.

As part of their initiation, the members of each generation must relocate and retrieve the gown of sovereignty and the firebird cloak, which keep getting lost. The rituals that carry boys and girls into adulthood are a means of reweaving these mantles of sovereignty, creating kings and queens, the "rulers" of society, out of the youths. The royal wedding occurs when an entire world has been remade symbolically through fire and water, sun and moon, male and female. This wedding may take place within an individual, between a woman and a man, or between the gender groups.

In many ways, the rift between women and men that has become so profound in modern society can be viewed as the separation and ordeal stages of a lengthy initiation—a prelude to the reunion that will take place when the symbols of sovereignty have been found again. Healing from losses, the rekindling of hope, and the beginning of change can all occur when masculine and feminine extremes meet at the center of the realm.

Once, at a conference with approximately fifty women and fifty men in attendance, the idea arose to separate the women and the men into different camps. I don't know whose idea it was; I wonder if anyone remembers now who thought of it first. But there was a camp across the lake from the camp where we were gathered, and there were enough canoes to carry half the group in a single crossing. The question was who should go and who should stay. If the men took the canoes and left, wouldn't that just repeat the usual pattern of men going off to work, off to war, off to hunt, while the women were left at home? Would the women feel abandoned and rejected? If the women took the canoes and left, would they feel better? Would the men feel left out or worried about the women in the camp over on the unknown side of the lake? Should the men experience that, for a change?

In trying to decide, the members of the group expressed an almost endless array of opinions and interpretations. In the end, the women decided to stay at the first camp. They liked it and didn't want to spend valuable time traveling. The men pushed off in canoes, forming random groups, learning to paddle in rhythm with each other.

The separation lasted several days, during which each group worked on issues pertinent to its gender. When it came time to come back together, both groups realized that the separation had increased their sense of loneliness and sorrow. But they had also experienced some of the joys of being separate. All had noticed that their language had become more direct, more certain, in these groups of all one gender. Still, there was a growing desire for the two groups to reunite.

When we did, someone suggested that we form concentric circles, with all the members of one gender in the center and the other group in rings around them. From these positions, the outer group would listen to what the inner group had to say. Once again we had to discuss, argue over, and feel through the issue of which group should speak first and which should listen. Each side felt that there were positive and negative aspects to going first. Eventually, it was decided that the men should speak first and the women would listen—or that the women would listen first while the men spoke. For a while it was like that; everything had to be said twice, focusing on each gender group in turn.

The men sat on the floor in a cluster of concentric circles, and the women sat in larger rings around them. There was to be no dialogue between the two groups. The men began to speak into the fragile silence. The separation had brought out many voices, many thoughts and feelings, and all of them wanted to be heard. There were concerns and complaints. There was weeping. There was screaming rage, rage that went all the way back to Mother. There was careful thankfulness expressed by a man toward his wife, who was present. There was deep anguish over what daughters would experience in the chaos of the world. As the men went on, many women began to weep, and as the telling continued, more and more men and women were crying. Throughout the entire presentation, not one woman spoke. Then it came time to change places.

The women moved to the center and sat in close circles, their knees touching. The men gathered in larger circles around them, but now everyone was closer together. Then, as the women began to express their feelings about men and make statements to them, a completely different thing happened. The men could not stop themselves from answering, correcting, and elaborating on what the women said. It was shocking. In order for the women to continue, the men actually had to link arms and hold onto each other to keep one another from bursting out with some statement of disagreement or even of agreement. The event was almost disrupted by the inability of the men simply to listen. Had we not locked arms and held onto each other, becoming as one body encircling the women, the women would have had to stop speaking.

So the men held onto each other, and the women got to say all that they wished to say. Included, once again, was the entire range of emotions—anger and rage, great fears and tendernesses, caring things that were said sometimes about an individual, at other times to men as a group. Afterward, it was clear that the men were more shocked by their inability to listen than the women were. Many of the women said that this was exactly what they had experienced in private. Some men said they just couldn't help themselves; words had come bursting out of their mouths before they knew they were going to speak. Several men said that although they weren't able to speak up in their private relationships, suddenly they had found themselves speaking out in this group.

Everyone found it valuable to hear what the other group had to say. It wasn't that everything that was said had been accurate, meaningful, beautiful, or even absolutely truthful. The importance of the event came from the careful listening that was done within the atmosphere of charged emotions and mutual risk. Throughout the rest of the conference, we all found it easier simply to hear each other, and certain things that were said echoed over and over inside each person. The ritual of listening had opened another ear inside, an inner ear that was intrigued by what the other gender group might say. Listening as a group also made hearing less personal. Some things that an individual man might have trouble hearing women say became easier to tolerate and hear as part of a group. Listening to this broad array of statements and questions also made it easier to identify with something said by the other gender. Sometimes a woman expressed most closely how one of the men felt, and vice versa. Women and men each contributed fire and water to the center. The fire can't all come from one side and the water from the other. During the separation the full range of heat and of cooling were available to each group, and part of the reunion requires the full expression from each. Desire, demands, accusations, griefs, and losses came from both sides. Eventually, the fearful feelings diminished, the angers were soothed by being heard, and the gentle feelings grew.

Many people have ambiguous feelings about "male bonding." This story offers one example of how bonding among men can be beneficial to both women and men. Separation increases fears of abandonment and rejection, as well as fears of negative things being said and planned by the other side. But if honest work is done in separated groups, the feelings can reach deeper and open up possibilities for mutual catharsis and reunion.

At the return after a separation, both harsh and healing words must be spoken, both fire and water must be displayed to show where each person or each group has been. In order to hear these words, men and women, both separately and together, must weave the knowledge and heritage of beauty and love into the work that they are doing. At this conference, we used art and little rituals to form connections within and across genders. We sang and danced as well as talked. Stories were told and interpreted by the gender groups as well as by individuals. Without these connections to others of the same gender, it becomes more and more difficult to open the inner ear. Men must feel connected sideways to other men in order to hear the difficult words that come both from within and from without. In these groups, men can act as the horse of power for one another; then, with a steadying presence nearby, a man can hear what's being said in the women's circle and can also hear what's being called for by the Vasilisa in his soul.

For a man must be able to hear both. If he does not sometimes hear the muses in his soul singing and demanding beauty, then he won't be able to appreciate the beauty in the world. If a man hasn't sat within his tent nourishing himself on the stories carried in his heart, he won't be able to hear the stories of others with his inner ear. If a man can't sense Vasilisa floating in her silver and gold boat on the sea of his soul, he won't be able to sense the soulful longings in a woman and won't hear her demands for sovereignty with sympathy. To experience a reunion of the masculine and feminine in the outer world, men must first find them together in their hearts.

By the time the hunter returns with the wedding gown, the order of the realm has already begun to change. The king has relinquished to Vasilisa the place of desire and the power to drive things forward. The old order, with the old king at its center, is about to end. The wedding and the cauldron are prepared at the same time; all the possibilities that the psyche can present are brought to awareness at once. Anything can happen, and certainly some great change will occur. Starting with the feather, the psyche has released a whole array of dynamic, ancient images. King and queen, phoenix and crab are all afoot. While one part of the realm prepares the great wedding of the queen and the king, the other part prepares the fire and water of the cauldron of death and rebirth. Now the story focuses on the cauldron, for through it a radical reordering of the psyche will become possible.

In the center of the great hall, at the center of the realm, amid preparations for both wedding and funeral, the cauldron heats up. The cauldron that was first seen in the story of the half-giantess has returned, but now its function as an instrument of change becomes evident. In contrast to the half-giantess's cauldron, which devours any form of life that happens by, this cauldron is central to the great feast that will renew the kingdom and reunite the feminine and the masculine.

As in the critical moments of an initiation or as with any of the dramatic events that erupt in life, what happens to the hunter at this point in the story is sudden and surprising. Where he expects death, he finds great fullness of life. Where he expects isolation, he finds marriage. Where he expects great sorrow, there is great joy.

When the hunter leaps into the cauldron, the force of desire has moved from the king to Vasilisa and from Vasilisa to him. Like the initiates in the Gisu rituals, he must ask for and desire the rites of initiation. Just before he is thrown into the boiling waters of change, he makes the leap himself. For the first time in the story, everyone wants the same thing at the same time. By the time he leaps, the king demands it, Vasilisa requires it, the horse advises it, all the people await it, and the hunter commits himself to it. It's a leap of faith and an act of fate.

In this moment, the hunter is an embodiment of radical change. In one sense, he has no choice about his actions, for every aspect of his life has become focused on the cauldron in the center of the hall. Yet as the horse of power points out, within these dire and narrow circumstances, he can still find a choice: to leap into the cauldron before he is dragged to it. The difference between pain and suffering lies in that leap. Suffering involves an aware participation while undergoing change; pain can be present with or without meaningful change. All resistance to going into the cauldron of change will create pain, and the pain alone will do nothing to change the situation. But as soon as the hunter moves on his own accord toward the cauldron that seems intended for his death, he begins the immersion that will transform his life completely.

When the old king leaps into the cauldron, he expects to acquire the new skin and youth of the hunter, but the hunter himself makes the leap with no expectations. The initiate leaps into nothing, into the unknown, into the probability of death. In the beginning of the story, expectations were necessary in order to find the firebird; at this point, expectations could be deadly. The cauldron combines the feminine powers of the womb and the tomb. For the one who lets everything go and dives in as if it were a tomb, it becomes a womb from which he emerges better than before. The moment of the reunion of the feminine and the masculine is not predictable, and it is not negotiated. It is sudden, stunning, and risky.

In the great hall of the old king, where the hunter has come and gone between the king and the horse, the wild dance of symbols culminates in the wedding of the hunter of the firebird and the queen of the seas. That which soars above all, rivals the sun, and quiets the forest now communes with that which stretches from shore to shore, reaches to the depths, and comes and goes like the moon. In the midst of turbulent emotions, both the height and the depth of the spirit are revealed, and the realm is remade through fire and water.

The story says that the hunter twice disappears into the boiling waters and finally comes out renewed and even better than before. The story doesn't describe what happens underneath the water. In an initiation, there is always something that remains secret. Even among tribal peoples who participate in age-old initiations, there are things that cannot be said about what has happened to each one individually. Part of the initiation remains mysterious and forms the secret around which the soul continues to grow. There is always mystery in the events that reorder and change the direction of a life. Only through metaphors can we express and still contain the turbulent events that change a life forever.

Something within the hunter changes enough during his immersion in the cauldron's waters that he becomes a king where once he was the servant of a king. He was being stretched between the poles of mentoring represented by the king and horse, and he survived that tension between extreme desire and determined strategy. Since he passes through the fiery waters and comes out ready to be a king, he must have integrated the qualities of kingliness into himself. He now carries a greater awareness of the force of desire and the capacity to know what is needed in the psyche and in the realm. And, he has incorporated the consistency, moderation, and faithfulness of the horse that carried him all along.

Embodying these characteristics allows him to take his place next to Vasilisa. When the story says that they rule the realm together, it also means that the hunter has learned how to be near the beauty and power of the feminine in his soul without falling unconscious and without losing his head. He has learned to love and respect the feminine powers and women. Now he has a greater capacity for relationships that risk the fires and waters of love.

When the hunter emerges from the cauldron, he appears with a new skin and an expanded capacity for life. Although the psyche presents radical change to us in images that are all or nothing, now or never, the awareness of what the changes mean can only develop more slowly. In the story, the new king and queen rule successfully together, but in an individual, the masculine and feminine may be integrated only intermittently. The three immersions in the fiery water may occur years apart. Actual initiations try to follow the sequences in this story so that the person can grasp consciously the nature and direction of the change he is undergoing. But a modern person without such rituals to aid him may have to pull together episodes from various times and places in order to see the same changes in his life.

Most of these stories were told over and over to both the children and the adults of a given culture, allowing the images to deepen and enrich the listeners' imaginations. For example, when this ending, too mysterious and glorious to be explained, claims a place in the imaginations and hearts of the listeners, it allows them to picture an outcome in which the extreme fires of the human heart benefit everyone. They can then see how the passions and emotions, instead of burning a path of destruction, can become forces for meaningful change that will renew the center of the culture.

At the beginning of the road through the land of fire, it's important to ignore the warnings of the horse of power and let the heart sing its fiercest and brightest songs. Eventually, the words of the horse echo with truth, and the hunter knows the meaning of fear and the size of the trouble that life can provide. Then, on the way out of the land of fire, the heart sings songs of survival, like this traditional song from West Africa:

> Do not seek too much fame,
> but do not seek obscurity.
> Be proud.
> But do not remind the world of your deeds.
> Excel when you must,
> but do not excel the world.
> Many heroes are not yet born,
> many have already died.
> To be alive to hear this song,
> that is a victory.

5

The Water of Life

Today is the day for crying in the kingdom.
Today my destiny is too much for me.

PABLO NERUDA

There once was a king who was sick, and no one thought he would live. He had three sons who were very sad. They went down to the palace garden and wept. An old man came by and asked them why they were weeping. They told him their father was sick and sure to die, for nothing seemed to cure him, nothing did him any good. The old man said, "I know of one more remedy: the Water of Life. If he drinks of that, he'll get well, but it's hard to find."

"I'll manage to find it," said the eldest brother, and he went to the sick king and begged to be allowed to go out in search of the Water of Life, since that alone could cure him.

"No," said the king, "the danger is too great. I would rather die myself."

The eldest son begged and pleaded until the king finally gave permission. In his heart, the eldest thought, "If I bring the Water of Life, my father will love me best, and I shall inherit the kingdom and be king."

The gates of the castle swung open, and the eldest son rode out on his horse, galloping straight down the road and looking straight ahead. He had not gone far when he came upon a dwarf standing on the side of the road. The dwarf called up to him, "Where are you going so fast?"

"What does it matter to you, stupid runt, little next-to-nothing?" said the prince. And he rode rapidly on.

The dwarf grew furious. He fixed his anger on the oldest brother and cursed him; he thought on him hard and befuddled him. The prince rode into a ravine. The further he rode, the closer the mountains on either side came together and the narrower his path became. Still, he kept going until the path was so narrow that his horse couldn't go another step forward. Nor could the prince turn the horse around, or dismount, or back out. The horse was stuck and so was he. He might as well have been in a prison.

The sick king waited in vain for the return of the oldest son. One day the second brother said, "Father, allow me to go look for the Water of Life." He thought to himself, "If my brother is dead and I succeed, the kingdom will fall to me."

At first the king said it was too dangerous, he would rather die himself. But eventually he gave his permission. The gates of the palace swung open, and the second son rode out on his great horse, charging straight ahead down the road. He looked neither left nor right but only straight ahead, much like his elder brother. He encountered the same dwarf at the side of the road. The dwarf asked where he was going so fast. "You little runt," said the second brother, "what business is it of yours?" He rode on without bothering to slow down or look back. The dwarf grew furious, fixed his anger on the second brother, and cursed him. Soon, this brother rode into a ravine that became narrower and narrower. He kept going until his horse couldn't turn around and couldn't back out. He was stuck; he might as well have been in a prison.

The sick king waited in vain for the return of the second son. One day the youngest son asked permission to search for the Water of Life. The king said it was too dangerous. Besides, if his two older brothers hadn't returned, how could he hope to succeed? How could one as foolish as he expect to do what his betters had not? But the youngest implored, and eventually the king gave his permission. The gates of the castle swung open, and out rode the youngest son, charging down the same road as his brothers. Once again, the dwarf was there, and he asked where this brother was going in such a hurry.

The youngest brother stopped, looked at the dwarf, got down from his horse, and said, "I'm seeking the Water of Life because my father is sick unto death."

"Do you know where to find it?" asked the dwarf.

"No, I have no idea," said the youngest.

"Since you've spoken well and have not been haughty like your false brothers, I'll tell you where the Water of Life is and how to get there. It springs from a fountain in the courtyard of an enchanted castle. But you'll never make your way through the gates of the castle unless I give you an iron rod and two loaves of bread. If you strike the iron gates three times with the iron rod, they will open. Inside await two lions with gaping jaws. If you accurately cast a loaf to each of them, they will calm down and not devour you. Then you must hasten and fetch the Water of Life before the clock strikes twelve, or the gates will close again and you will be imprisoned."

The youngest brother thanked the dwarf, took the rod and loaves of bread, and set out again.

Eventually, the youngest brother arrived at the castle with the iron gates, and everything was just as the dwarf had said. After three strokes with the iron rod, the gates swung open. He appeased the lions with the bread, went into the castle, and found himself in a large, splendid hall. Wherever he looked, he saw men standing stark still, all turned to stone. He passed among them and drew a gold ring off the hand of each one. As he was leaving the hall, he found a sword and another loaf of bread, and he took those as well. Farther on, he came to another room where a beautiful woman was standing. She rejoiced when she saw him, embraced him, and declared that he had set her free. "My whole realm will be yours and all the enchantments here broken," she said, "if you return in a year's time. Then we shall celebrate our wedding." Then she told him where to find the fountain with the Water of Life, encouraging him to hasten and draw the water before the clock struck twelve.

He went on and came upon a room with a newly made bed, covered with quilts finely embroidered with scenes from old stories. He was tired and thought he would rest a while. As soon as he lay down, he fell into a deep sleep and didn't stir until something awakened him at a quarter to twelve. He jumped up, ran to the courtyard, found the fountain, drew some water into a cup lying nearby, and hastened back the way he had come. Just as he reached the huge iron gates, they were swinging shut. The clock struck twelve as he went between them. The gates closed with such force that they cut off a piece of his heel.

All the same, he rejoiced at having found the Water of Life, and he started toward home. As he was going along, he heard a voice from the side of the road. It was the dwarf, who said, "Those are great treasures you've come by. With that sword you can defeat whole armies, and that loaf will always be the same no matter how much is eaten from it."

The youngest son did not want to return to his father without his brothers. He said, "Dear dwarf, can you tell me where my two brothers are? They set out for the Water of Life before I did, and they never came back."

"Don't worry about them—they're safe and secure," said the dwarf. "They are contained in a place well suited to their narrow views and haughty ways."

The prince pleaded, and at length the dwarf released them, though he warned him, "Beware of them. They have wicked hearts."

When his brothers appeared, the youngest brother rejoiced and told them all about his adventures. He told how he had found the Water of Life and brought away a cup full of it. He told how he had found and rescued a beautiful queen and how she was going to wait a year for him and then they would be married and would reign together. After he had told all about it, the three brothers rode on together and came upon a country where war and famine were raging and where the misery was so great that the king and the people thought that they must all perish. The youngest brother gave the loaf of bread to the king, who then fed all the people until they were satisfied. Then the youngest brother gave the king his sword, and the king destroyed the armies that were oppressing his people, and the land returned to peace.

The brothers entered two more countries where war raged and famine made misery, and each time the youngest gave the loaf and the sword. Each time peace and abundance were restored.

Then the three boarded a ship and sailed home across the sea. During the voyage, the two older brothers drew each other aside and said, "Our younger brother has found the Water of Life, and we haven't found anything. Our father will reward him by giving him the kingdom that should properly be ours. He will rob us of our birthright." They began to seek revenge and plotted to destroy him. They waited until he fell fast asleep and took the Water of Life from his cup and filled the cup with bitter seawater.

When the three arrived home, the youngest took his cup of water straight to the sick king, expecting that he would drink the water and be cured. But the king had barely tasted the seawater when he fell sicker than ever before. As the king was lamenting his state, the two older brothers came in and accused the youngest of trying to poison their father. Then they brought the true Water of Life and gave it to the king. At the first drink of that water, the king felt his sickness leaving him. Soon he was healthy and as strong as in his youth.

In private, the older brothers mocked the youngest, saying, "You certainly found the Water of Life, but much good it has done you—you have the pain and we the gain. You get the hardship, and we get the reward. You should have been more clever and kept your eyes open. We took it from you while you were sleeping on the ship, and in a year we will go to claim the beautiful queen as well. Even if you tell the king about this, he will never believe you, and you'll lose your life as well. But if you keep silent, we will let you live."

The old king was very angry with the youngest son and thought that the son had plotted against his life. He summoned his council. They said, "Indeed, indeed." He had them secretly sentence the youngest to be killed.

One day, the youngest brother, who suspected no evil, went hunting. The king's old huntsman was told to go with him. When they were alone in the forest, the huntsman looked so sorrowful that the youngest brother asked him, "Dear huntsman, what ails you?"

The huntsman said, "I can't tell you, and yet I ought to tell."

"Speak openly," said the brother. "Whatever it is, I'll forgive you."

"Alas," the huntsman said, "I'm supposed to kill you. The king ordered it so."

The youngest brother was shocked. "Dear huntsman, let me live. I'll give you my royal garments. Give me your common ones in their place. Pretend that I am dead and that you have taken my clothes."

"I'll willingly do that," said the hunter. "I wouldn't have been able to kill you."

They exchanged clothes. The hunter went home, and the prince, dressed in the hunter's common garments, went deeper into the forest, not looking ahead but into himself.

Sometime later, three wagonloads of gold and precious stones arrived at the king's castle. They had been sent to the youngest son as tokens of gratitude from the three kings who had defeated their enemies and sustained their people with the sword and the loaf. The old king began to consider, "Can my son have been innocent?" He said aloud, "If only he were alive. I can't forgive myself for having him killed."

At that moment, the huntsman spoke up, "He is alive. I couldn't find it in my heart to carry out the command." He told the king what had happened. Then a stone weight fell from the king's heart, and he had it proclaimed in all lands that his son was free to return and would be welcomed with open arms.

Meanwhile, it had come to the end of the year since the youngest brother had found the Water of Life. The lady of the fountain had the road to the castle overlaid with gold. She set guards at the entrance and told them, "If a man comes straight down the middle of the road, he will be the one waited for. Anyone who comes along either side is not welcome and should be refused entry."

As the time was close at hand, the eldest brother set out for the castle, intending to pass himself off as the savior of that realm. He fully expected to wed the lady of the place and to rule with her there. When he came to the castle, he saw the road covered with gold. He thought, "It would be a pity to ride on such a beautiful surface." So he turned aside and went along the right side of the road. When he reached the gates, the guards reviled him and sent him away.

Soon the second brother started out and eventually came to the golden road. His horse had put one hoof on the path when he thought, "It would be a sin and a shame to ride over that. What if I were to break it?" So he turned aside and went along the left side of the road. When he reached the gates, the guards reviled him, too, and sent him away.

At the very end of the year, the youngest brother turned toward the castle of the Water of Life in hopes of seeing the beautiful lady of the realm. As he went along, he thought about her incessantly and wished to be with her so much that he didn't see where he was going. He walked right down the middle of the road, and when he reached the gates, they opened without the need of the iron rod. The lady of the castle welcomed him with joy and said that he had saved the realm and broken the enchantment.

They celebrated their marriage with great joy. Then the lady told him that his father had sent for him and wished to forgive him. So the youngest brother returned to his father's realm. The old king welcomed him, and the youngest brother told the whole story of how his brothers had betrayed him and how he had kept his silence. The king wanted to punish the older brothers, but they had put to sea again and never came back as long as they lived.

CHAPTER 20

BREAKING DOWN

Working with stories is like waking up over and over again in separate parts of the forest. As soon as we have glimpsed the treasures of one story, we wake up in another one. The orientation of the psyche shifts; the flow of life pours into a riverbed that has been dry, and we must follow it or get stuck. There is no one story in which we can take up residence, living it out and learning all about it. Instead, we wander like Ulysses from place to place, story to story, trying to find home. We wake into another story before we feel that we've gotten everything from the previous story, or stage, that we were in. Life presents itself as dreams do: strangely, surprisingly, weirdly. In an initiation, the initiate always becomes disoriented and doesn't know what's taking place or where events are leading him. Initiations by water, in particular, are characterized by this sense of disorientation, by rivers that erode solid ground and chasms that suddenly appear. Our relations with people and things around us break apart, or the inner connections that make us feel solid and secure break down.

In the firebird story, there was the single hunter, the heroic figure alone against all odds. That's how fire is discovered, faced, and learned, how an initiation by fire feels. The way through water feels more multiple and more inclusive of others. Water offers a connection to family and eventually to community. The brothers at the beginning of this story are described as siblings who lament a sick father, but they are also brothers united by cultural illness, sons of a realm that is stuck and collapsing. The road of fire makes a great test of the individual; the road to water is full of aloneness but ultimately leads to the return of community and the proper flow of life. Through the metaphors of kingdoms collapsing and men being stuck in stone, this story shows how necessary watery emotions and imaginings are to the lives of individuals, communities, and cultures.

When a story starts with sickness, death, weeping, and the garden, it makes clear that the issues are those of the soul, for the sense of loss is a vital aspect of the soul's connection to life. Reconnecting to this sense of loss is one of the main tasks of an initiation by water. The garden of weeping is at the center of the castle, which is at the center of the realm. Like the small gardens that are tucked into city neighborhoods or the large parks with flowing fountains that stand at the center of a town, this image reaches back for the Garden of Eden where life flows from the center. Within an individual, the garden and fountain represent the source of the waters of the soul, which flow at the center of one's life.

At the beginning of this story, life is stuck and draining away from the center. The father-king is dying from a lack of the Water of Life, and the realm is drying up and draining away, as the life force drains out of the king. The tears of the sons as they contemplate death are the only water at the center of the realm. The three sons weep for the loss of father and king—for the lack of growth, for the damming up of the right flowing of life. Weeping seems appropriate when a reign is ending or when, in contemporary terms, the dominant images of an epoch are losing their energy and life force. If the brothers of the realm are not weeping, are prevented from weeping, or are never seen weeping, despair will solidify at the center. This may be happening all over the world right now.

It happens also inside a man when the accumulation of losses within grows too great. Listen to Pablo Neruda again:

WALKING AROUND

It so happens I am sick of being a man.
And it happens that I walk.
....

It so happens I am sick of my feet and my nails
and my hair and my shadow.
It so happens I am sick of being a man.

. . . . .

I don't want so much misery.
I don't want to go on as a root and a tomb,
alone under the ground, a warehouse with corpses,
half frozen, dying of grief.

. . . . .

I stroll along serenely, with my eyes, my shoes,
my rage, forgetting everything,
I walk by, going through office buildings and orthopedic shops,
and courtyards with washing hanging from the line:
underwear, towels, and shirts from which slow
dirty tears are falling.

As Neruda describes, even when a man is still "walking around," there can be acute sickness and stuckness at the center. There may be weeping and sorrow in his soul even if they have not yet risen all the way to his eyes. Such a soul sickness eventually causes a man either to become deeply stuck or to begin to weep. The trouble at the center can become a stuckness that spreads throughout a man's life and can turn into despair. Weeping, on the other hand, starts the search for a cure.

When sickness reigns at the center, when it's the king at the center of the realm who is sick, the kingdom has no clear direction. It feels like everything is breaking down, like life is becoming a wasteland or an empty tomb. The stuckness is a sign to stop and move toward the sorrow. Unless a recognition of the sorrow occurs at the center, the flow of life may stop in despair. Unless there is participation in the sorrow at the center of a man, at the center of a culture, at the center of the world, life will begin to be stuck "under the ground . . . half frozen, dying of grief."

The Water of Life can only be found by breaking down, by wandering away, by being and feeling lost. The world of water dissolves and wears away established patterns and accomplishments. Initiations by water begin with an accumulation of losses and sorrows, an expansion of emptiness inside, the feeling that life has stopped flowing in a natural and healthy way. A person begins to feel "out of touch"; communications break down; "things fall apart, the center cannot hold," to quote Yeats again. Somewhere below, in the water of the soul, a keening or lamenting begins. Now the danger is not that one may burn up but that one will get lost, not that one will die by the sword but that one will turn to stone. If a man in this condition cannot reach the waters that move the soul, he could go numb, dry up, or fall apart.

Initiations by water may precede or follow those by fire. Men go back and forth between the two in the tempering process. The discovery of fire is so basic to humanity that it easily occupies a bright spot in any psychic storytelling. But every light casts shadows, and in the shadows of the bright, burning stories of accomplishment and direct powers lie the waters of self-reflection. A man can't soar forever. To live fully, he must eventually descend to the ground and go still further down in search of his soul. Without the spirit symbolized by fire, life may not "get off the ground," but below the ground there always exists a well of sorrow. The sequence of first fire, then water, is common, and it reflects the way that sorrow and losses accumulate in a person's heart over time. Traditional initiations took this shape: first heating the spirit, then cooling it in the waters of the soul.

Some men, however, experience the opposite sequence: they go first into the waters of the soul. Their life stories begin in the shadows of a king and kingdom that are wasting away. They are born into a family in decline or in a period of depression. Or they receive a blow early on that throws them down too hard. For them, the sense of loss and breakdown dominates, while the fiery spirit burns below their awareness. When and if these men discover the heat of the psyche late in life, it is usually full of surprises.

In the story-making, inner, otherworld, sequences can easily be changed around. Although each person must touch both the warmth of fire and the cool of water in order to be fully alive, some spend most of their lives with the center breaking down, simply holding on.

In the sequence we are following, being heated by Litima is followed by falling into or wandering down into the labyrinths and waters of the soul. Here a man must learn to breathe "underwater," within the atmosphere of his feelings and emotions. Any attempt to force change is blunted, softened, and slowed by the dense elements of this underworld. The horse of power can't get going or goes the wrong way here. Stopping and listening become essential; without the ability to hear the voices of the soul and the body, all of life becomes stuck, just as the two older brothers in the story become stuck in the rocks. Time itself slows down. A man can feel imprisoned here, as if his purpose in life has left him, as if he's wasting time. Everything looks bleak and empty, as if a whole kingdom were wasting away.

The road of the firebird requires an inner fire that seeks risk and danger. On that road, it is appropriate to charge ahead, to ignore questions, and to look for a demanding, desirous king. The road to the Water of Life, on the other hand, doesn't lead to a strong king but wanders away from a sick one. In order to heal the king rather than replace him, to restore the realm from its condition of wasteland, we need a different approach from the beginning. Fire, sight, and heated vision all go together. Water, listening, and going ahead without a clear view mark this initiation. The powers at work here are smaller, lower, more easily overlooked, usually unheard, frequently dismissed. When a golden feather from the burning breast of the great firebird falls directly in front of a man, there are plenty of compelling reasons to stop. But when a small voice calls out or questions what is normally going on, it's easy just to charge on, even if the right direction is unknown.

Unlike the center in the story of the firebird, here the king has no resources; instead, there's sickness, want, and weeping. The fires may have burned too bright or burned out. The king is not threatening but withdrawn and ill, not demanding but rather distracted and seemingly uninterested. The question is not whether one can survive the demands and threats of the king but rather whether one of the sons can go from the deteriorating center to find the cure for the ills of the realm. The task becomes not just to risk but to heal. The way to go does not climb into greater and greater encounters with spirit; rather, it begins with stopping and descending and seeking more of the soul.

Learned from loss and brokenness and mistakes, the way of water consists of stepping down, allowing oneself to wander and to wonder what to do. The passport is not a golden, burning feather but the memory of things lost, of sicknesses endured, of collapses and depressions and times alone. Someone with a fire in his or her head won't be able to see the byways, the meandering paths, and the empty places where this story takes place. Not until all the other ways have been blocked, not until nothing else works, not until fire seems to be burning everything up or until everything seems to be turning to stone will most turn into the valleys and waterways of descent. Even a life of triumph, a life of success after success, a life lived for the burning of the spirit accumulates empty places and feelings of loss. Though these feelings may be overlooked for a long time, there comes a day in a person's life when there's "crying in the kingdom" and no place to go but down.

As at the beginning of the story, weeping blurs the vision, and it's hard to see where to turn. Fortunately, weeping draws a wise old man to the garden, and some hope of healing gets born of the tears of despair. The scene is reminiscent of the way the hunter would weep before receiving advice from the horse of power. Tears can be a creative force, for they release what's blocked in the psyche and the heart. They stir the Waters of Life. Some weeping is always going on in the soul. The tears of the sons draw the old man to them; the tears prompt the old man's questions and lead to his revealing the existence of a cure. The "old man" has the knowledge that the king and the brothers lack, and the weeping of the sons causes the knowledge to flow. Without the sons' tears, he might just pass by. This opening scene makes clear that the story is not about heroic searching and conquering; rather, it is about losses and feeling lost. The tears stir old resources of the psyche, resources that do not reside with the king "above" but that come from below.

Similarly, this is the direction that the story of the Water of Life will take: it winds down from the castle of the king onto the common road. From there it drops to the side of the road, the place of the dwarf. From there it descends further into the land of the fountain of the Water of Life. And even after the water has been found, there is a second descent brought on by betrayals and false accusations. The road to the Water of Life is found and refound by following loss and sorrow, by passing through the shadows of betrayal, misunderstanding, and exile.

On the way to the Water of Life, acceptance is more valuable than will, and surrender more meaningful than force. Stopping, letting go, and dropping down to suffer inner conflicts are necessary on this road. Fierceness turns aside from the outer world and toward the inner world. The road to the Water of Life feels crooked and dark, its direction uncertain. To follow it, we must take time away from the regular pursuits of life. But unless everything stops and bows to the sorrow of the world, the inner life will become stuck, and the king in the psyche will withdraw in illness. The story can't even get under way until the two older brothers are properly stuck and the remaining one stops as well. If we aren't prepared to wait, the radical change needed in our lives may never occur. But if, instead of continuing our drive for "hot power," we wait with the youngest son, we will get to see the workings of the world from below.

To revive the flow of the Water of Life within an individual and within a culture requires change that moves what is stuck and that water comes from below. If the stuckness has been of long standing, a radical change is needed. The story says that when the old ways of succeeding are empty and breaking down, change comes from going further down. The source and knowledge of change come from what is below, aside, and left out. The flow of life and the healing waters return from the depths below and from areas usually avoided and overlooked.

Unless things change, the older brothers will inherit the realm with the existing arrangements that hold it together. These brothers stand for the traditional way of sustaining order and systematically avoiding chaos. They represent the existing order in the family, the state, and the inner realm. When things are "in order," "as they should be," and "as everyone expects things to be," it is their realm. The older brothers are committed to the system as it stands, for the more one stands to inherit from the system, the more it appears to be the only alternative to chaos. Those who are upheld by the status quo don't want to change. Saying even quietly, "I don't know where I'm going," can seem like the loss of all order. From the fearful and hardened point of view of the dominant ego or the dominant class of the status quo, change can appear to be impending chaos. Stories often show how change occurs within a container that can stop the mechanisms of the regular world without destroying that world. So our story carefully sets up a structure that holds one realm in place while the second realm is opened up and entered.

What's the rush? Where's all this going, anyway? These are questions the youngest brother might ask. He can see the expectations that were placed on the older brothers. He can feel the sadness that the older ones can't afford to feel, can't drop down to hear, can't look back to see. The youngest brother can see what the older brothers and the sick king have dropped, pushed back, left behind. He can see all the stuff that we are encouraged to "put behind us" in our willful pursuit of life, happiness, and manifest destiny. And it's precisely the weight of all that's been put and left behind that is draining the life from the king. Now things must reach back and down before they can go forward.

In other words, the sins, mistakes, and illnesses of the fathers are visited on the sons. Not only the fires of a generation but also its problems and sicknesses are passed down. Families, businesses, and entire cultures can get stuck in the ways of the "older brothers" and those of the "sick king." Within a culture, the "youngest brother" or sister stands for the next generation, who are trying to get out of the old king's castle and find the Water of Life. These "youngest children" focus on the sickness in the realm, for they inherit the effects of it. The youngest brother is the part of a generation or of an individual that is closest to the source of illness. He can't be treated as an "older brother," for he won't respond to demands and direct challenges. Psychologically, he's the inferior function; within a family, he's the "identified patient." He's the part of a person or of a culture willing to try any direction that may lead to healing long-standing wounds. As a result, he is ready for initiation by water.

The search for the Water of Life is a story about turning aside, about finding what has been lost, and about healing wounds and sicknesses that call out with small, parched voices. For the water of the psyche to flow, the youngest son must get through to the fountain. Walking in the wake of the older brothers, he sees and hears what they and the king leave behind. On the yardstick of "success" in the outer world, the youngest brother may himself be a dwarf. He is not the glorified young son but the one left behind, the one of whom no one expects much. No one knows what to expect from him, and as a result, he doesn't know what to expect either. He is more able to take what comes to him than to will something to happen.

The youngest brother carries through the gates not the certainty of how his task must be accomplished but the uncertainty of whether it can be accomplished at all. The usual rulers of the psyche have given up. The last brother is only released when everyone else has failed and let go and nothing is being held back. Initiation requires that the whole psyche enter the troubles, with nothing held back. Initiation changes the shape of the psyche so that what appeared foolish, retarded, or despicable is brought forward, included, revalued, and given a new position. In initiation, restrictions are loosened, and the stiff-necked ego submits to what it considers below itself.

Despite being "the youngest" brother, the last remaining brother has been held in the castle the longest. He has been present as the king grows older and moves closer to death. He has been closer to the sickness and has become more aware of the nature of the illness than the older brothers. As the last brother, the youngest son, the little brother, he is closer to the trouble at the center and further from what everyone else expects. The little brother may appear slow, foolish, dumb, weak, overly emotional, underdeveloped, highly intuitive, or poorly prepared. And, the longer the little brother has been kept inside, the more strange and foolish he looks when he comes out. But in order to see his *true* nature, we need to enter the Territory of Brothers.

CHAPTER 21

THE TERRITORY OF BROTHERS

F AMILY CAN BE a storehouse of love and inherited riches. It can also be a source of sorrow and a prison made of fixed positions. When politicians and preachers call for a return to "family values," the heart may fill with warmth—while the skeletons in the closet dance. Which family? Which values? For family is also the locus of tragedy, as the Greek drama cycles demonstrated. In ancient Greece, tragic family flaws took center stage in a revolving calendar of plays that kept family values and family faults on display. Oedipus was one of many kings whose blind spots about both family and state resulted in disaster. In ancient cultures, the inevitable movement of family sins from fathers and mothers to daughters and sons was acknowledged through community ceremonies.

Family is the birthplace of human affection and nourishment as well as the source of illness and other troubles. Family also means fixed positions, relatives determined by birth, inherited structures that don't change easily. Sicknesses are passed through these structures; often we come by our symptoms and troubles honestly. Yet in pite of family faults and familiar sicknesses, the "older brothers" don't wish to change their positions; they choose to stay where they are in hopes of inheriting that familiar castle. The "youngest brother," on the other hand, inherits the full weight of the family trouble. He has been at home when the family skeletons were out and about. He has heard them rattling in the troubled dreams of parents when the "older brothers" were fast asleep. Often the gates of denial that close over family secrets cannot open until the youngest brother has broken out. The bottom of the trouble simply can't be reached by the "older-brother" parts of a family, a culture, or an individual psyche.

Each man has the three brothers from "The Water of Life" in his psyche, and each man was also born into an actual family position as a son. As the story shows, only the "youngest" is capable of finding the healing water. In order to look at the three brothers as parts of the psyche, men must start with the actual relations that they experienced in their family. The gates of the family have to open, and some skeletons have to be rattled in order to find the youngest brother within.

Usually, men who are working through this story feel compelled to talk first about their actual brothers. Of course, eldest brothers are quite willing to speak first, and they can say a lot about being the oldest. "The oldest receives adulation for no real reason," says one. "Not for me," says another, "I had to be super-responsible and achieve at a high level or the whole family would be let down." "For me it was like being a front-line soldier. I had to take all my parents' shit. My little brother could just duck and get by." "In my case, I was the point man. I went first into everything, and that made it easier for my brothers." "Well, I went first because if I didn't one of my brothers would have. I was sure I'd lose out if I didn't go first. I still act that way. I'm driven through everything I do, and I'm afraid to look back." "I always envied my youngest brother because he was carefree. He got to enjoy his childhood." "The strange thing for me is that my younger brother reveres me, treats me with adulation. I don't know why, and I don't return the feeling or the affection."

Then middle brothers begin to chime in. One says, "I adored my older brother. He would barely talk to me, but that added to the feeling. There's still that same distance and awe between us." "To me, my older brother was a father figure. Later, I acted as a father to my younger brother. I still do; we can't talk any other way." "I was the middle one, and I had to be the good boy. Part of being the good boy was being the scapegoat for the whole family." "For me, being stuck between my brothers meant being the go-between. I became the conciliator, the consensus maker, for the entire family." "For me, it meant being most connected to my mother. In our family, the middle one was supposed to be the priest, Mama's priest." "In my family, was expected to be the therapist; I don't know why, but I had to hear everyone's problems and not talk about my own." "I only got to deal with little things. My older brother was the big shot, and my younger brother was the baby. The older one had already done everything tried to do; I merely followed him, and my baby brother was so young he needed everyone's help. I was just filling in between them."

Finally, youngest brothers begin to tell their stories. "I was the youngest son and the favorite. Compared to my brothers, I was spoiled and indulged, and I feel guilty about it." "I was the youngest of many brothers, and I had to be tricky and quick or else I was beaten up by each of the older ones." "It was the opposite for me. I was the most held and the most held onto. Everyone wanted me to stay at home. was supposed to stay innocent of the world outside." "In my family being the youngest was like being the last victim, the last hostage, the last one caught in a crazy household." "I always felt like a serf, like would never get anything. My parents were old, and it was as if everything was used up when I got there." "I was just left alone a lot. It was as if I were handicapped, or too small, or too young to be part of things. I didn't like being seen that way, but it made me free to do what I wanted to, unobserved." "Exactly the opposite for me. I was expected to undo my brother's failures. I was the last hope. It was as if I had to rescue the family name." "My father died when I was young. As the youngest, it was clear that I would survive everyone else. always felt lonely and had a constant awareness of death. It was like was left in the shadows of my family."

"Wait a minute," a man says, "I'm an only child, and I feel really left out of this whole thing. Half the time I'm sad that I didn't have any brothers to play with, to remember, or have a feeling about. Then I get angry as everyone goes on and on about which brother he is. What if you're no one's brother?" Another man answers, "I was an only child, too. The expectations that an older brother gets were put on me, but I had the feelings of a youngest brother. To my father, was an oldest son; to my mother, I was a youngest. I've never been convincing as either one." The first man speaks again: "That doesn't make the issue go away—all this talk of brothers leaves me out. When I walk into a room full of men, like this one, I'm lost. I don't know how to act. This brother stuff doesn't apply to me." He's joined by other "only sons" who have been feeling left out in various degrees.

I offer that the three brother positions are a metaphor for relationships among men as well as for parts of the psyche. As a metaphor, they're available to everyone; every man can find the brothers in the relationship dynamics in which he participates every day. This idea doesn't satisfy the "only-child" group. There's something about being an only child that won't allow these men to accept the metaphor—at least, not right away. There is a literal isolation in the position of only child that demands recognition before a man can look at other psychological dynamics. One man, for example, says he just won't join the group because he doesn't trust that he'll be understood at all. Another says he was raised as an only child but actually had a brother who died shortly after birth; now the dead brother lies between him and feeling part of the group. He's part of the only-child group and yet he's not. This man's statement evokes a well of sorrow over missing brothers, known, barely known, and unknown. The sorrow brings everyone back together.

In daily life, men often unconsciously arrange themselves in the position of oldest, middle, or youngest brother. These positions readily transcend actual ages. When men have been working together long enough or closely enough, the sense of each one's position as brother can have a stronger influence on relationships than age or experience. The result can be both positive and negative, protective or destructive.

As the men at one conference came up with more and more examples, it became clear that the roles of brothers, their disappointments and jealousies, protections and ignorances, generosities and treacheries had been repeated through friendships, projects, and jobs with seemingly unrelated men. One oldest brother spoke about having abdicated his role as oldest and heir to the family expectations. Now he repeatedly found himself in work situations where a younger man was chosen over him, while he felt senior and more qualified. More and more instances arose where we could see the way an older brother's protective spirit was awakened by a younger-brother type, even when the "younger brother" was an older man. Men who had been bullied and ignored by actual older brothers found ways to reexperience that with other men, regardless of their ages or positions of seniority in the daily world. And we found that the less the men involved knew about these patterns, the more power the patterns could exert.

Men gravitate toward hierarchies. This behavior is common among animal kin, and humans slip into kin positions naturally and often unwittingly. The relations between actual siblings can be deeply painful, reassuring, even encouraging, and the same can be said for men who are "unconscious siblings." The rivalries for which brothers are famous form the basis for much of Judeo-Christian imaginings. Cain and Abel are never far away. They move closer when men gather together. The story of Joseph and his brothers is acted out daily not only on school yards and playgrounds but also in the halls of academia and in corporate boardrooms. Even if a man in this country hasn't been raised in the religions of the West, he has been raised in a culture informed by and styled from those religions. Part of the psychic inheritance of any man, then, are the stories of Cain and Abel, Jacob and Esau, and Judas and Jesus. They all sought to inherit the kingdom of the father-king. So although there may have been great filial love in any particular family, still as soon as "brothers" are mentioned, the seeds of struggle and betrayal are also stirring in the psyche.

When the territory of brothers extends beyond the family, it enters the area of initiatory brotherhoods where someone becomes "family" because of shared suffering and experiences. This area produces abundant metaphors that show the brother bonds among men: blood brothers; brethren of the spirit; brothers in crime; fraternal orders of Eagles and Lions; fraternity brothers; Christian brothers; brothers in orders, crews, bands, and gangs of all kinds. The intentions and values of these bands extend in all directions, and the names and styles that define them are in constant creative flux. But what connects all brotherhoods are common forms of hierarchy, rituals for entering and maintaining the group, shared intense experiences, and shared symbols. All of these groups have conscious and unconscious initiatory aspects and extend brotherhood beyond biology into emotional, ritual, and spiritual relationships. In initiation, relationships to actual brothers gets transferred to one's fellow initiates and often to the "elder brothers" who guide the initiation. The literal condition of being a certain type of brother or of being no one's brother is broken open and replaced with new potentials for brotherhood. In initiation, each one becomes the youngest brother or "little brother"; eventually, each plays "elder brother" as well.

In many initiation cultures, the initiate is assigned two elder brothers who have already been through the stage of initiation he is about to enter. The older brothers are there to protect, encourage, contain, and inspire him. Their role is to keep him from hurting himself or others while he lets go of who he has been. The initiate is letting his former self die metaphorically. His way of relating to everyone and his way of relating to himself will change radically. Part of the "death of him who was" occurs through the falling away of his fixed relationships. Temporarily, he is the "little brother," regardless of age or family position.

The initiation is made for the "little brother" within. The initiate connects sideways to the brothers who are his fellow initiates and connects upward to the elder brothers. They form the rings of initiation that expand from the initiates, the "little brothers" at the center, through the elder brothers who have recently passed through initiation, to those who are about to step into the ring of the elders. The elders themselves are held by the ring of the ancestors. Each ring contains the next group within it and looks out toward the groups beyond. All the rings are connected because each looks at a death, at the end of life or a stage of life.

Ideally, the elder brothers form the ring that contains and supports the fresh initiate. They can empathize with his fears and set limits on his excess while maintaining sympathy for him and his position. When the initiate's passion heats up, the older ones will keep him from harming others or burning himself up. While he swims on the sea of his passions, they can hold onto him and bring him back to himself. The presence of the elder brothers also allows the initiate to let go of his usual life and plunge into the sorrow and loss that he carries and must explore. This containing ring makes it possible for the initiate to fall away from and break down the dominance of his usual self.

During initiation, "normal" attitudes and beliefs break down through a process of surrendering, descending, and finding a way back. The emotions that are aroused carry us away and down to find out what is below and within us, while the "elder brothers" above hold the rings for our return. Those above must have been through this breaking down, or they won't know when to pull up and when to let go. They must be in touch with the foolish, surprising, little brother in themselves and more committed to him than to the status quo or to their own egotistical needs. When the elder brothers become self-interested "older brothers," the containing ring that they form breaks down, and they leave the little brothers to sink or swim on their own.

As I see it, in the first two rings of initiation the little brother is encouraged toward extreme expressions; he both takes flight and falls down. Later, when he enters the outer rings, he begins to take responsibility for family and culture, for children and ancestors. In each ring, he immerses in fire and water, and the ring outside him expands and contracts, cools and heats to contain him. When he's on fire, the heat needs to be contained and directed upward and outward. When he is drawn down by water, the water needs to carry him down through surrender or collapse into and under the ground. Then those in the containing ring need to be nearby and know when his return upward is necessary. The difference between the elder brothers of these initiations and the "older brothers" in the story lies in the elder brothers' ability to contain the little brother in a way that benefits both him and the community.

The shapes of initiatory rings and fraternal hierarchies lie dormant in the human psyche like empty containers waiting to be filled. When people cast about for a form that will hold, evaluate, and shape their ascending and descending spirits, they inevitably find and reshape this system of rings and the sense that people are moving from one to another.

Many modern systems of education adopt this form, but because it is used unconsciously or superficially, it cannot fully benefit those who participate in it. We keep the form of these rings without the knowledge of their deeper purpose and their power to change seemingly fixed attitudes and sicknesses in people. The structures of high schools and universities, for example, follow initiatory forms but deny the deeper needs of the students. The freshman is the initiate taking his or her first steps into a new stage of life. The sophomore has walked further into this new stage and stands at the next ring, still an underclassman but looking ahead more than looking back. From the point of view of the entering freshman, the sophomore seems wise (*sophos* means wisdom), but from the point of view of the upperclassman, the sophomore is still foolish (*moros*, as in moron). Then comes the junior elder and finally the senior elder; the latter is in the outer ring, about to become an initiate all over again.

Some variation on the rings of initiation underlies most learning systems, especially schools, fraternal organizations, military groups, cults, and gangs. They follow this lost form of initiation, and between grades or stages, they institute either hazing or honor ceremonies or both. Generally, the masculine psyche jumps at the chance to shape graduated, hierarchical steps out of life's events. Men carry an innate sense of graduation, a ladder of masculinity within. Usually, the fact that the ladders can be used to descend as well as to climb upward is overlooked, the way the older brothers in the story overlook the importance of the dwarf. Without the descent into the waters below, the emotions and memories that underlie the hierarchies are forgotten or avoided; then, the initiates may easily be exposed to the abuses found in hierarchies. In addition, when the elder brothers are not holding the ground from which the little brothers must descend and to which they must return, people begin to "fall through the cracks," and the rings of community break down.

Mostly, we get to experience the initiatory rings in a deteriorated state. Much of the anthropology of initiation focuses on the brutality of one group toward another. The initiatory rituals deteriorate to hazings that are hazardous for no genuine reason. Some of the elements that belong to initiations are present, but the purpose is forgotten, and the depths of feeling are avoided in favor of superficial exercises of control and dominance. These largely empty ceremonies persist because the need for an initiation arises whenever there is evidence of a transition or change. This ancient pattern and instinct won't go away, and ignoring its universal presence and potential depth directs its power to harm rather than heal those who experiment with it.

"Gangs" of boys will continually form, whether they consist of Boy Scout troops or "old-boy" networks. Entry rituals and graduated steps or rings are going to develop with or without societal approval. There are going to be "ringleaders," big brothers, and veterans in every group united by some common interest. The question regarding groups of males is whether the group will be self-initiatory like most street gangs—and eventually self-destructive and dangerous to others—or self-revelatory. Street gangs and army gangs kill each other off, and old-boy networks preserve the self-interests of old boys perpetually.

But it's not the form that perpetuates anguish and tragedy; it's the absence of the outer rings of ancestors and elders and the lack of a conscious orientation toward benefiting the "little brothers" and the community at large.

Since it is rare for modern men to have the full experience of an intentional initiation, we have to search for the pieces that have occurred to us accidentally. One of the purposes of gathering grown men together is to revive and reactivate each man's memories and feelings about his "brothers." A man who has never felt that he was protected by another man will not trust other men and will not be trustworthy either. If a man can't imagine being protected by a "brother" at a time when he is unable to protect himself, then he will feel a sense of threat and danger from all men. He will have an exaggerated fear of "letting go," a dislike of "little people," and no knowledge of where to look for the Water of Life.

On the other hand, many men have experienced the misuse of authority represented by blind loyalty, codes of silence, and absolute obedience. These can be ways in which men avoid individual responsibilities. If authority moves only from above downward and requires absolute obedience, then atrocities are in the making. One purpose of initiation is to awaken an inner authority in each person and to connect that force to the common ground of the community. Often this inner authority and the ground of community can only be found when the authorities "above" have become stuck; once again, they can only be found through descent.

To work on the sense of initiation through breaking down, through following the way to the Water of Life, requires finding memories of events where others held it together while we couldn't handle it, while we lost it or had to let go. Through whoever held things together for us, we can discover the sense of brotherhood that is not necessarily biological but psychologically true. These memories are those of ourselves as little brother. It is only from the youngest brother's place in the psyche, the place of the initiate, that we can find the tracks that lead to the Water of Life. Without a sense of who he is in us, we can't form a ring that will contain and keep safe the next group of little brothers. And a culture with no room for little brothers is about to burn up or sicken to death. To me, the various gatherings of men that look squarely at the skeletons in the personal, familial, and cultural closets represent attempts to stand within the rings. Men who are trying to handle the fires and waters of life together are becoming "sudden brothers" in order to encourage and contain each other.

In order to find the road to the healing waters, men need to get past the uprightness of the older brothers and enter the areas of themselves and of the culture that are sick, stuck, and broken down. In that sense, both dwarf and youngest brother are part of the shadow of the individual psyche, and they are aspects of the shadow of a culture. The cure for what ails individuals and communities can only be found by going down—through the shadows and the small openings that appear.

Once men have begun to acknowledge how brotherhood extends beyond the biological family, they are often ready to see that each of them also has the three brothers from the story inside, as part of the royal family of the psyche. As a metaphor, these brothers are available to everyone—they are even a necessity to everyone.

The "oldest brother" is the part of our psyches that believes it will inherit the realm. The oldest brother expects to gain control by right of law and rite of succession. He tends to be a fundamentalist. He has a fundamental interest in the current shape of the realm and in its continuance. He can't afford to deviate much to the left or right because the straight line of succession leads to him. For him, straight is the path and narrow the gate. Eventually, he becomes such a fundamentalist in his view of life that he gets imprisoned in rock-hard interpretations that turn his imagination to stone. His spirit of certainty leads him to a place where change can't occur.

The "middle brother" in the psyche shares the older brother's sense of inheritance. He believes that if he stays in line, everything will fall to him by default. So he becomes a follower, practicing the same steps, taking his turn, and getting caught in the same fundamental mistakes as the oldest brother. Although he has this affinity for the oldest brother, he also has some of the foolishness of the youngest. The second brother can be fooled. While the first brother is a man of facts, a hands-on, straight-ahead, no-detours son of the status quo, the second doesn't have the conviction of the first. He's more carried along by events and by the hope that the eldest will fall out of the picture one day. He may be more resigned than determined; he may be fond of saying, "It's always been this way." He may imitate the oldest brother or compete with him, but he won't step out of the line of direct inheritance.

Everyone has the two older brothers within; they are usually the first to respond when something needs doing. They are capable, in their own ways, and necessary. They keep things going. They manage and repair things. They defend and accept the comfort and order of the psyche. They keep the roads clear and oil the machinery. They ignore or exclude inclinations to deviate from the most direct route. They attack and insult anything or anyone that lies off the beaten path. They can't hear certain basic questions because they are so certain that things will go their way. They keep going without a clue as to what is missing from life. They are the CEOs and middle management of the psyche. They won't make basic changes unless they absolutely must.

Indeed, they won't see the need for change or understand the depth of the change that is necessary until it is too late, because they won't stop until they are absolutely and fundamentally stuck. They must be out of the way before the real story can begin. The strenuous ordeals and series of impossible tasks in stories and during initiations are used to confound and wear down the older brothers. Psychologically, they are two aspects of the ego that have to go ahead before what waits deeper in the psyche can really come out. In this sense, they are products that have been developed by the system that is breaking down, which is in need of change or else headed for death. They are the products of the realm as it stands, sicknesses and all.

Only when they are stuck will the king—the overseer of the psyche—allow what is truly foolish and unpredictable to emerge from the psyche's interior. Only when we are at the end of our wits do we turn to the deeper wit of the youngest brother. All the means of the other two must be exhausted before the strange ways of the youngest brother can slip past the gates of the ego. When we have failed twice and recognized the failures, the soul knows that this is not another "developmental task" to be managed. Now the entire psyche must be engaged and its resources released. The sickness of the king and of the older brothers lies partly in their exclusiveness. The cure begins with a foolish inclusion of everyone. Something begins to change when the king allows even the youngest son to try to find the cure, and it continues when the youngest son admits the truth to the dwarf: No one inside the castle knows where the Water of Life can be found.

One of the mistakes of the older, ego brothers is the certainty that they have all that they need to go straight to the goal. The idea that a cure exists is mistaken for actual knowledge of the cure. In modern cultures, the cult of the individual easily aligns with these "older, ego brothers." Often, when men first hear these stories, they ask, "Why should the brothers want recognition and permission from those old kings? What's the point? I'll do what I want. If I find a golden feather, I'll appreciate it myself. If I want to go after something in life, I'll just go. I don't need anyone's permission. I'll do what I want to do. It's my choice whether I do it or not."

That's the older brothers in men talking their way into the rocks. Such an attitude may even work on the road to fire, but on the road to water, permission is needed. Permission opens the pathway around the rocks.

Men may also ask, "Why can't I just initiate myself?" This is something that the ego is fond of doing. "Things seem a little stuck," it says. "Guess it's time for a radical change. I think I'll set up an initiation and put myself through it." The trouble is that the ego will just create more ego. Once the ego is strong enough to function it tends to go on ego trips. Initiation requires disorientation, not knowing; rather, facing some great "other" and leaving the ego out of it. The two ego brothers can convince themselves that they can initiate each other, but it's just a matter of time before they hit the rocks.

Seeking permission is a sign, a bowing of the head to the otherworld, to the world of the genius and the dwarf. We do it all the time and pretend that we don't. We present a sketch of something we really want before someone we respect. We don't call what we're doing "asking for permission," but if that person approves or encourages us, we're off. We use his or her authority to get going. Usually, we don't tell people that we're making them into a king or queen. But let them miss the point of our plan or dismiss it as too foolish, and we behead them, throw them down from the throne on which we had just installed them, and berate them to others in the bargain. Or else we feel crushed, dispirited, full of shame that we ever mentioned it, certain that they are so far above us that they know better and we'd best retreat to our room in the basement of the castle.

When we know we are seeking something that the soul wants, we ask permission from someone; we get someone to play queen or king for us. Or we pray. Which amounts to the same thing—it's just that the request is made higher, over the heads of kings and queens. We're asking for our effort, risk, and vulnerability to be blessed. We need blessed permission before we undertake the risk. It's a risk because we're feeling our wounds and incompleteness again; if we're not feeling wounded, the soul is not fully involved yet. The more we sense the involvement of the soul, the more we seek permission and blessing. Unless I invoke and acknowledge the world of otherness, I'm simply making the usual ego choices. Soon the older brothers are back in charge and we're heading for the usual rocks.

Some common forms of hero worship are also means of seeking permission. We see a characteristic of our soul in greater measure in someone else, and we study that person. We carry him or her in our minds, even in our hearts. When we have to step out on the fearful road that we know is the next path for our soul, we imagine that person and receive some permission to try. People read biographies to get the same permission. The question "How did they do that?" has an inner resonance: Can I do that as well? Through biographies and quotations and lines of poetry, we bow our heads to the authority of the author and take our permission.

Getting permission from someone who is dead but whom we revere is possible. Not only can the dying king give permission but the dead ones can as well. The concern that famous athletes and celebrities can mislead youth by bad example is partly based on the psychology of permission. The role model gives permission without knowing it. We've been led to believe in our own will and an ever-present "freedom" to do whatever we please. Meantime, students place the questions in their souls guardedly before teachers in hopes of catching a small nod of permission, approval, and blessing. Seeking the blessing awakens the mentor in the king and the king in a potential mentor. Even the headstrong older brothers know that some blessing is required before rushing into the dangers of life. Permission is a requirement of the soul. There is no mission without permission.

Denying the need for permission delays the release of the youngest brother and increases the anger of the dwarf when he's finally acknowledged. Denial is the first defense against change and against feeling the pain that accompanies change. Denial says that there is no problem, that things are not broken, stuck, or full of pain. When we break down the denial and seek permission, we have taken the first steps on the road to the Water of Life.

CHAPTER 22

SUBMISSION, SURRENDER

Permission from the king releases the energy of the psyche in the form of the three brothers riding out of the castle. The next step requires distinguishing among the psychic brothers in order to reach the part of the psyche capable of submission and descent. The story indicates that hearing, recognizing, and submitting to the dwarf is more difficult than receiving permission from the king. Encounters with the dwarf happen aside, off the beaten path, away from the usual ways of proceeding. From the point of view of the ego brothers on their high horses, the dwarf seems lowly and of no account. By personal and cultural standards, listening to the dwarf is weird. If the three brothers are treated as part of the same person, then the story shows that two-thirds of the psyche doesn't want to stoop to speaking to the dwarf. Bowing to the king may be humbling, but bowing to the dwarf feels positively humiliating to the ego.

One form of trouble comes when a person does not have enough ego to get going on the main roads of life. The other trouble comes when a person's ego won't relinquish the reins and won't stop. It especially doesn't want to admit that sometimes it knows nothing. The ego aspect of the self comes to believe that only it is capable of keeping chaos at bay and making a way through life. The ego feels humiliated when it's not in charge and crazy when it is disoriented. What feels appropriately humbling to the little brother feels humiliating to the ego brothers. That's why the king must get sick and the ego brothers stuck before meaningful, lasting change can occur.

The step after gaining permission can be called submission. This step involves stopping, getting off the horse of certainty, turning aside from the daily world, going within. It involves listening to small voices that may be intuitive or instructive and listening to feelings that have not had their say. For many people, it's difficult, even after they have received permission to seek healing, to ask for direction, to say, "I need help" or "I need guidance." For most men, it's more than embarrassing to ask for help; it causes a humiliating feeling of powerlessness.

In the first scene of the story, when the old man hears the weeping of the sons and informs them that there is a cure called the Water of Life, some hope is provided. Without the hope of some healing, submission becomes even more difficult. Often before the submission to the inner, under, otherworlds can occur, there needs to be some partial healing that revives the sense of hope and opens the belief in possible cures. Denial of the problem keeps everything stuck and ensures that there will be no cure. But accepting the problem and the weight of it must somehow be accompanied by the sense that life will be enriched and expanded through submitting to the search for a cure. The Water of Life is a symbol of the flow of emotions and spirits—a flow that may be missing now but that is possible to find. Along with the sorrows that must be carried, some sense of the joy of life returning must be felt.

After my experience with the military, I had a lot of resistance to the idea of submitting. In times of trouble, a voice inside me would say, "Well, I don't owe anybody anything. I can take care of myself." Owing something meant submitting to someone. Not knowing what to do or how to do something also brought up fears of having to submit to some unknown person or process. So I learned on my own and didn't owe anyone anything, though I often had a stiff neck and headaches at the "back of my neck," right where one might bow the head. I even managed to get married, father four children, and go through numerous occupations without really submitting. All the time the voice inside was saying, "I don't owe anybody anything. I'm free and clear." In a sense, I was attempting to keep the older brothers in charge, and I was trying to keep the youngest brother in the castle where he would be protected, since he had been clobbered for sticking his head out a couple of times. Meanwhile, the internal king, the ruler of the psyche, was not feeling well. Mostly he was feeling the weight of this life of responsibility—of being a father, not a daddy, and certainly not a little brother. So while the two older brothers were busy making a living and keeping things going, the inner world was wasting away.

When the king inside gets sick unto dying, there's a constant lament in the interior castle, whether it's being heard or not. Mostly, I didn't hear this lament, but one evening I happened to be listening to it, and this caused a bit of luck and opened me up to some small experiments on the road of submission.

On this evening, I was walking through the city, wrapped inside myself, listening to the inner song of pain. I wasn't sure where I was; I was just following my feet while the rhythm of walking helped to dislodge the stuck feelings inside. I happened by a store-front out of which strange music poured. The windows were painted over and the door was closed, but the music seeped out under the door and through other small openings. I couldn't help but stop. I was listening hard anyway, and the music fell right into the place that was listening inside me.

Moving closer, I recognized the music of Zimbabwe. I had heard this percussive music and seen groups perform the dances that go with it. I stood and listened for quite a while. Finally, my hand reached for the door and pushed. It wasn't locked. I quietly slipped inside and saw a great scene taking place behind the painted windows. Some people were working on dance steps in a line, while others were playing marimbas and a few were playing drums. In the center of the whole scene, a small African man kept everything going. He was showing a little step to the dancers, teaching more technique to the marimba players, and encouraging the drummers. I moved to a place beside the drums and watched in amazement. I felt as if I had stepped straight from my lonely, aimless walking right into the music. seemed to be standing at the same depth amid the music as I had been amid my own loneliness.

After a while, the African man came over to me. In a playful and inviting way, he said, "If you can walk, you can dance. If you can talk you can sing. If you can clap, you can drum. Now what is it going to be? Are you coming out here to dance? Are you going over there to play a melody? Or will you play the drum?" These questions and invitations slipped right past my usual defenses; I couldn't refuse the choice he had given me, and I stood there deliberating. On almost any other day, I would have said, "No, thank you, I'm too busy. No, thank you, I'm too arrogant. No, I'm too determined to keep pushing on. No if I was going to learn those things, I would have learned them when was younger." I would have had an endless number of ways to say no But on this night, I was standing in the midst of my own loneliness reaching for the lament inside. I had to surrender and choose one of these things.

Since the drums were nearby, I said, "I'll drum." With delight in his eyes and playful movements of his body, he showed me a pattern on the drum. The youngest brother had already begun to take over within me—after all, it was his foolishness that had led me to try the door to that place—so I had no resistance to the rhythm. Soon enough my hands were playing, and instead of watching the dance or listening blindly from outside the painted windows, I became part of the music I played and sweated and laughed and listened as hard as I could to all of the instructions until the session was over. It was a stroke of luck. had gone from feeling the sickness in my inner world—an aloneness that had been brewing there for a long time—to being part of a joyful expressive group. I had entered and played a part in the community of sound and rhythm. The youngest brother inside had found a way out.

It would be great to say that this African man became my teacher and that I learned everything I could from him about drumming and music and went on to great things. But this wasn't to be the case. As is often the way in encounters with mentors—or dwarves—that night represented the opening of just one little door into a big world. I learned something that night about bowing my head and stepping into the foolish place of knowing nothing and gratefully accepting what was being offered. I submitted to that man's teaching because I felt lost, and for once feeling foolish did not stop me. The ego brothers were worn out and not paying much attention. The youngest brother had come out, and he wanted to drum. And he knew a teacher when he saw one.

Had that man challenged me in a way that wasn't playful, had he insisted on something, I would have left. As it was, my capacity for submitting to a whole other world was very limited. But his kindness and playfulness, along with the confidence and joy in the world that he opened to me, allowed me to bow my head and try out being submissive. In his world, I was not afraid that the youngest brother would be tricked if I allowed him to submit.

For me, the man from Zimbabwe was like a dwarf putting a question before me that I was partially ready to answer. He handed me gifts, tools, some craft, a place to put my hands, somewhere to release my heavy load, a place where I could begin to learn and learn as a beginner. After that, I had several drum teachers. Some were generous, others were harsh. Some I could learn from, and some I couldn't. But to each of them I had to submit, for it's the nature of the realms where beauty and form are combined that one must submit. To learn drumming means bowing to the drum and bowing to the teacher of the drum as well.

Through drumming, I got close to the world of the dwarf, and through learning to submit—and submitting to learn—I found more and more dwarves inside more and more people. It's very difficult to learn about the dwarf inside ourselves and the gifts in his hands without getting near the dwarf in someone else. Dwarves can't be seen from a distance, can't be heard from above; only at close range do they hand over what they have to offer. Permission can be obtained from a distance, but submission requires proximity.

Healing and learning require getting down, drawing close to the source of the problem and the source of the cure. In terms of deep change, only the little brother can learn, and he only learns when he accepts his own ignorance, his not knowing where to place his hand or his foot next. The path to the Water of Life is the path to inner authority, but it requires submitting to other authorities first in order to learn the nature of true authority.

Before inner authority becomes familiar, it has to be lost and found many times. Usually, a person needs to become truly stuck before the voice of inner authority speaks. That's why the dwarf has an interest in stopping things, in slowing things down, and in teaching this business of submission. The issues of authority and submission are continuous problems for men. The dwarf likes to provoke authority issues; he'll enter a situation with the rod and the bread or other tools merely to test people's attitudes toward submission.

Once I was among a hundred men encamped in a towering redwood forest for seven days. Most of us did not know each other. We had come together to delve into issues of the soul, and we were mostly aware of our individual problems and prepared to work on them. At the beginning of the week, all the men agreed that there was to be no physical violence, and all agreed to engage seriously in whatever came up. Then each man was randomly assigned to a small group with six or seven other men. The members of each group were to focus on one aspect of what it means to walk as a man in the modern world. Then each group was to contribute a sense of what they were working on to the community at large through what we call a "group display." These displays are a kind of ritual designed to arrest the attention of the others and reveal an inner state; they are similar to the ways in which animals display themselves and communicate.

One of the groups was being led by Terry Dobson, a teacher of aikido, the Japanese martial art that studies the point where force and grace meet. The whole group had been getting up at 5:00 A.M. to practice working with sticks. You could hear the rattle of their staffs through the quiet of the camp each morning. They had been discussing the need for boundaries and limits in their personal lives and communities. They were looking at warrior issues: protection, force, limits, purpose, service. Questions arose: If there was to be no physical violence, then what was the point of martial skills? How do you hold a boundary without the use of force? What does a skilled warrior serve? They were wrestling with these questions and clacking their sticks in the rhythms of their martial exercises when a little idea—a dwarf idea—struck them.

They decided to place themselves between the men at the event and the food. Meals were taken in a large hall, a Civilian Conservation Corps lodge built by otherwise-jobless men in the 1930s. This building was both the main meeting hall and the dining hall. It was central to the camp and contained the kitchen and food storage. There was no other food available, and we all had great appetites because of the intense work going on.

At the sound of the lunch bell, the men from the other groups began to converge on the hall, ready to eat and socialize, only to find that no one could get in. Each of the four doors was blocked by guards holding staffs and wearing masks or painted faces. At the central entrance, these warriors announced that we could enter the lodge and eat only after we had spoken a poem at the door. The poem couldn't simply be read from a book or recited from memory; it had to be made up on the spot. It could be a song, a prayer, a rap, a blessing. It had to have some poetry in it and a breath of inspiration. The guards said no more but remained standing in their places, blocking the doors. It was a simple display, a clear request, and it had the dwarf in it. Everyone and everything stopped.

It was disconcerting. Each man felt surprised, trapped. The cleverness of the display unfolded slowly. We had already agreed that there was to be no physical violence, so what did it mean that the doors were blocked by armed guards? If we couldn't use force, neither could they, so what was to stop us from going through? They were counting on our keeping the agreement and not muscling our way in. They were also representing another world. Their masks and silence were effective barriers. We were stuck unless they made a false move, and they weren't moving at all.

I went to a side door where there was a single sentry. I thought I could slip in and watch the drama from inside. After all, I was part of the teaching staff, and we sometimes had to go to the front of the food line because of a meeting or some pressing demand. I suggested he let me go by. He didn't answer. I tried to pull rank, saying I had to get in. No answer. I tried to coerce him, distract him, duck through. I tried to think of a bribe. The masked face didn't respond. On one level, I knew every man in the camp; on another level, I didn't know who this man was at all. One of the effects of radical rituals is a reordering of hierarchies so that the status quo no longer exists. Getting to the front of the line in this case meant giving a poem, not being officious or in a hurry.

Back at the front of the lodge there was an extraordinary commotion, a storm of disbelief and dismay. Men couldn't believe they were being denied food with no warning and no chance of appeal. Some shouted that they had paid for the damned food, and they weren't about to pay again. Many were outraged. "We have rights to that food," they claimed. "This is ridiculous, it's childish, it's fascistic, it's abusive, it's illegal," they said. Men were threatening to leave, to attack, to go to town and eat burgers.

In the midst of this tumult and confusion, some men were beginning to give poems at the entrance. A man would say his poem, the
guards would pull back their staffs, and the man would disappear into
the hall.

So while some men were arguing over, refining, and sharpening
the point of their protest, others were composing and humming their
songs and poems. It was becoming clear that the warrior group had
pulled off the display through their silence and their masks and the
strange disconcerting request. Whatever had been rushing through
the minds of the hundred men had stopped. Everything was focused at
the entrance to the hall, and everyone was either forming a poem or a
protest.

After a while, the focus shifted to the words that the men were
saying in order to enter the hall, and a second stage of the ritual began.
It takes a long time for each one of a hundred men to compose a poem
and tell it out. Rituals alter time and space; they affect habits. Now
everything was slowing way down. Even the men on the inside began
listening rather than eating. The food was mostly forgotten. Our
appetite for food had been transformed into an appetite for hearing
what each man offered. And poetry is, after all, a form of food.

Someone had picked up a stone and placed it by the entrance
while giving his poem. There was something right about that, so
everyone started putting a stone by the entrance. Now a kind of grace
entered into the event, as each of us stood in line, advancing slowly
up the stairs, one at a time, waiting for men we couldn't see to give a
poem or the semblance of one, trying to hold onto the thread of our
own verse while hearing the others. One man made a quiet prayer
because it was the anniversary of his mother's death—this took the
edge off another's protest. Another converted his protest into a poem
that rhymed, and he killed two birds with one stone. Some of the
verse was good, some was bad. By the time I finally reached the door,
it had become clear that a real grace was occurring. This was not
prayer by rote but a real bowing of the head. There was genuine reflection before each poem was given; conflict and uncertainty were contained in it, and disagreement surrounded it. Each man's reflection
was different; none of it had ever been said before. The ritual couldn't
be explained or dismissed, and it wasn't finished when all the poems
had been said. There was a mysterious quality to the event that
affected the entire meal and made it a continuance of the ritual. No
one who was there will ever forget it, and we never did it again.

That night everyone gathered together for a community meeting, and the entire display had to be reworked. The feelings provoked by the events were undiminished by the hours that had passed since they occurred. Some men were still outraged. But there were different reasons for each man's feelings, and they all had to be spoken. We were back in it. Each of us was carrying a piece of what had happened, and when we reconvened, the emotions of the event recurred. This symbolic event had caught us and held us in its web.

We had submitted to something we didn't understand. We were still chewing on it; it was still working on us. We argued and fought about it, praised it and defamed it. We couldn't let it go. The blocked doors and armed guards had stirred painful memories of past outrages. In the 1960s, some of these men had faced off with National Guards during protests over the Vietnam war or civil rights. Others had been through battles, incarcerations, or union lockouts. Men had been locked out of houses, kept out of jobs, forced to submit to endless rules and regulations. Any number of doors had been slammed in their faces, and this event had brought all the memories back, complete with the emotions they evoked. The guardian group was accused of everything from a desire to bully to conspiring with the military-industrial complex.

When the group that had staged the display finally spoke, it was clear that they were as astonished as everyone else. It had seemed a simple idea at first, but they were amazed at their own emotions that had emerged in the process: fear, sympathy, determination. They had been caught up in it as well, surprised by the other men's intense reactions but committed to seeing it through.

The teachers were criticized for not interrupting the thing early on, for allowing the injustice of it to continue. But the teachers had also had their own experiences, and those didn't agree either. Meanwhile, another group defended the outpouring of poetry and the value of being made to slow down. Some of the men had never worked on a poem and had found themselves delighted to try. Others wanted to repeat the entire thing at every meal.

Even after the community meeting was over, the life of the event continued, for the stones lay by the central door for days, piled like pillars marking the entrance to a ceremonial house. Everyone approached meals with a keen eye and ear and the beginning of a poem.

The warrior display had the dwarf in it, for it forced the issues of submission out into the open. The flip side of the warrior's ability to defend is his meaningful submission. Remember the question of the border guard in the story of Cuchulain: are you looking for a battle or asking for a poem? At various times in his life, a man must surrender, bow his head, and give a poem or something else that displays his heart. If not, his life will consist only of battles, of offense and defense, of keeping his guard up. Without submitting to something greater than himself, a man cannot locate the flow of the Water of Life—or make a good poem.

Submission is not the same as obedience, although the two are often confused. Often people are forced to obey rules that humiliate them and offend their sense of self. To the wounded self, any rule or requirement can look humiliating. But the wounded self also feels a desire to let go, to drop the defenses and protections, to surrender to something bigger than the well-defended "me." Besides the drive for success and recognition, men feel a desire to play a part in something meaningful yet mysterious. Submission is the act of surrendering and giving up some control in order to experience life as the little brother again. Inevitably, this causes the ego brothers humiliation, and it means that the little brother inside must suffer once again the pain of past failed attempts to be part of meaningful events.

Most men resist acts of submission because they faced early on an overly dominating parent or culture to which they had to submit in order to survive. Some kind of obedience was required that was excessive for that person. To protect some inner core of spirit and self-worth, they learned to respond like warriors. Defiance, toughness, strength, quickly activated defenses, and attack attitudes formed around a wounded core and now habitually protect it from further mistreatment by authorities. The sense of injustice is easily inflamed in many men, and they are quick to pinpoint potential misuses of power. This attitude keeps alive but imprisoned the injustices that have already occurred and keeps out any additional attacks on the inner core of integrity and wounded dignity.

Another, less martial response to early abuses to authority involves trickery, humor, and misdirection. Like the "wise guys" in school, some men keep their wounded spirits alive and protected by converting issues of power into jokes. The jokes and tricks deflect any direct use of power, and the sharp wits reveal weaknesses in authority figures. The wit can see the other side of anything that's presented, can see through any facade and can juggle ideas, words, gestures, theories, compliments, criticisms—all things genuine and not genuine.

Some internal integrity is maintained by pointing out the lack of integrity in outside authorities. And the need to submit is avoided.

The trouble with this "trickster defense" is revealed when the trickster grows tired or begins to age; then, what was ironic becomes bitterly sarcastic, and what was sharply witty becomes darkly cynical. The wellspring of wit begins to dry up or becomes poisonous. Similarly, the well-defended warrior eventually begins to suffer feelings of emptiness and paranoia, like a besieged town. The sword that could cut through any outer force also keeps allies away. All the inner resources are consumed or dried up, but the habit of not accepting help is still in place. The head so capable of scanning the surroundings for enemies can't allow itself to bend to any blessing, even when the body and soul are in great pain.

The defenses necessary to preserve the integrity of one's spirit during early stages of life become life-threatening later on. They will eventually keep one isolated from the flow of life and poison the inner waters of the soul.

The third defense against submitting to any authority is to be an authority oneself. In my attempts to avoid having to submit at the front door of the dining hall, I tried all three of these defenses at the side door.

Once it was clear that I couldn't force or trick my way into the hall and that I couldn't simply use my authority to get through the side door, I began to give up and slow down. While waiting to give my prayer or poem at the central door, I held a stone in my hand like everyone else. As I held the stone, I began to think about my father and recall his funeral and burial. The stone became a little weight pulling me toward my father's grave. In my hand, the stone became the sorrow I had felt at that time but had been unable to express completely.

When I received word that my father had gone into a deep coma on the opposite side of the country, I had been writing a letter inviting him to come and visit and simply spend time together. It was a lonely, broken time for me. My marriage was ending, and I was separated from my children. I was feeling an inexplicable gratitude toward and sympathy with my father. I suggested that we could find a boat and go fishing, though neither of us fished. The letter was interrupted by the news of his impending death. By the time I got to his bedside, it was clear that his soul was leaving this life. As the oldest brother in the family, I wound up arranging for the various machines to be disconnected so that he could continue his way into death. As the oldest brother, I made the funeral and burial arrangements. As the oldest brother, I tried to help my mother and younger brothers and sisters. But as the oldest brother standing at the grave site, I was dry of tears. There was a gap between the sorrow inside and the stiffness and determination necessary to carry things through on the outside.

As I stood in line to give my poem, I felt as if I were standing at that grave site again. I made a small prayer that carried some of my sense of sorrow at my father's death; I said it quietly and placed the stone at the entrance to the hall. During that prayer, the tears that had not been able to flow at the grave site began to come. Once they started, there was a gushing of sorrow, a flow of tears that went all the way back through childhood, picking up rages and angers along the way. The prayer awakened the sense of loss and even anger at my father for dying before I could make contact with him and when I needed his strength myself. The tears washed over those feelings and over the humiliation and guilt of not having finished and sent the letter to him before his death.

The submission that I had tried at first to avoid opened up a well within me, and the flow of water moved obstacles that had been sitting like stones inside, blocking sorrows as well as other feelings.

Sometime later I finished the letter to my father. I addressed it not to his former home in New York but to where he was now. It wasn't for sending in the mail, but I finished the writing of it and also began speaking to him in small ways. One night after I had finished the letter, he came to me in a dream, dressed in fine Sunday clothes, wearing a brand-new fedora hat. He stepped from behind some trees, tipped his hat and smiled at me, then turned and walked off to a lake beyond us. That was his letter back to me. It was his way of saying he had received my letters and my tears. Had I not dropped my older-brother certainties and submitted to this whole chain of mysterious events, I might not have felt that stone in my hand, I might not have felt that prayer in my heart, and I might not have opened the well of those tears. If the head won't bend, the heart won't open, and grief held too long can make a stone of the heart.

The story of the search for the Water of Life is guided by the dwarf. He's in the middle of the story, located near the gates between worlds, and he is the middle figure of the three old men who help. The architecture of the story shows a sick king in the above world and an enchanted queen and stone men in the below world. The upperworld needs the Water of Life in order to be healed, and the lowerworld needs to be remembered and returned to or it remains encased in stone. In between are the three brothers and the three old men. The first old man appears in the castle of the upperworld with the general knowledge of what is missing. The third wise old man appears when the hunter refuses to kill the youngest brother and gives him the common clothes. In between waits the little old man, the dwarf. It's time for us to look at who the dwarf might be and why he appears by the gates of the world above and by the world below.

The symbol of the dwarf is easier to point at and describe than to define. The dwarf is condensed and quick and focused. He attends to details and sees the value of whatever he handles. He's not ponderous or obvious. Rather, he appears and disappears, cultivating invisibility. He's at play with things, always tinkering with the inherent powers in the stuff of nature and culture. In many stories, the dwarf is crafty; often he is actually a craftsman. He can work at the forge, smithing minerals, and he can mine gems. He knows the veins that run through the earth and what treasures lie therein. But he also practices and teaches the skills of culture: he bakes and tailors and makes shoes. He has a great interest in shoes and heels and how the foot touches the ground; he can be a dancing master as well. Because he is constantly in touch with the elements and the patterns of things, he can predict the weather and foretell the future.

The dwarf is the opposite of a giant. In the language of stories, the dwarf contrasts with and can be the antidote to the giant. Giants are huge, clumsy, oafish, stupid, and committed to hoarding. Giants have things of great value that they don't use and don't understand. Giants are concentrated on their appetites. They consume great quantities, sleep heavily, and are oblivious to the destruction they cause; they step on people and don't even notice it. They are easily disoriented. They hold fast to maps and treasures that they acquire but don't really use. They act like the big psychological complexes that block change and waste energy in people's lives. Dwarves, on the other hand, offer ways out of and through complex problems.

The dwarf himself is like condensed matter and condensed time. He's both explosive and generous. His ambiguity is disturbing to our usual frame of mind. He's child and old man compressed together. He's a carrier of old traditions, and he's completely unpredictable.

Dwarves are the original indigenous people. They are deeply connected to the earth and what's in it and of it. They are experts in the connections between things; they see what holds things together. They are short, like children, so they see the legs of things, the way things reach down to the ground. They are old like the earth and know the time it takes for metals and ores to form. They have the basic interests of children: where are we going, why do you do that, what is that for, do you want to know what I know? But they have the wisdom of the age-old earth, so their questions don't spring from ignorance or innocence. The questions of the dwarf aim to find out if the people rushing around have learned anything about who they are and where they are being pulled by destiny. Like children, dwarves don't like to be talked down to. Unlike children, dwarves can do something about it.

The appearance of the dwarf represents an interview between inner need and outer circumstances. Denying one's actual inner needs causes an anger that can stun the imagination and stop the life of the person who is in denial. The stuckness and befuddlement operate as a curse. They are the other side of the blessing that is also available. The real choice in the situation is not about where I want to ride my high horse. The choice that the dwarf forces is whether or not I am going to deny the true circumstances of my life. The dwarf dwells in the circumstances, the details, the elemental situation.

The dwarf knows something of the future because he is a knowing carrier of the past. If he has a map, he knows how to read it and how to mislead with it. He knows what's hidden in the earth and in people. He knows the directions of the roads and byways and observes who is traveling where. His connection to shoes lets him see how a person walks, and from that he sizes up the person's motivation and true destination. His knowledge of clothes allows him to see the typical feelings with which people wrap themselves. He knows wells and streams and the whereabouts of water. He knows where the inner streams originate and where the water goes when it's gone. The dwarf tests the qualities that are essential for a person to travel his or her road in life. If you don't exhibit some of the qualities essential to that road, he'll send you back, turn you astray, or plague you with difficulties. If you think you are pure or innocent, he'll teach from his ample knowledge of shadows and dark emotions.

Although small and coming from the shadows, the dwarf's voice is imperative. In the story, he's aware of where the healing water can be found and what instruments and timing are needed to effect the change from sickness to a healthy flow of life. Unlike the general knowledge that the first old man carries, the dwarf's guidance is specific and insistent. In a person's life, the voice of the dwarf can be an inner whisper that questions one's habitual attitudes and assumptions. When it comes time to deal with a malaise that has taken hold at the center of a person's life, the voice of the dwarf can speak from within, asking questions that were never before considered seriously. Where are you going, really? he asks. If the dwarf's voice is ignored, he will try to seize the person's attention by tripping him or her. He can be seen in things that keep going wrong and at times when there are dead ends no matter where we turn. When he's overlooked, the world becomes narrow and hard. And the longer he's overlooked, the harder we fall.

In one three-month period, I encountered three middle-aged men, each of whom had fallen from a rooftop and broken numerous bones. Each was incapacitated, stuck in bed, pulled out of the flow of life. Two of them volunteered that they had been resisting a voice telling them that they needed a career or life change. An inner voice had been saying, "You'd better stop what you're doing." They had known that a change was being called for, but they couldn't stop. When we hear this voice, it often doesn't make sense to us—or not enough sense until everything crashes down. The dwarf is part of an underside of life that has to be lived or else life becomes a prison. He represents a force in the life of a person, a group, or a culture that will cause gridlock, engineer an accident, or deepen an illness in order to force a change of direction.

The dwarf won't talk about the Water of Life until most of the ego has been contained, either shut down or locked up. The big outer noises need to quiet somehow; the incessant mantra of the ego has to stop or get absorbed into the surroundings so that this other voice can be heard. Often there is a fateful interruption of the course of our lives. Something becomes seriously the matter with us, or something that matters a lot is taken from us. The death of a loved one leaves a space that demands that we fill it with tears and prayers and serious amounts of time and care about the details and objects of their lives and our lives. An accident or illness forces us to turn our attention to matters of the body and issues of the soul. Like the king, we are forced to stop and recognize the presence of death nearby. We are forced to seek healing, which begins with stopping, getting down, and submitting to forces below us.

Part of what the dwarf has to say is always hard to hear. It makes us face some darkness from which the ego wishes to turn away; it calls us to a shadow area that the ego would flee. Whatever a person imagines the Water of Life to be, whatever could cure a dying king and return the flow of life to a wasteland, can only be reached through iron gates. For reasons the dwarf knows, the healing waters of the soul are guarded and kept away from the sight and touch of the regular self. We only get to those gates by giving all else up and letting go. If we don't force the gates a bit, they just won't open. If we use only an iron-fisted approach, the lions beyond the gates will devour us. We either won't get in or we won't get out. The dwarf is offering tools and skills for entering and leaving the realm of water.

Entering this territory means immersing in emotions that can be as ferocious as the lions at the gate and as healing as the water in the fountain. No one can have the benefit of one for long without the tempering of the other. Between the two waits the hall of stone men and an enchantment that must be broken.

CHAPTER 23

MEN OF STONE

A MAN CAN get caught between an outer life whose meaning is draining away and an inner life dominated by lions enraged from lack of nourishment. After a while, stuckness becomes numbing—one of the most fearful states men experience. Turning numb happens in all kinds of ways and has become so common that it's considered part of aging; certainly, it is one of our fears about aging. Whatever the primary emotional style of a man may be, numbing can occur. His anger may turn cold and form a hard shell that blocks his inner and outer life. Even a warm heart may become stone cold and kill intimacy of any kind. Fear may become petrified, keeping people at a distance and blocking change within. Shame may build to a point where any close attention will shut everything down; it can stop a man from doing something before he even gets started. Sorrow may begin to feel like a weight that can't be moved, and a wasteland can grow out of this numbness.

In our story, the sickness of the king in the first realm is mirrored by the enchantment of the second realm. The "stuckness" of the older brothers becomes multiplied into the hall full of stone men. In the first realm, there is a lack of water; in the second, there is an excess of stone. The old idea was that what is wrong in one realm will be cured from another. What is wrong in the human realm finds its cure in the otherworld. But it goes the other way as well: the youngest brother must return from the human realm to the realm of the queen in order to break the enchantment there. Initiation through water begins new exchanges between the realms.

The dwarf waits at the gates of both realms. He can be in either or in both, and he reminds humans that they have the same capacity. It's an old Celtic idea that a person can step into the otherworld at any time; any moment can act as a door into the otherworld. In the other world, each person sees and feels more fully what he or she carries through that doorway. The otherworld is a reflection and an elaboration of what is carried through the gates. The gates keep out what hasn't gathered enough iron and substance to get through. There needs to be enough force of life gathered to strike the door three times and enough iron in the strokes to make the gates ring.

Striking the gates awakens the sleeping lions who are not fed often enough and who are tired of being thrown crumbs from the daily world that land like pebbles on their side of the gates. There must be enough nutrition in what is being carried through the gates to satisfy the hunger of the lions. They need to be fed the bread of intentions and the attention to a person's inner life, a bread that is made from the emotions active in the person. The lions require a taste of what is really being baked in the regular world.

One of the old details about lions who serve as guardians of the gates is that they are awake when their eyes are closed and sleeping when their eyes are open. The gatekeeper, whether wise old man or wise old woman, informs the one seeking the other realm of these facts. The facts of life—even the facts about sleeping and waking—change when we go through the gates. Change and knowledge of what's changing become the most important facts upon entering the otherworld. On the other side of the gates, the inside world awakens as the eyes look inward. The lions are blind to the outside but see fiercely what is going on within. They must be fed or they will put the inner life back to sleep. The lions are a test of whether the seeker is actually awake or simply disturbed. They function like demons at the gates of awareness, and they see into the emotional and spiritual truth of the moment. They are both sides of an issue seen at once. They don't want to be awakened until there's something to bang the doors about and enough ferment to raise the bread.

A man suddenly awakes at 3:00 A.M. A dream or nightmare has tossed him from one side of the gates to the other. Something has happened that has struck the gates between the worlds three times, and now the dreamer is sitting bolt upright and "awake." His eyes are wide open before he knows it. For a moment he's awake in his dream. What does he do? If the voices of reason rise to their usual volume, he'll dismiss the dream and try to close his eyes and go back to sleep. The oldest brother stirs: there's important work to be done later that day; he needs to be clear and sharp for it—better sleep. The second brother says he'll remember the dream in the morning; the inheritance of the dream will be there. The gates that sprung open begin to close. The voice of Mother comes all the way back from childhood, awakened by the sound of the gates opening. She's reminding him that he needs at least eight hours of sleep, that rest is important for a balanced life. Father, too, is suddenly there, feeling stern. He bangs on the gate: what the hell's going on here? Someone close the door before we lose everything.

If the gates are always pushed closed again, then the lions aren't fed the attention they require. The trouble that was banging on the gates goes from being a specific problem to a general feeling of anxiety. When the lions are agitated on the other side, everything in the regular world takes on a troubled, anxious, rattling quality. Or, we fall asleep to the real issues of our lives; when we should be awake and aware, we close our eyes. The gates to our inner life close tight; we can't find any openings, and we can't see where we are really going.

To find the Water of Life, we must pay the price exacted by the lions: we must open our eyes when most are sleeping; we must see as the lions do, looking beyond the "gates of reason"—the usual reasons people have for doing things. If the lions are given some of the food of our attention just as they awake, then even though their demands are inconvenient, they calm down. In other words, *we* calm down, and eventually a deeper rest occurs. The lions don't require an endless series of sleepless nights, just enough bread to show that we acknowledge the otherworld.

If we feed the dream, we feed the lions. Something fell from the daily world into the otherworld and stirred up a dream. The dream wants to bring something from that world into this one. Sometimes, just turning attention to the dream calms the waters of both worlds and returns something that was missing to this one. If what fell into the inner world was a big chunk of reality—something that is deeply disturbing to the dreamer's "lions"—then approaching the gates will cause a great roar from the other side. It feels like someone will be eaten. We may know that if bread goes in, then water will come out, but in this case, fear of the lions may become too great. We worry that the bread may not satisfy them—what then? Maybe if I wait, they'll go back to sleep on their own, we say. What if I pile stuff against the gates on this side? Now I can't hear them. Out of sight, out of mind. But this, of course, is another form of denial. Instead of the gates opening and closing and both realms calming down, there's a shutdown. Denying the lions makes them obsessive.

Denial is always a possibility at the gates between the worlds. It can be directed at either world. The inner world may be denied because of the pain kept on that side of the gates. For the Water of Life to flow again from the inner toward the outer world, the pain held behind the gates must be suffered. But when we have been in denial for a long time, we begin to believe that this suffering would be so painful that the lions at the gate would go mad before the water could get out. So the gates are kept shut. We may also try to deny the pain of the outer world, believing that if the truth of the outer world were allowed to come through the gates, the pain of it would be too great. In this case, the rocks of denial are piled against the inside of the gates to keep the outside from ever stirring things up again. Denial can hold the gates closed from either side.

The trouble is that once the eyes have opened to something they weren't supposed to see or weren't ready to see, they never completely close. If a person has caught a glimpse of the flight of the firebird, has seen the movement of the spirit, he can't simply deny it. If he has suffered some loss, it's known on both sides of the gates. The dwarf keeps track of what's going on; the youngest brother keeps trying to get the gates open. The lions begin to stir, and the pain at the gates can be felt. Some substances and habits can fool the lions at the gate, cool them and calm them down, but only for a while. Eventually it requires more and more to keep them calm, for it's not exactly what they wanted. They can be bought off with substitutes for the bread and wine of the soul, but the price always becomes higher and higher to keep the doors open. In cases of addiction, the doors between the worlds are continually but partially open. The mechanism for closing them is broken, gone, or stuck, and the addictive material is being used to quiet the lions. There is no end to the appetites of the lions when the gates are open. A means has to be found to close the gates.

Denial is the part of the process that claims that the gates are not open, maybe even claims that they never did open. The stones may be piled so high against the gates that we will try to claim that the inner, other world does not exist and that what happens in the "real world" is all that matters. Such denial begins to turn everything in the inner world to stone. The fact is that going through the gates always involves some pain and always involves some payment to the lions. Never going through the gates leads to a tremendous numbness. The pain is not felt fully, but neither does the Water of Life flow. The gates are kept blocked, and nothing changes. The pain is still there, but it's buried, encased in stone. The feeling for life is on hold, stuck. The inner life becomes a mausoleum—or a museum with great stone lions at the gates and the feeling that it would take tremendous effort to move all the statues that stand in the halls.

We all hold an innate knowledge that going from the daily world fully into the inner world is painful. A change occurs at the gates that causes suffering. Addictions and some habits are substitutes for the painful learning of more genuine rituals that can open and close the gates, that can feed the lions and find the way to the fountain of the Water of Life.

When a man is all alone, the pain at the gates may seem too much to bear. The purpose of a radical ritual is to allow a person to suffer what one needs to suffer but lacks the courage or the information or the will to suffer on one's own. When a group of people arrives at the gates together, there's an increase of courage, a deepening of determination, and the possibility that a man will go through the gates when he would not go on his own. The group events that I describe are attempts to knock on those gates and then hold them open long enough for everyone to get through, at least for a moment, so that each person can feel what is encased in stone on the other side—and then feel further, getting a taste of the Water of Life that's beyond the hall of stone men.

When I speak of the gates to the "inner world," I'm referring to the gates within a person, guarded by his or her own personal "lions." When I call them the gates to the "otherworld," I'm referring to the gates that can appear before a group. Behind these gates are collective lions that need to be fed as well. Because the gates are found by going down, back, and in, they are also the gates to the underworld. Stories are like dreams that can open the individual and group gates at once. Stories carry mysteries that can move an entire group while also containing and moving each individual in the group.

The story of the Water of Life describes an inner territory that is both painful and joyous. Once past the lions, the youngest brother enters the hall of stone men. Each person gets through the gates in his own way and with his own issues. Then everyone meets on the other side, each as a little brother. If they get all the way through, they will see the queen and be welcomed, but the place is enchanted. Something has turned the men in the hall to stone. Each of these stone men was also a "youngest brother" once; otherwise, he would never have made it to the castle at all. Each knows the king is sick unto death and carries this knowledge in his own way. Just so, every man carries a little brother turned to stone in his heart. You can only see this stone man on the other side of the gates; he's rarely visible in the daily world. Between each man and the Water of Life is a stone brother within. Unless he touches this brother and allows his story to come out, the man will remain stuck; he will go no further. Each passage through this hall is painful, for it requires breaking through something that has hardened. On the other side of the room are the sword that defeats armies and the bread that feeds all—and beyond these things are the queen and the Water of Life itself—but in between are the stories of the stone men.

When a group of men begins working in the inner hall, musing on what turns to stone in life, we never know where the opening that cracks the stone will come from. Before things crack open, there's a little chill. A man makes a joke about his kidney stones, but another treats it seriously because that's what he felt near the stone men. He says passing stones was the most painful thing he'd ever done. It stopped him in his tracks and made him look at other pain in his life.

Another man says he has a pain that won't move. It stays stuck in him; he can't put words to it, and he feels he's slowly turning to stone. His statement releases a torrent of stories as men echo the theme of losing their passion, feeling passion draining out of their lives, and feeling stuck or turning numb. A man says losing his job has led to his shutting down inside. But other men who still hold positions of authority and have experienced outward success speak of the loss of passion that has brought change and growth to a halt for them, too. The room grows heavy with the weight of sorrows that were there all along but not seen or felt clearly until now. Each man had carried in these stones almost unseen when he joined the group.

Now a man says he's stuck in a marriage that is going nowhere. "There's no passion in it," he says. At first it didn't matter, he had plenty to do, but now it's killing him. Another man says he is frozen with fear that if he leaves his marriage, he'll die old and alone, and if he doesn't leave, he'll die lonely anyway. The next feels that somewhere he lost the purpose he had early in life. Now he's just going through the motions; there's no point to what he's doing, and he's not going anywhere. Another says he's held his feelings in check for so long that he feels encased in stone; people can't get to him, and they know it, so they leave him alone. That's what he wanted at one time, but now he feels like he's a small voice locked way inside the stone, and no one can hear him. "Cold," a man says—his life has become cold. He used to have friends and dreams, but now he feels isolated, standing outside his own life. Soon, it's as if tears are running down the faces of the stone men in the hall. At some other time and place, the stone men might talk another way. Right now it's the weight of sorrow. Something has died—a lot has died—and everyone knows a piece of it.

There's a huge weight of grief inside American men. When the heart knows sorrow and never weeps, it becomes blocked; it turns to stone. But when men stop and talk about the stones they are carrying in life, the weight begins to drop and the heart begins to open. Once the outside world has been left behind and men have a chance to talk about their lives, the inner gates open. Sorrow rolls through the gates, pushing forth tears.

An African tribesman was once in one of these rooms full of a hundred American men when each began to talk from a place of stone. He was overwhelmed by the weight of what was said. Not that he didn't know the weight of his own grief and the many griefs of his people, but he was amazed that so much of this grief had been carried for so long. He had never seen so much solid grief. A group of war veterans stood together to speak about the Vietnam war. They had to stand side by side, as if stuck together, as if the only way to move the weight of each man's stone was as a group. As each man spoke, the room dropped, the floor went down. Each had carried the weight of dead bodies and dead dreams for twenty-five years, and their words rolled on the floor, stones that could break a heart. You could feel and hear the cracking of hearts. Griefs carried like gravestones were being pushed out. Inner funerals that had become stuck or been halted were moving forward.

Another time in another hall, men erected altars around the room, some for friends left behind on battlefields or streets, others for loved ones who had died but had not been grieved. It started when five Latino men who had lost many friends in Vietnam made an altar of what was at hand and put candles on it. Each of them stood at the altar and addressed their lost friends. They poured out anger and anguish and grief in both words and wordless sounds at the altar. They banged at the altar with their rage and anguish. They fed it the bread of their grief. The room began to feel like a battlefield after a battle.

The sorrow of those men began to unlock sorrows that were carried by others. Men of different generations were present. Some began to talk of the Korean War and parts of their lives or people they had lost but still carried inside themselves. These losses needed to be grieved over and over again, especially since they had not been grieved by the culture. Older men recalled the Second World War and the grief that the films about that war did not convey. Soon enough, it was hard to tell what war was being grieved, but it was evident that everyone in the room felt as if they had been through a war. It was too much for words, yet words and tears made the outpouring. Much of it had waited many years to come out.

We began to sing an old lament, giving both words and tears a place to flow, keeping the weight moving lest it crush someone. We sang an old Irish dirge that lamented the loss of life and limb through war. The weeping intensified, but now it was carried a little bit by the song. Some vehicle was needed to carry the weight of the grief. Often, the lack of a vehicle is what stops men from grieving—that, and the belief that they are alone, that other people's grief is not like their own.

In the midst of this lament, a man stood up and angrily protested, "Not everyone dies in a war; not every loss comes because men are soldiers and street warriors. Other things kill. Other things take life and limb and leave gaping wounds." It was a shock, the song quieted, and everyone listened. This man worked with people dying of AIDS and had buried many of them. He was afraid that this attention to those lost through war excluded the grief that he carried and the grief of many whom he knew. He was afraid that gay men were being excluded, that the tragedy of AIDS was being excluded, that women were being excluded from this opportunity to lament and grieve as a community. A small argument started, for some men felt that their grief was being intruded upon.

Finally, someone said, "Listen, this whole thing is a war. Whenever great numbers of people are dying, no matter what they're dying of, there's a war going on. No one is excluded from the war, and no one is outside the lament." The truth of this struck everyone. The weeping increased. The song rose up again. And it went on until the weight was so heavy that it seemed as if we would never get out of the room. At that point, one of the older men said, "Let's just get up and carry it outside to the trees."

The whole group went out among the huge redwood trees. There the lamenting and weeping continued; now the trees became a part of it. Someone began to pick up stones from the forest. Soon each man had carried a stone back into the hall. We made a pile of those stones, a cairn, a monument to the sorrow that we could no longer simply carry around inside ourselves. It was a way for the men to see the size of the grief inside them, a way to see and move and carry the weight of it. For days, we passed back and forth among the stones of our grief. Later, all the stones were carried down to the river that runs through that forest. At that point, the tears flowed into the river, and the stones fell among those already lying in the water.

All of these tears are part of the Water of Life. Shedding them moves the soul, opening a place where change can occur. Some of the water flows back into the daily world; some stays within. Once, after weeping like that, a man said that he felt that his dead friends were able to see through his tears from the otherworld into this one. Others have said they weep for the little children inside who were knocked about by parents or by the world. Many of the tears are shed for others, for harms to or the loss of loved ones, for things unsaid to one's children, for things said wrongly, for blows given, and for blows taken.

Many times the weeping begins with one man, with one small stone of his story, and it grows until the whole group is weeping for the world. Living at the end of the twentieth century is like walking through a great weeping. It is like an ongoing funeral, a huge shedding of the life of the world. All the hopelessness felt about the loss of forests and animal species comes out in the tears. The anguish over lives wasted and shot down on city streets also washes out in these tears. The losses that pile up as statistics in news reports about this or that atrocity cannot be carried without the heart turning to stone. From the lions' side of the gates, the world looks like a continuous funeral. When the heart knows sorrow and never weeps, the sorrow gets locked like a storm inside the heart. When the storm can't pour out, it turns solemn, it becomes a stone weight. Grieving clears the heart and keeps it open. The old saying is "Too much grieving makes a stone of the heart," but you could also say that too little grieving fills the heart with stones.

In almost every culture, men have inherited rituals for grieving. Often in the past, beginning to participate in funerals and grief rituals was part of entering the life of initiated men. Until modern times, men have always taken part in lamenting for the world. Frequently, learning grief rituals occurred among men gathered together as a group, for men can draw the sorrow out of each other. On the other hand, it's often true that if men don't see the sorrow in each other, they can't even recognize that it's there. Men of one race or culture are often surprised at the depth of sorrow in men of another culture. Seeing another through his tears changes the heart more thoroughly than any facts or arguments. When tears are shared, the stones that might have been thrown at each other become part of the cairns of grief instead.

The reasons for the grieving can defy translation, and attempting simply to speak them can cause conflict rather than tears. Songs and chants are a universal way of carrying individual and group grief. The sound of the song sets the river of grief flowing. Once, a conference brought together Asian American, Native American, African American, Latino American, and European American men all in one place. In the midst of a fierce conflict that was beginning to seem like it would burn the place down, a man, from the heat of the fire, began to sing, "Wade in the waters, wade in the waters, God's gonna trouble the waters."

This old gospel song called on the battlers to "wade in the waters." Despite the burning fires all around, singing converted the sounds of conflict to the sounds of sorrow. The fires of conflict came first; they couldn't have been repressed or hidden. There were fierce angers that had to have a voice and had to be heard. There were rages that burned a path back through history and across oceans. If there had been no room for the rages to storm, there would have been no room for sorrow. But there comes a point when rage will burn the heart or turn it stone cold. The song was started just before we reached that point. It was a legitimate call, a lament born of fire that didn't deny the depth of the trouble. It didn't separate God from the trouble either but put everyone and God in the same troubled water.

In spite of the language of conflict and because of the honesty of it, men began to sing. Now the song carried both conflict and sorrow, carrying things that had just been said to each other, carrying things that had been said for hundreds of thousands of years to each other, carrying things that had never been said to each other. Eventually, all the men began to sing: "Wade in the water, wade in the water, all God's trouble in the water." The flow of the feelings of the group moved from conflict into sorrow so that weeping was going on within the singing. And this went on long enough that it moved from weeping into a kind of joy. The song began to multiply in harmonies; the sound began to grow. It carried the grief that had been born out of conflict all the way into notes of joy. "Wade in the water. All God's children in the water."

When the weeping and grieving reach enough men and there is a true outpouring of the weight and anguish that each person carries, then a radical change occurs within each man and in the group. The flow of life changes within the individual, between members of the group, and between group members and the people "outside" with whom they are connected. As in many situations that move parts of the inner life, outer relationships change unpredictably.

If a man is overwrought with burning heat and inner rage, deep weeping joins him to the sorrow of the world and diminishes that rage. It calms an excess of aggression and cools his heart. The heat pours out in the tears, and the sounds of sorrow clear the heart and mind. The clearing goes as deep as the grieving. And the opposite happens as well. If a man is too cold or frozen in stone, weeping cracks the stone. Bottled-up emotions can be paralyzing; being part of the deep lament releases these emotions and frees the soul to move.

Weeping will raise the temperature of this man's psyche. Whereas it cooled the heart of the other man, it will heat the heart of one too cold. That's the nature of grieving, and it is what happens when the Water of Life returns.

I have seen how this change has occurred in groups by the end of these events. Those that entered too hot, too fiery, ready to burn someone else or even themselves are cooler and calmer. Their water is more stable. Those that entered afraid to move, stuck in some passivity, or numb to the whole inner world are more flushed with feeling. Now they want to do something. One type of man is calmed, sometimes even put to sleep like the youngest brother in the story, for it's a great expenditure of energy to grieve. Another is suddenly awake, suddenly has found the lions inside himself that had turned to stone.

In this way, the Water of Life, sought in the story and sorely missing from the modern world, has a general healing effect. It cools the excessive heat of an individual or group while it heats up those who are passive. In both individual and group, the split into violence or passivity, excessive aggression or excessive lethargy, can be brought into balance by deep grieving.

There's even some biology to back this up—or at least some mythobiology. Some research indicates that deep, convulsive weeping affects the testosterone level in a man's system. For men with an excess of this hormone—often true for those who are excessively aggressive and violent—weeping reduces their testosterone level. Men with low testosterone levels will have theirs raised through weeping. The more extreme the levels of testosterone beforehand, the more radical the change. In other words, a man who has not wept in a long time can make a dramatic change in his life by allowing himself to lament. The missing passions of his life can return, or the excessive passions can be cooled for some time.

In order to maintain this balance, a man must return periodically to weeping. The grieving may not be as deep after the first time nor the effects as radical, but when this ritual is incorporated and new and old sorrows are grieved as they arise, a man is able to go further into his life and further into relationships.

On another level, participating in one's own sorrow makes a person part of an inclusive, fully human community. The Water of Life makes a community from below. When a group has gone through the gates, calmed the devouring lions, and cracked the stones of sorrow together, it becomes very difficult for those who have shared the lament to attack one another. A change occurs below the level of language and culture; ancestors nod wordlessly to each other. One part of the initiation by water has occurred; the men have traveled to the other side of the fires of Litima. Learning to carry both the fires and the waters of the soul is the process that tempers men; alternating between the rituals of outbreak and the rituals of breaking down continues the tempering. Breaking down the stone that grows around the sorrow in the heart and then carrying that sorrow can steady the wings of desire.

Men learn how to grieve most easily when they are in a group with other men. When a man reveals the incredible sorrow that he has hidden all his life, other men perceive him differently and begin to look at themselves differently. Recognizing his sorrow gives other men the courage to recognize their own. Having the grief shaped into a song, made into an altar, put into some form moves the sorrow from a stuck or waiting place within a man to the world outside. Then the Water of Life begins to flow into the world, and water inevitably changes the shape of whatever it touches.

As the little brother in the story moves through the hall, he takes a gold ring from each man of stone. Is he stealing from the dead? Is he a common thief benefiting from their inability to stop him? The rings are never mentioned again. But they are a reminder to him that he is a member of this group and that his purpose is to bring the Water of Life to the sick king and the world above. In order not to get stuck in this hall, he needs to recall his purpose; later, he'll need to recall the hall and the movement from sorrow to joy in order to avoid feeling exiled in the upperworld.

The gold rings are symbols of loyalty, of a passionate faith. The stories that men tell of deep passions that have turned to stone inside carry a sense of deep faithfulness to an ideal or a purpose. Even when the purpose has become paralyzed, the ring represents a man's marriage to that purpose. It stands for the story of that purpose in the man's heart; what has turned to stone is connected to gold. Carrying this type of gold leads to the other treasures and makes the beauty of the underworld queen visible.

Once the youngest brother has collected the gold rings, he receives the sword and the loaf. After passing through the alchemy of this hall of stone, the iron rod has become the sword that can defeat all armies. The two loaves that fed the lions reappear as one loaf that replenishes itself endlessly and can feed others. Learning to feed the inner lions enables the youngest brother to feed others. Learning to open the gates to the inner life and to communal emotions makes a sword that can defeat any army. The process of feeding the inner life and facing the sorrow that has turned a man to stone returns abundance to the outer world. There is no way to defeat the attacking armies or feed the starving hordes without breaking through the stone to find the rings. The sword that protects and the bread that nourishes don't come out of simple good intentions and wishful thinking. Rather, they are made from the stories of benumbed emotions and passionate purpose once these are released from stone.

Between the stone hall and the Water of Life is the queen, the lady of the fountain who appears if one doesn't turn to stone. Who is she? She's the Queen of the Underworld, Dark Persephone, the one who made Vasilisa's gown. She's also Our Lady of Sorrow, the Queen of Mourning, the keeper of the Water of Life and the Water of Death. Whatever is lost eventually reaches her castle.

In the Welsh myth "The Lady of the Fountain," the water in the fountain can be the Water of Life or of Death. Whoever enters the lady's realm and survives the challenges of the place becomes the Black Knight, the protector of the Water of Life and observer of funerals. When the hero of that story first sees the lady of the fountain, he is awakened from his sleep on a beautiful bed in a peaceful room by the sound of wailing and weeping.

He leaps up and rushes to the window and sees below a long funeral procession, with hundreds of people carrying candles that light the casket being carried. Behind it walks a woman who is weeping louder than all the rest. He is stunned, struck by the beauty and majesty of the woman walking behind the casket.

He falls in love with the sadness of the queen. He sees the nobility in her lament. Eventually, he becomes the Black Knight and agrees to embody the darkness of the castle as well as to wear a golden ring to remind him that he must return to the lady of the fountain. This tale reminds us that being near the Water of Life means seeing the nobility in sorrow and awaking to the lamentations not just of the sick king but also of the lady of the fountain. In order to reach the Water of Life, the Black Knight must know more about grieving and death. His rest is partially a participation in the mourning of the otherworld; it also deepens his sense of beauty. He sees into his own sorrow as well as hers, and that leads to both of them finding joy again.

The man's recognition of the sorrow of the lady and his desire to don the dark garments of the Black Knight are part of the radical changes that bring the possibility of joy back into the otherworld and the possibility of the curing water into the upperworld. Near the Water of Life is the Water of Death; the pouring of libations and the weeping of tears for the dead precede our reaching the Water of Life.

The lady of the fountain in "The Water of Life" represents the sudden appearance of beauty and joy to eyes that have been washed with tears. She seems to awaken when the brother makes it through the room full of stone men. She seems to benefit from what he has experienced there. What he has learned with the men of stone, the rings, the sword, and the loaf affect her. She rejoices. Some spell around her is broken, at least temporarily. She raises the sound of joy and directs him to the Water of Life.

When the spell of stone breaks, the lady of the fountain is released. If a man doesn't get far enough into the genuine suffering of his soul, he'll forget that this source of joy even exists. If he loses all sight of her, then he won't be able to see the sorrow, joy, and beauty in women, in men, in anyone he loves.

In the realm of the lady of the fountain, heroic battles accomplish nothing. So once the youngest brother has seen the queen, he falls asleep; he rests and dreams. This lady doesn't need to be rescued from a tower or saved from a villainous king. Getting through the stone men and seeing her sorrow and joy are what's required. Acquiring the Water of Life is not about heroic effort. Falling asleep doesn't deprive the hero of any opportunities; rather, it prepares him to draw near the source of life. He joins the group of men who know the difference between stopping in time and being stuck. He puts on the dark garments that cause a man to move slowly, the way deep feelings and deep waters move. He learns the value of sleep and dreaming. The little brother sleeps and wakes in the rhythms appropriate to the land below.

But when the little brother does awake, there's no time to consider what has happened. Now he must act quickly, so he finds the water and rushes back the way he came. At the last moment, he gets through the heavy gates and escapes being turned to stone—except that his heel is caught. A piece of him remains behind; he loses something on the way out. A small death is required for a cup of the Water of Life. There is a marking of the body, a scar that inscribes the dark knowledge of mortality.

The youngest brother doesn't get through this initiation unscathed or come out better than before. Instead, he limps out of the realm of the Water of Life. He comes out of the underworld with a wound that will affect his stance and all his movements in life. His hands and heart are full—he carries the cup of the Water of Life, the sword, and the loaf—but he also carries more knowledge of stones and sorrow. The "little brother" carries more life and knows more death; he has been darkened.

where a piece of himself remains. Initiation leaves certain wounds and scars that make a person specifically who he or she is. And the little brother can now be known by what he's lost. Something is lost on the way back with the healing water, as if staying in touch with loss were part of the healing. Part of the youngest brother is left behind in the underworld with the stone men and the queen, making him partly of them.

The price for carrying some of the water that flows at the depth of the inner world is to carry a wound at the lowest point of the body. While the youngest brother's hands are full of the water and bread of life and the sword that can defend them, the foot carries the mark of the underworld. The wound is in the backward, downward place, opposite of and far from the glorious head. Some knowledge is deposited in the foot as a reminder of where the brother has walked, of what he has felt. It's a funeral scar, a limp that becomes part of every step to remind him of the spell of stone that still grips the otherworld. He may be able to cover the wounded heel, but every baring of his soul will reveal it again. This wound is the mark of failure to get through cleanly. Ultimately, it's his passport for crossing between the world of the older brothers and the world of the fountain.

It is only after being cut by the gates that the brother learns the value of the sword that will defeat attackers and the bread that will feed all. So it's only through awareness of the wounded walk and of the stories of the stone men and of the entrapment of the queen that the knowledge of how to defend and feed others becomes more than a fantastic ideal. Of the three brothers, only the one who has sacrificed a heel to the underworld can help others. It is not his wholeness or lack of woundedness that heals; rather, the healing lies in his involvement in loss, a loss that he now carries in every step. It is the ability to carry the wound and experience the sense of loss in each step that makes it possible to get the sword and loaf through the gates.

As before, the dwarf is by the gates and at the side of the road when the brother comes out. The dwarf tells him the purpose and value of the sword and loaf and warns against the wicked hearts of the brothers. But the youngest will not be deterred in his determination to restore everything. Whereas in his first meeting with the dwarf, he submitted readily and fully, now he won't submit at all. He's inflated; the lost heel seems a small price to pay to be able to carry such abundance in his hands and such glorious potentials in his heart. Whereas before he didn't know where he was going, now he is certain and knows what he wants. He is imbued with the flow of life and the desire to include all in it. Since his heart is open and abundance overflows from his arms, he feels that everyone will surely embrace the same inclusive joy.

The effects of this return from the castle of the Water of Life are not at all straightforward. The youngest brother has changed radically, and all the relationships to which he returns must change as well. The relationship with the dwarf is immediately altered; now the mentor has to listen to the requests of the little brother. The older brothers are partly driven to treachery by the abundance of gifts the youngest carries. The king is cured but condemns the son who brought the cure. The connection to the world of the Water of Life makes one an exile in this world. For a while, matters get much worse as a result of being in touch with the men of stone, the lady of the fountain, and the gifts of the other world. In this way, the story shows how initiation changes all relationships.

The youngest brother can't refuse the expansiveness caused by the contact with the water even when this means a deepening involvement with the "wicked-hearted." He has to tell the story of his experiences on the other side of the gates. On the one hand, this is a naïve thing to do, and on the other, it's impossible to resist. He can't contain what has happened. What he has in his hands and heart has become too much for him to keep to himself. What he has is not simply for himself; even the dwarf bows his head to that.

The Water of Life is not simply a cure-all; it cures some and exiles others. It throws life and death into question. The Water of Life and the Water of Death are always connected. From the closing of the gates until the little brother sleeps on the ship floating toward home, he rides on the abundant charm of the sword, loaf, and water. He acts with the magnanimity of a king and is able to provide protection and abundance to any and all. But when he sleeps on the ship, he loses the whole thing. From the moment when he falls asleep until he stumbles back to the gates, he goes from being everyone's savior to being lost within himself. His sleep within the castle was part of the steps for getting close to the Water of Life. Being near the water causes a sleepiness, for in sleep we find the dreaming that is also a part of the Water of Life. When he sleeps on the ship, it precipitates losing the water— but it leads eventually to finding something more.

At this point in the telling of the story, men begin to argue over whether the youngest brother should sleep or not. Various ways to guard the cup of water are suggested. Finally, though, it becomes clear that avoiding sleep and devising protection plans are older-brother reactions. The youngest brother is bound to sleep. In this way, he stays connected to the source of the water and keeps himself from moving into the position of older brother. If he were to use older-brother tactics, he would be bound to enter into negotiations with the king over the water. There would have to be affidavits signed by each side that this was in fact the water desired. Lawyers would rush in; the ministers would begin saying, "Indeed, indeed." Congress would be called to form committees. Soon enough, the whole thing would become merely a furtherance of the dying structure that was the problem in the first place.

Bringing the Water of Life doesn't mean pouring new life into a corpse that has lost touch with its own depth of being. Bringing the water doesn't mean shoring things back up so that they can continue as before. The realm gets worse before it gets better. The Water of Life is both bitter and sweet medicine. The king must learn to see who carries a wicked heart. The youngest brother can't simply become a heroic older brother who forgets about his heel and never hears a dwarf speak again. The older brothers can't, through treachery, simply become everyone's helpers. Bringing the Water of Life deepens the condition of each person. The water doesn't wash away all faults; it follows, widens, and deepens the fault lines that are already there. Bringing the water from the fountain of life and death means deepening the passions of all who handle the cup. The cure can be worse than the disease. Or as Goethe said, "Great passions are incurable, their very remedies make them worse."

The youngest brother, who has carried the capacity for great ideals and the genuine desire to heal father and kingdom, gets those passions activated fully. He can't help but include his brothers and everyone else in his good fortune. The dwarf's nature is intensified by the water as well. He does his job of saying what's what, of going to the heart of matters and revealing what is in the hearts of all the brothers: "They are in narrow prisons that well suit their wicked hearts, while you are carrying the water and bread of openheartedness." But he can't force the issue; he can open the prison of the older brothers, but he can't close the heart of the youngest.

The Water of Life seems to have this effect on everyone in proximity to it. When the older brothers touch the water, their greed, envy, and drive for power increase. Their self-importance expands; their mutual support of their false selves deepens into treachery. While handing the cure to their father, they poison his heart toward the youngest brother and intrigue him into trading his life for the death of his youngest son. When the king drinks his sip, the fault in him widens. There's a glimpse of what sickness the king suffered in how he acts in recovery: He's quick to judge, hasty to condemn. The king's ear is too open to the poisons of the older brothers, and his counselors emulate his vindictive traits.

At first, bringing the Water of Life seems to revivify the worst traits of the kingdom, and the youngest brother has to survive the increases of death that are stirred by carrying the water of the other-world back into this one. He can't simply run back to the castle of the lady of the fountain. There's a ritual requirement that he return at the end of a year, when all the things set in motion by his entering the gates in the first place have been played out. If he returns to the castle of the lady too soon, he won't change her imprisoned state, and he'll join the men turned to stone. If he stays in the outer world, he'll be put to death.

Now he is in the terrible territory of betrayal. When a group of men is working in this story, each man can identify the point of betrayal in his own life through some memory and feelings of anguish and exile. A man says, "He should have listened to the dwarf the second time as well. It was the youngest brother who betrayed the dwarf by not following his advice, and that's what begins the betrayals." But another man disagrees completely, saying, "It was the dwarf who betrayed him. The dwarf should have insisted on keeping the wicked brothers frozen in the rocks. The dwarf betrayed the youngest brother." But another says, "The youngest brother betrayed his mission—that's the first betrayal. He was naïve and foolishly full of himself. He should have known not to tell the brothers about the Water of Life and about the beautiful queen at the fountain. By telling them, he betrayed his mission and the queen herself." And the next man says, "It was the queen who betrayed him. She should have told him that he would be betrayed in the upperworld, that the Water of Life would have the opposite effect on those above than it has on those below. She should have told him that he could get stuck up there as well as turn to stone down below."

Another man says, "If he hadn't fallen asleep, the betrayals wouldn't have started at all. It's his own fault. He betrayed himself by sleeping." "Everyone has to sleep," says the next man. "It was simply the two brothers who started all this betrayal by switching the real water with the saltwater and betraying their own brother."

"It's the betrayal by the father that's killing me," says another man. "The father should have seen through the tricks of the older brothers. He should have been interested in the story of how this water got there. He should have been more observant. He should have known his sons better." Someone else says, "The last question in the main story of Western culture is 'Father, why hast thou forsaken me?' How could this father be expected to know more than God, the Father?" Another man wants to blame the counselors of the king for not holding a genuine trial to arrive at justice and for once again just following the dictates of an obviously deranged leader.

Yet another says, "It was the youngest brother who betrayed himself by not defending himself. He had the sword that could defeat all enemies, and he could have defeated every one of them. And he had the bread that could feed endlessly, and he could have made a show of the power of that bread. Then it would have been obvious who had brought the Water of Life. He could have defeated the brothers and counselors and proved to the king that he was the right one. He betrayed himself." Someone else says, "He betrayed himself from the very beginning when he came out of the gates and did not talk about the wound in his heel but only talked about the glorious things he had seen. He betrayed himself, he betrayed his wound, and he betrayed the stone men in the underworld."

In the story, the youngest brother can help the realms besieged by enemies and famine, but he can't defend himself against those closest to him. "You're always betrayed by your own!" That's the old saying. Betrayal can only come where trust has been placed. In this sense, every betrayal is self-betrayal. Touching the Water of Life causes betrayal; betrayal and the wounded heel go together. The place of betrayal is a terrible place. But I've never met a man over thirty-five who hasn't been betrayed and who hasn't betrayed at least himself. If a man is playing at innocence after thirty-five, he's either asking to be betrayed or is setting up a betrayal of someone else. This is a prison of one's own making. Protests of innocence are just another form of betrayal.

The story says that clinging to innocence after a certain age is a betrayal of the source of the Water of Life. At some point, a man must hand himself over; that's the meaning of "be-tray." At some point, a man either hands over his innocence and walks on in the common garments of the betrayed, or he joins the betraying brothers in their guise of innocence. The youngest brother chooses to relinquish the outward appearance of innocence; wearing the dark cloak of mortality that he received in the land below, he now wears his innocence on the inside.

Once again there's no way for the youngest brother to go but down. The water presses at the faults in him as well. In the strangest way, it's his fault that things have gone awry. His capacity for stopping to hear the dwarf means that he now must hear the condemnations of father and brothers. Now, he must listen to the echo of the dwarf's warning about wicked hearts. His ability to state the obvious, to avoid denial and admit that he has no idea where he's going, means that he can't now deny the judgments laid on him.

The outer, upperworld becomes a wasteland if the soul is abandoned. Once an initiation into the watery realm of the soul has occurred, there is no way to avoid the pull of the soul. The youngest brother forgot that what propelled him into the upperworld was the connection to beauty and sorrow in the underworld. He forgot that the older brothers and the king had not listened to the voice nor visited the halls of the lady of the fountain. He confused one world with the other. He didn't realize that despite the deep sense of community in the underworld, each person from the upperworld must get there on his or her own.

So the youngest brother had another step coming, a further breaking down. From the exhilaration of finding the water, he must descend again. He must step out of his royal garments into the common garb of the old hunter so that he can see life and death from the hunter's point of view. He's in his own healing now—exiled, thought to be dead. Traversing the wasteland of betrayal is the second part of this initiation of the soul. It is another part of the initiate's process of learning about and becoming who he really is and must be.

When the youngest brother leaves the king's castle for the second time, it is not to search for the Water of Life. He leaves under a sentence of death. He is escorted out of the castle by his executioner. His life is in the hands of the old hunter, the third appearance in the story of the wise old man. The first old man gave all three brothers the basic information that there was a cure for the illness of their father. He gave to the brothers equally, and they each set off on the same road. Then came the ambiguous dwarf, who first divided the brothers based on their attitudes and the genuineness of their intentions on the way to the Water of Life. Later, he joined the three together again, despite the threat this posed to the life of the little brother. The third appearance of the wise old man is full of sorrow, like the weeping at the opening of the story. But now the one under threat of death is the youngest son, not the king. Now the healing needs to come to the little brother. The old hunter recognizes the limping of the youngest son and reveals his own sorrow; finally, they are joined in their griefs.

In this scene, the cracking open of hearts that occurred in the hall of stone men is repeated. What the old hunter and the youngest brother share are the closeness of death and the sorrows it awakens in them. They talk about these sorrows, and that's what leads to the exchange of clothes. The youngest brother exchanges all the evidence of his royal birth and high rank for the clothes of the hunter. He steps inside himself and into the common guise that allows one to wander about, limping along, carrying one's own grief. The old hunter hands the brother over to his wounded heel, gives him a cover that allows him to dwell in the common ground of lost innocence. Now the youngest brother is on the other side of the need to redeem his father and the desire to save the kingdom. The way back to the Water of Life is exactly through this wasteland of betrayal.

This exchange of royal garments for common clothes also begins a series of reversals and radical changes in all the realms of the story. While the youngest son begins his second descent and his wandering in exile unseen by anyone, the caravans of gold and gifts from the once-famished kingdoms begin to arrive at the center of the realm. The recognition that could not come from his father comes from the kings of the other realms. Suddenly the sick king realizes his mistake and has a change of heart. The old hunter reveals that the youngest son is not dead, and the king rejoices above as the youngest son goes further in his descent. The king sends messengers of forgiveness and declarations of the openness of his heart to the youngest brother, even as the oldest brothers, typically, are heading out to reap the benefits of the other realm.

While the caravans of gold are going toward his father and his older brothers are going down either side of the gold-covered road, the youngest brother is hunting in his own heart. While the king is finding the youngest brother innocent and declaring it to all lands, the brother is learning the darker side of innocence. Forgiveness is moving from father to son and from youngest son to father. But this is not a simple-minded, innocent forgiveness. This forgiveness means learning to trust again despite betrayal. Loss and death are contained in this forgiving. The king knows he condemned the son, even believed he caused his death. His forgiveness comes *after* that. The youngest brother is returning to the hall of stone men and doesn't see the golden road of forgiveness.

Forgiveness can't occur to the ego brothers; they are still going for the gold. As the story winds down, the older brothers become more rational and thoughtful, and they exercise a sympathy for the gold road that they never show for people. They take a side road, leaving the self-centered high road of their arrogance. They have finally encountered something that exceeds their estimations of their own self-worth, a road foolishly covered with gold. This time the dwarf doesn't have to stop them, for their own distorted values lead them away from what they want. While they are watching where they are going and thinking once again that they know where they are headed, they miss the goal.

The little brother doesn't see the golden road, but what he is contemplating deep within himself opens the gates again. He doesn't enter as the conquering hero, the rightful heir, or the dutiful groom. He arrives at his destination unknowingly. When he reenters the gates of the castle, he isn't a prince but an exile, wearing the common clothes of the hunter and the hunted. He finds himself in the realm of the lady of the fountain at the right time, in the right approach, in the right manner of appearance, without knowing that he has found it all again. He doesn't manage it, direct it, command it, regulate it, or empower it. It happens through his hunting inside and limping along.

The youngest brother returns on the grieving road wrapped in the cloak of sorrows, not charging in as a white knight or savior. The lady of the fountain waits for just such an approach; then the Water of

Life is released again. The ego brothers can never see this. The unforgiving can never see it. The princes of domination can never see it.

When the youngest brother comes out of his deep reverie, everything has changed. The spell on the realm of the lady of the fountain has been broken. There is a feast with great rejoicing and some weeping. News arrives from the father's kingdom; forgiveness is being offered all around—except for the brothers who sail away on the salt sea, afloat on the bitter waters that they made others drink.

Both realms are revived. The state of abundance, which was lost, has been refound. Father and son embrace in mutual forgiveness. Queen and prince embrace in unfettered joy. Nature is renewed, culture is revivified by the sorrow-laden Water of Life. The grieving road turns out to be the golden road.

The road between the upperworld and the otherworld is not the main road, the freeway without obstacles; rather, it traverses the land of the dwarf. The way between the realms requires a descent through stuckness and the fury of the dwarf, through banging on the gates and paying the lions. Returning from the otherworld requires giving up a piece of oneself and experiencing the loneliness of betrayal. By the time the little brother returns to his father's realm and all is forgiven, he has been back and forth among three realms, and three layers of his own life. The first is the world of the king, the realm we're calling the ego world, where the sick king and the ego brothers dominate. It is also the ongoing, upper, everyday world, the world of fact and matter-of-factness. From another point of view, it's the world of simple survival. If that world is not maintained, if there isn't actual food to eat, if there isn't actual work to do and a job to provide a way of living, then there is no hope of healing what ails us. The upperworld is also the realm of common courtesy where simple agreements allow us to continue on the path of basic survival as long as possible.

We'll look into the second realm, the realm in between, in a moment. In the third realm lies the room of stone men, the golden rings of loyalty to purpose, and the community of the openhearted. Here are found three tremendous treasures: the Water of Life that can heal the illnesses of the upperworld, the sword that can defeat all enemies, and the loaf of bread that can feed the disenfranchised, the besieged, and the starving of the world above. The third realm is also the place where the queen of joy, dignity, and beauty is found. In her presence, sorrow can change to joy, and even betrayal can be washed in healing waters.

In this third realm, the flow of life can move from the songs of grief and lament to the sounds of joy. The hardness of life can break down, and a feeling of tremendous union among people of all kinds can be experienced. When the opening of the hearts occurs and the wounds begin to sing with voices of sorrow and joy, the healing ground of universal brotherhood and community has been reached. Then, the Water of Life flows into the first and the third realms, and both are released from their stuckness and sickness.

When the rulers of the upper realm become sick and near to death, the cure can be found in the third realm where the fountain of the Water of Life lies. When the older brothers in an individual psyche or a group become stuck, imprisoned, caught in narrow views of life that exclude the "little people," then the healing that can crack that stuckness is found in the realm below. This is the promise of the first old man.

The trouble lies in this: Going from the first realm to the third requires crossing the second realm, the territory of the dwarf. Each visit to the third realm requires stopping whatever is keeping us in the first realm and listening to the questions being asked in the second. If the dwarf has been ignored for a long time—if the small things, the little feelings inside, or the "little people" of the world have been avoided, overlooked, or ignored for a long time—we will have to get through some fierce rage before the road to the third world opens up.

Between the worlds, the gates have to be dealt with, and as we've seen, each pass through the gates requires suffering some pain. There needs to be enough ferocity in a person's inner life, enough fierceness among the people of a community to bang the gates open. The lions must be fed the food of real issues and genuine emotions.

The water that's eventually released benefits those who are besieged and undernourished, those who are trapped and near death. The older brothers, who would steal from others who have suffered and not get down into the second realm themselves, never benefit from the release of genuine emotions or the flow of life. Their authority comes only through inheritance, the maintenance of the status quo, and betrayal. They always wind up betraying the source of healing and supporting the systems that get stuck and exclude the common emotions, the common people, the indigenous world, and the need of the soul to descend.

Everyone becomes familiar with the sick king and the stuck brothers somehow, and each person also inherits a little brother who waits to descend. The little brother must get to the third realm at certain times in life and must get there often enough to hold onto both a taste of the Water of Life and the hope of tasting it again. But always the movement between the upperworld and the underworld, between this world and the otherworld, between the outer world and the inner world, requires going through the gates of suffering.

At the end of the story, the Water of Life is flowing again, and all's well that ends well . . . except that the lady of the fountain doesn't leave the source of the Water of Life. After a while, the old king seems ready to begin placing judgments and laying down rules again. The youngest brother has no more brothers. The caravans of gold may stop coming. People forget. Things wear down, dry up. One day it seems as if something important is missing again. . . .

6

The Companions

The other refuses to disappear: it subsists, it persists... in what might be the incurable otherness from which oneness must always suffer.

ANTONIO MACHADO

THE COMPANIONS

In the old times, not long ago but way before anything else, there lived an aged queen, who was also a sorceress, and her daughter, who was simply the most beautiful maiden under the sun. The old queen, however, had no thought but to lure mankind to the edge of destruction. When a man would appear and seek the hand of the beautiful princess, the old queen would awaken and require that he complete a task or die. Many had been drawn by the beauty of the daughter and had taken the risk, but they never could accomplish what the old woman required. Then, no mercy was shown. They had to kneel on the ground, and a blade would sing in the air between their heads and their bodies.

A certain king's son heard of the maiden's incomparable beauty and said to his father, "Give me your permission to seek the daughter of the old queen and ask for her in marriage."

"Never," said his father the king. "If you go in that direction, you go to your death."

Hearing this, the son fell into a sickness and began to waste away toward death. For seven years the youth lay ill. Physicians of all kinds came, but none could cure him. When the king perceived that all hope was over, when he realized that there was nothing else to be done, when he grasped that this was not in his control—then, with a heavy heart, he said to his son, "Go and try your luck, for I know of no other means of curing you."

When the son heard this, he rose from his bed and was well again. And no sooner had he arisen than he joyfully set out on his way.

As he was going along, he came across a field and saw a huge mound rising from the ground like a heap of hay. As he drew closer, he could see that it was the stomach of a man who had laid himself down there, but it was a stomach that looked like a small mountain. The prince walked all the way around the side of the mound until he encountered a head. The huge man turned toward him and asked, "Where are you going? Where are you headed these days?"

The prince said, "I'm seeking the beautiful daughter of the old queen."

The huge man rose slowly, saying, "If you're in need of company and would like assistance, take me with you."

The prince replied, "What can I do in the company of a clumsy man that I couldn't do better on my own? How could it improve my condition to be in the company of such an oversized person?"

The Stout One said, "Oh, this is nothing; when I really expand and puff myself out, I'm three hundred times this size."

"If that's the case," said the prince, "you're welcome to come along."

So the Stout One and the prince went on, and after a time they came upon another man lying on the ground with his ear laid close to the turf.

"What are you doing down there?" asked the prince.

"I am listening," answered the man.

"What is it that you listen to so attentively?"

"I am listening to what is just now going on in the world. Nothing escapes my ears. I even hear the grass growing out of the ground."

"Tell me, then, what do you hear at the court of the ancient queen who has the beautiful daughter?"

"I hear the whizzing of the air moved apart by the sword that is descending on the neck of a youth who was wooing the beautiful maiden."

The son of the king said, "With ears like that, you are welcome to travel the way with us."

The three went on, and after a time they saw a pair of feet lying on the ground and saw behind the feet a pair of legs, but they could not see the rest of the body because a forest got in the way of their looking. They walked on a great distance and saw how the body continued; finally, after another extended hike, they encountered a head.

"You are a tall rascal," said the prince.

"This isn't the full extent of the story," said the Tall One. "When I consciously stretch out my bones and my limbs, I am three hundred times as tall as this—taller than the highest mountain on this earth."

"If you have an interest in travel, you are more than welcome to go the way with us," said the prince, and the four traveled on.

After a time, they came upon a man standing by a tree at the side of the road. His eyes were bound and bandaged like one who had wandered off a battlefield. The prince asked him, "Have you weak eyes that you cannot look at the light?"

"No, but I must not remove the bandages, for whatever I look at with my eyes shatters into pieces because of the power of my glance. If you are going somewhere, I should be glad enough to go along with you."

"You are welcome to travel the way with us," the prince replied.

And on they went. After a time, they came upon a man standing in the direct sunlight in the heat of the day, but he was trembling and shivering all over so that not an inch of his body was still.

"How can you shiver when the warm sun is striking your body?" asked the prince.

"Alas," said the man, "I am of a different nature. The hotter it is, the colder I am, and the frost pierces through my bones. Now, the contrary is also the case: the colder it is, the hotter I am. In the midst of ice, I cannot escape the heat; in the midst of fire, the cold assails me."

"You are a strange fellow," said the prince, "but you are welcome to travel the way with us." And they all traveled onward.

After a time, they came upon a man standing and stretching out his neck, squinting his eye, looking all about him, and searching to a great distance.

"What are you looking at so eagerly?" asked the son of the king.

The man replied, "I am exercising my sight, polishing my vision and my searching. I have such sharp eyes that I can see into every forest and field, every hill and valley throughout the world."

"What do you see at the court of the old queen?" asked the prince.

"I see the bits of dust in the air being divided by the edge of a sword that is descending on the neck of a man foolish enough to court the beautiful daughter of the queen," the man said.

"You are welcome to come along, then," said the prince. "We can use such a man as yourself." And they went along together.

After a time, they came to the realm where the aged queen had her dwelling. The son of the king went directly before the old queen. He did not say who he was, but he spoke out, "I have come seeking your beautiful daughter. I will perform whatever tasks you require of me."

The old queen was glad to have the handsome youth caught there in her net, and she said, "I will set you three little tasks; that is all I require, no more or less. If you are able to perform them all, you shall become the husband of my daughter. If you should fail, well, don't hold it against me, but your head must come off."

"I agree to the terms. What is the first task?"

"First you must fetch me my ring, for I have dropped it somewhere. I haven't been able to find it for years. It may be in the depths of the Red Sea, though."

The king's son went to his companions. "The first task is not easy. The old queen's ring must be gotten from the bottom of the Red Sea. How can we do it? Can you help me on this matter?"

The Man of Great Vision said he could readily see where the ring lay. He looked in the deepest waters and said, "The ring hangs there in the depths, caught on a pointed stone."

The Tall One said he would readily snatch up that ring with his long arm, but he could not see through the water.

"Is that the only problem?" said the Stout One, and he lay down, put his mouth to the water, and began to drink. The waves formed and moved toward his great mouth and fell into him as if he were a whirlpool. In a short time, he had drunk up the whole sea, and all that remained was a dry plain. Then the Tall One reached down and plucked the ring from the stone.

The son of the king rejoiced when he had the ring and took it directly to the old queen. The queen was astonished. "Yes, it is the right ring," she said. "You have done it, and you are safe into the bargain. Well, then, it is time for the next task.

"Look there. Do you see that meadow there, that plain lying beyond my palace? Do you see those three hundred fat oxen feeding back and forth there? Those you must eat. The skin, the hair, the bones, the horns, the flesh, the entire heft and hoof of each one of the three hundred must be eaten. That may cause you a thirst or a dryness in the mouth, so in the cellar below lie three hundred casks of wine. Those you must drink as well. If one hair of one oxen remains in that field, if one drop of wine remains in the corner of one of those barrels, then your life is forfeited and your head must leave your body."

"Well," said the prince, "a dinner, whatever its size, is a poor thing if it is taken without company. Can I not invite guests?"

The old woman laughed with malice, "You may invite one for the sake of companionship, that is all."

The king's son went to the companions and called the Stout One, saying, "You shall be my guest today, and you shall eat your fill." The Stout One was ready for this event. He first puffed himself up and then began to capture oxen. Some he pounced on, others he caught on the hoof as they ran by, and still others he rolled over as he went about. Whatever way he caught them, he treated them all similarly, devouring each one, skin, flesh, bones, and marrow, down to the last organ, to the last hair. After finishing the three-hundredth ox, he began to complain that it was unfair, false advertising, seriously misleading to invite someone to a brunch and then provide nothing but little snacks, when one was expecting a combination of breakfast and lunch.

The complaining engendered a thirst, and the Stout One was glad enough to enter the cellar and drink the wine that was there. He drank it by opening the spigot of each wooden barrel he came to and drawing the wine out. He would draw out the wine until there was not a drop left in the barrel, until there was no moisture at all, until the barrel was as dry as bones and collapsed. He treated three hundred large barrels of wine in that fashion, and when he was done, he berated the keepers of the cellar for the paucity of their stock, saying that it was a crime of another order to have such a limited supply that a man, just as he was beginning to appreciate the fine qualities of the grapes, should find himself already at the bottom of the barrel.

When the meal was over, the prince went to the old woman and told her that the second task was completed. She was amazed, saying that no one had ever gotten this far before. "Still," she said, "one task remains." And to herself she thought, "You shall not escape me, nor will you keep your head connected to your shoulders after this night!"

"Tonight," she said out loud, "I will bring my daughter to you in your chamber, and you shall put your arms around her. But you must keep your arms about her and beware of falling asleep. When the clock is striking twelve, the last hour, I will come. If she is no longer in your arms, you are lost forever."

The prince thought, "This task is easy and pleasurable. I will keep my eyes open gladly." Nevertheless, he called the companions and told them of the task, saying, "Who knows what treachery may lurk behind this. Let everyone take care that once the maiden is in my room, she does not leave it again."

Night fell, and the old queen brought her daughter and gave her over into the prince's arms. Then the Tall One wound his arms around the two of them, and the Stout One placed himself in front of the door so that no living creature could gain entrance past him. The rest of the companions arranged themselves around the room. There the two sat, and the maiden spoke never a word, but the moon shone through the window on her face and the prince beheld her wondrous beauty in that soft light. He did nothing but gaze at her; he was filled with love, and his eyes did not weary for all he looked. He held her in his gaze and in his embrace until eleven o'clock. At that time, the old woman cast such a spell over all of them that they fell sound asleep, and in the same moment the maiden was carried away. They slept a deep sleep until a quarter to twelve, when the spell lost its power.

"She is gone and I am lost," cried the prince. The companions all began to lament the loss of the whole thing.

Finally, the Listener called for quiet. "No more laments, no more noise, I want to listen." He listened. "She is stranded on a rock far from here, bewailing her fate and isolation. Only you can reach her quickly, Tall One, with your long strides."

"I'm off," said the Tall One, "but the One with Piercing Eyes must go with me, that we may destroy the rock." The Tall One took the one with bandaged eyes on his back, and quick as an eye can blink, they reached the enchanted rock. The Tall One took the bandages from the head of Piercing Eyes and turned him toward the rock. One piercing look shivered the huge rock into a thousand pieces. The Tall One caught the maiden in his arms and carried her back in no time, turned her over to the prince, returned and fetched his companion, and in short order all were sitting exactly as they had been before.

The clock struck twelve and the old queen came abruptly in, certain that the maiden was stuck on the enchanted rock and that the prince was in her power. What a shock when she beheld her daughter gazing into the eyes of the prince and the prince raptly gazing back on her as the moonlight bathed them both! "Here is one who knows more than I do," she said in alarm. She feared to set up any further opposition to him, and she promised her daughter to him.

But she whispered one little thing into the sweetly formed ear of the beautiful maiden: "Isn't it a disgrace and a shameful thing that you have to obey common people, to give yourself over to a common man and not even be allowed to choose a husband equal in quality to you and suited to your own liking?"

The daughter of that old and powerful queen began to think about what had been said. She knew nothing of this man; he seemed common enough. What if he meant harm to her, and what of all these strange companions?

The next morning she caused three hundred bundles of wood to be brought to the palace hall. She called the prince and said that although he had accomplished the three tasks, she would not consent to be his wife until he had seated himself in the midst of the great fire that she was about to set burning. The prince asked if it were allowed that someone do the sitting for him. The princess said that it was allowed, for she was sure that none of the companions would let themselves be burned for him, that he would have to enter the fire himself, that he would be burned, and that she would regain her freedom.

The companions gathered and said that each had done their part except the Man of Temper, so he must now set to work. He was placed in the middle of the great heap of wood, and it was set on fire. The fire blazed up and burned with intense heat, driving away all the onlookers. It burned that way for three full days, until all the wood was consumed and the flames died out. Then as the smoke settled, to the great surprise of all, the Tempered One was seen standing in the pile of ashes, trembling like an aspen leaf, saying, "Oh, it was a killing frost. I never felt such a frost in my whole life; had it lasted any longer, I would have been benumbed and turned to stone."

The last test being done, no other pretext to delay was found, and the beautiful daughter of the old queen was forced to take the unknown youth to wed. When they set off together, the old woman said, "I cannot endure it, the loss, the disgrace." So she sent her warriors after them to cut down everyone and bring her daughter back. But the Listener had his ear to the ground and heard the secret discourse of the old queen.

"What shall we do?" he said to the Stout One.

The Stout One didn't speak but turned back and spit out some of the water he had earlier consumed and caused a sea to form suddenly and catch the warriors as they rode, drowning them. One escaped and reported back to the queen, who railed at him and sent another army.

This time when the Listener heard the sound of the soldiers' pursuit, he undid the bandages of Piercing Eyes and turned him toward them. Piercing Eyes looked rather fixedly at the charging troops, and they all broke into so many pieces like shattered glass.

There were no more attacks, and they were able to go on their way. At a certain point the companions said, "Your wishes are now satisfied; you need us no longer. We will go our ways." After many embraces, each went his way.

Near the palace of the prince's father was a village, and near that was the hut of a swineherd. When they reached the hut, the prince said to his new wife, "I wish I were the prince of the great palace, but truly I am a herder of swine, and this is our family hut, and that old man is my father. Now that we have arrived, we two must set to work and help him with the swine."

He passed word of what he was doing to the villagers, and in the morning the princess was given an old gown and was escorted to the herd. To herself she thought, "Well, he accepted the fire I set for him, so I guess I must accept the little hut, the common clothes, and a number of pigs." She set to work and so did he.

One day, people came and asked her if she knew who her husband was. "Yes," she said, "he is the swineherd, and you can find him now on his way to market with pigs and ropes, hoping to drive a good bargain when he gets there."

They said, "If you'll come with us, we will take you to meet him." She agreed, and they took her straight to the palace. There, they didn't hesitate at the entry gate, didn't stop at all until they were in the throne room. There stood her husband in kingly raiment. She did not recognize him in her amazement. But when he came close and they gazed into the each other's eyes, she knew at once who he was. It was as if they were gazing at each other again, bathed in moonlight, guarded by the companions. After that they began to prepare a great wedding feast.

CHAPTER 25

INCURABLE WOUNDS

THROUGH THIS STORY, once again, the young hunter of the psyche is released and wanders from one realm to another. Once again, he follows the pattern of every initiation, separating from what is known, suffering ordeals and unusual events, and returning in a deeply altered condition. This time, before he departs, he must endure seven years of breaking down and realizing his own incurable condition. The sickness of the soul has moved from the king of the realm in the last story to the son of the realm in this one.

In the very first story in this book, "The Hunter and His Son," the son received a wound from his father. In a sense, that wound has been working its way through all the stories and appears now as seven years of incurable illness. The stories can be seen as a series of adventures that begin with a boy exploring the world without and the world within, which leads to temperings that will now culminate in an initiation as an elder.

At first, the son followed in the footsteps of his father and walked directly into a wound that was being passed down from father to son. Next, he set out on his own and found the half-giantess, symbolizing the incompleteness of his vision in the world of the mothers. In the story of Conn-Eda, the son separated from the world of the mother and the realm of the father and descended through water and fire to find an incredible brother within. As a result of that episode of initiation, he began to find the resources within himself and in the "otherworld." Conn-Eda's "great black steed" seems then to become the horse of power that advises him and carries him throughout the ordeals in the land of the firebird. After completing the tasks on the road of fire, the tempering of the son requires that he go in search of the Water of Life in order to cure a sickness in the king and a sickness in the realm. Now he discovers an ache and a sickness in himself; he is stuck in a place that no one can alter or cure. The only thing that will allow him to get unstuck is the king's permission to seek that which is at once the most beautiful and the most dangerous thing in the world.

For the son has heard of a woman of compelling beauty; although all who have sought her have lost their heads, he will lose his life now if he cannot pursue her. Previously, the son of the realm has gone on his missions alone, having to separate even from his older brothers in the last story in order to accomplish his task. He has been aided by a variety of strange and resourceful animals and by a series of old men who have both driven him and guided him. This time he will take hardly a step along the way by himself. Rather, he will encounter the strange companions who seem to rise up from the depths—from the ground and from below the ground.

This time the son of the realm has entered the outer initiation ring, the ring of the elders, and he must join with those who can bring together the two extremes: the realm of the king and the world of the ancient queen. At one extreme stands the realm of the king and the father, with its incurability, its inability to heal the wounds of the soul. At the other extreme waits the world of the old queen and the mother, where most lose their heads even before the beauty of the daughter can be seen. Connecting the two worlds lies the road of the strange companions, the ancient helpers from below.

This story appears under many names and in many guises. It is called "The Six Servants," "The Six Who Went Through the World," or something else altogether. I call it "The Companions" to focus on the company of ancient helpers who awaken because of trouble, illness, and danger and who seek the cure for the conditions of the soul in that which is most beautiful. In different versions, the companions themselves take on various shapes; they take on the characteristics of the local culture so that they can be seen, recognized, and understood. But they always appear after the severe illness of the prince and join him as soon as he moves toward the vision that made him incurable. They are connected to what seems incurable in him, and they connect him to the cure he seeks. They appear when a certain depth of desire becomes set in the heart and when there is nowhere else to go. The companions are part of the human heritage; they are ancestral forces that become available at the last hour. As we will see later, they are the last chance, the only way left to turn, and they provide a connection to the world of ancestors.

One day, the son of the king, the little brother in the psyche, the hunter of the realm, begins to waste away. All the cures are tried, but nothing helps, nothing changes. He has become a symbol of the wasteland, of what's ailing at the center of the realm. He has heard something that has fallen all the way through the labyrinth of his ear into the place of destiny in his heart. From there it has worked its way all through his bones and organs until he has become sick in his soul. What he heard has knocked him off the path of regular life and onto the path of destiny.

The story he heard was not new, but ongoing: That which is most beautiful is held in a distant place; she can only be approached through difficult tasks; many have tried, but no mercy has been shown, and they have all lost their heads. The prince must have heard this story before, but this time he hears it differently—it speaks to him specifically. A scene that combines beauty, terror, imprisonment, and release calls to an ancestral place in him. This story is constantly being remade in the soul of each person and in the soul of each generation. The object of desire may vary, but always there is a place in the soul that is longing for beauty, even as the spirit senses the danger.

What has thrown the prince into the wasteland of his own soul is an awakening that he cannot reverse. In this story, the son knows from the onset that he will face danger and death. He heard it all at once— that beauty and the danger of death lie in the same direction. He is not following in his father's footsteps; his father would prevent him from going. He's not naively stepping out to see what's in the wide-eyed world; he knows the old hag-queen-giantess waits for him. It's not the order of a king that sends him after what is most beautiful, and it's not the wasting of a king that awakens his desire for a cure. Something in *him* has heard the call of destiny. He's in another initiatory state: If he goes, he'll face death, and if he doesn't, he will surely die.

What he has heard holds both sickness and cure, both beauty and terror, both present and ancient conditions. The prince has become weirdly sick, sick in a way that avoids all cures for seven years. No amount of rest can cure this illness, and all the physicians together can't manage to heal it. It doesn't respond to less pressure or more pressure. Being the child of the king doesn't help. Other people's versions of the story don't help. Hearing that his desire is impossible to achieve won't change anything. Self-medication won't help. Improved self-esteem won't help.

The seven years signify the amount of time required to clear everything out of the way in order to open the door to the extraordinary and weird. This is the time spent gathering permission to go on the strange road of fate. This time when the prince remains incurable represents a "stripping down," a shedding of all the rational and familiar approaches to what is an unchanging condition of the soul. Everything gets stripped away except the vision that struck the soul. Ulterior motives, the usual concerns for others, even the idea of returning are all stripped away.

Before most people can admit to the incurable condition of their souls, they have to describe and diagnose and prescribe and recast it many times. But this condition speaks most clearly when it is permitted to be simply incurable. The only way to treat the condition is to get everything out of the way and allow the sickness to speak for itself. It can only be heard when all the possible cures have been eliminated and its incurability has been admitted. The soul sickness needs permission to be the strange story that it declares itself to be.

In a sense, people have within them a room or a chamber where a part of them is always lying incurably ill. The illness comes from being separated from the beauty and full range of life the soul desires. The cure can be found in the place of greatest loss and fear, where all have lost their heads. Unfortunately, all appeals to normalcy will only drive further away the beauty that is missing.

Each culture has an incurable wound as well, and life conditions have to become serious before that chamber is entered, before what's sick and wasting away in there can speak and be heard.

I learned about this chamber through telling stories. The story-teller is trying to say, "Beauty was trapped somewhere once upon a time, once under this time. In the timeless water in the pond of this moment, there is something beautiful that only you can imagine. Head after head has attempted to find it, to free it, to cure its ills, but they all rolled on the floor. Have you heard of it? Does opening the door to that sense of beauty bring back every illness you've ever faced?" The storyteller knows that each person is sitting in or near the room that contains his or her own illness and own sense of beauty. Why else would anyone want to hear a genuine story, except that it might touch the conditions of his or her soul and ease them, or incite them, or both? A story such as this one unites the prince and the princess, the incurably ill and the endlessly entrapped, who reside in each soul.

The many versions of this story allow its listeners to enter their own room of incurability and find permission to wander out on their own road of the companions toward what is specifically beautiful and dangerous to them. There's no description of the son of the king, for example, nor is there a description of the beautiful daughter of the old queen. The prince is incurably ill and she's incurably beautiful, or she's incurably dangerous and he's always lost. Both are inside each person and each epoch. They are repeatedly lost and rediscovered again. The story asks each person who listens to find the incurable room inside and to invent a new way out of that place. Everyone must respond inventively to the story; it makes a re-searcher, a novelist, a painter out of all who listen. And, it opens the ears of the "inner elder."

The prince has fallen ill because of a vision; he has fallen into a creative illness. Soul sickness is the preparation for going where he must go. He allows himself to be pulled down. He admits physician after physician, diagnosis after diagnosis. He is not fighting the illness. He waits until everyone has made his or her attempt to name the condition and change it. He suffers the ailing soul until permission arrives to go further into it.

In the incurable area of the psyche, the matter at hand is always an issue of life or death. It's always the last hour, always the end of one stage and the beginning of another; it's always the millennium. And the last minute is not just a time for heroes and saviors but also the time for radical change from below. When the structures have broken down in a culture, that which has been denied and repressed can return. This return brings with it new potentials, energies that were long held back and that have a capacity to burst through old illnesses. The results can be both terrible and beautiful. How people deal with change determines how much terror and how much beauty they experience. But in the deep psyche, it's always the dark time when everything is about to change. Curing the soul sickness means learning to see despite the increase of darkness.

> In a dark time, the eye begins to see,
> I meet my shadow in the deepening shade;
> I hear my echo in the echoing wood—
> A lord of nature weeping to a tree.
> I live between the heron and the wren,
> Beasts of the hill and serpents of the den.
>
> What's madness but nobility of soul
> At odds with circumstance? The day's on fire!
> I know the purity of pure despair,
> My shadow pinned against a sweaty wall.
> That place among the rocks—is it a cave,
> Or winding path? The edge is what I have.

> —THEODORE ROETHKE, FROM "IN A DARK TIME"

The incurable condition of the soul appears as a "dark time," as a "dark night of the soul," that can envelop an individual, a community, an era. For the incurable condition of the son of the realm can also represent the condition of contemporary life, as if he were standing at a threshold similar to that which we face in the modern world. What is it that the "eye begins to see" when the dark times occur? In what direction do people turn when "the day's on fire" and when weeping and pure despair make an edge that is also like a threshold? In this story, one of the answers is to turn toward, rather than deny, the incurable condition of the soul, to enter into the darkened areas of a culture. The path to releasing the beauty in the otherworld takes the prince right into the most extreme symptoms of the illness and follows where they lead.

We see this story through our own "dark time," in the darkening light at the close of the second millennium of recorded history. City lights glow for twenty-four hours at a stretch, lighting both day and night because everyone knows it's a dark time. It is a time full of the echoes of the last thousand years—echoes that reverberate each day in the morning papers and the nightly news, repeating a litany of loss, destruction, conflict, and confusion. The news stories are repeated over and over because they hold off the sound of nature weeping among the trees. A thousand years ago, the forests were wide and impenetrable, and news traveled slowly. Now, the news eats the forest in order to print itself, it speaks on lines that cross through the trees, and it leaps over them with the ease of a fire driven by the wind. As the wind of the rapid-fire events in the modern world whips through, over, and around the trees, forests grow smaller each day.

The trees, meanwhile, stand there like empty icons. As the life force drains out of forests, it also drains out of the institutions of culture. Losses in nature are paralleled by losses of vitality in the systems of culture. Eventually, the threshold of basic life is reached and the question becomes: Do we cross the threshold and find another way of existing, surviving, and celebrating life? Or does everything stop on this side of the threshold?

It is partly the nature of the end of a life stage or the end of a historical age that some aspects wind down and some collapse. Loss is an integral part of major changes. The modern world stands at the threshold that ends one age and begins another. At the edge of the millennium, the dying age sees the history of the past thousand years pass before its eyes, just as a person who is dying may see his or her life flash by. As we draw near the threshold of change, we face the question asked at the end of each age and each stage: is this the end of reality, or is it a metaphorical ending that is occurring? Is it the shedding, breaking down, and falling off of old forms so that the threshold can be crossed into another stage of culture, another age of life? Or is this the final curtain?

That has been the question hanging on the threshold of life since World War II and the dawning of our capacity to destroy the world by exploding small pieces of it. At the threshold, the facts of life, the inner truths of psychology, and the timeless wisdom of myth begin to merge. Outer world, inner world, and otherworld coincide briefly. The actual, the incurable, and the impossible meet. The end of an age or a stage is like a near-death experience. Is it necessary actually to die, or is this cultural brush with the great wing of death the prelude to a new era? This serious and mysterious question can only be answered in the minds and hearts and imaginations of people who find themselves standing on the threshold. During the last throes of an age, the psyche is absorbed in looking back and looking ahead. Looking back can consist of deep searching for origins or of simple nostalgia. Looking ahead can contain visions of possibilities viewed through cracks in the collapsing culture, or we may see only darkness and shadows.

On the threshold of an age, time seems to flow backward and forward at the same time. Battles that have been treated as parts of history turn out to be part of the present and of the future. The political agreements made at the close of World War II now unravel. Old battlefields are revisited. Old kingdoms try to resurface. Nations form and reform more quickly than even "instant news" can travel. Money changes value faster than it changes hands. The "new order" is both disorder and many orders at once. We witness the return of the incurable, of the sins of the fathers visited on the sons, of the old wounds and conflicts refusing to be covered over or treated symptomatically.

Old battles for sovereignty, struggles among religions, and surges of tribal revenge resurface from their hiding places below the ground-cover of modern times. The incurable returns in the form of issues that won't go away, won't stay buried, won't allow themselves to be "put behind us." Once again, the great question of a woman's right to choose abortion lies on the legislative tables and in the courtrooms of America. Once again, the death penalty is in question in state after state. Once again, the demand for civil rights flares up in burning fires in various urban centers throughout the country. Again, the question of racism in America demands attention. Once again, the great questions that divide the genders rattle within houses and institutions throughout the country.

Can there be female and male faces in positions of authority, and if so, what is the nature of the authority enacted by each? Can the multiple faces of the diverse cultures that are thrown into the great sea of America surface and be seen? As the number of incidents of violence increases in city after city, can America survive only as an armed camp? Can a country founded in colonial wars, indentured servitude, and slavery and therefore dreaming of freedom and democracy survive the return of its own origins? Does the "right to bear arms" ultimately mean that we have to live under siege? Must people become "billeted troops" in their own homes? Will the experiment in democracy end in a democratic shoot-out—or through holes shot in the ozone?

Whole cultures are passing now through a period of initiatory ordeals, shedding forms with which they have lived for hundreds of years, being stripped of even basic aspects of life, being forced to submit to the radical changes that are sweeping across them and the planet. The changes are so sweeping and rapid that they are quicker than the eye of the TV camera. Film has to be slowed down in order for us to see what has actually happened, and even then, there are as many interpretations as there are viewers. The same questions are asked over and over, the same films rebroadcast, the same battlefields revisited. This is not history repeating itself but history defeating itself and ritual emerging. History can't change anything because its place is in the past. Instead, what repeats are the great symbols of the psyche, the crucial images of a culture, the startling forms of nature, and the incurable dilemmas of life.

There's a feeling of loss for all of us when we allow the immovable and incurable to enter. The weight that each person has been carrying is felt; the darkness beyond the laser beam of light is revealed. In the shadows of modern culture, there are many myths to be glimpsed; in the shadows lie the refuse of old cultures tossed out of sight and the memories of feelings too dense or too subtle for the news. In a dark time, the eye begins to see into the pieces of things. In a dark time, things need to be stumbled upon and felt in order to be learned and pieced together anew.

In the story, the movement toward the cure begins with acceptance of the incurability of the condition. The son knows that beauty, terror, and death are all calling from the other side of the door and that he has no way to heal the conditions of his soul except to go across the threshold. But the king will only give his permission when all else has been tried. The king has a great resistance to the opening of that particular door. He'd rather have a sick son than a healthy son who goes through that door. The last thing the ruling figure in any psyche wants is to cross that threshold. In story after story, we are warned, "You can go anywhere you wish, but don't open that door." In most stories, the protagonist receives both the key to the door and the warning against opening it at the same time. In "The Companions," as in "The Water of Life," the key to the door consists of becoming so ill that the choice is between dying or going on the perilous path that has led all others to death.

But a story always says more than it appears at first to say. When permission is given, the health of the man returns; simply opening the door to that road changes the nature of the sickness of the soul. It's as if the king were actually resisting something else—not just the son's passing through the door but the son's taking the path that leads to the strange companions. The king avoids what actually has to happen if the son is to be healthy, if beauty is to be found. Everything else must be tried, but "not that." Everything beyond the door is the "not that" of the king, of the family, of the culture. Beyond the door, in that direction waits the repressed of the culture. Only when death comes knocking at the door will that way be permitted, and one can enter into what has been hidden and forbidden in the culture.

A cure is first of all an airing out. What gets cured first gets exposed to the light and air. In this sense, the king's son has been a curator of his ailing soul; he has exposed the illness to every possible cure, and he has stayed with it until he knows it well. He has held and harbored his condition and followed what ails him. In the other realm, the old queen has been chopping off heads, cutting away until the only path that can lead from the incurable to the unreachable has been cleared—and this is the path that weaves through the land of the strange companions.

As usual, the opening scene lays out the story's major themes. There are two realms, two castles, two rulers, and each has a problem. Actually, they are more than problems; they are the troubles at the root of the problems and illnesses that keep cropping up. One trouble arises when what is most beautiful is imprisoned and all who try on their own to free it are slain. They are beheaded one by one, as if to demonstrate that their approach is wrong, that a single heroic head can't accomplish the tasks that the old queen sets. The queen wants something other than the headstrong, heroic types who think they're saving girls from towers. And she will keep appearing as a sorceress, an old hag who cheerfully takes the heads of all, until she gets what she wants. She, too, is incurable. Her daughter agrees in part, for partly she is held, and partly she remains of her own choice.

Between the two realms, a tremendous tension builds up. On the side of the king, the son of the realm wastes away while the king refuses to allow him to seek the beauty that his soul desires and requires in order to live. On the other side, the old queen won't release the beauty of life that the world is missing unless both she and her daughter are recognized. The tension between the two realms grows until the continuance of the culture depends on the son being released by the king and the daughter being released by the queen. But the daughter will not be seen until the realm of the old queen is recognized. Head after head will roll until the power of the queen over life and death is acknowledged. After the prince acquires permission for his journey, the next step of the cure requires the recognition of some great "other." The queen insists that the king bow his head in the direction of her realm.

In the world of the king, everything is in collapse. The son represents the next phase of the realm. If he remains incurable, the wasteland will extend everywhere. The only possibility of renewal waits within the daughter of the old queen. But she is stuck in her own incurable room behind the tasks required by the queen. Sure enough, the first task is to find and return the lost ring—the gold hoop of sovereignty—that has fallen to the very bottom of the sea. While the great structures of the kings of the world are collapsing, the beginning of the cure lies at the deepest place. The old hag of the world waits by her well; if someone retrieves the ring from the well, beauty will return to the world. If not, the collapse will continue because the source of sovereignty has fallen to the lowest place. The ring connects the king and queen, the two realms, the son and daughter, and the incurable with the most beautiful.

What is missing above can be found below. The powers of beauty and healing lost in the above world can be retrieved below. As usual, there are tasks to be undertaken. This time there are four tasks after acknowledging the trouble: bowing to the sovereignty of the other realm, accepting the enormous appetite for life that resides there, learning to see beauty and love at the right time, and finding the temperament to withstand fire and ice. But before all the tasks can be accomplished, the companions must be found, or else another head will be lost. Between the realm of the king and the world of the queen wait the ancient companions.

CHAPTER 26

THE TERRITORY OF THE ANCESTORS

Separating from the dominant way of life—from king, family, and the usual prohibitions on and protections from the soul's desires—means stepping onto another initiatory road. The prince departs from the place where he is weakest, most inferior, closest to his own death and steps onto the road of fears and phobias, where he will meet the strange and the weird. This is the road of the return of the repressed, the road that releases all that stands between the soul and the sense of beauty that wounds it, wastes it, and holds its deepest intentions. Stepping onto this road means releasing the repressed aspects of both the individual and the culture. The strange companions are both the radicals of the soul and the fears that accompany what has been repressed in the psyche. But they are also aspects of the ancestors, carrying the capacities to accomplish any task. They dwell in the initiatory ring of the ancestors and act as guides along the road between the incurable and the impossible.

Part of what the king doesn't want the prince to encounter is this assembly of the weird. Seen from above, they are bizarre and exaggerated, ridiculous and extreme, each in a different way. They are ancient aspects of the soul, as radical as each task is impossible. They are the guardians and curators of the masculine soul, and they are equal to the wild imagination of the old queen. They are the root images that underlie the companies of men who form into bands, gangs, and brotherhoods of all kinds. The companions are interested in healing incurable wounds and undertaking impossible tasks. They are the aspects of the soul that awaken when a man finally turns toward what he must become and what he truly desires.

Each companion embodies capacities and powers beyond the normal. Each represents a connection to the *wyrd*—that is, to fate and destiny. Young people quickly perceive any essential strangeness in a person and label it "weird." To the young, this quality is both attractive and repulsive. It is often the actual point around which a friendship forms, the place where the friends are connected. Gangs, tribes, communities, and cultures all require diversity and extremes. It's the weird parts of people that make unusual contributions to life. Denying the strange extremes and the deeply different aspects of people can turn their strangeness into something damaging to themselves and others. For the strangeness does not leave a person; it always finds a way to live itself out. Later in life, deeper in life, the "weirdness" in one person can help another move closer to his or her purpose and can remind each of a shared meaning in life.

On a cultural level, what is incurable in one culture can often be healed by a weird or extreme aspect of another culture. Culturally diverse societies can find healing in the variety of medicines carried inside the traditions of original cultures. In this way, multiplicity can unite what has been separated, and the "weird" can offer cures.

The companions are not, of course, literal people. They represent the extremes of imagination, purpose, and capacity that are awakened when the psyche reaches the point of incurability and impossibility. They are capacities and powers acquired through conscious suffering and a genuine sense of purpose. They are made of the same stuff as the dwarf, the horse of power, the little shaggy horse, and the lizard in the fire. They are not the trappings of another culture but the carriers of the medicine of that culture.

The strange companions are an extension of everything that participates in the weird in the previous stories in this book. The willingness to enter and engage fully in any struggle finds its source in these old companions of the soul. They become interested, stirred up, and begin to speak when a man steps onto a path that connects to the genius in him, when he hears a call that cannot be refused. Their appearance is always strange and must be gotten used to. If the soul is bound to have troubles and symptoms, it is also bound to have strange helpers whose speech must be learned. As we learn about and accept the weird conditions that life has placed on our souls, we have the potential for hearing this speech. When Conn-Eda agreed to drop the reins and enter the waters, the little horse began to speak. When the hunter reached for the burning feather, the horse of power began advising him. And when the youngest brother stopped, the dwarf filled him with knowledge.

The companions of the soul can appear as animals, strange beings, trees, or tools. In this story, they are many, and they are connected to the creative sickness that has called the son away from life. Their purpose is to find beauty and release the fullness of life again. They are the embodiment of symptoms and the source of ritual behaviors. In that sense, they are the "elders" at work. They are the knowledge of what underlies our personal and cultural symptoms and the knowledge of how to move toward a cure. The symptoms of personal and cultural illness are always aimed at something; they are purposeful. In the story, this is represented by the relief that the king's son experiences from his incurable illness as soon as he has permission to move toward his purpose. Feeling a sense of meaning and purpose in life changes the way a person suffers even the worst blows to the soul.

"The wise man seeks the reason for the symptom, not in the past, but in the purpose the symptom aims at." That's what John Layard wrote while working through the story of Kilwch and Olwen, considered by many to be the oldest story in Europe. The companions are symptoms carried to the extreme, and they are capable of carrying extremes of purpose. They relieve each other's symptoms, and they reveal the purpose in each other. What is seen at a great distance by the Man of Great Vision can be reached by the Man of Great Extension. What blocks his ability to reach it is removed by the endless appetite of the Stout One. All are radical aspects of an individual and of the ancestral psyche, helping each other.

The wisdom of the son of the king resides in seeing the extreme purpose in each companion. He doesn't do the tasks, yet he's not above them. He "suffers" the tests of the old queen and her daughter, but the weird companions carry them out.

Wisdom is attained by going to the depths, finding meaning below in the dark tangle of emotions that appear as illness above. It's important not to take the darkness out of wisdom, for wisdom begins in the half-light where the upperworld meets the underworld. Those who try to be wise without descending to the level of the strange companions lose their heads. What's missing has fallen below, and true ascension starts from those dark depths, not from the head upward. When people try to ascend using only their heads, those heads are chopped off.

The first test of the old queen requires several of the companions, and it requires retrieving something missing from the depths. Strangeness and multiplicity work where the single heroic head has failed over and over. The old queen is teaching the wisdom of the weird.

The wisdom of the elders consists of the darkness and strangeness that lie at the radical roots of human life. The road that descends and extends from the incurable condition, which has separated the man from regular life, is made of encounters with his radical roots. Six radical characters wait along the way; each is an opening to roots that lead beyond the known personality toward its extreme origins.

A man's radical roots tap family and ancestral sources; they contain all the repressed, compressed matters that can nourish life up above, but they also carry truly ancient fears and passions. As someone grows older, the "elder" waiting inside is nourished by these roots. The youthful branches that launch into the sky each year are being fed from the roots of the "elder" in the ground. The life below can be much more extensive than what is seen above. The tree grows downward as well as upward, and the tree of a person grows more within and downward once the young growth stages of life are passed. The strange companions represent a radical aspect of the soul that won't be fully repressed, no matter how many years of mundane matters are pressed over it. If a man has tapped into one of these radical roots, he will either have to accept what grows from it or spend an increasing amount of time cutting off its persistent productions.

Radicals are what can't be eradicated, which literally means "pulled up by the roots." The radicals are our roots, and our roots are radical. There are roots in the individual psyche that run so deep that they draw nourishment from deeper ethnic root systems and from even deeper roots fundamental to all humans. A person's originality comes from the roots that work their way down to extreme places of origin. That's where the elder in a person originates from, that's where the purpose in a life is found, and that's where the passion for living can be located and renewed.

Even after seven years of wasting illness and involvement with a deep need and purpose, it is not clear that the king's son is ready to accept this strange world of ancestors. The meeting with the huge man appears as a test of the initiate's ability to tolerate and value the extreme appetites of the ancestral world. Theirs is a psychological interview in which the huge man explains himself, the other companions, and the nature of this strange territory. He is not just a fat man who can't control his appetite and eats himself to a standstill. He's not lying on the ground because he can't get up. Rather, the huge man waits like the dwarf was waiting, until someone recognizes the need for his insatiable appetite for life. If you think he should be ashamed of himself for overeating, you're mistaken. If you think that pointing to his excessive weight and awkward state will get him out of the way, you've got the wrong man. He isn't ashamed of himself; in fact, he points out, "This is nothing. When I puff myself up, I'm three hundred times this size." He knows that this is who he is and how he's valuable. He's an aspect of the soul allowed full entry into life and an image of the ancestors of humanity and their insatiable appetites.

The huge man seems to be connected to the wasting sickness of the king's son. After seven years of wasting away, the prince encounters appetite personified, desire and hunger for life fully released. The huge man is like a symptom released and allowed to reach its full extension. The word *symptom* means "to fall together with." The *ptoma* is a falling body, and the symptom falls into the body and pulls us into an area needing our attention. From the point of view of the huge man, the cure for his overeating isn't dieting; the cure lies in falling further into his appetite. Beneath the overeating of food is an appetite for life that is not being satisfied. Below the hunger for food that won't be controlled is an appetite for participating in the great dramas of the psyche and of community life.

The oversized person in our culture is conspicuous and usually ashamed of it. He'd rather hide, but his condition keeps making him conspicuous. That's the huge man speaking through the body, saying that something even bigger waits hidden behind an addiction; something that intends to be seen is at the root of his appetite. The huge man turns our usual perspective upside down: In contrast to the idea that inside every fat person there is a skinny person trying to get out, the huge man says that inside every fat person stirs an even bigger person trying to get out. Inside what appears to be a clumsy, fat being is a huge appetite for life that is being forced to satisfy itself with literal food. Behind the doors of shame and guilt lies an even bigger person, a bigger appetite that wants to contribute to the quest for what is beautiful and to the cure for what wastes the culture. The appetites and capacities of the huge man are what uncover the lost ring of sovereignty and help release the most beautiful being in the world.

The old queen wants the desire for beauty to be felt to the depths where it originates. If it can't be felt in depth, then it must be experienced compulsively at the surface. If a person or a culture won't descend to the depths of the old queen's realm and seek the cures that sent the symptoms to the surface, then the symptoms will be lived literally. Appetite will manifest itself in overeating. Desire for beauty will become greed that remains stuck at the literal level of accumulating and hoarding goods and gold. Ambition will keep conquering the same pieces of ground and never look to discover why those grounds are fought over again and again. When the symptom is taken literally, the voices that are trying to speak through the symptom are missed and dismissed.

Stepping onto this road began with accepting the choice between death and finding a radical cure; now, the huge man teaches the son of the realm what is needed on the road to the impossible tasks. As they encounter more strange fellows, the prince becomes alert to the point at which symptoms open into a huge capacity. He talks to the symptomatic place in each companion. The excessive, obsessive listening of the man with his ear to the ground would be considered paranoid if seen merely as a symptom in the above world. But on this road, the man's obsession becomes hearing all the way into the ground of things and knowing if they are headed the right way. The listening man is like a dream interpreter who hears everything happening in the soul. The prince needs him because moving on this ground is like following a dream and learning the languages that dreams speak.

Seen as a group of people, the prince and the companions each attend to their own extreme focus and help each other along. It's as if by suffering his own condition long enough, the son of the king attracts and is attracted to others similar to himself. They are similar in that they have come to know who they are in at least one extreme way. They each have suffered their stuckness, their symptom, their problem until they have reached the strength within it. They recognize in each other not sufferers in the same disease but sufferers experiencing the same intensity of "dis-ease." They see into each other's trouble in a way that permits them to go along together, forming a group based on having suffered something to its very roots and being no longer stuck with the weakness of it but finding the radical power in it. Knowing oneself at the root level is a requirement for an elder and a connection to the ancestral helpers.

The prince cannot be cured of his desire to seek what is most beautiful. The huge man can't be talked into a diet or shamed into another form; he is the possessor of and is possessed by a huge appetite. If you are going to take him along, you have to take the radical appetite as well. And he isn't asking for the usual sympathy, nor for good advice, nor for support for his problem. He is beyond help. He has fallen below the symptom to the ground of its origin.

Tribal imagination has long grouped illnesses under the name of the ancestor or god who rules them. By digging down into the ground below any culture, we can find some system of tracing the shape of a disease to the particular style of a god, ancestor, or saint. Ultimately, the diseased person had to seek the cure in the temple or on the sacred ground of the god who claimed that disease and its victims. The victim of trouble or disease was seen to be in a complex condition. The old idea was that the "afflicted were sacred"—not because they were better people but because they had been touched by a god. In touching the victim, you were touching one who had been touched by a god.

Part of the purpose of the affliction was to draw that soul to the service of that god, to introduce the individual to the ritual ground of that deity or ancestor. The ritual style of the particular deity indicated the way to withstand or relieve the affliction. All who survived the touch of the god became followers of the god. The symptom was the otherworld trying to break through; one might experience the touch of the god through his or her disease even if one didn't know the ritual style of the god.

So the old sense about any severe illness, persistent symptom, or incurable condition was that a god or goddess was behind it, in it, below it. The afflicted one could find his own cure if he was in touch with the god in the disease. Falling into the condition was also falling toward a certain divine area. "Why me, God?" can, then, also mean, "Why am I falling in this direction, in this way, at this time?" The one who is falling must look to the god behind the disease for an answer.

The symptom leads to a core area that must be ritualized or else it becomes a habitual way of "acting out," of acting in the style toward which the psyche is compellingly attracted. If one continues to resist the deeper call of the symptomatic area, then the habit will intensify and the symptoms increase, but there will be no benefit from the pain or humiliation experienced. If the resistance is broken through, the deeper ground of the habit, the radical area of the soul that it represents, can be entered. Habits are repeated surface ripples in a body of water that has deep currents. If a man drinks only at the surface, he knows nothing of the deep currents that keep the life of the sea circulating. By staying on the surface, the drinker will also never experience the depth of calm that is part of the water.

Finding a core ritual allows one to find that deep sense of calm and permits an immersion in the currents that sustain life itself. The huge man accesses his insatiable appetite in order to expose the missing ring, as if his purpose were to devour obstacles. Each of the strange companions contributes a weird power to accomplishing the common quest. Each is like an ancestor calling the elder in a person to a ritual ground where symptoms can be transformed into potential power.

Psychologically, ancestors, saints, and deities represent ways of approaching the "unconscious," mediating and containing the myriad of forces that lie below conscious attitudes. After a man has undergone some tempering by fire and water, his emotional life is activated toward a purpose, and what lies below consciousness begins to demand attention. The attention is drawn in many ways: toward the body and its intense drives and subtleties, toward the imagination and its persistent creations, and toward the ground, the roots that a person's spirit aims to reach. The process of initiation insists that a person keep going further; there is no turning back. The trouble in the soul gets worse; the troublesome parts of life and culture become intolerable. The tension within a person grows, and the heart, soul, and mind have to expand to relieve the pressure. In the story, the tension between the two poles, the two realms, the king and the queen, stabilizes temporarily when the king releases the son and his wasting away stops. But that tension is replaced by encounters with the wild and strange array of capacities and powers that could overwhelm the prince. He needs to restate where he is going to each ancestral figure he meets. His vision of beauty and of the restoration of life makes the weird encounters tolerable and keeps him purposeful.

The companions represent capacities that have been glimpsed before during those life-defining moments that were steps of initiation in a person's life. In initiatory moments, the fear of not surviving the ordeal grows great, and the feeling of expanded life afterward is just as great. Temporarily, a person feels like one of the companions. The huge man's appetite for life is present, and the heights and depths of feeling and imagination are experienced. The ear of the Listener hears all the way into the ground of the person's being and suddenly can tell where the road is leading. Often the capacity to hear at that level remains present just long enough for the person to make an important turn—one that saves a life, gives meaning to it, or finds love.

Momentarily, a person can see with a keen eye right into the destination for which his or her genius aims. Another looks within with a vision that shatters the walls of denial and opens an inner world that had gone dark with pain and numbness.

Such experiences are shocks to one's regular system of awareness. When these capacities of the soul are admitted, there is an increase of both sorrow and joy. Along with expansive feelings of unity with everyone and everything, one experiences a deeper awareness of the shadows and conflicts of life.

The companion experiences don't fit well into daily life. The Stout One disturbs everyone with his insatiability and his complaints about the inadequacy of the daily fare. People may laugh at him, but they feel uneasy at his lack of boundaries and limits. The Man of Shattering Vision is invaluable when trying to see all the way to the essence of a problem or a life. He's stunning when turned loose on a problem or when attacking arguments or enemies. But after he's looked at the problem, everything seems shattered, deconstructed, and torn down.

The companions of the soul are too much to bear all the time. If just one is encountered, he comes across as an addiction or an obsession. When the whole group is present, the impossible tasks that the old queen dreams up are done quickly and joyfully. But one person, alone, can't survive the huge motions and emotions the companions initiate. The "I" is swamped, like the old queen's soldiers. A person could drown. As with most of the radical figures in the psyche, the point is not to become one of them but to develop conscious relations with them. After death, a person goes to join these ancestral forces; until then, the idea is to remain human.

The story makes clear that going into this territory only happens when all else has failed. This adventure usually begins after the land of fire and the waters of life have been experienced. The seven years of preparation sharpen and clarify the vision the prince has had, clearing, cleansing, and eliminating anything in the way. Without this preparation and the shaping and containing forms of myth and ritual, walking into the territory of the ancestors can feel like one has taken on a multiple personality disorder. But within the protection and shape of myth and rituals, powers that could seem overwhelming become capacities for tolerating change and finding inner resources.

Fairy tales about the companions are connected to old root stories that underlie modern cultures and that remind us of the ancestral helpers in the psyche and in the world. With the loss of myth and ritual from the common life of Europe and the New World, however, we have also lost a sense of the meaning of "ancestors." And when we lost an understanding of this territory, the meaning of "death" narrowed to a literal end. With the door closed to the ancestors, layers of inner resources and ways of understanding were cut off. "Original" came to mean "new" and the origins of troubles and cures were forgotten. The elders working at the ailments of the community, the companions solving the impossible tasks of the old queen, and the resources of the territory of ancestors are all connected to each other. The initiations of the elder involve entering the territory of the ancestors and beginning to see into the ring that holds the world.

An old proverb says, "The elders are wise because they know more dead people." The land of the dead, the territory of the ancestors, and wisdom are all connected. Knowing more dead people also means knowing more of the land of the dead, the other underworld. It also means paying attention when death brushes one's life. The "dead people" are ancestors, not corpses, and ancestors are those from whom we are derived: our forefathers, foremothers, forerunners. We are descended from ancestors both known and unknown, and we have inherited physical, emotional, and spiritual aspects of ourselves from them. But ancestors are also those who precede us in entering death while we remain among the living; they "go to join the ancestors." Knowing more dead people means paying attention to those who enter the ancestral world before we do. In that sense, ancestors are ahead of us as well as behind and below us. Knowing more dead people means realizing that life is an island surrounded by the ancestral world.

In the tribal world, ancestors are involved with the living and must be honored, placated, learned about, and listened to. The ancestors form a community that surrounds the living community; they frequently include animal and plant spirits. In the modern world, we have the "problem of the ancestors" and a problem with death. The problem with death lies in seeing it as a literal "dead end," a solid, standing stone that ends the path of a life. Originally, the gravestone marked where the dead person entered the land of the ancestors, and it could serve to connect the living to them as well as to keep the dead in their place. When modern ideas began to reject the old connections to the dead, we developed the "problem of the ancestors." Before the tremendous migrations of people in modern times, a person would commonly be walking near or even on the ground that held his or her ancestors, literally and figuratively. Now, people often don't know who their actual ancestors were or exactly where they lived. But there is a psychological as well as a geographical aspect to the ancestor problem: People don't want to be connected to ancestors who remind them of inferior ways or terrible deeds.

Often, the objection to one's ancestors as a group comes from viewing them as perpetrators of great harm or as part of an undeveloped, inferior way of life. Some immigrants try to shed their foreignness; others try to escape the shadow of injustices and atrocities enacted by or to their ancestors. But attempts to ignore or escape don't make the ancestors go away. The inheritance of the dead resurfaces at least psychologically, as witnessed by the number and popularity of horror stories, especially those concerning characters who refuse to die. Americans come to the New World and leave behind ancestors all over the globe, but eventually we export films about the "living dead" back to our ancestral lands.

Another aspect of the problem of ancestors surfaces when a person reaches a turning point in life and begins to wonder where his or her roots can be found. Often, the interest in roots and origins is precipitated by a loss or separation in life or by the death of a loved one. These roots may have been covered over and lost or abruptly cut off, and they may now seem impossible to find. When we only think of ancestors as our literal predecessors, then we feel that we have no roots on which to rely in times of trouble and darkness.

There is also a common fear that by entering the imagination of one's tribal ancestry, a person may automatically begin to repeat the atrocities that have been enacted by that group. The increased incidence of tribal warfare, renewed on the same ground where it was fought long ago, provides evidence that people can get caught up in this aspect of their ancestors. But the return of ancestral wars and cycles of revenge also reflects the approaching end of the age, when events are repeated, just as a life flashes before the eyes of a person facing death.

Fortunately, there are several ways to look into the land of ancestors. Besides the specific forerunners and members of one's family tree, there are those ancestors who represent the best qualities of the tribe or culture—specific individuals who have lived in a meaningful way and who, after their death, are claimed as ancestors by many unrelated people. In this sense, people can choose from among the deceased those whose good qualities or purposeful lives can help them in this life. A chosen ancestor can replace something that is missing or desired in a person or in a family. There is also a third set of ancestors who are the cumulative ancestors of all human beings. These are the archetypal ancestors, the radical roots of humanity, the very deepest roots of the human family tree.

The importance of these three levels of ancestors becomes apparent when we begin to seek deep roots in order to cure a personal or a collective problem. From the first level of ancestors—the actual family members who have lived before us—we know that we have inherited diseases and other troubles. Our mothers, fathers, grandmothers, and grandfathers are specific people who cannot be chosen, and if these ancestors acted in a brutal or destructive way, then that is part of our heritage. If we are trying to change some cycle of damage passed down through our family and if we look only at the first, literal level of ancestors, then we may turn away altogether from any attempt to connect to our roots. We may turn away from the idea of ancestry altogether and lose the sense of deep support and resources.

Strangely enough, though, we can find a healing ancestor on someone else's family tree. The second level of ancestors—those who are chosen for their admirable and desired qualities—can help to heal problems inherited from the first type of ancestor. Revered individuals who have died and are unrelated to us by blood can become like tribal or clan ancestors; we can honor them, and they can connect us to inner sources of strength, endurance, and healing.

Still, we have inherited woundings and troubles even from this second type of ancestor. For instance, leaders of tribal and national groups have caused tremendous atrocities, causing people to deny their ancestry from feelings of inherited shame and guilt. No group of humans has managed to avoid being involved in the history of atrocities, and these disasters are carried in tribal memories and can resurface many generations later.

It is on the third level of ancestors that healing for the atrocities and the wars of vengeance enacted by those on the second level can be found. The problem with renewed tribal wars doesn't come from simply reentering the ancestral imagination; it comes from not going into that imagination far enough. The way to approach ancestors is similar to the attitude of the huge man in the story when he says, "If you think this is large, you should see me when I become three hundred times larger." In other words, the healing capacity of ancestors and the greatest imagination of ancestors comes from going all the way through the levels of ancestry. The third level of ancestors is like a great pool in which reside types, archetypes, and figures of great imagination and great power. They can dispel the harm seen on the other levels and renew the capacity for healing. On this level, the ancestors are common to us all.

One aspect of living at the end of the second millennium of modern times involves the accumulation of knowledge in the form of information. One of the trails of knowledge traces the human tribe, step by step, back to a common origin in Africa. Both anthropology and history arrive at a similar place in Africa where human beings stepped off or made a great leap from what had gone before, causing a new branch on the tree of life. Science, doggedly following its own paths, has arrived at a similar conclusion, even stating that all human beings can be traced back to the womb of a single mother, also in Africa, in the ancestral past. The old queen in our story, the old hag of the earth in others, can be seen as that original source of life, the womb from which beauty springs, the mother of leaps of imagination.

The six strange companions can be seen as part of the general ancestral pool that exists below all cultures. The seemingly impossible tasks set by the old queen before she will release the beauteous sense of life in the form of her daughter are set up in order to force a connection for the prince with his deep ancestral roots of healing, imagination, and spirituality.

The story is very specific when it says that the old queen had no purpose other than to bring "mankind to the edge of destruction." But as we pointed out earlier in the story of Conn-Eda, if the old queen wanted to end life, she could do that with one snap of her fingers. Clearly, what she really wants is for the prince to enter into and travel fully the road of the companions, the road to the ancestors.

In many old stories, the grandmother or Grand Mother of the people waits in her cave at the end of the road of life. She offers the simple fate of death or an encounter with destiny—that is, with one's actual destination. At the entrance to the cave, she conducts an interview and administers a test. The old grandmother draws half of a design in the dirt; the suitor for destiny must fill in the missing half so that it fits the design of the life she has drawn. If he is able to match her design with an equal design in himself, he touches his destiny; if not, his head rolls . . . again. The old woman never tires of the encounters, nor does her daughter. Each time the design is a little different, and the place for the meeting moves around as well. But one way to find it is to look for the place where the radical companions appear. They can each offer a piece of the design, if they're allowed to display it. The worst thing that can happen is the loss of your head—and actually, it would be a worse fate never to encounter the radical origins of your own soul and take a look at your destiny. That's a fate worse than death.

One of the meanings of the word *symbol* is to throw or fit pieces together. The old grandmother draws a part of the symbol of a life, and the one trying to be an elder has to find the other part of the symbol inside. When drawn together, the two halves symbolize who the person must be, who the person has been trying to become. Becoming an elder is a puzzling problem that can only be solved by putting together the pieces held by the old woman of the soul with those from the ancestors and from the knowledge a person has acquired through suffering. The elder, then, becomes a symbol made of pieces of ancestry and pieces of an individual life, pieces from the land of the dead and pieces of one's life now. The elder winds up with a foot in each world.

The old woman of the soul is an essential image that waits at the end of many roads, handling the destinies of people and cultures. She is one of the radical images that moves in the depths of both the individual and the collective psyche. Earlier we looked at her appearance as the Three Sisters of Fate. She has a hand in every birth and a hand in every death. She waits at the fountain of life and at the well of healing and inspiration. She presents the horrid face of death, but behind her waits the daughter of renewed life and inspired beauty. Sometimes all she requires is a kiss that shows courage as well as a knowledge of beauty and of her connection to it; more often she also requires the accomplishment of seemingly impossible tasks.

She may appear as the hag at the well, the old mother at the cave, or simply an old woman asking for food. An individual and a culture can be destroyed by not handling the initiatory fires of its youth, and they can also be destroyed by overlooking the old hag at the well. She knows the designs that keep life going and insists on the sovereignty of that knowledge. When a culture ignores her, life drains of meaning and hope, and the world loses beauty and grace.

The beautiful princess is nourished at the old hag's well. The Water of Life is returned to a culture through that well. The elders of a culture, both women and men, sip at the well. The old hag who waits there will abide the foolishness of youth, the extremes of someone who has found one of the deep roots of life and feels a reckless love of beauty, but little else. An African proverb says, "Some say this world is a virgin; others say this world is a wise old woman." Some say the old woman made that riddle in order to catch your head . . . again. Some say the first time you get to see what your soul finds most beautiful, you are a virgin getting your first look, first taste, first touch of the water in the well of life. Some say that if you are ever to see it again, you'll have to see the hag as well.

The old hag is one of the ancient radicals of the soul. She will strew the path with whatever needs to be encountered in order to open the soul. She will gather a vision at the end of the road that is so infused with beauty and danger that it becomes irresistible. She knows that the prince won't accept the bizarre companions of his soul if he's unaware of either the beauty or the dangers of life. She knows that her lovely daughter won't return to the world unless her fire is accepted and her connection to the ring and the water is seen. She knows that a person all alone will tend to succumb somewhere along the way to the encounter with her. The roads are littered with lost heads. When they speak, they say that if you want to see the beauty of the soul again, you'll have to learn how to approach her through the ancient helpers.

By the time the prince reaches the place of the old hag, he's not calling himself a prince, and he's ready to undertake her tasks. He's ready to see life through her eyes. They are eyes that have seen everything. She's always looking for a living response to the dilemma she poses, a solution that is crafted on the spot. Such a solution is what I call a "radical ritual"—a mixture of the known and unknown that changes life and moves the soul. Ultimately, it moves the old queen, too; it relieves her old sorrows and stirs the return of her sense of love.

CHAPTER 27

CONFLICT, SHADOWS,
AND COMMUNITY

THROUGHOUT THEIR LIVES, people try to see aspects of the old radicals of the soul in each other. Men try to touch the old companions by making myths of and with each other. From battlefields to sports pages, from classrooms to concerts, from corporations to dance halls, men compete with each other and try to inspire the old companions in each other. In seeking a mentor, a man often seeks a quality he feels glimmering in himself and sees glowing in the other. In seeking a friend, a man often seeks a strange quality undeveloped in him but apparent in the other. Like the companions in the story, friendship often occurs where contrasting people share similar goals. William Blake even said, "Opposition is true friendship," and "Without conflict there is no progress." One of the ways of opening the road to the resources of the companions is by following conflicts to their sources.

The circumstances that cause the companions and their extreme capacities to be present can be accidental or intentional. In other words, the companions stir from the ground during crises and during rites of change. When the full attention of a person or a group can be brought to one place, inner or outer, the ancestral companions awaken. The extremities of crises and the intensities of radical rituals get the attention of the "old ones." The companions are an image of the radical forces that can convert an overwhelming crisis into an initiatory step. In that sense, they are the resources that make a person an "elder," and they are the roots that connect elders to ancestors.

But the aspects of the companions can also appear in a negative light; they have a shadow side. When a man is out of touch with the sense of the companions in himself and in other men, he's truly alone and in danger. If a man is emotionally isolated or too much alone, any of these weird figures in the psyche can take over a man's life. The Stout One can move into his life and consume everything, through addiction after addiction, and never be satisfied. The Listener can take over and sprout ears in all directions; an exhausting paranoia takes over and conspiracy theories are generated out of anything he hears. The Man with Shattering Vision turns every outward gaze into fault finding and every inward feeling into a weight of shame. The Visionary may move in unnoticed, take over, and keep pushing everything away, so that things can be seen only from a distance or only in the future. The Man of Tempers walks through fires and freezes out the feelings of pain and joy, but he takes on the wrong battles, or sweats bullets over cold facts that won't change. All alone a man can be dominated by any of these, even by the old hag herself, or by moon-eyed visions of princesses.

On the other hand, random groups of men often become dangerous to themselves and others. What is to keep a group from becoming a collective version of one of the companions? Aren't corporations organized versions of the huge man, consuming water, wine, animals, oil, any "product" that can be snatched from nature and regurgitated at people for momentary pleasure and endless harm? Can't the Listener become the CIA, the FBI, the KGB, and Big Brother all rolled into one big ear? The basic form of men bound together toward some transcendent goal is both universal and ambiguous. Under this guise men have wreaked destruction, simply passed time, or made sustained, creative communities. If a man is solitary, he can become numb to his inner life and to other people. If men form groups, they can become fanatically self-absorbed and brutal toward non-members, or they can become dedicated protectors of communal life. It's as if there is no innocuous place for men. Isolate men from each other and they can become individually dangerous; form groups of men and further dangers can arise. There is a "collective Litima" that permeates a group of men. At one extreme, brutality can occur, and at the other, they enter the service of beauty and common good.

How can a group of men avoid adding to the broken visions, dashed hopes, and rampant oppressions that already populate the world? The only models I've seen are in these stories and in the ritual involvements they allude to. In most stories it is the last hour when radical change occurs. In most stories it becomes a close call whether the destruction increases or there is a return of tempered hope. In all the stories, meaningful change requires recognizing what has to be sacrificed at critical moments. In most stories, if the conflicts within are faced and endured, there is a return of the sense of beauty and a restoration of the feelings of community and abundance. The route is full of ambiguous encounters that have to be communally digested, and any balance that occurs is temporary. Inside one story is another one, and the end of one starts another on its way. The only constant is the group or community forming around inner and outer troubles.

The old stories carry the bones of rituals that until modern times were used to change and heal communities. The bare bones of community rites include birth, initiations into adulthood, rituals of conflict, marriage and celebrations, rites of death and burial. When any of those are omitted or unfinished a whole culture can become disoriented. Today, most people experience parts of each type of ritual but nothing feels completed, not even death. The incompleteness grows into a general anxiety, loss of purpose, and a lack of evident meaning for individuals and communities. The loss of all the connective rituals feels like apathy, despair, and deep loneliness. People trying to move toward the ground of these rituals wind up going against the cultural drift and entering areas of great loss. Finding a meaningful orientation in a disoriented culture puts people in more danger than usual.

There isn't always a choice between the dangers of sudden crises and the mysteries that suddenly appear within radical rituals. But, when there are no ritual spaces, within which the course and meaning of a life can be changed, there will be more and more crises and an increasing need to deny the intensity and subtleties of the human soul. If the radical nature and the extreme elements in the soul are denied and ignored, they have to surface through the broken ground of dangerous crises and conflicts. As the old saying goes, "If you don't hunt the snake, the snake will hunt you."

These stories say that the human soul will try to reach as far out as it can and as far in as is possible. The soul conjures a story that will draw and lead itself through the inner and outer worlds, as fast as it is possible to go. Individuals will someday face more terror and more beauty, more sorrow and more joy, than they would choose on their own. The distance between the "I" and the depth of the soul will be experienced by each person and each community. But similar to stories, rituals don't prescribe emotions or predetermine insights; stories and rituals invite emotions and offer containers for symbolic learning and change. Radical rituals invite the expression and release of the entire range of human emotions, even those as extreme as the companions display. The release of these emotions is physically, psychologically, and mythologically necessary.

When emotions are avoided or held too long people become stuck in repetitive experiences of old pains, rigid in attitudes, more likely to project negative opinions on others, and unable to change in meaningful ways. Participating in rituals where emotions are awakened, felt, and expressed helps heal old harms and losses that would have been impossible to heal at the time they occurred. "Time heals all wounds" partially because it makes a distance between the wound and the wounded.

Approaching the wound again with actual and symbolic support and safety allows the emotions to be released and to flow through the wounded area. Besides the purging and clearing that can occur, troubling events are opened to the light of day and insights into the individual and into life in general are gained. The release of pent-up emotions clears the ability to see past, present, and even glimpses of future. By experiencing and surviving the basic feelings of anger, fear, grief, and loss, joy and hope are also found and released. Rituals that reach the point of releasing long-held or overwhelming emotions can bring a relief to the individual and return them to the sympathies and empathies that connect people one to another. The benefits of participation in ritual expressions spread from the individuals through their relationships and into the community at large. The discussions that go on before and after group rituals also provide opportunities for sharing and for the fixing of insights that come from the release of emotions and the mutual inspiration of community.

In modern times a sense of genuine community is often missing or only encountered through disasters and tragedies that suddenly bring people together. The conferences I have been describing are most often attempts to find community by establishing a common awareness of loss and pain. Since the center of community is always getting lost, each conference has to try to find community all over again. When the common center is frequently lost, conflicts become the primary thing that everyone holds in common. Often the lost sense of community can be hiding in the shadows of conflict, so that finding community means finding conflicts. Each conference is a struggle to find a vision that can be held and entered in common. The vision has to be big enough to let everyone present in. And it has to have many entry points because people come from various angles and many places.

The entry points to community are doors of emotion that can open and close, even slam shut. All of the doors have locks that are little masterworks of protection and denial to keep some things inside and other things outside. The gathering of the community is a ritual undoing of the locks and opening of the doors through a combination of artful vision and released emotions. The combinations are different every time because what's found at the center of the community is a mystery, and because the members change and undergo change. For meaningful change to occur, the mystery at the center has to be rediscovered each time.

If it's to be a community of men, the observation and handling of conflicts becomes essential. Every man carries an inner knowledge that men have argued, struggled, competed against, fought with, and killed each other since the beginning of time. This sense of conflict with other men is an inner history combining personal stories, family plots, ethnic styles, and a complex array of displayed and hidden emotions. These styles and emotions are awakened immediately upon entering some old camp hall, as each of a hundred men begins looking for some lost sense of community.

Entering a conference that is seeking the unknown attracts fear, like shadows among trees. You can feel it and see it gather, encouraged by the ghosts that frequent these camps and the surprising way that night falls in a place that is unfamiliar. Fears separate and isolate people, and fear of the unknown moves faster than any other fear. The inner conflicts of the men sense each other, awakening fear and the instincts of "fight or flight." Actually, it feels like fight *and* flight, both happen—the push and pull of fight and flight are the essence of conflict. Just the minimal intention of conferences to gather around serious issues awakens the soul and provokes inner conflicts that are smoldering.

Since there is such a diversity and mixture of ancestry in America, a conference room can become filled with descendants of peoples who were perennial enemies. And then there are descendants of peoples who never had mutual history. By the time everyone gathers, the spirits of one's family and ancestors are poking around the room asking, What the hell is going on? What is stirring up here? When part of the intention is to seek a lost sense of community, one that may never have had a shape before, the fears and conflicts feel mysterious.

In the odd light of an old CCC lodge, it's hard not to notice the strange variety of spirits that gather when men try to find community. Even in the beginning of these events when almost all the men were "white," the diversity was calamitous. Beneath American veneers, the endless history of European wars entered the room in the barely disguised glances of tribal eyes. The histories of urban struggles between Irish, Italian, German, and Jew in America, and old troubles from the War Between the States, lurked around. The civil wars that drove the ancestors of those present in search of new communities entered as well. At these conferences, ancient enmities and the spirits of old conflicts are reawakened. Part of the time is spent trying to find ways of keeping men and spirits all in it without having a tragedy. Every man comes out of some tradition of seeking and avoiding conflict, and there's not enough time to introduce all the personal conflict styles to each other. Besides, the older spirits that awaken are resistant to learning new ways, and some of these spirits refuse to "get along."

As soon as the group starts to form, the shadow of the group starts to form. The group shadow is greater than the sum of the shadows of the men in the group. The group shadow is capable of growing rapidly and grows best when ignored and avoided. The shadow areas will become depositories of heat and energy. In addition to coping with the natural rise of conflict, conferences become attempts to see and understand their own shadow.

The difference between what life "ought to be" and what it actually is can be called the "shadow." Every move toward what life ought to be or what we hope it to be requires encounters with the shadows of self and community. Refusing to admit your own shadow doesn't get rid of it; rather, it requires that you put it on someone somewhere else. Each person does it; every group does it. But the shadow aspects can't be taken in all at once, so people tend to enact multiple shadow plays with each other. The quickest way to form a group is to evoke an aspect of the shadow, hang it on some people not wanted in the group, and then begin pointing at it. As long as the threatening or repulsive thing can be kept outside and hung on someone else, the group can keep its form by the simple exclusion and opposition of what people fear in themselves. The trouble comes when the group loses energy and direction toward its original goal because more and more attention is needed to keep pointing at the shadow on the other and fixing it back on whenever it begins to slip. When people do not face their own shadows, they create prisons inside themselves and also outside, where angers and fears are locked up. Eventually, it takes more energy to keep the prison inside, and the shadow figures outside, than to deal with the rage and fear. Eventually, the shadows and repressed emotions have more energy than the community.

A person, a group, a country can be consumed by its own shadow. We see it played out all the time. Whatever "sin" a TV preacher keeps pointing at keeps gaining power until he himself is caught in a brothel or in a fraudulent deal that reeks of greed and hunger for material power.

I use an example from the church and ministry because of their association with the sacred, for the sacred and the shadow are always found close together. In fact, the church is the place where "sinners" gather. The sinners are like a group dragging their shadows into a common space. When a common space is made for the shadows to come in, the space becomes a church. By church I mean a "sacred space," an *ekklesia* as the Greeks called it, an assembly of everyone with their shadows, a meeting in the great hall of humanity.

At most conferences, within twenty-four hours of arriving in camp there is a shadow forming that is peculiar to that event and that group. There are new and old conflicts being activated. One way we have learned to address these troubles is through conflict rituals. Conflict rituals are a way of uncovering the individual and group shadows and establishing deeper levels of trust. These events allow everyone opportunities to "eat" some of the shadow of the group rather than to feed it blindly. If the shadow is not consciously kept present in the event, genuine energy will drain out. Conflict rituals are the opposite of projecting shadowy materials on other people. Beyond releasing the fears, tensions, and angers that occur when we encounter each others' shadows by surprise, the ritual seeks the really deep conflicts that divide any group.

Before we learned to seek out underlying troubles, conflict would break out on its own. Heat would gather over a certain issue or a statement, and there would be an outburst. Usually one individual would become the focus for all the unexpressed conflict and would explode. Eventually, it became clear that expressing conflicts was an essential need in every event.

We began to experiment with forms of intentional conflict. There's more in the shadow than conflict and anger, but the sparks they make light the way in the dark. Among a hundred men the range of conflicts can be enormous. We were always faced with a question: How much appetite for heat and for tasting the shadows is in this group? One way to tell is simply to gather the whole group, sit in the hall, and agree to raise whatever conflicts are present.

At first it seems artificial. A man says, "I don't get angry when I intend to. It just happens. I can't just show up and be in conflict." If you have an ear for conflict, you can hear that he's conflicting with the idea of intentional conflict. More than that, he's defending a supposed spontaneity of conflict. "It just happens" implies that it's not coming from him but from elsewhere. Often people believe physical violence "just happens" as well. But, Americans, like many other groups, carry the effects of so much violence that it can't be allowed to "just happen." Part of the tempering by fire is an education in conflict. Expressing inner conflicts and managing outer ones can be learned by practice.

The basic idea is to engage everyone in a meaningful conflict, to encounter the heat, the spirits, and the shadows of the group. There's an immediate sense that though a complaint can mask an underlying conflict, a complaint isn't enough to warrant everyone's attention. So complaints are weeded out. Ultimately, complaints will divide and conflicts can unite. There is something artificial about it, but in the sense of artifice in the form, not artificial emotions. It's a skillful, artful contrivance whose purpose is to increase the skills of those in the community for handling conflict without violence. It's also intended to break any inertia of emotions and to find solutions to conflicts at the community level.

The ritual begins by finding an ember burning in the center of the community and feeding it with the large and small sticks of conflict that come up in the course of interaction. Every now and then a man says he isn't interested in that fire. He wants to be above petty arguments and wants to get beyond the conflicts that keep people apart. This is the above-and-beyond argument. It's an argument with conflict itself, which implies there is a stable place out of the human fray. It implies there is an escape from the shadow of living. One trouble with above-and-beyond is that it usually means above others and beyond the common human turmoil. It usually means sticking some people deeper into the turmoil so others may rise above the fray. The old saying is, "He who is closest to the light, casts the greatest shadow." The making of a man who is above common conflicts is also the making of a big shadow life for others. How many people must suffer great conflict for one person to stay in peaceful bliss?

Entering this life was partly a bloody struggle from which we emerged covered with blood and feces, our own and our mother's. If something else is going to be born, it will have to have some of the odor and mess that accompany birth on this planet. Entering community means entering the mess of life; community has blood and conflict and shadow in it.

The conflict rituals are a way of exploring the courage of the group to wander into the minefields of power, trust, and love. Each ritual finds uncharted territory. The map is made as we go, and it gets made from the sightings of the whole group. There's an implicit understanding that the area aimed at is mystery. We are wandering together in search of mystery, in search of the opportunity to see and feel the mystery of community. The destination of each ritual is unknown, and once it's over, the map of each event is thrown away. There are recognizable landmarks, but the complexion of the group and the lay of the land are different every time.

The leaders take the role of ritual elders and try to regulate, speed, heat, and direct by glimpsing the pieces of shadow trying to come out. Rituals like this are full of opportunities to learn quickly. Men who can't enter heated conflicts in their workplaces, in projects, or in their relationships get to observe how other men act and to try that out. Men who have inherited great fear can sit with that fear and not run. Men who go quickly from anger to rage can be tempered by other men and learn where the line of rage lies in themselves. Leaders can learn how their manner and how their shadow drag across men who are interested in being led somewhere and, sometimes, not wishing to be led to avoid carrying their own authority. As the mysterious point of the ritual emerges, it's not clear whose voice will have what kind of authority. And, it's not clear until being there what emotions will author the center of the event.

Anger tends to begin the movement in this territory of conflict, as if the foothills we enter are magnetized toward anger and populated by insects and buzzing flies and people slamming doors. But once inside the territory, many emotions occur. Fear is never far away, and the point of the ritual may become to grab hold of the scurrying fears and sit with them, sit with the conflicted feelings of fight or flight. For some men, just being in a room of potential conflict requires full courage. Or, the feelings may plunge into a pool of grief that is waiting below the frustrations and arguments. The room just had to get warm enough and safe enough to make the waters of grief approachable. For its part, grief can have bitterness and screams in it, so that it carries conflict in its own stricken way. And there's a joy of conflict, which can be as surprising as a sun break on a stormy day, and it has to be appreciated when it shows. Meanwhile, humor often plays at the edges of conflict and can tickle places that used to be sore.

In this context, safety means being secure enough to risk exposure to the unknown. Since the intention is to locate and suffer conflicts, discomfort becomes part of the territory. In this case, safe doesn't mean untroubled or predictable; safe doesn't mean no mistakes, no harsh exposures, and no sudden emotions. Safety has to be re-established and shaped for each event.

The effort to engage conflict has to be genuine enough that the leaders are involved and not completely apart. It seems essential that there be more than one leader sitting in the ritual positions. If a leader is pulled into the center of a conflict, there need to be others to hold the ground and regulate the heat.

And it seems essential that the conflicts primarily involve those present. In other words, it's not a conflict ritual if the other side of the conflict isn't present. At a men's gathering, conflict can't be aimed at women or at some group not represented. That's simply blaming. It doesn't engage the shadow; it only increases the shadows that lie between groups.

Sometimes the sense of conflict builds very fast, or the group meets during a tragic time, and the only way to express the anguish and outrage is to direct it at God. That's called conflict with God, and it can be very appropriate. If you think it's disrespectful, remember that anger connects and respects its object. Besides, who was it that invented this ever-present conflict? There is an old idea that says that any conflict followed far enough leads to an opposition between the left hand and the right hand of God. And, like fight and flight, instincts eventually conflict with each other causing tensions in the soul and in the body. Maturity and moving closer to God involve dwelling longer and more deeply in life's conflicts, not denying or avoiding them.

Once we had a conflict session where men had to choose between a life based in passion or one dedicated to purpose. Each man had to choose and join one side or the other, physically. Moving the body commits the mind, the emotions, and the imagination, gets head and heart on the same side. Moving breaks the abstract plane of the questions and creates separations that make it possible to discriminate the feelings in each group. Moving tells the psyche that there may be something going on besides the play of ideas, and moving increases the tension in and between the groups. After moving, each group began to argue their position and establish their emotional territory.

Soon, there was one group identified as men of passion and another as men of purpose and there was a third, a middle group. There's almost always a middle group that argues against joining either side. Someone always argues, "I have both in my life. I can't exclude one." "But," we must reply, "right now which would you choose? Which is lacking and needed in your life? Which keeps you connected to what is most important right now? Which have you always been afraid of and can try out now? Which does your wife, your lover, your children, your friends say is missing? Which did you wish you had dwelt with more in your earlier life or in your youth? Which do you want to find more of in old age? Which did you come here looking for?"

The passionate men begin to speak, gradually becoming more and more impassioned, eventually yelling out their comments. The purposeful men keep pointing out that the passions miss the point. At first, it's part play acting as each side gets used to its position. Then, men are asked to speak from their life experience, not simply to state an opinion. It gets serious. Men have had their lives destroyed by uncontrolled passions. Others have served a purpose to the exclusion of everything else. One man says he dies a little each day because he feels no purpose in his life. Another has watched the passion drain out of his marriage and desperately wants to be among the men of passion. A man talks about the purpose that he knows has always been in him, but that he has always been afraid to live out.

A man changes sides after this, as if drawn by the feeling in the other man's voice. He says he's always followed his passions this way and that and defended his right to do so. Suddenly, he's feeling the loneliness of abandoning himself to passions that may have no purpose. A man who had argued eloquently for the absolute necessity for us to build things around a purpose and a plan in order to reach goals, or we would face the collapse of society, decides to drop the whole thing. He heads for the other side and looks to be shedding years of constriction as he goes. The "purpose men" let him go, but lay claim to his arguments as part of their territory.

Another man says he's a "passionate type" who feels things strongly and writes about them. But, the devastation to the youth in his neighborhood has made him take up a purpose. He works daily with troubled youths and feels that they need to sense his purpose in order to find and to trust their own. He's weeping and stating his purpose clearly. Is he in passion or purpose? A few more men change sides, more quietly though. Someone says the teachers haven't chosen sides. The teachers go through a separation, surprised after sitting so long together to be going different ways. The teachers are required to speak for their choices and say how passion or purpose pulled them in life. The hierarchy that was necessary to begin with is replaced with a complete division into two groups, and it will only be reinstated if needed for stability.

Now, the whole room is divided . . . or is it. The room is actually softer, more congealed. If anyone new walked into this room, they would stand out like an alien. After that afternoon, anyone entering the camp would be noticed immediately as different. They would be asked, "Passion or purpose?"—as if there were now totem groups. Looking in at the end of that conflict you would see the men in each group close together, connected by something not quite visible, and looking across at the other group as if there was a mystery to be seen. A few men say that they were most impressed by something that was said on the other side. After a while, each side sings a chant, each a different chant. Everything ends on a single resounding note, a shared sound, the holding of a single note of resolve. The next day at a community meal a man stands up and says that he has decided to switch sides. There are long thoughts going on about passion and purpose, spontaneity and order. The thoughts are mixed with emotions and stories from other men's lives. A ritual like this deepens the sense of each side of the question, and a sense of community grows from holding the tensions between opposite directions.

It's not always so sweet. On other occasions the primary conflicts arise with the teachers. The teachers have proposed ideas that are disturbing or contradictory, or a man in authority has offended a participant. The whole weight of authority issues comes up. It's always amazing how carefully men watch the demeanor of those in authority and the ways the "authority figures" interact with participants. Part of what men get to do at these events is to observe each other very carefully with less risk of being misunderstood than in the daily world. One of the areas studied most carefully is authority. In the business world, the academic world, the legal world, it is difficult and dangerous to question authorities. Men lose jobs, promotions, status, and friends for doing so. Men lose freedoms, rights, even their lives for questioning authority. Freedom and authority have an innate conflict with each other. When the rule is "no physical violence," there's a great opportunity to work on authority issues. Authority not held by force can be challenged more thoroughly, and challenging authority is a way of learning about how to hold it and how to relinquish it, and it's also a way of testing a developing community.

We learn about our own authority by risking authority in others. Men need to project or hang their sense of inner authority on outer figures in order to see how it works and in order pull their inner authorities out. In close interactions, the lights and shadows of inner authority get acted out and observed in depth. How the teachers and leaders handle authority, mistakes, and challenges affects everyone. If there isn't enough sense of authority present, the events won't go very deep. If there is too much authority at the top, there will be few risks taken. If the authorities are not able or willing to disagree with each other, everyone else will hold back. If the leaders are not somehow separate, the authority issues won't get focused. If the leaders are always separate, the group will be divided over how much authority the leaders should have. There's no "right way" to do it. Everyone wants to push around in the tricky areas where authority is given over and demanded back.

America was founded in and is remade out of unresolved conflicts. The United States are barely united, and they are seething below the surface with clashing expectations, old wounds, and even older desires. America is not what it thinks it is, not ever. America is not what it pretends to be either; the unity of the states is founded on disputes and conflicts. The origins of America are continually in dispute. Ultimately, the fascination people have with America is with the wild diversity of it's peoples and with the question of whether it will survive it's own conflicts and passions and ideals.

The first time we did an intentionally cross-cultural, interracial conference in this style, fifty black men and fifty white men met at a remote camp for six days. Due to great good fortune, there was one Asian man, two Latino men, and one Native American man. The focus was men and racism, especially the clash of black and white. The teachers were respected black men and white men. There was an agreement of no violence. The room was not very big, and no one waited for the conflict session listed on the schedule. After some opening blessings, the first of many impromptu conflict rituals began. The container of the group had to be tested, the rule of no violence had to be tested, the teachers had to be tested. There was no doubt that a conflict was present. The only real questions were who would begin it, how hot would it get, how would it ever end?

A black man tore into it right away. He'd already heard some things and tones of voice he didn't like, like it was cool to be at such a hip event. Well, fuck that! Of course, in an atmosphere drenched with historical conflict and glistening with fear, another man assumed he was being referred to. Off we went, quickly, heatedly, not knowing where to and soon enough not caring. To be directly in the heat of this conflict was better than to be in the daily shadow of it. And, conflict goes its own direction before it ever reveals what it was trying to get everyone to see.

But no sooner had we come together, surprisingly, by surviving the first conflict than a man insisted that the black men and the white men meet separately. That raised ghosts of all kinds and threatened the shaky unity of the newly met leaders of the event. Just as a sense of a community began to surface, it was to be tested.

That's why I say, great good fortune that there were men who were Asian, Latino, and Native American present. Where would they go if the group were divided into black and white? It wasn't that they would mind taking the side opposite "white," but they didn't wish to be absorbed into either of the great colors of opposition. They would lose something essential to themselves and their ancestors. In the face of such immediate conflict, everyone desired to be a part of a distinct group before facing the raging battles, but many also desired to form a community big enough to hold everyone. Many men insisted on staying with this first community before meeting in separate groups. By attending the fire at the center of the whole group, we had a place to return to, and a pattern was established that deep conflicts would in no way be denied, yet they would be kept in view, in the center of the community. Each man got to put a stick in that fire, some carried in cords of wood. The fire was rekindled over and over. While some stoked, others cooled things off. Once, the only cool spot in the room came from a wise, little story told by the lone Native American man when the fires of conflict had become blinding. At another dangerous point, the oldest black man present told how he survived the abuses of racism and of alcohol. From each story the "cool" grew and spread until the group and the room settled to a simmer.

But, this wasn't a new attempt at "the melting pot." The men present didn't want to be fused into a new amalgam; they didn't want to disappear into some solution. They wanted to contribute to the fire rather than being melted in it. The melting pot seems like a manufacturing image, as if there could be a manufacturing of people, an industrial approach that melts people into acceptable molds. Fortunately, the melting pot doesn't get hot enough to melt core memories and ancestral spirits. It never will. Individual people get melted down because the heat is too hot for some and they can't find a place to cool off; they get melted or go up in a puff of flame.

Meanwhile, the fires that flare up in cities are not attempts to heat the melting pot, they are more like an attempt to display the ashes of burnt hopes. They are more like the making of funeral ashes to memorialize the dead. They are more like using last embers of communities to make a statement: We are burning. The houses of our souls are burning with rage and frustration. Our ancestors are burning from disrespect not given to them and from the mistreatment of our families. Our hearts are burning over the refusal to accept our children in the fullness of their human needs and aspirations. The fires are also a call for water. Not the hosing down of the buildings, but a request for the Water of Life and the pouring of some all-heal and cooling waters that restore the soul.

Some things at the core of people won't melt down, however. There are old pieces of radical soul that can't be reduced in the manufacturing of modern cultures. The radical aspects of the psyche are like the Man of Tempers. You set up a melting pot, a cultural smelting industry, and he'll step right into it. But contrary to melting down, he'll freeze. The hotter the fire, the more he'll move into the opposite state. You won't wind up with a smelted, molded "individual," you'll come face to face with a frozen radical. Right now it's displayed in rap lyrics. "Ice" is one of the premiere images, as if to say, "the more firepower you bring here, the more 'ice' you get. You think that's hot, I think it's 'cold.'" On the other hand, if you try to freeze people out, treat them real cold, keep them out in the cold, without food, without hope . . . some radical part of the soul begins to burn. The more cold shoulders you turn on him, the more the temper of a man heats up. When justice has a cold eye, the Man of Tempers is on fire.

There's another aspect to this process of engaged conflict: Once the old radicals of the soul start awakening, they all wake up and show up on the road. It's as if each area of the soul hears that there's another attempt at finding community and sustaining the "gaze of beauty," and they each decide to go along and see whether it's more heads rolling or something that reaches to all the old souls.

At the multicultural conference, when everyone was getting used to the idea that various races could be in this hall together as long as we kept putting our sticks into the fire and not using them as weapons, two men stood up and spoke of the necessity to recognize gay men. One was a black man, one was white. You could hear the fire crackle and blaze up again. It was as if the pattern was established and the community fire had to accept whatever radical aspects of life were present. It was also another aspect of great good fortune. Part of the point of lighting the fires of conflict is to burn away phobias, including homophobias, fears of men, of other men not like me. Many of the men gathered had never faced the homosexual radical in others or in themselves. Suddenly, here it is. Does the fire go out? Do the messengers from another radical piece of the human soul get shut out? Or, does each man turn the shattering vision into himself, and by looking at the fear that becomes a hatred of others, shatter that fear? These men represented another piece of our multiple culture, which is also a piece of every culture that has ever been, a piece that won't melt down in the melting pot. So, do these radical messengers get to speak at this community fire trying to be?

The strange thing about beginnings is that they set a style and that style gets repeated. Anything new causes a return to beginnings. A man yells out again, a different man, but he's saying he's heard something he doesn't like. He doesn't want men kissing men, or educating his sons, and he doesn't want to give white people another way to demean black men. Out of one conflict has come another, and once again seeing and hearing it directly feels better than walking in the shadows of it daily. Another man says that he didn't know that there were gay men present, and he's having a kind of reverse-phobia, as if to say, "How could I have slept peacefully when there were gay men sleeping nearby?" Various fears crackle about the room. Even the racial fears get revived in new ways: Are there more gays among my culture? Do other groups deal with this better than we? The room wobbles; cracks appear, chill winds blow dark shadows across the fire, which had started to feel familiar. The same questions arise that were there at the beginning: Can the group hold together? Can the respected leaders encompass realities that were not mentioned before the event in any of the literature? The men look at the teachers.

One teacher says emphatically that though he is heterosexual, two of his mentors in the world of art were gay men. If he accepts the gifts that they have given to the culture and to him, how can he refuse their need to be who they are sexually? He praises their courage and their generosity to him and their integrity regarding the sexual orientations of others. Now, the two men standing here have to be seen in that light. Another stick has gone into the fire, and there's less shadow in the room. Another teacher recites a Whitman poem, as if to say, "Are you going to keep Walt Whitman out? If you do, you'll wind up burning books to keep false fires burning."

The two men have remained standing. One wept as he told how his uncle was the only one in his family who saw him with an open heart and had blessed his way of walking into life. It's clear that he will keep walking if there's no room at this fire. The other man stands defiantly, ready to fight for a place at the fire.

Two more teachers, one black and one white, speak about the role of gay people in many cultures, but specifically in African tribes and European groups, in which they stand at the gates between two worlds and hold them open. If someone doesn't fit into the simple division of two genders, they stand between the two and go between the two. They show how aspects of life go back and forth between fixed positions. At different ceremonies they may put on the clothes and manners of either group. Since their basic way of being in this world has this quality of in-between, they also can learn to open the gates between the spiritual worlds, between spiritual positions that are usually fixed, and even between those in opposition. The result is more sticks in the fire, fewer cold shadows in the room. More room at the fire.

But there was also more room at the rivers and pools of the water of life. Surviving conflict releases the joy that was being held back, but it also increases awareness of the grief that flows below the surface of any conflict. Active and meaningful conflict requires the process of grieving. The wound needs to be washed as well as exposed. Healing seems to require descent, and old wounds often have to be dipped in the waters of the ancestors. Those fires would have burned too far had not many of the men been privately and openly grieving and weeping. Some obstacles get moved through fire, but grief gets moved by water, by the tears and laments that wash memories of loss the way rain washes stones. The poet Vachel Lindsay wrote:

> Men thank God for their tears
> Alone with the memory of their dead,
> Alone with lost years.

The end of conflict is found in grief for what has been lost and in gratitude to the dead. One of the sacred places in the unsettled land of America is the Vietnam Memorial Wall in Washington, D.C., which seeks a ground of unity below ongoing cultural conflicts. The blackness of the Wall, the fact that it descends into the ground, and the fact that the names on it come from the sorrowed array of ethnic groups throughout the world symbolically unites these groups. The ancestral names combined on one wall, which shares the commonality of death as well as the tears of mourning that are brought to it, are a symbol of the capacity of America to rediscover the rites of grieving and descent. Differences of color and belief and status disappear into the dark uncertainty of the Wall. And if the imagination continues where the Wall enters the ground, you join in a common lament that pours past the scars and the woundings. America begins to become itself somewhere below the base of the Wall.

It's not insignificant that the Wall was designed by an Asian American woman, and it is significant that there is a continual ritual of grieving going on at the Wall. Unlike heroic statues that stand alone, the black Wall acts as a conductor that moves emotions from the living people to the land of the dead. It is more of a ritual center than a memorial edifice. The mourners come and go, pouring tears that fall to a well deep below the fires of conflict, which spit and flare throughout the capitol.

There are inequities even at the Wall. Names of the missing and the lost do not appear. Descendants of slaves who gave their lives as certainly as anyone else are buried within and listed in the names of their enslavers. But groups that cannot find a common language to this day find a common silence at the Wall. Women align with men, gay align with straight, immigrants align with unwilling travelers. The accumulation of grief and tears moves all of them along the road of death. For the old idea—known to native people in the Americas, in Asia, Europe, Australia, and Africa—was that the dead have to be helped along the road to the underworld. If the living don't release their grief through tears and song, the dead get stuck on the road to the ancestors.

I first went to the Wall to look for the names of friends who had died in the war, but I soon found myself in the confusing waters of my own grief over that war. I entered the ritual of the place, following the names on the Wall, chronologically, day-by-day, as in a procession of death after death, until the name of a friend stopped me like a blow newly struck. Then I read all the names around his, imagining that they were connected to him because they had all died on the same day. I stood among the families of the dead who took rubbings of the names of the deceased the way people take rubbings of art in old cathedrals. Meanwhile, others were feeling their way along the Wall, touching the dead as they went.

I returned a few times just to feel that place, and then I wanted to sing as well as cry. I wanted to return at night and sing the dead on their way, the old way. So once, at a public presentation in Washington during the Persian Gulf War, we decided to make a procession to the Wall at night in order to sing to the dead.

Several hundred men went. We walked out into the street where candles were handed out, and we began to sing an old lament for the dead. At dusk we went down through the streets, singing, but the police arrived to announce that since we didn't have a permit, we couldn't continue as a group in public. Maybe they thought it was a protest or simply a political statement. Whatever the reason, they didn't want it to continue. But there is often chaos at the beginning of a rite; it seems necessary. We kept singing and kept going. We knew it wasn't a protest or conflict ritual, but we were underway, and to discuss the issue would have turned sorrow into conflict. So we kept singing.

When we reached the vicinity of the Wall, we were told that it was illegal to sing there. But we had come to sing the dead along—we couldn't not do it; we couldn't discuss it either—so we began to hum our song. As we moved on, we were told that as a group we could not enter the area, so we formed into a single file and prepared to enter one at a time. And when they said that lit candles were not allowed at the memorial, a man offered to blow out each candle, one by one, as each man in the procession descended. Along the entire stretch of the Wall, our candles blown out, we entered the dark and became one with the Wall and with the dead who are remembered in it. As we came out of the dark a man stood and relit each candle, and one by one we climbed the hill beyond the Wall.

By this point, the police had realized that we had no intention of being disrespectful, so they joined us as we moved up the hill and away from the Wall. Our intention was not politics, but ritual. Our focus was the dead, not the living. We had kept going where we were going, to lament in song and with tears the dead, to keep them going toward the ancestors.

If you had observed the event from the hill above, you would have seen a crowd of men approach, singing and carrying a myriad of lights. At one point, the song changes to a hum that begins to stretch out along the Wall. The lights stretch out to form a line, and at a certain place, the lights disappear, one at a time. Then you have to imagine these men walking a dark road and humming a lament until they appear at the other end and their light somehow returns. Where the candles are relit, the song begins to grow words again until everyone who disappeared into the dark returns with voice, carrying light again. You tell me who made that ritual and what happened at that Wall, and what the ancestors may have seen.

Rituals that reach for the ground of the radicals of the soul can awaken any and all of the radical elements of human nature. The story of the companions seems to say that all the radicals are needed to keep a meaningful vision alive. When the obstacles in the world become greater and more complex and seem to be coming from all directions at once, there are two great tendencies in the psyche. One is to simplify and quickly adopt some fundamentalism, and the other is to accept the multiplicity and the great tension that come from embracing the world. The weird companions represent a person's sudden, increased capacities when he or she accepts the incurable nature of the world. Accepting the companions also means being willing to travel along the road that is most fearful, remembering that there is a great beauty the soul desires, and trusting that the capacities of other people will be equal to the dangers of the road.

CHAPTER 28

AT THE WEDDING

AFTER GATHERING WITH the ancestral companions, the prince arrives in the realm of the old queen. He announces himself as a common suitor for the hand of life, not as the son of a king or an initiate who has been through fires and waters and been schooled by the ancestors. The influence of the companions has helped him to state that he has come seeking the daughter of the old queen of life, and that he stands ready to earn his way.

In the strange style of myth and of ritual, the tasks he is assigned are very specific but the methods for achieving them are not. The oxen and wine must be consumed to the last hair and the last molecule of moisture, but it's quite all right if the suitor doesn't do it himself. The fire must be endured to the last ember, but not exactly by the betrothed. Getting through the designs of the old queen requires both attention to detail and getting out of the way so the inner resources and ancestral forces can arise.

If the suitor for the hand of life begins to lose sight of the vision of beauty that caused his soul to waste away, he'll lose his head . . . again. The job of the prince is to accept the impossible tasks the way he accepted the conditions on his soul in the story of Conn-Eda. His actual task is to keep going toward the source of life despite and because of what he has learned of breakdowns, wasting, dying, and death. Whatever he has learned from his companions now serves to reinforce his vision; whatever he has learned of tempering his spirit has to serve that vision as well.

In the first test, the old queen wants her lost ring of sovereignty back—can he find it? Does he understand descent and how to find gold and silver in the depths of the sea? Or, does he wish to quibble over whose ring, lost when, is there a certain way to go about this, is there a time limit? If so, it's too late; if he doesn't know by now where to find help, he'll lose his head. If he can't recall the descent to retrieve Vasilisa's gown, it's too late to start over. The companions are partly made of his own memories and partly made of ancestral memory, and if he can't get to both . . . he'll lose his head . . . again.

Next, his desire is tested: Does he have an appetite for the whole thing, for all of life, the gristle, the bone, and the shadows as well? Or, will he simply get drunk when the wine is opened and the heady stuff of life flows out, with no rules or limits except his own ability to enter desire?

When he gets past that, there is the third test: Will he be able to keep his awareness while looking straight into the eyes of the beauty of being alive? Will he be able to stay awake as he actually comes close to what the longing in his soul has aimed for and sought? For a moment the extremes of life touch each other; the old queen has brought them all together. The eyes of the daughter of the queen are gazing into the eyes of the son of the king. They are surrounded by the old companions, and moonlight pours into the room.

For a moment, everything stops. The embrace of the daughter and the son of the realms joins everyone. The ancestors are awake and see the gaze of beauty. The old queen pauses from making designs on the ground, placing obstacles, and whispering plots. In the embrace on the other side of incurability, the future is conceived. Before the midnight of the soul strikes, the next round of life begins. For a moment all were "blessed and could bless." Life got blessed, beauty was blessed, the ancient longings were blessed. The moon poured a light of blessing down, live hearts were full to the brim, and the cup of the Water of Life was passed around.

A moment in a recessed chamber of the soul is captured and held by the companions, a moment of beauty and love that radically alters the conditions in both realms. The flow of life reaches that point and turns, reverses. Life reverses itself. All that was wasting away and falling into years of incurability and headed for its last moment reaches the end of its fall and turns back again. A millennium occurs in the soul. For a moment everything was awake in the depths of life, and that releases life to flow again. The next direction of life is begun, initiated. The huge efforts of the companions, the designs of the old queen, the suffering of the prince and princess meet in the depth of that moment. It can't be held any longer. The moon moves past the window, its soft rays suffusing the night but no longer bathing the moment in full, unbearable light. Even the companions fall asleep when the mysteries at the center of the chambers of the heart are seen and felt.

The daughter of the old queen is whisked away and chained to a rock at sea. She now has to be found much the same way the queen's ring was found and similar to the way the wedding gown was found for the beautiful Vasilisa. If this can be accomplished—just as in the sequence in the story of the firebird—then the tests and tasks will no longer be orchestrated by the old ruler, the queen, but by the one being prepared for the wedding.

The old queen whispers in the ear of her daughter that the man looks common enough when the moon withdraws its light. It's true, and the companions look stranger than ever. When not engaged in great tasks, they look exaggerated and awkward. The daughter realizes that marrying and leaving the moment of love and the protection of the mother's realm will be a great exposure. What if this common fellow forgets, or falls asleep again? The old queen has tested the prince with water and food and her great spells of sleep, confusion, and despair. Now the daughter will test him with fire. At the pivotal moment of midnight, the queen's daughter has become the central figure in the realm, and she requires that the one who has broken her mother's spell enter a great fire.

The only companion who has not been tested, who has not entered one of the tasks, is the Man of Tempers. For the daughter of the old queen to leave her mother's realm and return with the son of the king, she must see for herself where all this tempering has brought him.

As the fire is being built in the center of the hall, you can look across the flames and see the preparations being made in the hall of the firebird. Beyond those flames you can see the villagers stoking the fires in "The Lizard in the Fire." In that story, a son of the king was suspended in some state between full life and full death. The only one who would enter the fire to return him to life was a young woman. When she leapt to the center of the fire and pulled out the lizard, the son returned to life. Or, it could be said, he entered life more fully and stepped out of death. Then, for the young woman to stay in life, the youth's mother had to die as his "mother." Only the daughter entered the fire, and her leap demonstrated that the father could not save the son and the mother had to let him go. This was necessary in order for the son and the daughter to be in life together. Now, it's the other side of that fire, will he enter it for her?

Once again the question is being asked: Is this the son of a king or a common man? This time the old queen prompts the question, and the daughter sets the fire. It's as if the old hunter wanders over from the lizard story and says, "Now, the situation is this: If the son can stand in the fire that the daughter of the old queen makes, they can reenter life together. If he can't survive the tempering, then he'll die altogether and the daughter will remain with her mother and wait. For her to return with him, he must survive her fire."

The prince is being drawn through the fires one more time. His tempering has become one of his companions; the repeated immersions in fire and water have connected him to the old soul who waits for just those tests of extreme temperatures. When he asks whether his companion can enter for him, he has passed another test. The son answers the question: When the fires grow hot does he stand it alone, or does he have a sense of "the other"? If he leapt into the fire himself, he might find himself working in the firebird story again. If he insists that she enter the fire, it's "The Lizard in the Fire" all over again. If he refuses her fire on the basis that he's already been through the fires demanded by the king in the form of the firebird, and he's already passed the fire tests of Conn-Eda, then he loses his head and she returns to the sea. His dilemma is that he can't refuse the fire for the loss of his head, and he can't enter it either. Part of the test is whether he remembers that one of the companions seems to enjoy the heat that no one else can stand and can stand the cold no one else could endure. Once the Man of Tempers is invoked, the fire will be survived. The true question becomes whether the son will remember that the Man of Tempers is ready whenever the fires are set.

These are the fires of Litima once again. On the one hand, the son is once more immersed in the forging of his character. On the other hand, he may accomplish all of the tasks of the old queen but fail to stay in touch with the daughter who represents new life. Looked at as an interior event in the psyche of the son, the question is, Can he handle the flames that she sets in his life now that he has become himself? Taken as a test of where the hero is in life, the question could be, Can he enter the fires of relationship and not burn himself up, or burn his spouse?

In tribal initiations, it is often at the end of a long period, perhaps ten or twelve years of ongoing initiation, that the elders see that a particular man is ready to move from the stage of struggle, often called the warrior stage, to the stage of elder. The young men may enter initiation as a group, but they are called out when individually ready. They are called after they have been in fire enough and been in water enough. From the point of view of the warrior, the question is whether this son is ready to leave behind the stage of having to find fire in every event in life and having to match fire with fire. Can he enter the hut of a relationship and be able to recall the companion of tempers when necessary? Can he endure the demands of love and community without burning up? Can he stand the fires of community and not burst into violence or lose his tempering? Can he become cooler as the fire burns and become cold if there's too much fire being set at his feet?

From the point of view of the daughter of the old queen, of the old hag of the world, it's an important question. It is closer to the central question than the concern of whether he's the son of a king or of a common man. Is he the son that can stand in the fire that is required in order for the energy of the feminine to return to the world? Is he knowledgeable enough about the tempers in himself to join the elders and remember the ancestors?

Part of the cure of the incurable lies in developing the capacity to withstand the fires and remember the Water of Life when the fires are burning hot. The Man of Tempers acts as the elder acts—he cools his heart while the fires intensify. He knows how hot he can take it and how cool is far enough before cold occurs. He says upon emerging that if the fire had gone on much longer, he would have frozen to death, so that even within the tempering some tempering is required. The coolness is remembering the Water of Life, but if he begins to turn cold, he's headed toward stone again. The tempering lies in the memory of fire when things become too cold and in the recollection of cool waters when events become too hot.

When the practice of this is demonstrated, the elder has been born. Then the daughter of the old queen of the world is willing to travel with that son. Of course, there are difficulties on the return. The old queen has further tests to see if these events have entered and settled deeply in the soul or not. She sends a couple of armies to see whether the listening ear is kept open and the capacity to look with a shattering vision remains ready.

There seems to be a last danger as well. If the Man with the Shattering Vision is left standing at the border between the worlds with his head turned toward the daily world, he will shatter anything he sees. The piercing quality of his vision will look too hard at the outer world, which, after all, is not as extreme as the inner, other, under realm. So an army is sent to attract his attention. The Listener hears what is coming and turns the Man of Shattering Vision at the army charging from behind, below. This act leaves him looking deep inside and shattering the enemies within. The risk is that if he is left at the border facing the other way, he may mistake people running about in the daily confusion for the army rushing from within and shatter them. It's another test of the temper of the psyche and a reminder that the great battles are first won within.

At the border between the worlds, the companions remain behind. Those old souls return to their places, where they lie on the ground of the soul, or stand by the tree that is forever growing, or else stand at the edge of a cliff in the inner world, gazing and gazing at whatever moves. The bandages go back over the Man of Shattering Vision. The huge man lays down again and looks like a great hill in the terrain of the psyche. Things calm down within.

The son of the king and the daughter of the queen continue on together. All is well in the psyche, but a test is required in the daily world as well as in the otherworld. From the point of view of the upperworld, the inner, otherworld is always inflated, and it is too much to tolerate on a daily basis. The otherworld is always exaggerated; it's always living in the last minute; it's always about to explode or fall into the caverns of love. Something must be done to reduce, contain, and bring to the everyday ground the excessive and extreme excitements of the soul.

The son of the king and the daughter of the queen return as common people. They enter a pig herder's hut and live with herders and people who work with animals and move the waste of the world. They exchange the royal clothes of the inner, otherworld for the common clothes of this world. It's necessary that they be able to share a hut together, despite each knowing in some way that he or she is the child of royalty. They both have to live in a community and in a common life together.

The camp of the pig herders represents a return to daily life and the period spent seasoning their experiences in the world of the companions. The extraordinary occurrences and the changes in the depths of the soul are too much for consciousness to bear for long. The princess and the prince must be brought to a further sense of calm. In the manner of the half-giantess, after the great eruptions in the waters of sorrow and in the fires of rage, they must calm down and enter a hut. They must dress for work; they must dress for dinner. They must put on common clothes as the youngest son did in "The Water of Life." After the hugeness of events and the wonders of descent there needs to be calming down.

Looked at another way, the value of what has happened in the depth of the soul and in the far reaches of the inner world must be shaped to fit the daily world. The pig herder's camp is the place for construction of a mutual life, made of real exchanges anchored in daily living. The pig is the oldest animal of herding and the first domesticated animal. When Ulysses returns from his wanderings through the worlds, he returns as a pig herder. The old grandmother, the matriarch of the keepers of pigs, accepts him and inspects him. He arrives worn and tired from the excess and extremes of his journey. While washing him she sees the scar of his old wound and recognizes that he is Ulysses returned from the otherworld. So, living among the camp of the pig herders is also the time when the son of the king and the daughter of the old queen are recognized as two who have gone into the wondrous and terrifying otherworld and returned. And, they are recognized through some scarring that they bear. Before they can enter the palace, there needs to be a settling, a healing over of the scarring experiences found in the otherworld.

And there is also another reversal going on. If the son entered the realm of the mothers as a common man ready to earn his way to reach the daughter, then she must put on common clothes to work with him. Also, being with the pigs means working for the "sow mother." They both have become children of the earth mother, or they are seen again as her children. When they enter the palace, they are recognized as the son and daughter of the king's world, and they are also seen as the son and daughter of the queen's world.

The question that was asked in the very first story of the book is answered in this multiple way, after traveling through all the stories. Who is he? Is he the son of his father or the son of a king? Is he the son of his mother or the son of the great queen? Who is she? Is she the daughter of the hag at the well? Is she also a woman in the real world? Is she the daughter of the half-giantess? Is she also a part of his soul? Eventually, the answer is . . . yes.

Eventually, the prince and the princess will go back and forth between the pig herder's hut and the palace, and from the pig herder's hut to the deep world of the companions and the old queen. Like Conn-Eda, they have gained access to both worlds and have an obligation to live in both. Upon returning from the otherworld, they reenter through the hut of common living, the hut of equality of scars, the hut of memory that reaches to the world of the old queen. The hut becomes the opening to the world of the radical old souls below.

The radical rituals that can change a life, that can change a relationship, that can change a group, cannot be sustained for great lengths of time. The extremes of the human soul, represented by the companions, the tyrannical old kings, the old hag at the well, the dwarf, the lady of the fountain, the half-giantess, the old king who demands the firebird, cannot be suffered for extensive periods of time. They come and they go. They are seen and they disappear.

People cannot dwell in the otherworld, for people are intended to be human. There must always be a passage through the pig herder's camp, for it returns us to human conditions. The otherworld is like a utopia; it isn't anywhere exactly. It's found in different places at different times. It moves around and is always temporary. It can be found through the pig herder's hut, but the door to the lower world can open to any place. Utopia means nowhere, and utopias are momentary glimpses into our communal, mysterious core. The living out of utopian ideas never works because people cannot remain in those intense, radical spaces, that is, until they are ready to join the ancestors.

The point of initiations, whether accidental or intentional, is to touch the mysterious core, pass through change, and return. It is like touching the fire that continually burns at the center of the earth or touching the depth of a great ocean. A touch is all that a human being can stand. One touch can change the course of a life forever. Trying to dwell in those depths, trying to live in the flames of those fires, makes people crazy. The pig herder's hut means a return to the daily needs. But if we return from our rounds in the fires and waters of life, we may carry healing to the wounds that seemed incurable above, a healing that moves the world again.

As elders, the prince and princess will construct the huts for the initiations of the next group of young men and women. Inevitably, making the ritual huts will stir up the old stories they have heard and lived. In maintaining the huts, they will reopen the scars and wounds of memory and keep in touch with initiations and ancestors.

Meanwhile, the story of the companions is not quite complete. The time spent in the hut of the pig herder can be a long time or a short time, or whatever time it takes for all of the elements of the soul to find their situation in the human psyche again. Then one day, they are summoned to the castle. The princess has mostly forgotten everything that happened in the otherworld. The prince has likely forgotten it too. When the princess is invited to come see her husband, she expects to find him, as usual, on a market day, holding the ropes of the pigs, bargaining and arguing for a good price—then trying to reduce the tax when the tax collector comes by. He's in the usual human circumstances, she thinks, with some pig shit, trying to hold together something that never comes out quite right. She is in the common clothing of the pig herding woman.

There aren't great expectations here. If the meal that evening is a little better than usual, it's something to be thankful for. If there's a little less work the next day, it's enough to give thanks. If a little more love flows between the two, it's something worth savoring. But, on this occasion, things go differently; some of the wonder of the otherworld slips into this one. Instead of arriving at the marketplace and seeing her husband in his stall with the pigs, she's taken to the palace. She's brought before the prince sitting in his raiment, in his garments of royalty. She has never seen him this way. She doesn't recognize him until she looks into his eyes.

As she stands in some confusion about what is transpiring, people begin running in every direction. They are gathering all the things that are needed for the making of a great feast. The prince and the princess look into each other's eyes. Once more she recognizes him through the soul that she sees in his eyes. And he, once more, sees in her eyes that vision he saw when he was wrapped in her arms and embracing her. Once more they feel the presence of the old companions around them. Deep memories move in each of them, and they are lost in that gaze, feeling the rays of the old, silver moon falling all around the two of them.

While they are embracing each other, the feast is being rapidly brought together. Fine juices, coffees, teas from all the lands of the earth are being gathered so there will be no thirst on this occasion. Great old barley beers are hauled up from the basements of the palace. Fine wines are brought from the vineyards of Chile, from the slopes of France, from the valleys of California. Dark stouts are brought from Ireland and fine lagers from Germany. Honey gathered in Mexico and South America is mixed with grain from Africa by old women making fresh beer and preparing to watch the young men dance through their initiation fires.

People come from all the places where stories are made, so that those people gathered in the hall are of all origins, ages, and shapes. They appear in the many-colored garments that people wear to show their relationship to the earth and to the stars above. Among them come musicians bringing an array of instruments made from the shells of animals, from trees, and from the sinews of whales. They bring drums that have to be answered with dances and stringed instruments that draw out laments and the great joys of humankind. And with them come dancers, women who can move great distances so gracefully that they appear hardly to move at all. There are men who can leap into the air, then turn and pivot at the top of the leap and dive for the floor, only stopping their head from hitting the ground by the arrival of their hands at the last moment.

Women and men dance forth carrying the dark, burning fires of flamenco. So that if a man comes forward stamping into the ground and reaching for the sky above, he is soon met by a woman sparking the ground with her heels. The arch of his body is answered with the toss of her skirt, as if to say, Everything that spreads from these heels out belongs to me by right of the Great Mother living below. She answers his movements with exaggerations of her body that are both delicate and powerful. He responds to her, and they gesture back and forth in a language of water and fire.

When the singers arrive, groups of women sing notes that cascade through the ear as if rain is falling through trees, the drops on each leaf making a rhythm inside the notes like patterns in a pool of water only they can see. Groups of men begin singing a lament, remembering all those who could not live long enough to reach this feast but whose memories will live into the feast and out of it again because of the lament being poured for them. Poets begin to catch images and shape them into words in ways that cause the old, original meanings to come out and mix with the living activity. The mixture of old meanings with the joy in the world causes the path of words to be so impeccable as to be remembered by anyone who was present at the feast.

King Lion, who stays awake in the center of the village while all others sleep and waits for orphaned sons, returns in the dance of those words. Of course, wherever he goes, the troop of counselors goes as well, questioning everyone and sampling everything laid out at the feast, only stopping between bites to say, "Indeed, indeed." While the Half-Giantess roams the tables grumbling, "People have been taking from my food. I thought such a great feast would satisfy me, but I can see now that people have picked little pieces out of all those things baked just for me." Soon, she is finding that the level of wine and stout and juice poured into each glass is not right and that people drink a little too quickly, a little too much, and she is unsatisfied once again.

Meantime the men's chorus has joined the women's chorus, and they're singing songs that praise horses. They invoke the little shaggy horse that carried Conn-Eda to the water of Lough Erne and the great black steed that carried him back up from the fires and waters of the world below. That reminds them of the horse of power, and they sing of how he was ever standing at the foot of the stairs waiting for the hunter to return to exchange tears for advice and the encouragement to go on. And that brings to mind the beautiful Vasilisa floating in her boat of silver and gold. They sing her song and raise it to the roof of the hall so that all can hear and never forget the sound of silver oars dipping into the great blue ocean of her soul.

While the daughter of the old queen and the son of the king hold the gaze of beauty, they begin to recite again their marriage vows to each other. The excitement and the commotion of the event awakens the old ones in the earth below the castle. The singing and punctuation of the dancers' feet stirs the old king and queen of the underworld. The Old Hag of the World and the Old Tyrant King participate in the wedding vows, though no one seems to notice. While the two above promise to see the source of beauty in the other's eyes for better or for worse, in sickness and in health, "till death do us part," in the hall in the earth below, tasks are being named by the old tyrant, his eyelids propped open with forks, his wit kept sharp by the presence of the old queen with her sword. They are cheerily making a list of tasks that get entangled with the marriage vows. They reel off the actual requirements for sustaining the gaze of lovers, just as they gladly invent tasks for each attempt at marriage and each attempt at culture.

Since this is a wedding of a king's son and a queen's daughter, a son of the firebird and a daughter of the fountain of the Water of Life, the old ones layout some fine tasks. "See those fields," they say. "We want them cleared, the growth burned, and the ashes used to fertilize it. Then plow it and sow it and harvest the ripe grain, but before the dew is gone from it. For it must furnish food and drink for all the guests at the wedding, and the wedding won't be over until it's done. By the way, you can't cut any 'old growth' trees because they are part of us, and you can't disturb the owls that inhabit them or the marriage will end in disaster. No pesticides either; they discolor our teeth. There's no way you can do that unless you find the old, wild son of the field, and he's in the underworld and won't come with you unless you bring an oxen from the ancestors of each of your families and yoke them together with a rope made of the wedding veils of each of your grandmothers and all of your great grandmothers. Do you agree to that?" Up above they each say, "I do." Some at the wedding laugh, some cry.

Down below the old ones say, "Though you accomplish that, you won't accomplish the next task." Says the old giant, "For the wedding,

I want my hair washed and my beard shaved, and nothing can soften these hairs and stretch them out except the blood of this old, black hag. And the blood must be taken warm or it is of no use, and nothing can contain it and keep it warm but the bottles of the old dwarf, and he won't give them unless you find him. And you won't find him by looking but only by hearing what each other are trying to say when your own blood is boiling. Do you agree to that?" Up above they each say, " I do." Some at the wedding laugh for joy, some weep again

And the old queen says, "Though you accomplish that, there's something you won't accomplish. Every marriage requires music, and we require that you find the old harp that plays itself when some truth has been told and falls silent when empty promises are being made. And we wish to sip wine made from honey nine times sweeter than the honey made by the first swarm out of the hive. And when it comes time to rest, you must bring the birds of Rhiannon that rouse the dead and allow the living to sleep, but who do the opposite when you harbor enmity and envy of each other. They will torment your rest whenever you fail in this. Do you agree to that?" Up above they each say, "I do." Some at the wedding raise the sound of joy, some weep. And this continues until all the tasks are listed, all the ancestral problems are raised, and all the "I do's" are said.

Then toasts are given from the women to the men, from the men to the women, from the people of one world to the people of another. Everyone imagines that they are drinking the Water of Life. The toasting goes on until everyone has said what is on the tip of their tongues. The feast draws to a close, although hearts are open and wishing to continue. Then someone hears the voice of the little dwarf at the side of the room saying, "Where are you going in such a hurry? Where are you headed at such a speed?" And realizing that this is no time to rush straight ahead without knowing where they are bound, they begin the feast over again.

The dancing begins again, and this time is seen more clearly, and the singing this time is heard from a deeper place. The food is all tasted again; and the toasts are made more elaborate. The second feast is such a fine event that they decide to have a third feast. And by the time they have reached the center of the third feast, they begin to sense the presence of the six companions.

The third time makes such a great feast that the son of the king and the daughter of the queen embrace each other in joy and sorrow, so much so that the tears from his eyes run down her back and the tears from her eyes fall down his back. The whole event seems such a fine dance that the old queen below feels warmed and inspired once again to create new tasks before she will let go of those things that people need most in the world above.

Where one thing ends another begins, and a wedding is the feast that prepares the place for new life to enter. And everyone watches the marriage ritual: the children as well as the ancestors, for what happens at the wedding is the stage upon which new life will play. The children that are present will never forget the sight and sound of all those people dancing and leaping, singing and weeping. The memory of it will encourage them at their tasks.

At the wedding, everyone is bride or groom, or even both. Through the symbols and rituals of marriage, all of the characters of the "otherworld" are remembered and invoked so that they are at the wedding, too. Does the couple live happily ever after? No. There has been a small error in the translation of that phrase. The saying originally was, "They lived happily in the ever after." In this world, they found happiness as often as they found sorrow, and that was enough.

Acknowledgments

I would not have ventured far into the telling and writing of stories without the example set by, the guidance given by, and the love offered by my wife, Erica Helm Meade. More than once when I stood hesitating before a road that was dark to my eye, Erica told me to go on, to not look back and to hold nothing back. My gratitude can't find enough words. Without forgiveness from my children, Oona, Aram, Fionn, and Bran, and the certainty of their courage, I would not have hope in the future.

To Lucille, my mother, who never loses faith, and to my Aunt Florence, who has given to me freely, I say prayers of thanks. To Brother Rudolph, who spoke directly from his heart, I am thankful for permission to try to speak from mine.

I am grateful to two men, returning from the fires of Vietnam, who protected me when I couldn't have covered myself and who showed me that surviving a fire was more important than arguing over the size of the flames.

For long-term encouragement and many helping hands, I thank Susan Plum, for inspiration and for saying "just close the door and write"; Rick Simonson, for long thoughts of friendship and for being there when there was no work, no money, too many shadows; Barbara Thomas, for saying "let the images rise from the roots and the ground"; Bob and Pat Johnson, for never being far when there were tough distances to cross; Dumisani Maraire, for opening the door for me and saying, "No one owns music. It can only be given. No one can take it from you."

I thank Robert Bly, for opening many roads through the forest, inviting me along on the adventures, and gathering poems, sorrows, jokes, and insults to nourish everyone along the way; and James

Hillman, for insisting on going where the road gathers shadows, but also for remembering to bring candles to light the way and soften the night for dreaming.

I pay my respects to Etheridge Knight, for poems and songs, no matter what the pain, and for leaving the rule "no physical violence" before making the turn toward the ancestors; Terry Dobson, who uncovered his heart and gave it away many times before anyone could take it from him and then did one last "jump . . . down"; Walter Meade, my father, for speaking with awe of writing and songs; and St. Patrick, who got confused about snakes and wells but remembered in time to transcribe the old stories and pass them along.

I'm grateful to Van Morrison, for finding the Muse in the radio, the song in the street, the healing in the common; Aidoo Mamadi Holmes, for walking in the door first, breaking it all down on the drum, pouring libations; John Densmore, for finding groove after groove and carrying many brothers along; Riccardo Morrison, for steppin' out, finding many feathers, leading the dance.

I offer thanks to Malidoma Patrice Somé, for extending a brother's hand, teaching me ritual, carrying old healing to new wounds, pointing out ancestors, stepping on crocodiles.

For making old roads brighter and opening new tracks toward "home," I thank Haki Madhubuti, Clarissa Pinkola Estés, Jack Kornfield, Coleman Barks, Onaje Benjamin, and Miguel Rivera.

For seeing this book before it was visible to me, I thank Robert Moore, Ned Leavitt, and Tom Grady.

For keeping all of it visible, for keeping me going, making work a reward in itself, Jim Alkire.

For exacting work under trying ordeals and seeing the book through right to the last minute, I thank Jeff Campbell, Nancy Palmer Jones, Margery Cantor, and George Brown at Harper San Francisco.

Any faults or omissions are my own, or else they are errors made when my little horse stumbled in the dark as I was trying to write this down.

Select Bibliography

Epigraph

Mann, Thomas. From a 1936 lecture entitled "Freud and the Future," quoted in *The Gods of the Greeks* by C. Kerényi. London and New York: Thames & Hudson, 1951.

Introduction

Eliade, Mircea. *Rites and Symbols of Initiation*. New York: Harper Torchbooks, 1958.

Hamilton, Edith. *Mythology*. Boston: Little, Brown and Company, 1942.

Knight, Etheridge. *The Essential Etheridge Knight*. Pittsburgh: University of Pittsburgh Press, 1986.

Van Gennep, Arnold. *Rites of Passage*. Chicago: University of Chicago Press, 1961.

Part One: The Road of the Two Fathers

Bly, Robert, James Hillman, and Michael Meade, eds. *The Rag and Bone Shop of the Heart*. New York: HarperCollins, 1992.

Feldman, Susan, ed. *African Myths and Tales*. New York: Dell, 1963.

Kerényi, C. *The Gods of the Greeks*. London and New York: Thames & Hudson, 1951.

Knappert, Jan. *Bantu Myths and Other Tales*. Leiden, The Netherlands: Colon Brill, 1977.

Moore, Robert, and Douglas Gillette. *King, Warrior, Magician, Lover*. San Francisco: HarperCollins, 1990.

Rees, Alwyn, and Brinley Rees. *Celtic Heritage*. London and New York: Thames & Hudson, 1961.

Somé, Malidoma. *Ritual*. Portland, OR: Swan/Raven and Company, 1993.

Vallejo, César, Robert Bly, John Knoeple, and James Wright, trans. *Neruda and Vallejo: Selected Poems*. Boston: Beacon Press, 1972.

Part Two: Moving the Mother

De Banville, Théodore, and Stuart Merrill, trans. "The Goddess." Reprinted in *The Rag and Bone Shop of the Heart*, edited by Robert Bly, James Hillman, and Michael Meade. New York: HarperCollins, 1992.

Feldman, Susan, ed. *African Myths and Tales*. New York: Dell, 1963.

Ford, Patrick, trans. *The Mabinogi and Other Medieval Welsh Tales*. Berkeley, CA: University of California Press, 1977.

Frobenius, Leo, and Douglas Cox. *African Genesis*. Berkeley, CA: Turtle Island Foundation, 1983.

Hall, Nor. *The Moon and the Virgin*. New York: Harper & Row, 1981.

Johnson, Buffie. *Lady of the Beasts*. San Francisco: Harper & Row, 1991.

McLean, Adam. *The Triple Goddess*. Grand Rapids, MI: Phanes Press, 1989.

Neumann, Erich. *The Great Mother*. Translated by Ralph Manheim. Princeton, NJ: Princeton Univesity Press, 1963.

Walker, Barbara. *Crone*. San Francisco: Harper & Row, 1985.

Part Three: Ceremonies of Innocence

Campbell, Joseph. *The Hero with a Thousand Faces*. Princeton, NJ: Princeton University Press, 1968.

Estés, Clarissa Pinkola. *Women Who Run with the Wolves*. New York: Ballantine Books, 1992.

Hillman, James. *Puer Papers*. Dallas, TX: Spring Publications, 1979.

Mahdi, Louise, ed. *Betwixt and Between*. Peru, IL: Open Court Publishing, 1987.

Yeats, William Butler, ed. *Fairy and Folk Tales of the Irish Peasantry.* New York: Dover Publications, 1991.

―――. *The Collected Poems of W. B. Yeats.* Edited by Richard Finneran. New York: Macmillan, 1983.

Zimmer, Heinrich. *The King and the Corpse.* Princeton, NJ: Princeton University Press, 1948.

Part Four: The Land of Fire

Afanasev, Aleksandr. *Russian Fairy Tales.* Translated by Norbert Guterman. New York: Pantheon Books, 1945.

Beckwith, Carol. *Maasai.* New York: Harry N. Abrams, 1990.

Eliade, Mircea. *Shamanism.* Princeton, NJ: Princeton University Press, 1964.

―――. *Myths, Dreams and Mysteries.* New York: Harper Torchbooks, 1960.

―――. *Rites and Symbols of Initiation.* New York: Harper Torchbooks, 1958.

Evans-Wentz, W. Y., ed. *Tibet's Great Yogi Milarepa.* Oxford, England: Oxford University Press, 1928.

Kinsella, Thomas, trans. *The Tain.* Oxford, England: Oxford University Press, 1969.

La Fontaine, J. S. *Initiation.* New York: Penguin Books, 1985.

Lane, Edward W., trans. *The Arabian Nights' Entertainments or One Thousand and One Nights.* New York: Tudor Publishing, 1927.

Manheim, Ralph, trans. *Grimms' Tales for Young and Old.* Garden City, NY: Doubleday, 1977.

Paz, Octavio. *The Labyrinth of Solitude.* New York: Grove Press, 1961.

Sagar, Keith, ed. *D. H. Lawrence: Selected Poems.* New York: Penguin, 1972.

Saitoti, Tepilit O. *The Worlds of a Maasai Warrior.* New York: Random House, 1986.

Saitoti, Tepilit, and Ole Saitoti. *Maasai.* New York: Harry N. Abrams, 1980.

Shorris, Earl. *Latinos: A Biography of the People.* New York: W. W. Norton, 1993.

Part Five: The Water of Life

Bly, Robert. *Iron John.* Reading, MA: Addison-Wesley, 1990.

Chernoff, John Miller. *African Rhythm and African Sensibility.* Chicago: University of Chicago Press, 1979.

Diallo, Yaya, and Mitchell Hall. *The Healing Drum.* Rochester, VT: Destiny Books, 1989.

Dobson, Terry, and Victor Miller. *Aikido in Everyday Life.* Berkeley, CA: North Atlantic Books, 1993.

Dobson, Terry. *Terry Dobson Teaches.* Grand Ilse, VT: Soft Power Video, 1993.

Guest, Lady Charlotte. *The Mabinogion.* London: John Jones Cardiff, Ltd., 1977.

Hillman, James. *Loose Ends.* Dallas, TX: Spring Publications, 1975.

Manheim, Ralph, trans. *Grimms' Tales for Young and Old.* Garden City, NY: Doubleday, 1977.

Part Six: The Companions

Kazin, Alfred, ed. *The Portable Blake.* New York: Penguin, 1946.

Layard, John A. *Celtic Quest.* Dallas, TX: Spring Publications, 1975.

Madhubuti, Haki. *Black Men—Obsolete, Single, Dangerous?* Chicago: Third World Press, 1990.

Manheim, Ralph, trans. *Grimms' Tales for Young and Old.* Garden City, NY: Doubleday, 1977.

Palmer, Laura. *Shrapnel in the Heart.* New York: Random House, 1993.

Rolleston, T. W. *Celtic Myths and Legends.* New York: Dover Publications, 1990.

Sanford, W. B. *The Ulysses Theme.* Dallas, TX: Spring Publications, 1993.

Strehlow, Theodore. *Aranda Traditions.* Melbourne, Australia: Melbourne University Press, 1947.

———. *Journey to Horseshoe Bend.* Sydney, Australia: Angus and Robertson, 1969.

Turner, Victor. *The Ritual Process.* Ithaca, NY: Cornell University Press, 1969.

The Limbus catalog is the source for all books and tapes by Michael Meade. In addition, Limbus carries hundreds of titles on the subjects of mythology, psychology, poetry, and world music, including nearly every title mentioned in the bibliography of this book. For the latest free catalog, please write: Limbus, P.O. Box 364, Vashon, WA 98070, or call toll free, (800)233–6984.

Purchases through Limbus benefit Mosaic—a non-profit foundation that produces conferences bringing together people from various economic, racial, and cultural backgrounds. For more information on Mosaic, call, (206)463–9387, or write: Mosaic, P.O. Box 364, Vashon, WA 98070, or call toll free, (800)233–6984.

Other titles by Michael Meade

Books edited by Michael Meade

The Rag and Bone Shop of the Heart: A Poetry Anthology,
edited by Robert Bly, James Hillman, and Michael Meade

Books including contributions by Michael Meade

Walking Swiftly: Writings and Images on the Occasion of Robert Bly's 65th Birthday, edited by Thomas Smith

To Be a Man: In Search of the Deep Masculine, edited by
Keith Thompson

Wingspan: Inside the Men's Movement, edited by Christopher Harding

Audio Tapes

The Dance of Gender: When Women Went One Way and the Men Went Another, Michael Meade

The Mythology of Gender: Conflicts, Truces, and Harmonies Between Men and Women, Michael Meade

Men and the Life of Desire, Robert Bly, James Hillman, and Michael Meade

Images of Initation, James Hillman, Michael Meade and Malidoma Somé

The Great Self Within: Man and the Quest for Significance, Michael Meade and Robert Moore

The Lizard in the Fire: Male Encounters with the Feminine, Michael Meade

Off With the Rat's Head: Tales of the Father, Son, and King, Michael Meade

Video Tapes

On Being a Man, Robert Bly and Michael Meade